RADIO FIELDS

Radio Fields

Anthropology and Wireless Sound in the 21st Century

Edited by Lucas Bessire and Daniel Fisher

Afterword by Faye Ginsburg

NEW YORK UNIVERSITY PRESS
New York and London

NEW YORK UNIVERSITY PRESS
New York and London
www.nyupress.org

References to Internet websites (URLs) were accurate at the time of writing.
Neither the author nor New York University Press is responsible for URLs
that may have expired or changed since the manuscript was prepared.

LIBRARY OF CONGRESS CATALOGING-IN-PUBLICATION DATA
Radio fields : anthropology and wireless sound in the 21st century / edited by Lucas Bessire
and Daniel Fisher ; with an afterword by Faye Ginsburg.
p. cm.
Includes bibliographical references and index.
ISBN 978-0-8147-7167-9 (cl : alk. paper)
ISBN 978-0-8147-3819-1 (pb : alk. paper)
ISBN 978-0-8147-6993-5
ISBN 978-0-8147-4536-6
1.   Communication in anthropology—History—21st century. 2.   Radio—History—21st
century. 3.   Communication and culture—History—21st century. 4.   Technology—
Anthropological aspects. I. Bessire, Lucas. II. Fisher, Daniel.
GN12.8.R34   2012
070.1'94—dc23   2012024953

New York University Press books are printed on acid-free paper,
and their binding materials are chosen for strength and durability.
We strive to use environmentally responsible suppliers and materials
to the greatest extent possible in publishing our books.

Manufactured in the United States of America

10 9 8 7 6 5 4 3 2 1

CONTENTS

ACKNOWLEDGMENTS

Many people have been instrumental in bringing this volume to fruition. In addition to the patient and hard-working contributors, we would like to particularly thank Tom Abercrombie, Faye Ginsburg, Steve Feld, Fred Myers, Harald Prins, and Bambi Schieffelin, and as well as our editor, Jennifer Hammer, and two anonymous reviewers at NYU Press for their help in shaping this volume.

1

Introduction

Radio Fields

LUCAS BESSIRE AND DANIEL FISHER

Radio is the most widespread electronic medium in the world today. More than a historical precedent for television, film, or the Internet, radio remains central to the everyday lives of billions of people around the globe. Its rugged and inexpensive technology has become invested with new import in places on the other side of the "digital divide," where topography, poverty, or politics limit access to television, computers, or electricity. In metropolitan centers, radio also remains a constant presence, sounding and resounding in public space. It is broadcast from satellites into cars and jets, streamed through laptops and loudspeakers in shopping malls, classrooms, and waiting rooms, and it fills the air at parades, weddings, military bases, and squatter settlements. It is beamed into war zones and native villages, broadcast from cellular phones and homemade transistors powered by the sun. Urban taxi companies, Pacific Islanders, and indigenous people in Amazonia alike use it as a channel for two-way dialogues. Radio quite literally seems to be everywhere, but it is the technological form that has been least studied by anthropologists.

This collection arises from the recognition that radio is ubiquitous around the globe, and the following chapters are testimony to the geographic breadth and diversity of radio media's social presence. Yet this volume offers more than additional evidence for radio's far-flung travels. Here, we take the diversity of radio itself as a provocation for anthropology and its comparative endeavor and draw on this diversity to frame our central problematic. What, we ask, is widespread about radio? Is radio the same phenomenon or thing in Aboriginal Australia as it is in cosmopolitan Zambia? And if, as we propose here, radio is best imagined not as a thing at all, how might anthropology better conceive of radio as a domain of ethnographic research? How might ethnography illuminate the power of this media and the different social worlds it calls forth?

The authors in this book have all begun to answer such questions. They demonstrate how media anthropologists are increasingly turning to radio to illuminate broader disciplinary concerns with emergent forms of kinship, political agency, religious life, subjectivity, and other social domains. The following chapters explore the social reach and nature of radio technology to ask what is at stake in its practical entanglement with people's lives. These essays describe how one particular technological form animates the political, linguistic, strategic, or emotional registers of lived experience in concrete ways that are amenable to ethnographic analysis and comparison. This volume collects pioneering efforts by anthropologists to take radio seriously, efforts that often are relegated to the margins or footnotes of other anthropological projects. In doing so, the volume aims to identify and energize an emerging anthropology of radio and its orienting concerns.

Each contributor reveals the ways in which ethnography, as a loose set of methods and claims, is uniquely suited to grapple with radio's dispersed social life. At the same time, the contributors suggest how ethnographic attention to radio may enrich the concerns of anthropology. This book, then, is intended as an argument for what ethnographic methodologies may contribute to the study of radio, as well as for the ways that radio offers a rich terrain for exploring the concepts, methods, and praxis of contemporary anthropology. It demonstrates how radio fields are being newly imagined as ethnographic sites by a broad range of anthropologists and compares how radio's particular capacities inflect and transform social life in concrete ways. Anthropology and its signature methodology of long-term participant observation makes a fundamental contribution to how we might understand radio and ask questions of its social life. Although each of the contributors draws inspiration from a wider body of scholarship on radio, they also suggest several ways in which their work is fundamentally distinct from important intellectual projects currently under way in the fields of communications, media studies and history, sound theory, and cultural studies. Each contributor shows how an anthropology of radio may simultaneously further and redirect these broader trends in radio scholarship and media analysis.

One of the principal questions that emerge from our contributors is that of the social definition of radio itself. From investments in two-way radio by recently contacted Ayoreo-speaking people to Nepali engagements with liberal conceptions of the self, radio is never a single technology. Rather, it gains force and traction according to wider formations of meaning, politics, and subjectivity that often remain inaudible to short-term, focus-group or questionnaire-based research. For instance, radio means something different to two different female Muslim radio preachers in Mali or to a development worker in the same place, let alone to a DJ in Mexico City or Nepal. And beyond such hermeneutic questions, radio acquires its form within specific practices, politics, and "assemblages" that give it shape, including its digital transformation and extension through the Internet (Collier and Ong 2005; see also Born 2005). In such ways, it might be approached as an "actor-network" (Latour 1991, 2005) or "apparatus" (Foucault 1980, 1988; cf. Agamben 2009), social theoretical terms which call attention to emergent constellations of power, social relations, and things, as well as the historical moments in which they acquire durability and specificity. Radio's boundaries thus cannot easily be assumed a priori; its objectness is always potentially unsettled by shifting social practices, institutions, and technological innovations and by the broader domains within which it finds shape, meaning, and power.

At the same time, radio matters for such domains in ways that can productively be compared across time and space. Diversity of form and content, or effect and distribution, may be most noticeable to ethnographers in the field, but unexpected similarities between radio's varied apparatuses or assemblages are also strikingly apparent and impossible to ignore. It is no coincidence that Ayoreo-speaking people in the Gran Chaco and Appalachian radio preachers both imagine radio as a suitable prosthesis for the metaphysics of prayer, or that radio stations were occupied by women marchers in Oaxaca in 2006 and Libyan protestors in Benghazi in 2011 and were targeted by FARC guerrilla fighters in Colombia in 2010, or that radio's historic role as a wartime media technology is being reprised in present-day Iraq and Afghanistan (Ahrens 1998). The challenge for an anthropology of radio is to put such tensions of difference and commonality to work. It means developing a set of analytics capable of drawing together substantive, experience-near research on radio's plasticity with wider questions about the recurrent dynamics associated with radio's broader assemblages. The authors collected in this book suggest several ways that such a project could be imagined.

As editors, we use the concept of "radio fields" to signal this complex intersection of radio technology and social relations (cf. Williams 1974). Here, we imagine radio fields as unruly ethnographic sites, as well as zones where social life and knowledge of it are organized in specific and comparable ways. The authors of this collection show how the diversity of such entanglements defies any single notion of radio's social labor, even as they emphasize how radio matters across time and space. They describe how radio's voice gives force and texture to news, music, and events. From two-way conversations about the weather in South America to Appalachian Pentecostal faith healing and narratives of national crisis in Israel, radio's electronic sound marks the urgent as well as the ordinary, the mundane alongside the metaphysical. It crosses borders of all kinds: national frontiers for Turkish immigrants in Germany, ethnic and caste markers in South Asia, and even prison walls for incarcerated Aboriginal peoples in Australia. Radio may be put in the service of governance and empire, and it is central to state and imperial projects around the world. Yet it also lends material and means to a wide range of minority claims and social movements, from Oaxacan marches for women's rights or indigenous mobilization against the state to Somali pirates or Zulu musicians in South Africa.

Radio routinely intensifies and elicits novel forms of imagination, meaning, and desire that exceed its informational content. This, along with the profoundly embodied nature of listening and sounding, makes radio deeply entangled with the inner lives and political agency of its users. What does it mean, for instance, for young Indian boys to come of age listening to BBC broadcasts of cricket matches or for people living on the dispersed islands of Vanuatu to valorize *kastom* on the radio in the context of a newly independent, postcolonial nation (Appadurai 1996; Bolton 1999)? And radio also creates expertise around its material constants of microphones, wires, and antennae, or iPods, audio streaming software, and wireless networks. Historically such expertise has been inseparable from the forms of imagination and desire that have underwritten nationalist and postcolonial social movements, even as any media technology always exists as only one element in a larger and complex "media world" (Ginsburg, Abu-Lughod, and Larkin 2002b). Today, radio is being transformed and extended by digital technologies and new web-based networks of distribution, a process that demonstrates how the technological specificities of audio mediation alter the reach of radio sound and its availability to different social projects at different times (Bull 2004; Tacchi, chap. 12 in this volume). Radio fields, as Frantz Fanon noted, are thus impossible to assess in their "quiet objectivity" alone (1959, 73).

This collection thereby offers several arguments for the ways culture matters for the study of radio—as the context in which it is deployed and gains meaning but also as the object of its transformative potential. The contributors show how cultural forms and radio's technologies are mutually constitutive across time and space. As several chapters make apparent, odd things happen to both "culture" and "radio" at their intersection. It is a central premise of this book that the anthropology of radio must begin by taking both radio and culture as ideal forms and ethnographic questions rather than a priori contexts. This inductive framing also entails rethinking many of the other concepts commonly used to describe radio. The chapters thus take ideas of "community," "autonomy," "voice," "public" or "counterpublic sphere," and even "mediation" as terms for critical analysis and ethnographic specification rather than preexisting, stable analytic categories.

In sum, this volume does not aim to encompass the entire field of radio studies or history. It is instead composed of diverse examples of what anthropologists offer to the study of radio's culturally varied worlds and of what radio fields offer to anthropology. In this introduction, we first locate an emerging anthropology of radio within history and wider bodies of radio scholarship. Then we use the insights of the work collected here to suggest several conceptual axes that may be useful for future anthropological engagements with radio's sociality.

Anthropology and Radio

People have been intensely interested in radio since its inception. Thought to travel through an invisible "ether," the disembodiment of radio voices and its ability to separate spirit from flesh was initially understood through reference to spirituality or magic (see Houdini 1922). The 1920s have been described as a time of widespread "radio fever" (Sterling and Kittross 2002), and by 1926, radio broadcasts had "become one of the most essential elements of public life" in Europe and the United States (Weill 1984 [1926]). Radio technology soon figured in a variety of national, colonial, and imperial projects, even as artists and writers such as Gastón Bachelard (1971), Bertolt Brecht (Strauss and Mandl 1993; cf. Kahn 1994), and Felix Guattari (1978) hoped that radio and "radiophonic space" (Weill 1984 [1926]) could provide a "veritable feedback system with listeners" and, thus, "turn psyche and society into a single giant echo chamber" (McLuhan 1964, 299). Intellectuals including Brecht, Rudolf Arnheim, Theodor Adorno, and Walter Benjamin began experimenting with radio technologies even as they sought to understand their implications. Benjamin alone wrote more than seventy radio "models" for Radio Frankfurt between 1929 and 1933, including twenty intended for children (Mehlman 1993; see Benjamin 1999a–f). These echo features of Brecht's "epic theater" by questioning radio's mass distribution of culture as "stimuli" and encouraging "the training of critical judgment" (Benjamin 1999f, 585; see also Mehlman 1993).

The parallel histories of radio and the consolidation of anthropology as a discipline have created a unique relationship between anthropologists and radio as well. Franz Boas, for example, was an advocate for using radio to spread anthropological insights (E. Boas 1945), while Margaret Mead, Alfred Kroeber, Robert Redfield, and many others regularly appeared on radio programs. Moreover, many anthropologists in the 1930s and 1940s were involved in large-scale projects involving radio, such as the Rockefeller Foundation's "Radio Project," which began in 1937, and, beginning in the late 1940s, UNESCO's Division of Radio in its Department of Mass Communication, which produced radio programs and distributed radio sets—efforts that established community-based radio stations around the world (see Lind 1950). Other anthropologists were involved as administrators and consultants for colonial projects in Africa, India, and Asia, to which radio was central. By the 1930s, for instance, the British Colonial Office required its administrators to use radio as a tool for "imprinting British culture and ideas into the minds of native listeners" through daily broadcasts, often on the battery-powered "saucepan special" receivers manufactured throughout the 1940s specifically for African audiences (Head 1979; Posner 2001). In Nazi Germany, the Reich Broadcasting Company aired extensive nationalist propaganda over a series of affordable radio sets subsidized by the state, called the Volksempfanger, or "the people's receivers." Between 1933 and 1939, more than seven million of these sets were produced, each stamped with a swastika and an eagle (Aylett 2011).

During World War II, Axis and Allied anthropologists alike were involved in radio propaganda, including Gregory Bateson and Ruth Benedict's "black propaganda" radio programs, which successfully undermined Japanese morale in the South Pacific (Cummings 2001; Jelavich 2006; Price 1998; Soley 1989). After the war, public anthropologists also were regular contributors to radio programs in the United States, Canada, and the United Kingdom, such as BBC's *Third Programme*. Aspiring to bring social anthropology to a broad public audience, the program featured lectures by E. E. Evans-Pritchard,

Mary Douglas, Max Gluckman, Raymond Firth, and Audrey Richards throughout the 1950s and 1960s. By the late 1940s, anthropologist Edmund Carpenter was also hosting his own radio show, *Explorations*, for the Canadian Broadcasting Corporation (Prins and Bishop 2007). Such widespread radio use by anthropologists produced a substantial corpus of skill-based tacit knowledge that prefigures an explicit research paradigm for the anthropology of radio (see also Eiselein 1976). Carpenter (1972), for instance, later theorized the implications of his experiences with visual and aural media in Canada and Papua New Guinea.

Meanwhile, radio was broadly reshaping the diverse sites in which anthropology was practiced as an academic enterprise. This global spread of radio included its use as a "portable missionary" for proselytizing Native groups, beginning when HCJB went on air in Ecuador in 1931. This was followed by the Far East Broadcasting Company in Manila in 1948 and Trans-World Radio in Tangier and Liberia in 1954. By 1964, there were forty international Christian stations operating around the world. The reach of such missionary radios has been so effective that missionaries estimated that only ninety-three major language groups were not reached by Christian radio a decade ago (Gray and Murphy 2000; see also BBC 2005). Radio sound was an instrumental tool for much early "contact" work by missionaries in lowland South America (see Capa 1956).

Latin America was also the site of the earliest experiments in community-based radio stations (see Dagrón and Cajías 1989). In 1947, Aymara and Quechua silver miners started a group of radio stations focused on collective advocacy for better wages and working conditions. By the 1950s, twenty-three of these stations had taken root in the Bolivian Altiplano and became known as the Miner's Radio. Also in 1947, the Catholic priest and liberation theologist Joaquín Salcedo started Radio Sutatenza / Acción Cultural Popular in the Colombian Andes. This project eventually developed approximately twenty thousand "radio schools," which combined broadcasts and group discussion and focused on what Salcedo called "integral fundamental education" (Fraser and Restrepo-Estrada 1998). Such trends not only spread across Latin America (see Early 1973) but in the 1960s and 1970s were echoed across Europe and the United States, where an explosion of illegal or pirate radio stations developed the idea that small-scale and local radio practices were an antidote to mass media and crucial tools for claiming citizenship and rights (see also Shields and Ogles 1995).

Throughout the mid-20th century, colonizing powers and postcolonial nation-states alike turned to broadcast radio to air programs aimed at economic development, the disciplining of national subjects, and the consolidation of state power (Larkin 2008; Mrázek 2002). Yet anticolonial and pro-tonational movements also organized around radio technologies. As Fanon wrote of Radio Algiers, radio technologies could become a tool for decolonization, insofar as radio sets "develop the sensorial, muscular and intellectual powers of man in any given society" (1959, 71–72). Radio's social effects were never entirely contained within any single colonial agenda (see also Appadurai 1996).

This was true in the colonies of the colonies as well. Australian colonial administrators in Papua New Guinea and Bougainville also imagined radio as a technology for the pacification and modernization of "natives," who soon incorporated it into their own independence movements (see Bolton 1999; Carpenter 1972; Hadlow 2004; Seward 1999). In some cases, such as the New Guinea highlands and parts of Amazonia, radio and other mass media were used to introduce the very idea of the nation-state and to cement its authority over indigenous populations, often by self-conscious staging of its technological capacities. Missionaries and government officials found that passing a vocal message over radio could intensify its desired effects of authority, solidarity, or both. Carpenter, for instance, describes how the orders of patrol officers in Papua New Guinea were at times only obeyed after they were broadcast over the radio (see Prins and Bishop 2007). Internally colonized indigenous peoples and other minority groups also appropriated radio for their own ends from a very early date, such as the Shuar Indigenous Federation of Ecuador, which began indigenous-language broadcasting in the mid-1960s.

In short, the social effects of radio have always exceeded any single colonial or governmental agenda, even while provoking forms of nation building and national identifications in the (post)colony. British and Portuguese "radio-colonization" broadcasts, for example, shaped the foundations of independence movements in parts of Africa by popularizing senses of regional unity based on linguistic homogenization (Power 2000; Spitulnik 1998; Zivin 1998). Marianne Stenbaek (1982, 1992) reports a similar effect of 1950s Inuit language radio broadcasting in Greenland. Even the "people's receivers" radio sets produced by the Nazi government were capable of picking up foreign broadcasts, a fact which led Hitler to make listening to anything but German radio a crime punishable by execution (Aylett 2011). Radio B92 —an early Internet-facilitated "guerrilla radio" in Serbia—provides another striking example of the ways radio's unruly voice can destabilize projects of totalitarian governance (Collin 2002). Such scholarship draws attention to radio's historical embeddings in the very concept of the (post)colony, as well as the unpredictable relationships between radio technology and hegemonic or imperial formations (Mbembe 2001; Mrázek 2002; Stoler 2002). Driven by such diverse agendas, as well as corporate interests in radio's commercial potential and common hopes for radio as a tool of democratic emancipation, radio technology was soon a worldwide phenomenon. Long before the re-invention of anthropology made it audible to ethnographers, radio was present in even the most remote, rural, or traditional anthropological fields.

Anthropologists and sociologists have long noted the social importance of radio practices (see Barton 1937). In the Lynds' famous 1937 study of Mid-dletown, for instance, they noted the transformation of American public life caused by the radio and family car (see Lynd and Lynd 1937). Yet de-spite several significant precedents for focusing on the social effects of radio —including W. Lloyd Warner and William Henry's (1948) monograph on the uptake and composition of daytime radio "serial" programs, Daniel Lerner's (1958) study of the Voice of America in the Middle East, Hortense Powder-maker's (1962) interests in radio and cinema in the context of her central Af-rican fieldwork, and Carpenter's (1972, 1975, 1978) prescient analyses of the specific sensory qualities of radio (see also Eiselein 1976; Eiselein and Top-per 1976)—anthropologists did not begin to develop their tacit knowledge of radio into a systematic analytical project until the 1990s ushered in the rise of "the anthropology of media" (see Ginsburg, Abu-Lughod, and Larkin 2002a, 3). Within such paradigms, radio sociality again became audible and relevant to a larger set of scholarly concerns. Indeed, Powdermaker's early media eth-nography was perhaps initially more influential for scholars in development and communications through its importance to Wilbur Schramm's writing (Schramm 1964), while Carpenter's work was vigorously engaged by "media ecologists" and sound theorists but largely overlooked by anthropologists until relatively recently.[1] While pioneering work on radio was being done in the context of communications and media studies, these projects were often quite distinct from the concerns of anthropologists (see Girard 1992).

We draw inspiration from media anthropologists such as Abu-Lughod (2005), Appadurai (1996), Askew and Wilk (2002), Born (2004), Boyer (2005), Carpenter (1972), Ginsburg (1991, 1994, 1997, 2002), Ginsburg, Abu-Lughod, and Larkin (2002b), Larkin (2008, 2009), Latour and Weibel (2006), Maz-zarella (2004), Michaels (1994), Peterson (2003), Powdermaker (1950, 1962), Prins (1997), Spitulnik (1993), and others who have been instrumental in constituting media as central ethnographic sites. The ethnography of radio fields shares their central concerns: it takes a global perspective on media practices, foregrounds the diversity of media practices within expansive "media ecologies," and emphasizes that "media" and mediation are defined through social relations and in social practice (Ginsburg, Abu-Lughod, and

Larkin 2002a). However, a focus on radio sociality also requires shifting analysis away from the "visualist bias" and central concerns of visual anthropology and film theory to engage with another set of debates centering on the relationships between sound, technology, and power (Askew and Wilk 2002; Fabian 1983; Ginsburg, Abu-Lughod, and Larkin 2002a; Hilmes 2005). To do so, the contributors to the ethnography of radio fields also draw inspiration from scholarship on relationships between music, audio media, and the voice (Erlman 2004; Feld et al. 2004; Fox 1997; Greene and Porcello 2005; Hirshkind 2006; Meintjes 2003; Samuels 2004; Weidman 2006). This is to rethink the defining questions and conundrums outlined by media anthropology through the specific issues of language, the senses, and sound that radio's entanglement with social life entails (Gaonkar and Povinelli 2003; Kapchan 2008; Miller 1992).

Approaches to Radio in Other Disciplines

Although there are few anthropological efforts to describe radio in comparison to the explosion of anthropological scholarship on television or film, in the past two decades an increasingly sophisticated and growing number of ethnographic analyses have focused on radio in a variety of contexts. This pioneering work includes not only Powdermaker and Carpenter but also Bolton's (1999) groundbreaking work in Vanuatu, Tacchi's (1998) efforts to understand radio sound as material culture in the gendered space of home, Spitulnik's (1994, 1996, 1998, 2002) development of linguistic ideological and material culture analyses in her work on Zambian radio, Vargas's (1995) work on participatory media in Mexico, Fardon and Furniss's (2000) collection on radio in Africa, and Larkin's (2008, 2009) historical treatment of broadcast infrastructures and listening publics in Nigeria.

Anthropologists today approach radio in a variety of ways, using a broad range of theoretical perspectives. Many have assembled their analytic frames from the ground up, drawing from a wide range of radio research and broader schools of media theory to make sense of what they have found. This somewhat fragmented scholarship includes academic and applied scholarship on alternative and community media; cultural studies and art critical analyses of radio aesthetics and poetics; and sociolinguistic work on radio as a distinct domain of speech pragmatics. In framing radio as an ethnographic question, anthropologists have thus drawn inspiration and insight from well beyond their disciplinary boundaries, while also endeavoring to reframe or question the analytical categories on which such studies often rely. We briefly sketch these important literatures here, before turning to the chapters and the ways they amplify and intervene in these conversations.

Early Tensions in Radio Theory

As Srinivas Melkote and H. Leslie Steeves (2001) and others argue, the social effects of radio have long been understood through divergent theories of communication. These in turn have shaped how radio technology has been imagined as a demagogic tool of capitalist expansion, deployed as an apparatus of national public making or colonial discipline, or adopted as an instrument for social change. Certainly, much radio writing continues to be shaped by enduring concerns over, and questions about, the homogenizing or dystopic effects of mass-media technologies, the capacity of "hot" media to "swallow culture" (McLuhan 1964), to impose state, colonial, or imperial projects, and to circulate a narrow sense of modernity (Tomlinson 1991). Yet scholars have also found in Jürgen Habermas's (1989) concept of "the public sphere" or Benedict Anderson's (1983) idea of "imagined community" a more nuanced vision of media sociality than that presumed in models of cultural imperialism. In doing so, work in media and communication studies has drawn from theorizations of "counterpublic spheres" and resistance (Calhoun 1992; Fraser 1991; Hall 1980, 1997; Radway 1984; Warner 2002) to recuperate radio from the critique of mass culture, signaling instead its capacity to generate alternative social forms at the local level. Rosalia Winocur (2003, 2005), for instance, has written extensively of radio's expansive entanglements in negotiations around citizenship and political participation, while Clemencia Rodriguez (2001) has described how community radio practices create a "fissure in the global mediascape" where unexpected forms of political agency may arise.

Such tensions between a critique of popular and commercial cultural production and efforts to identify modes of counterhegemonic media production were already present in early 20th-century studies of radio media. Brecht's (1979–1980 [1930], 1993 [1932]) interest in reshaping radio as a communicative, rather than distributed, media remains an inspiration for community and alternative media scholars and activists (cf. Hartley 2000). Similarly, Rudolf Arnheim's (1972 [1936]) interest in the aesthetics of radio sound and editing extended to the ways this had the potential to transform perception in politically consequential ways (cf. Cardinal 2007). While it is often observed that in this period many observers were preoccupied with the threat mass communications presented to functioning democracy through the stultifying effects of media's mass "distraction," Adorno and others also saw in media technologies novel possibilities for critical cultural production and began to develop methods for its analysis (Adorno 2009; Benjamin 1999a, 1999e; Levin and von der Linn 1994; cf. Born 1995).

Paul Lazarsfeld's Radio Project, first at Princeton University and then at Columbia, focused on the empirical study of radio audiences and provided a North American research home for both Arnheim and Adorno. This project produced foundational studies of North American media audiences, from studies of audience consumption of radio news to Adorno's own writings on radio's mass reproduction and sonic miniaturization of musical form (Adorno 1941, 2009; Cantril 1940; Lazarsfeld 1940; Lazarsfeld and Stanton 1941; cf. Hullot-Kentor 2009). While the Princeton Radio Project initially lent material support to Adorno's emergent critique of mass culture, under Lazarsfeld's direction it also conducted some of the first large-scale market research that was to fundamentally shape much 20th-century corporate media practice (Hullot-Kentor 2009). The tension between these quite different methodological perspectives—the aesthetic and cultural criticism of Adorno, the gestaltist phenomenology of Arnheim, and the empirical and comparative efforts of Lazarsfeld (and later Wilbur Schramm)—echo through much of the scholarship and critical cultural analysis of the past seventy years.

Community and Alternative Media: From Political Analysis to Political Praxis

This emphasis on radio's particular social properties took on increasing importance in the 1970s and 1980s, as media activists and academics began to seek fissures in dominant mediascapes in which alternative media forms could engender resistance, open spaces for participatory democracy, or find recognition, tolerance, and occasionally state support (Murillo 2008; Rodriguez and El Gazi 2007; Rodriguez and Murphy 1997; Tufte and Metalopulos 2009). These developments emerged in concert with increasingly sophisticated critiques of dominant, corporate, and national media monopolies and arguments that community-based media catalyze forms of citizenship and inclusion (Huesca 1995; Ojebode and Akingbulu 2009). This has been most vigorously engaged by scholars working on, alongside, and within minority, diasporic, and indigenous communities in diverse sites around the world (compare Barlow 1999; Meadows 1992; Meadows et al. 2006; Valaskakis 1983, 1992). Lorna Roth (1993, 2005), for instance, describes how call-in radio became a central site for negotiating Mohawk claims to sovereignty and self-determination, a process that also illuminates the longstanding dis-juncture between First People's efforts to appropriate media and the forms of governance implied by media regulation. Like Roth, many radio scholars are also media activists, and their work links scholarship with political praxis (Girard 1992; O'Connor 2006).

Such trends are particularly evident in scholarship that focuses on the decades-long use of small-scale or community radio transmitters as tools for promoting development and democracy by a variety of communities, international funders, and national NGOs. Extending the normative, teleo-logical perspective of many colonial projects, the predominant paradigm of development in the 1970s assumed that development was a process of mod-ernization "via the delivery and insertion of technologies, and/or inculcating values, attitudes and behaviors in the population" (Melkote and Steeves 2001, 38). Throughout the 1980s and 1990s, such models of development commu-nications were effectively challenged by scholars pointing out the persistent inequalities and forms of dominance occasioned by these projects (Esco-bar 1995). For such critics, communication and radio technologies were the means to develop class awareness and foster resistance, "antibodies to the . . . neglect, insensitivity and insanity" of both conventional media and neoco-lonial projects (Lewis 1993, 15; also Berrigan 1981; Mody 1983). Building on these insights, communication scholars and activists throughout the 1990s and 2000s increasingly began to assert that small-scale radio was more ad-equately seen as an ideal tool for an "emancipatory" communication (Raboy 1993; see also Couldry and Curran 2003; Critical Art Ensemble 2001; Down-ing 2001, 2007; Garnham 2000).

Drawing heavily from liberation theology and the writings of Paolo Freire (1973) on "dialogic communication," proponents of this view argued that communication is not an exchange of information but a complex in-terplay of information and culturally specific context that will give voice to the voiceless and "free people to determine their own futures" (Melkote and Steeves 2001, 38; Querre 1992). This emancipatory paradigm presumes (often uncritically) that empowerment is the actual and the ideal result of small-scale radio practice. Empowerment, in turn, is increasingly viewed as a crucial element for developing civil society, strengthening institutions, and promoting democracy (Hill 2003; Rozario 1997; Stern, Delthier, and Rogers 2005). As the goal of much development work shifted from a "trickle-down" model in the 1980s to a "bottom-up" approach of "participatory develop-ment" in the 1990s, empowerment has become widely used by development agencies and international organizations as the justification for founding and funding small-scale radio stations around the world (see Brownlee 1983;

H. Fisher 1990; Myers 1998; Norrish 1999; Tabing 1997). The primary definition of community radio—as a "powerful source for empowerment, especially for disenfranchised and marginalized groups in society" (Center for International Media Assistance 2007, 4)—is now echoed by development officials, media activists, and communication scholars alike.

UNESCO itself has been an important funder of radio research from the early 1960s (see Schramm 1964). It has been particularly influential in promoting the spread of community radios in Africa and Asia, a commitment which has also entailed actively developing new, widely accessible radio technologies (Fraser and Restrepo-Estrada 2001; UNESCO 1997). In the preface to the 2001 *Community Radio Handbook*, Claude Ondobo, the director of the Communication Development Division, describes a vision of community radio that has now become standard (see AMARC 2008; Panos Institute 2008; Shanks 1999).

> UNESCO sees community radio as a medium that gives voice to the voiceless, that serves as the mouthpiece of the marginalized and is at the heart of communication and democratic processes within societies. With community radio, citizens have the means to make their views known on decisions that concern them. The notions of transparency and good governance take on new dimensions and democracy is reinforced. (Fraser and Restrepo-Estrada 2001, iii)

This framing of alternative and community media finds strong empirical and critical support in studies of Latin American radiophony. Such works often draw on a Marxist critique of commercial and state-produced media as forms of ideological domination. They commonly underline the necessity for participation in noncommercial media production by politically marginalized groups and those uprooted by capitalist economies, such as migrant Bolivian communities in Buenos Aires (Grimson 1999) or the Andean migrant radios of Lima (Llorens 1991; Martín-Barbero 1988, 1993). Many accounts of radio in Latin America thus describe radio technology as an ideal tool for popular or class protest (Dagrón and Cajías 1989; but see Martín-Barbero 1993). Thus, a number of ethnographically oriented works on radio in Latin America focus on the preconditions for political participation (see Winocur 2003). Anthropologist Diana Agosta (2004), for instance, points to the ownership of new alternative radio stations in El Salvador as an emergent civil society in which participation is itself a value emerging from the practice of radiophony. Robert Huesca's (1995) account of miners' radio in Bolivia stresses the ways in which production techniques maintain the anonymity of women speakers, enabling critique as a form of participation. While these issues are clearest in environments where radio clearly speaks in the voice of state interests, this perspective has traveled to other social contexts as a normative trope for radio's real voice. Small-scale radio, then, becomes described as a technology that produces a predictable democratizing effect opposed to the alienation of mainstream media (cf. Spinelli 1996).

From Media and Communication to Radio Studies

While this stress on media's democratizing potential informs a significant strand of radio writing, it should be read alongside historical and cultural studies writings on radio that question the legacy of the Frankfurt School's critiques of popular culture. Valuable historical scholarship has demonstrated how commercial and popular cultures became increasingly linked through radio's development and national integration (Hilmes 1997), exploring in detail the imbrications of popular media and national publics in the early 20th century. Others have described the ways radio media—commercial, state sponsored, and community based alike—may provide the building blocks for a range of social identities and social movements (Chignell 2009; cf. Hall 1980). While such work embraces a holistic approach to understanding the significance of media as the foundation of cultural production in modern life, and such projects have grown increasingly important in a broader "radio studies," there remains a tension within much recent writing on radio between critical celebration of noncommercial, alternative, and community media production (as in Howley 2009 and discussed earlier) and the tacit valorization of popular culture and the vernacular or idiosyncratic uses of commercial media by different audiences and individuals (see Hilmes 2002; Scannell 1995, 1996). Bull (2004), Schiffer (1991), and Zilm (1993), for instance, each draw attention to the ways that the portable nature of the radio set, including its important status in the automobile, shapes its social uptake.

Emerging in part from the broader attention to media within British cultural studies and coalescing around the term "radio studies" and a listserv under the same title, more recent radio research aims programmatically to transcend the older normative frameworks that might divide commercial from public or governmental from pedagogic (see Chignell 2009; Hendy 2000; Hopkinson and Tacchi 2000; Scannell 1995). For instance, John Hartley's (2000) neologism "radiocracy"—or government by radio—makes explicit the frequent co-occurrence of the governmental and commercial, the instructive and the entertaining, the demagogic and the distracting. While Hartley and his interlocutors are preoccupied with the promise of radio to elicit forms of public identification and imagined community, they observe that the actual practices that such communities engage in can vary widely (Hopkinson and Tacchi 2000). For David Hendy, the tension between accounts of radio's demagogic potential and its popular, democratic appeal has instead been a powerful rubric for questioning the degree of power we lend the medium itself. Hendy (2000, 202–214) observes that Rwandan genocide and Bolivian popular resistance have both been linked to radio broadcasting (see also Des Forges 2007; Kellow and Steeves 1998; O'Connor 1990; Thomson 2007), and he suggests that such entanglements cannot be attributed only to "radio's power." Rather, broader features of mediascapes, national publics, and the politics of popular culture are crucial for how radio voices are understood to address and constitute their audiences (see also Shandler 2009).

The contributors to this volume take such features as central ethnographic questions, but not merely as empirical problems to be solved with better data. For instance, several contributors to this collection note the social variability and complicity between forms of liberal governmentality and the understandings of voice and subjectivity encouraged in forms of participatory communication. Such ethnographic analyses suggest that we question the givenness of both "communication" and "community" as ahistorical categories and thus as the paradigmatic lenses through which to analyze or understand radio media. This perspective also benefits from broader analyses within both anthropology and media and communications studies that open the very concept of communication to historical and metapragmatic critique (Axel 2006; Peters 1999; cf. Kittler 1999).

Radio and Place, as Art and in Cultural Studies

Cultural studies and art writers have also provided significant critical frameworks for rethinking radio's relationship to place and the particular ways it builds an audience through appeals to the local. Influential critical writings posit that radio's seeming local character and intimate address may in fact conceal radio's industrial production of locality and profound relationship with capitalist logics of space, time, and commodification (Berland 1990, 1993, 1994; cf. Schafer 1977). Jeffrey Sconce (2000), for example, locates the anxiety and panic surrounding Orson Welles's famous broadcast of the *War of the Worlds* in the loss of media's mysteriousness and its new link to entrenched institutions of broadcasting and the bureaucratic machinery of modernity. R. Murray Schafer (1977) echoes Edmund Carpenter and Marshall McLuhan (1960) to argue that radio's schizophonia (the splitting of sounds from their sources) "ventriloquizes modern life" and that radio sound colonizes space. Jody Berland (1993, 1994) echoes these anxieties about radio's spatial expansion, arguing that the voices of commercial radio DJs interpolate a local listening community in the interests of a nonlocal dynamic of market expansion. Such perspectives begin to theorize the mediated sonic environment and point to the interactions between capital, technology, and expressive form by which radio emplaces listeners in a variety of ways (see also Corbin 1998).

While such trends support the efforts of alternative radio activists and scholars, they are also in critical dialogue with earlier efforts to rethink radio as a practice by artists such as Glenn Gould, John Cage, and Pierre Shaefer, among others[2] (Cage 1961; cf. Bazzana 2004; Strauss and Mandl 1993). Their explorations of the aesthetic implications of audio media have inspired a range of recent radio criticism that lends insight into how radio's possibilities encourage reexamination of the relationship between sound, technology, and social life (Kahn and Whitehead 1994; Weiss 1995). The English-language publication of Jacques Attali's *Noise* (1992) also stimulated scholars, artists, and producers to assess the transformative potential embodied in digital media (see also Augaitis and Lander 1994; Kahn and Whitehead 1994). In Attali's celebratory account, we are on the brink of a new age of "composition" —in which the tools of music production are dispersed to act as "noise" in the stockpiling and commodified distribution of music as product. We are all, Attali's text suggests, producers. Such experiments in writing and radio continue to prove inspirational both within anthropology and without (Erlman 2004; Feld 1996; Westerkamp 1994, 2002) and have been an important resource for reimagining radio as both art and expressive culture.

Indeed, Attali's writings have been a catalyst for broader conversations about audio media that now provide a new set of coordinates for thinking about radio beyond the dichotomous opposition between an alienating mass media and empowering community voice. This emerging scholarship on the social life of sound frequently places audio technology at its center and often employs conceptual frames drawn from science and technology studies. Such work includes writings about the acoustics of concert halls (Thompson 2002); the soundscapes of infirmaries (Rice 2003) and village squares (Corbin 1998); the history of sound reproduction, telephony, and radiophony (Gitelman 1999, 2006; Sterne 2003); and anthropological attention to the institutional production of expertise around digital music and the engineering of sonic culture (Born 1995; Greene and Porcello 2005; cf. Pinch and Bijsterveld 2004; Pinch and Trocco 2002). This work builds on a broader effort to bring together social history and cultural analysis with an interest in the technological entailments of media forms more broadly (cf. Kittler 1999; Liu

2004). For example, Jonathan Sterne (2003) deploys the concept of transduction, a term from physics which refers to the conversion between one form of energy to another, to gain critical distance on the materiality of sound (cf. Helmreich 2007), while Lisa Gitelman (2006) writes of the broader protocols and conceptual claims that coalesce around new media technologies (by comparing recorded sound and telephony with the World Wide Web). In this more recent work, the question is less one of a relationship between an electronic medium and its audience and more between technology and epistemology. While not about radio per se, such expansive attention to sound and its mediation provide significant axes for thinking about radio fields.

Radio and Language

While writings from communications and cultural studies provide powerful suggestions for rethinking radio, perhaps more familiar to anthropologists are sociolinguistic approaches to radio speech, which frequently refer back to Erving Goffman's (1981) attention to distinguishing features of broadcast speech as significant for establishing the routines of everyday talk, and to Allan Bell's (1983) descriptive account of broadcast news registers as prestige standards and normative frames for speech communities (cf. Bhimji 2001; Coupland 2001; Scannell 1996). Others have focused on the complex ways in which media language practices interpellate listeners into wider constituents of a nation, ethnicity, or social collective (see Barnett 2000). Such sociolinguistic research has entailed substantial (albeit not thematically coherent) contributions from anthropologists and ethnographically focused scholars. Craig Palmer's (1990) interests in two-way radio communication among commercial lobster fishermen in Maine emerges from extended ethnography and focuses on radio's potential to amplify the availability of valuable information and on the ways this may shed light on forms of secrecy and sharing of information around scarce resources. Martin Spinelli (2006) extends such concerns by examining how the editing practices entailed by radio's recent digital extension affects the language practices and rhetorical forms around which radio speech is organized. Linguistic research has also been an important source for articles on indigenous radio production as a kind of archival resource for further exploration of the pragmatics of speech genres (Shaul 1988).

   Although a good deal of such work presumes radio's transparency and neutrality as a channel for language rather than as constitutive of its socially specific forms and practices, many such scholars also foreground the effects of audio media on speech pragmatics. Much of this work has focused on the particular format of talk radio (see Katriel 2004; Matza 2009). Ian Hutchby (1999), for instance, describes the initial turn-taking sequences of calls to talk-back radio shows, drawing on Goffman's notion of "footing" to discuss the ways that participants, callers and hosts, creatively entail the interactive contexts of the broadcast frame. Douglas Coupland (2001) draws on Bakhtin's work with speech genres to analyze the "dialect stylization" and ironic distance established by Welsh DJs, whose phonological performances both index their Welsh identities and yet, by virtue of their heteroglossic play, also deauthenticate and distance themselves from that identity as well. This harks back to Goffman's sense that to speak on the radio is to perform in a very literal sense. Linguistic anthropologists working within this broad domain focus on the interanimation of media and linguistic form, foregrounding how radio has provided new forums for valuing language practices for many minority and indigenous communities (see Browne 1990, 1992, 1998; Cormack 2000; Eisenlohr 2004; Fava 1989; Luykx 2001), including Aymara (Albó 1974; Swinehart 2009), Navajo (Klain and Peterson 2000; Peterson 1997), Lakota (Smith and Cornette 1998), and Kuna (Gerdes 1998). Such scholarship begins to suggest the numerous linguistic resources speakers engage on the radio in order to key social difference and to establish effective mediatized communicative frames. Such accounts also begin to locate such media practices within a wider set of social, political, and economic conditions.

Introduction to the Chapters

This volume defines an anthropology of radio in relation to the intellectual trends and projects discussed in the preceding sections. In doing so, it draws a crucial distinction between radio scholarship based on fieldwork methodologies in general and the specific conceptual concerns of media anthropologists as applied to radio. Moreover, such concerns are not homogeneous or uniform. In this section, we bring the insights of the chapters into dialogue with one another, as well as with some of the major questions in radio scholarship detailed earlier. The aim is to illustrate the diversity of radio sociality and productive tensions within analyses of it.

Here, we argue that the anthropology of radio fields opens expansive and provocative ways to rethink foundational assumptions about how media creates social collectives within complex political fields, the changing character of expressive economies in the context of neoliberal state reforms, phenomenological questions about how sound influences the subjective experience of space and time, or radio's capacity to alter and key distinct contexts of perception, affect, and everyday politics. Radio encompasses a range of electromagnetic frequencies, broadcast formats, wireless networks, and pro-gramming genres, which range from two-way dyadic handsets to corporate news broadcasts or from live link-ups with cell phones to Internet streaming of popular music that extends far beyond the reach of actual radio waves. To-gether, the contributors illustrate a staggering diversity of radio technologies, even as they reveal the unpredictability of their social effects. Each contri-bution follows radio into unsettling and provocative questions. The authors underline radio's excessive nature and make it clear that it is impossible to understand radio sociality without taking seriously the interlocking cultural meanings that radiate outward from any particular radio field.

All the contributions, however, share a basic focus on the complex inter-section of radio technology and emergent social relations. The authors ques-tion the givenness or stability of both "communication" and "community" as analytic categories and thus as the paradigmatic lenses through which to understand radio media. Rather, they describe how the communities em-powered by radio technologies must be understood as constituted, to some degree, by the very media forms they adopt. In the examples described in this volume, the contributors each show how this relationship is shaped by the particular qualities of radio, as an assemblage of expertise, material cir-cuitry, listening practices, and sound. In doing so, they expand on the central insight of such different writers such as Frantz Fanon (1959) and Friedrich Kittler (1999) and more historicist analyses of communication (Axel 2006; Peters 1999).

The chapters are loosely organized along five conceptual axes. Each axis represents a widespread approach to radio's sociality. At the same time, how-ever, we have argued that radio is a compelling ethnographic site precisely because it exceeds any singular analytic heuristic and entails putting multiple interpretative frameworks to work. This means that each of the chapters may offer a distinct set of orienting concerns, even while speaking to multiple axes or approaches. Such groupings, then, are far from rigid or deterministic. Instead, they are intended to reveal some of the central resonances and ten-sions around which this volume has taken shape. In what follows, we signal the divergences and overlaps of the concerns illustrated by the chapters, both singly and in dialogue with one another, and suggest what theoretical signifi-cance they may hold for the future anthropology of radio fields.

Axis I: The Voice

Several contributors make "voice" a central focus of their work. As a figure, "voice" frequently links the social potentials of vocal address to longstanding tropes of social agency and liberal personhood. To have a voice is, in this understanding, to "have" agency (Bauman and Briggs 2003; Weidman 2006). Yet such generic equations risk overlooking the specific ways this figure has become widely compelling and consequential. The voice has thus been problematized by ethnographers concerned with theorizing agency, with pursuing a phenomenology of social interaction, and with detailing the ways in which new media technologies inform or problematize local expressive economies (Feld et al. 2004; Hirschkind 2006; Inoue 2006; Weidman 2006). As the contributors to this volume make clear, radio offers a unique site for the ethnographic analysis of the mediatized voice; the specific and variable ways it interpellates listeners as members of audiences, collectives, and publics; and the means by which it shapes and shades affective experience. At the same time, they call attention to the ways such dynamics vary according to the particular forms of radio transmission (commercial, pirate, small scale, two way) and to how they are embedded within larger social, political, and historical contexts.

Such questions are taken up explicitly in the first two chapters by Laura Kunreuther and Daniel Fisher. Kunreuther (see also 2006) draws from extensive fieldwork to trace the cultural history of FM broadcasting in Nepal and its significance for the democracy movements of the 1990s. She analyses a local equation of radio with "free speech" and "voice" as agency, a correspondence that became prominent following the 1990 People's Movement that ushered in a democratic government. She describes how, in many accounts of modernity, the voice is nostalgically recalled as a primordial site of agency and authenticity, in contrast to the presumed distancing effects of sight. Kunreuther notes that while vision is often figured as the quintessentially "modern" sense, the figure of voice, as a cultural construct, has gained significance in this modern moment of neoliberal democratic reforms and with a corresponding explosion of new media. Yet while Nepalese discourses of the modern foreground the immediacy and transparency of a radio voice, Kunreuther also describes how older forms of social relations persist in forms of radio-station ownership and programming.

Fisher (see also 2009) describes how Aboriginal radio producers at FM stations in urban Australia negotiate tensions between their understandings of the voice as a technologically malleable site of expressive practice and as the foundation of indigenous identity and political agency. As with Kunreuther, this chapter questions the global spread of a particular expressive ideology and its problematic relationship to media technologies. Voice here comes to matter as a relationship between a global discourse of "the voice" as a sign of agency and therapeutic self-expression, even while the technological practice of producing the voice for radio destabilizes and unsettles its a priori character. The techniques of radio and its globally mobile musical content make the sounds of Aboriginal voices provocative and problematic. They become imbued with an uncanny character, at once of particular Aboriginal selves and other to them. Fisher describes how Aboriginal radio producers bring two poles of "voice" together. In Fisher's analysis, then, the voice becomes a lively terrain for political negotiation and indigenous self-fashioning, while indigenous radio stations figure as institutions that enable insight into the emergence of a local "voice consciousness" (Feld et al. 2004).

In these chapters, as well as in contributions by Dorothea Schulz, Jeffrey S. Juris, Kira Kosnick, Lucas Bessire, Anderson Blanton, Jo Tacchi, and Debra Vidali-Spitulnik, the voice is inseparable from its technological and institutional mediation. More than an expression of resistance or personal expression, it gains its social life through particular technologies, local linguistic ideologies, and specific institutional practices. Expression, in different degrees, is shaped by the particular social practices and materials (institutional, technological, and cultural) by which radio sound is produced. Yet these broad suppositions emerge from particular historical moments. Thus, Kunreuther's description of the voice of the democratic, neoliberal citizen claiming equality shares in a globally mobile linguistic ideology but remains quite distinct from the voice of Aboriginal Australians grappling with the ontological ramifications of media technologies and their appropriation of global musical genres, as well as from the voices of Free Radio DJs in Mexico City described by Juris, the female Islamic radio preachers in Mali described by Schulz, or the self-conscious stagings of the voice in German "MultiKulti" radio documented by Kosnick. Kunreuther and Fisher thus join other contributors to show how particular radio publics are constituted in dialogue with local and changing conditions of cultural production. Together, they illustrate a variety of distinct domains in which radio media—as institution, technology, and discursive provocateur—creatively entail those forms of social relation they often seem merely to reflect.

Axis II: Radio and Nation

Chapters by Danny Kaplan (also 2009) and Dorothea Schulz similarly comment on the technological production of radio's voice but foreground its power to interpellate audiences. Whereas Kunreuther and Fisher focus on social poetics and discourses of personhood and identity in a national context, Kaplan and Schulz turn to the nation as an explicitly central frame for exploring such questions. As Benedict Anderson's (1983) landmark book

Imagined Communities suggests for print media, media forms such as radio have been conceptualized as central technologies for constituting a national "public sphere" and regimes of citizenship (Born 2004). Pioneering scholarship by Martin Hadlow (2004), Rudolf Mrázek (2002), and Lissant Bolton (1999) underscores the crucial role that broadcast radio plays in constructing national imaginaries. Bolton (1999), for instance, describes how lingua franca radio programming in the dispersed islands of Vanuatu enabled the postcolonial emergence of an image of the nation and citizenship based on a shared discourse of "kastom." These contributions to the collection show that while globalization may have restructured such identifications, the nation—as both assembly of hegemonic institutions and as a potent social imaginary—remains a vital part of everyday life for many people around the world (Ginsburg, Abu-Lughod, and Larkin 2002a, 11).

Kaplan and Schulz reveal distinct ways that radio sound is intrinsically entangled with the narratives, sentiments, and images of a national imaginary or the "unevenly spread" authority of governing institutions (see also Abu-Lughod 1990; Postill 2003, 2008; Tsing 2003). Kaplan (see also 2009) underscores the role of radio engineering as "a bottom-up practice of nation-making" in Israel. He describes how radio sound is self-consciously "crossed" in editing practices with shared public events, from banal shifts in weather to profoundly fraught events of commemoration or violence. Radio stations across Israel, he argues, use such crosses within their broadcasts to intentionally shift "the national mood" by evoking well-rehearsed narratives of nation and self. Favoring the logic of live editing over predetermined programming, radio engineers become active interpreters of what it means to be an Israeli citizen. They use radio sound to mark certain events as nationally significant, including the states of emergency that are all too familiar for most residents. Moreover, Kaplan describes how such strategies are taken up by private broadcasters as a way to remain publicly relevant in a rapidly changing media environment. For Kaplan, the conditions of broadcast radio production play a crucial role in defining events and imbuing them with significance within wider imaginaries of the nation. Radio sound, in his analysis, is explicitly imagined to evoke and "engineer" the nation.

Broadcast radio and talk programs do not always reinforce or produce a shared imaginary of the nation. Rather, this technology may also reflect profound tensions implied by negotiating gendered citizenship within the variety of competing social interests organized within a single state. Such frames are complicated even further in cases where citizenship is overlain or held commensurate with the moral values of a dominant religious faith or a foundational narrative of persecution. Schulz describes broadcast radio's central role in widening public discourses of Islamic moral renewal in Mali. She explores how the terms of public debates around Islam are related to the recent proliferation of private FM radio stations and examines the increasingly prominent public presence that radio practice implies for Muslim women, specifically female "radio preachers." Cautioning readers against interpreting such media effects as evidence that media use results in "resistance" by oppressed Muslim women or a "democratization" of religious interpretation, Schulz argues for a less instrumentalist notion of radio technology—an argument supported by many of the other contributions to this volume. Like Kunreuther, Fisher, Lynn Stephen, Bessire, and Blanton, Schulz explores how radio broadcasting, as a relatively new technology of mediating religion, inflects the message it publicizes with culturally specific notions of voice, sound, and authority. In the case of Mali, radio broadcasts circumscribe audience engagements with religious texts and reconfigure public debate by fostering new imaginations and norms of religious community as well as moral difference. Rather than assuming that audio reproduction technologies introduced radical ontological changes or focusing on the disruptions in the foundations of religious authority they generate, Schulz illustrates several significant continuities in how authority is claimed and assigned over the radio, as well as the ways in which listeners attribute significance to a variety of social practices or discourses through their media engagements.

Citizenship, for Kaplan and Schulz, then, is indelibly shaped by radio technology. As in the chapters by Kunreuther, Fisher, Kaplan, Juris, Kosnick, Bessire, Tacchi, and Vidali-Spitulnik, it arises from complex negotiations organized by radio networks whose social effects routinely exceed any single national project or state agenda. While broadcast radio plays a central role in setting the terms of discourses of the nation, a process intensified when listeners are able to call in and talk back to the messages they are hearing, as in the talk radio described in chapters by Schulz, Melinda Hinkson, and Blanton, or the two-way radio described in the chapter by Bessire. Each of the chapters signals that such relationships between radio production and national imaginaries are deeply linked to the experience of listening to and speaking with radio's voice. The chapters of this collection draw attention to the phenomenological and affective components of citizenship, or how it arises from particular bodily practices and cultivated sensibilities. In doing so, tracking radio sociality also comments on a central concern for anthropologists interested in the senses and the critical ethnography of sentiment (Hirshkind 2006; Seremetakis 1996). The contributors to this volume suggest that it is precisely such qualities of radio sound that may allow it to reinforce or subvert projects of governmentality and to graft public/private boundaries onto living bodies. In the case of Russian radio call-in programs examined by Tomas Matza (2009), for example, radio technology enables widespread anxieties about neoliberal political economies to be envisioned as an interior subjective space and mediated over the airwaves. Such processes open new spaces for surveillance and subjection but also point to the ways radio technology promotes complex entanglements of self-making and public-making that can be channeled into a variety of agendas and outcomes, including but not limited to those controlled or regulated by states.

Axis III: Community Radio

Earlier we described a prominent trend in radio studies that focuses on community or alternative radio forms as the clearest expression of radio's emancipatory and empowering potential. Scholars have located such potentials in the free circulation of information within a "counterpublic sphere" that gives "voice to the voiceless" and is opposed to the dominating policies of the state and the corroding local effects of mass media produced elsewhere (Fraser 1991; Tacchi 2002; Tamminga 1997; UNESCO 1997; Urla 1994). Often these notions are taken as givens when radio use involves members of indigenous, peasant, or minority groups that have historically been figured in both romantic and derogatory terms as outside of history and radically other to modernity and its projects. Mario Murillo (2008), for instance, describes Radio Payu'mat in northern Colombia as intrinsically resistant indigenous radio but labors to distinguish this resistance fundamentally from the support it receives from the state as well as the marketing of commercial music it at times includes.

This volume follows sophisticated accounts by Kathy Buddle-Crowe (2002, 2008) and Lucila Vargas (1995) in taking the relation between community and radio as a primary ethnographic question. Chapters by Lynn Stephen, Melinda Hinkson, and Jeff Juris describe three distinct modes of small-scale, local radio practices in relation to larger social and political contexts. Stephen describes what happens when a popular uprising targets radio, in this case a landmark 2006 women's march in Oaxaca, Mexico, that took over state-owned and commercial radio stations. She explores why community radio suddenly spread across the area after the march and relates new opportunities for participatory democracy in Oaxaca to the postmarch integration of testimonial speech genres as central to regional radio broadcasts. Stephen argues that the potential of broadcast community radio to become a political force in this case arises because it provides a forum for expanding the speech genre of personal testimonial. Such testimonials, which emphasize inclusive participation and emotional expressions, are a longstanding feature of local community governance in Oaxaca. The women marchers, by inserting their voices into radio broadcasts, effectively claimed a valid space for participation within the democratic process of the nation, precisely because they made personal testimonials a central part of radio sociality. For Stephen, the antihegemonic or empowering potentials of radio broadcasting depend on direct action and language ideologies or communicational style. The ideal aim of the community uprising in Oaxaca was not generalized resistance but, rather, the specific inclusion of a variety of minority voices within the democratic political process; radio technology played a pivotal role in realizing this aim.

Hinkson describes a distinct relation between local communities and broadcast radio in central Australia. Whereas Stephen focused on the ways commercial stations became a negative catalyst for community mobilization, Hinkson describes how local broadcast practices are related to Aboriginal cultural reproduction. The Warlpiri Media Association was established in Yuendumu, central Australia in 1984, two years before national broadcasting was introduced into remote Australia. Over the subsequent two and a half decades, the activity undertaken by this organization has been influenced by changing funding and policy circumstances as well as the shifting dynamics of intercultural collaboration. In this chapter, Hinkson explores broadcasting by the Pintupi Anmatyerre Warlpiri radio network, which operates across eleven communities spread across a vast region.[3] She focuses on the distinctive approach of young Warlpiri people to on-air broadcasting and locates their media practices within particular Warlpiri cultural imperatives. In this chapter, Hinkson describes how Warlpiri people utilize on-air dedications to publicly proclaim and cite an expanding field of mobile and dynamic interpersonal relationships. Radio, for Hinkson, does not simply reproduce "tradition" in the present. Rather, she shows how broadcast radio is a critical tool for reproducing the defining values and subjectivities of a contemporary Warlpiri community within the complex conditions of postcolonial Aboriginal Australia.

Juris explores similar questions from the perspective of illegal urban radios in Mexico. His chapter explores the role of radio within grassroots movements for social change, specifically examining the relationship between illegality and autonomy among Mexican "free" or pirate radios. Given the extreme concentration of Mexican media in the hands of two large conglomerates, one response has been to attempt to build a democratic movement for communication rights. The work of the World Association of Community Radio Broadcasters (AMARC) to promote the legalization and proliferation of community radios in Mexico represents one example of such an approach. The free media movement proposes an alternative strategy: instead of pushing for legal access, free radios encourage communicational autonomy by taking the airwaves through illegal transmissions, posing a significant challenge to both private and state-oriented media. Through an ethnographic account of the politics of excess and transgression within Radio Autónoma, an urban, largely youth-based free radio station in Mexico City, as well as comparative interviews with their counterparts in other urban and rural/indigenous communities, Juris develops the notion of communicational autonomy and considers the consequences of illegality for Mexican free radios within the domains of autonomy, security, and repression. On the one hand, free radio activists view their refusal to apply for legal permits as part of a growing politics of autonomy among Mexican grassroots movements. On the other hand, this oppositional stance means that free radios are under constant surveillance and threat of repression. Juris thus argues that illegality is a necessary condition and also an obstacle to the politics of autonomy among free radios in Mexico. In his account, such free media are "privileged institutional arenas for the construction of autonomy as a discourse, ideal, and mode of social practice."

These chapters describe three distinct kinds of relations between minority or indigenous communities and small-scale broadcast radio. Along with contributions to this volume by Fisher and Bessire, they reveal how such technologies are used to expand a wide range of practices and social projects, as well as the range of technological assemblages grouped under the label "community radio." These include locally controlled AM or FM stations intended only for regional audiences—the classic "radio by the people, for the people"—as well as community-specific programming embedded within wider broadcast networks, unlicensed FM broadcasters transmitting illegally or diverting satellite signals, or even commercial stations that are taken over by direct action. Despite these differences, the contributors to this volume are in accord on four main points. The first is that the terms of community, resistance, and autonomy are each set to varying degrees by local radio practices. Radio technology is generative of such effects in ways that are specific to both auditory media and particular contexts of control and adjudication. Second, each of the accounts illustrates the central role of mediated voice and vocal address to the constitution and circulation of authority at various social scales. Third, a key component in radio's ability to shape forms of authority in each case derives from the fact that its users hold multiple subject positions simultaneously. Radio use itself may be seen to constitute a unique form of subjectivity across these domains: that of "the media producer," host, or participant. Thus, the voices of Oaxacan marchers simultaneously figure as the voices of gendered subjects, members of a "peasant" or lower class, representatives of domestic labor, universal citizens, and savvy, progressive media makers. Juris's chapter draws attention to the ways illegal radio broadcasts enable a recursive relation between the idealized autonomous space of radio and the personified sites for the romantic or stigmatized oppositions often located in the wilderness or the rural, including the subject position of the "peasant," "youth," "guerrilla," "laborer," or "Indian." Such insights also resonate with descriptions by Kunreuther, Fisher, Kosnick, Bessire, and Vidali-Spitulnik. Finally, these dynamics unsettle the notion that small-scale radio use necessary implies an antihegemonic stance. Rather, community radio use can further a variety of contradictory social agendas (see also Flueckiger 1991). Even in cases where resistance is the explicit aim, each of the chapters shows how the technological features of broadcast radio imply a series of complex negotiations and outcomes.

Axis IV: Transnational Circuits

A common theme linking all of the chapters is the tension between local social projects and the border-crossing potentials of radio technology. For many anthropologists and each contributor to this volume, attending to radio and its vocality has called attention beyond explicit staging of identities in a single place to the highly mobile and fluid registers of belonging that characterize much everyday engagement with uncontainable radio waves (cf. Appadurai 1990, 1996). Radio has proven a particularly apt technology of dramatic emplotment, sentimental scripts, and feelings of longing, nostalgia, desire, or hope as they move over time and space, including international borders (see Abu-Lughod 2005; Fink et al. 1981; Grimson 1999). Chapters by Kosnick and Bessire, as well as other contributors, examine how radio offers a unique vantage onto the debate about how deterritorialized media practices within a global mediascape reorganize a variety of identifications and senses of belonging to the local, the nation, and diasporic communities. Despite some claims to the contrary, the new order of globalized interconnection often noted by scholars has intensified local anxieties about social boundaries of all kinds and has produced new forms of distinction, even within discourses of "multi-" or "pluricultural" states.

In this volume, Kosnick in particular tracks radio practices among peoples and institutions whose social lives contest old boundaries and create new spaces of imagination from which to engage the global reordering of politics and economics. Her chapter presents fieldwork material gathered in the context of working as an intern and freelance journalist at Berlin's public-service radio station Radio MultiKulti. Given that the station's stated mission is to give a voice to ethnic minorities on its airwaves, Kosnick describes how it negotiated the manifold difficulties associated with rendering ethno-cultural diversity audible on its airwaves. Contrasting the station's claims to inclusiveness with the day-to-day processes of constructing audible representations of ethnic difference, she demonstrates the strengths of participant observation in being able to reveal the actual power dynamics that inform daily practices of audio representation. She analyzes how difference was constructed through various aspects of Radio MultiKulti's production, including the use of accents in its German-language programs in order to denote a "foreign view," questions of editorial control in the backrooms, and the construction of an imagined "native" target audience. Kosnick's account shows how such self-conscious participation in a global discourse of "the voice" as a site for resistance undermines the station's claims to give a voice to immigrants and to contribute to minority empowerment. Kosnick troubles the notion that giving voice is itself a transparent process or alone sufficient to allow for expanded political participation, even as she shows how radio technology may be a central technology for imagining political sensibilities through recognizably foreign sounds. In doing so, she offers a distinct perspective on the transnational politics of voice and vocal citizenship.

Bessire's chapter approaches similar questions from a very different perspective, by describing the intensive use of a transnational, solar-powered, two-way radio network among recently contacted Ayoreo-speaking people of the Bolivian and Paraguayan Gran Chaco. Ayoreo-speaking people use two-way radio sets to build cross-border alliances around formulaic expressions of everyday emotion and news of suffering or ill bodies. Such expressions, in turn, are believed to catalyze the circulation of a metaphysical soul-matter that is widely considered to have been reconstituted by contact and conversion and that provides the source of radio's power to heal and assist its participants. Two-way radio becomes an effective technology for collective self-objectification by linguistically standardizing a unique Ayoreo vision of moral modernity around phatic exchanges in a transcendent acoustic space. Yet Bessire also argues that such Ayoreo media practices have long been misrecognized by outsiders, who have either ignored their generative effects altogether or only interpreted these relative to the artificially limited set of practices that count as indigenous tradition or cultural authenticity in the region. Thus, Bessire's chapter locates the political potentials of Ayoreo radio in a fundamental disconnect between fluid ontological understandings of radio's voice and encompassing discourses about what electronic media entail for relatively isolated indigenous populations.

For both authors, radio tunes the researcher in to the complex social interplay that renders borders simultaneously porous and surprisingly durable. Like other scholarship on this area, Kosnick and Bessire, as well as Kunreuther, Fisher, Hinkson, Schulz, and Blanton, emphasize that radio may increase access to a global set of signs and symbols that are always locally coproduced and that the meaning of this access is rooted in particular ways of understanding the relationships between voice, information, power, and space. Similarly, Andrew Skuse (2006), writing about the production of BBC radio soap operas intended for audiences in pre-2001 Afghanistan, has examined the fraught process by which corporate and state agencies attempt to anticipate, activate, and export such sentimental sequences. Such soap operas are not intended for entertainment but rather seek to cause "discrete development goals" around human rights, hygiene, and education. Georgina Born has brought ethnographic attention to the BBC, figuring such institutions of cultural production as "cultural states," intentionally designed to cultivate a "normalized" citizenry through radio broadcasts (2004, 66–67). Viewing such scholarship on radio as a governmental instrument from the perspective of Kosnick's and Bessire's work, as well as that of other contributors, we begin to see the ways that radio's travels at times may also exceed such governmental aims, becoming instead a resource for a variety of border-crossing projects that are by no means predictable or predetermined.

Axis V: Language and Perception

Ethnographic analyses of radio's social life commonly foreground issues of language practices and bodily perception. Each of the chapters shows how radio technology may act as a sociolinguistic catalyst or resource, while radio sound may itself "key" contexts of speech and conversation, shape practices of listening, popularize or stigmatize dialects, and extend or extinguish speech genres, codes, and dialogic conventions (Goffman 1981; Myers and Brenneis 1984). It may also pattern or structure other kinds of perception. Bennie Klain and Leighton Peterson (2000), for example, describe the emergence of a "broadcast Navajo" in vernacular commercial radio. Through rapid tempos of speaking, lexical creativity, and liberal code switching, broadcasters bring together cultural practice and technological innovation to provide a space to index the limits of a Navajo community. At other times, broadcast styles or vocal inflections associated with elsewhere are mimicked or parodied.

Aurolyn Luykx (2001) addresses the significance of satellite radio technologies for vernacular broadcasting and language maintenance programs in Quechua-speaking regions of the Andes, arguing that the significance of this technology emerges in the *lack* of support it receives from state agencies and the not-unrelated sense of ownership its listeners experience through hearing familiar sounds. Karl Swinehart (2009) describes a distinct dynamic, in which programmers at Radio San Gabriel, the oldest Aymara-language station in Bolivia, intentionally edit content for linguistic purity. These chapters, as well as chapters by Kunreuther, Fisher, Schulz, Kosnick, Bessire, Blanton, and Vidali-Spitulnik, emphasize how radio's sociality emerges at the juncture of speech practice, language ideology, and political context.

Chapters by Blanton, Tacchi and Vidali-Spitulnik explicitly make language and perception central to their analyses and extend existing insights in unexpected ways. Blanton draws from ethnographic observations of Appalachian radio faith healers to explore the unanticipated centrality of tactile experience within listening to prayer over the radio, usually understood as an exclusively auditory phenomenon. He describes how the faithful listener in "radioland" must put his or her hand on the radio apparatus in order to receive the healing power of the Holy Ghost. Charismatic practices such as skein prayer and radio tactility, he argues, can be seen as performative negotiations of a specific technologically mediated environment just as much as attempts to influence and instantiate supernatural power. He suggests that there are crucial moments within the ritual context when the performance of prayer and the technical apparatus of radio become indistinguishable. For Blanton, the phenomenon of radio tactility shows how radio technology becomes a "prosthesis of prayer" and an "apparatus of faith" that supplements and extends the spiritualized language practices and rhetoric of faith healing. In his analysis, the language of prayer is fundamentally altered when it is passed through radio circuitry, even as radio sets themselves function to extend the perceptual and tactile capacities of the listening, praying subject.

Whereas Blanton examines how radio practice organizes subjective dispositions, Tacchi is concerned with the ways the digital extension of radio sound organizes the affective management of the everyday in what she calls the "(i)home," a digitally enabled private sphere with multiple channels for the reception and circulation of media content. Informed by a long-term ethnographic study of people's perceptions of radio sound in Great Britain, she notes a striking generational shift in ways of defining radio as a technological form. While young adults nostalgically associate radio with the past, their uses of digitally mediated audio, including streamed radio, closely mirror the domestic role occupied by radio some two decades ago. Tacchi argues that this tension between a changing technological form and a durable domestic utility should be understood in terms of a consistent subjective need for "stillness" and domestic privacy, a function that is at the heart of contemporary digital media's social appeal in the metropolitan north. In her analysis, the digital extension of radio sound reveals the degree to which "the technological" has become central to defining perceptions of the novelty or urgency of the present moment and the appropriate techniques for affective management these entail. In such ways, Tacchi's chapter also exemplifies some of phenomenology's key methodological insights and their applicability to radio ethnography. When Tacchi describes her interlocutor's apprehension of mediated sound as a form of "affordance" (Gibson 1979; cf. Merleau-Ponty 1962; Norman 2002), she provides an experiential account of continuities between radio's domestic life and contemporary digital technology in the (i)home.

While Blanton and Tacchi foreground the relations between the nature of mediated sound and social experience, Vidali-Spitulnik uses radio to describe a relationship between language and perception. Her chapter draws from long-term Zambian fieldwork to locate radio within a range of arenas that are "tangential to the immediate moments of media production and media reception," and she uses linguistic evidence to describe how radio technology and mediated talk changed local ways of perceiving modernity. Vidali-Spitulnik makes this argument, in large part, by describing nouns and verbs for radio broadcasting from the Bemba language. She shows how different orders of linguistic data—such as nicknames for radio personalities, modes of address, circulating radio phrases, word choices of radio listeners, and the very words used to denote radio, including their grammatical patterning—provide important arenas for exploring the entanglements of meanings and experiences within sonic cultures and ways-of-hearing. For Vidali-Spitulnik, radio also fundamentally transforms language, meaning, and perception (see also Fox 1997; Kapchan 2008; Morris 2000; Pazderic 2004). This also suggests a particularly potent avenue for analyzing radio's broader social life and its increasingly complex entanglements with other "new media" forms (Black 2001; Priestman 2002; Spinelli 1996, 2000).

Taken together, these five axes by no means exhaust the potential conversations suggested by the following chapters. For instance, Vidali-Spitulnik, Tacchi, and Blanton join Fisher, Bessire, and Stephen to illustrate how phenomenologically influenced methodologies make radio's varied social lives newly available to ethnographic understanding. These contributions each

employ phenomenological approaches to denaturalize experience and perception and to foreground the varied "somatic modes of attention" radio af-
fords (Csordas 1993; see also Buck-Morss 1996; Desjarlais and Throop 2011;
Husserl 1999 [1919]; Merleau-Ponty 1962). Other potential conversations
focus on the particular orientations toward speech entailed by radio. Chapters by Schulz, Bessire, and Blanton, for instance, identify a similar relationship between radio sound, the perceptual constitution of religious faith, and
the efficacy of prayer (Oosterbaan 2008, 2009). Chapters by Fisher and Kosnick suggest that radio production may encourage a broadly reflexive understanding of vocal expression, opening speech to both technical manipulation
and social examination (cf. Hirschkind 2006; Silverstein 2008). The contributions of Kunreuther, Schulz, and Stephen, in turn, raise important questions about how radio informs a range of gendered expressive repertoires (cf.
Buddle-Crowe 2008; Imam 1991). And as the contributions from Fisher and
Tacchi both suggest, radio technologies are being transformed and sustained
through their imbrication with digital media. This latter potential conversation represents an exciting area for further research that may clarify how the
specific capacities of any media technology are fundamentally consequential
to its social uptake (cf. Black 2001; Postill 2003, 2008; Wall 2004). The aim
of this collection, then, is not to restrict analysis to only five axes but rather
to suggest both the potentials and the challenges entailed in developing a
programmatic approach to radio as a terrain for anthropological exploration.

Conclusion

This volume brings the conceptual tensions described earlier to an emerging
anthropology of radio. We note that this project is only possible to imagine
because of important interdisciplinary interlocutors, but we also suggest how
anthropological methods and concerns may further and reorient work on
radio's social life. The following analyses of radio fields begin to unsettle a
common trope in media studies that there is a single "radio" that spreads
over the globe as if it were an ontologically coherent blanket, differing only
in its cultural content or institutional organization. But these essays also provoke us to think comparatively about what radio does in fact unsettle, alter,
create, or evoke across such diverse domains. While this volume aims to de-
essentialize the boundaries of its primary object, it also seeks to encourage
conversations about relationships between social context and technological form, radio sound and governance, and between transnational forms of
media activism and political agency. These conversations necessarily attend
to the daily practices and embodied perceptions by which radio's ontology

is made intelligible and effective within a given social context, as well as the material, institutional, and technological features that link such practices in any locale with those in another. In short, the chapters that follow ask us to approach radio as historically specific assemblages of technology, technique, and social relations that are also interconnected, of consequence for one another, and amenable to comparative ethnographic analysis.

We offer the concept of "radio fields" as an alternative heuristic to radio as an abstract singular. We understand radio fields as interrelated domains in which radio technologies, audiences, and electronic sounds shape the social lives of our subjects, even as they enliven the anthropological imagination and orient ethnographic research and analysis in new directions. Radio asks anthropologists to think about the relation and disconnect between their different fields in a distinct register. The contributors point to the fact that radio may be about circuits of kinship or personhood, as much as about communication or the aesthetics of electronic sound. Indeed, we argue that such distinctions themselves pose new questions. The contributions that follow demonstrate how ethnographic attention to radio enriches anthropological perceptions with the insights from media and sound studies, and vice versa. This may begin with a productive hesitation and a willingness to tune into radio's social circuitry, wherever it may lead.

NOTES

1. Schramm read widely in anthropology in his studies of global media and development, and both Malinowski's Trobriand work and Powdermaker's attention to media informed his writings on the role of media in social change and economic development.
2. This notably includes Glenn Gould's early radio documentaries and their orchestration of "contrapuntal voices" and the musicalization of sound in 20th-century avant-garde composition, most famously in John Cage's writings and compositions but equally significantly in Pierre Shaefer's *Musique Concrete*. Cage, for example, used the "kinesthetic input ports" created by analogue synthesis pioneer Don Buchla to draw electronic music from an FM radio receiver (Pinch and Trocco 2004, 44).
3. These are three predominant languages of the region served by the Warlpiri Media Association.

REFERENCES

Abu-Lughod, Lila. 1990. The Romance of Resistance: Tracing Transformations of Power through Bedouin Women. *American Ethnologist* 17 (1): 41–55.
———. 2005. *Dramas of Nationhood: The Politics of Television in Egypt*. Chicago: University of Chicago Press.
Adorno, Theodor. 1941. The Radio Symphony: An Experiment in Theory. In Paul F. Lazarsfeld and Frank N. Stanton, eds., *Radio Research 1941*, 110–140. New York: Arno.

———. 2009. *Current of Music: Elements of a Radio Theory*. Edited and with an introduction by Robert Hullot-Kentor. Cambridge, UK: Polity.

Agamben, Giorgio. 2009. *What Is an Apparatus? And Other Essays*. Translated by David Kishik and Stevan Pedatella. Stanford: Stanford University Press.

Agosta, Diana. 2004. Naming the Future: How Salvadoran Community Radio Builds Civil Society and Popular Culture. PhD dissertation, City University of New York.

Ahrens, Frank. 1998. Radio Free Iraq's Strong Signal: U.S. News Service Heats Up for First Time since Cold War. *Washington Post*, December 18. http://www.washingtonpost.com.

Albó, Xavier. 1974. *Idiomas, radios y escuelas en Bolivia*. La Paz: CIPCA.

AMARC. 2008. *Citizen Empowerment for Good Governance through Community Radio in Western Africa*. Montreal: AMARC.

Anderson, Benedict. 1983. *Imagined Communities*. New York: Verso.

Appadurai, Arjun. 1990. Disjuncture and Difference in the Global Cultural Economy. *Public Culture* 2 (2): 1–24.

———. 1996. *Modernity at Large: Cultural Dimensions of Globalization*. Minneapolis: University of Minnesota Press.

Arnheim, Rudolf. 1972 [1936]. *Radio, an Art of Sound*. New York: DaCapo.

Askew, Kelly, and Richard R. Wilk, eds. 2002. *Anthropology of Media*. Malden, MA: Blackwell.

Attali, Jacques. 1992. *Noise: The Political Economy of Music*. Minneapolis: University of Minnesota Press.

Augaitis, Daina, and Dan Lander, eds. 1994. *Radio Rethink: Art, Sound and Transmission*. Banff, Canada: Walter Philips Gallery.

Axel, Brian Keith. 2006. Anthropology and the Technologies of Communication. *Cultural Anthropology* 21 (3): 354–384.

Aylett, Glenn. 2011. Hitler's Radio. Posted on *Transdiffusion*, http://www.transdiffusion.org/radio/features/hitlers_radio (accessed March 10, 2011).

Bachelard, Gastón. 1971. *The Right to Dream*. New York: Grossman.

Barlow, William. 1999. *Voice Over: The Making of Black Radio*. Philadelphia: Temple University Press.

Barnett, Clive. 2000. Language Equity and the Politics of Representation in South African Media Reform. *Social Identities* 6 (1): 63–90.

Barton, D. R. 1937. Radio, the Drum, and the Indian. *Natural History* 40:527–530.

Bauman, Richard, and Charles L. Briggs. 2003. *Voices of Modernity: Language Ideologies and the Politics of Inequality*. New York: Cambridge University Press.

Bazzana, Kevin. 2004. *Wondrous Strange: The Life and Art of Glenn Gould*. New York: Oxford University Press.

BBC. 2005. Ecuador: HCJB World Radio to Air Daily Broadcasts in Cofan Language. *Monitoring International Reports*, February 21.

Bell, Allan. 1983. Broadcast News as a Language Standard. *International Journal of the Sociology of Language* 40:29–42.

Benjamin, Walter. 1999a. Bert Brecht. In Michael Jennings, Howard Eilad, and Gary Smith, eds., *Walter Benjamin Selected Writings*, vol. 2, *1927–1932*, 365–371. Cambridge: Harvard University Press.

———. 1999b. Children's Literature. In Michael Jennings, Howard Eilad, and Gary Smith, eds., *Walter Benjamin Selected Writings*, vol. 2, *1927–1932*, 250–256. Cambridge: Harvard University Press.

Benjamin, Walter. 1999c. Demonic Berlin. In Michael Jennings, Howard Eilad, and Gary Smith, eds., *Walter Benjamin Selected Writings*, vol. 2, *1927–1932*, 322–326. Cambridge: Harvard University Press.

———. 1999d. The Railway Disaster at the Firth of Tay. In Michael Jennings, Howard Eilad, and Gary Smith, eds., *Walter Benjamin Selected Writings*, vol. 2, *1927–1932*, 563–568. Cambridge: Harvard University Press.

———. 1999e. Reflections on Radio. In Michael Jennings, Howard Eilad, and Gary Smith, eds., *Walter Benjamin Selected Writings*, vol. 2, *1927–1932*, 543–544. Cambridge: Harvard University Press.

———. 1999f. Theater and Radio: The Mutual Control of Their Educational Program. In Michael Jennings, Howard Eilad, and Gary Smith, eds., *Walter Benjamin Selected Writings*, vol. 2, *1927–1932*, 583–586. Cambridge: Harvard University Press.

Berland, Jody. 1990. Radio Space and Industrial Time: Music Formats, Local Narratives and Technological Mediation. *Popular Music* 9 (2): 179–192.

———. 1993. Contradicting Media: Towards a Political Phenomenology of Listening. In Neil Strauss and David Mandl, eds., *Radiotext(e)*, 209–217. New York: Semiotext(e).

———. 1994. Toward A Creative Anachronism: Radio, the State and Sound Government. In Daina Augaitis and Dan Lander, eds., *Radio Rethink: Art, Sound, Transmission*. Banff, Canada: Walter Phillips Gallery.

Berrigan, Frances. 1981. Community Communications—The Role of Community Media in Development. *Reports and Papers on Mass Communication* (UNESCO) 90.

Bhimji, Fazila. 2001. Retrieving Talk from the Past and Present Progressive on Alternative Radio. *Journal of Pragmatics* 33:545–569.

Black, David. 2001. Internet Radio: A Case Study in Medium Specificity. *Media, Culture & Society* 23 (3): 397–408.

Boas, Ernst P. 1945. Foreword to *Race and Democratic Society*, by Franz Boas. New York: Bilbo and Tannen.

Bolton, Lissant. 1999. Radio and the Redefinition of Kastom in Vanuatu. *Contemporary Pacific* 11 (2): 335–360.

Born, Georgina. 1995. *Rationalizing Culture: Ircam, Boulez, and the Institutionalization of the Musical Avant-Garde*. Berkeley: University of California Press.

———. 2004. *Uncertain Vision: Birt, Dyke, and the Reinvention of the BBC*. London: Secker and Warburg.

———. 2005. On Musical Mediation: Ontology, Technology, Creativity. *Twentieth Century Music* 2 (1): 7–36.

Boyer, Dominic. 2005. *Spirit and System: Media, Intellectuals, and the Dialectic in Modern German Culture*. Chicago: University of Chicago Press.

Brecht, Bertolt. 1979–1980 [1930]. Radio as a Means of Communication: A Talk on the Function of Radio. Translated by Stuart Hood. *Screen* 20 (3–4).

———. 1993 [1932]. The Radio as an Apparatus of Communication. In Neil Strauss and David Mandl, eds., *Radiotext(e)*, 15–16. New York: Semiotext(e).

Browne, Donald. 1982. *International Radio Broadcasting: The Limits of the Limitless Medium*. New York: Praeger.

———. 1990. Aboriginal Radio in Australia: From Dreamtime to PrimeTime? *Journal of Communication* 40 (Winter): 111–120.

———. 1992. Radio na Gaeltachta. *European Journal of Communication* 7.

———. 1998. Talking the Talk on Indigenous Radio. *Cultural Survival Quarterly* 22 (2).

Brownlee, Bonnie. 1983. Regional Radio for Development: The Information Environment of Miskito Village Women in Haulover, Walpasiksa and Krin Krin, Nicaragua 1978–1981. PhD dissertation, University of Wisconsin, Madison.

Brunetti, Vicente. 1997. *Emergenica de las radios comunitarias en Paraguay.* Asunción: Facultad Politécnica de la Universidad Nacional de Asunción.

Buck-Morss, Susan. 1996. The Cinema Screen as Prosthesis of Perception: A Historical Account. In Nadia Seremetakis, ed., *The Senses Still: Perception and Memory as Material Culture in Modernity.* Chicago: University of Chicago Press.

Buddle-Crowe, Kathy. 2002. From Birchbark Talk to Digital Dreamspeaking: A History of Aboriginal Media Activism in Canada. PhD dissertation, McMaster University.

———. 2008. Transistor Resistors: Native Women's Radio in Canada and the Social Organization of Political Space from Below. In Pamela Wilson and Michelle Stewart, eds., *Global Indigenous Media: Cultures, Poetics, and Politics,* 128–144. Durham: Duke University Press.

Bull, Michael. 2004. Automobility and the Power of Sound. *Theory, Culture & Society* 21 (4–5): 243–259.

Cage, John. 1961. *Silence: Lectures and Writings by John Cage.* Middletown, CT: Wesleyan University Press.

Calhoun, Craig, ed. 1992. *Habermas and the Public Sphere.* Cambridge: MIT Press.

Cantril, Hadley. 1940. *The Invasion from Mars: A Study in the Psychology of Panic.* Princeton: Princeton University Press.

Capa, Cornell. 1956. Martyrdom in Ecuador. *Life,* January 30.

Cardinal, Serge. 2007. Radiophonic Performance and Abstract Machines: Recasting Arnheim's Art of Sound. *Liminalities: A Journal of Performance Studies* 3 (3). http://liminalities.net/3-3/cardinal.pdf (accessed October 1, 2011).

Carpenter, Edmund. 1970. *They Became What They Beheld.* New York: Outerbridge and Dienstfrey.

———. 1972. *Oh What a Blow That Phantom Gave Me!* New York: Holt, Rinehart and Winston.

———. 1975. The Tribal Terror of Self-Awareness. In Paul Hockings, ed., *Principles of Visual Anthropology.* The Hague: Mouton.

———. 1978. Silent Music and Invisible Art. *Natural History* 87 (5): 90–99.

Carpenter, Edmund, and Marshall McLuhan, eds. 1960. *Explorations in Communication: An Anthology.* Boston: Beacon.

Center for International Media Assistance. 2007. *Community Radio: Its Impact and Challenges to Its Development.* Working Group Report.

Chignell, Hugh. 2009. *Key Concepts in Radio Studies.* London: Sage.

Collier, Stephen, and Aiwa Ong. 2005. Global Assemblages, Anthropological Problems. In Aiwa Ong and Stephen Collier, eds., *Global Assemblages,* 1–21. Malden, MA: Blackwell.

Collin, M. 2002. *Guerrilla Radio: Rock 'n' Roll Radio and Serbia's Underground Resistance.* New York: Nation Books.

Corbin, Alain. 1998. *Village Bells.* New York: Columbia University Press.

Cormack, Mike. 2000. Minority Languages, Nationalism and Broadcasting: The British and Irish Examples. *Nations and Nationalism* 6 (3): 383–398.

Couldry, Nick, and James Curran. 2003. *Contesting Media Power: Alternative Media in a Networked World.* Lanham, MD: Rowman and Littlefield.

Coupland, Douglas. 2001. Dialect Stylization in Radio Talk. *Language in Society* 30:345–375.

Critical Art Ensemble. 2001. *Digital Resistance: Explorations in Tactical Media*. New York: Autonomedia.

Csordas, Thomas. 1993. Somatic Modes of Attention. *Cultural Anthropology* 8 (2): 135–156.

Cummings, Richard. 2001. The Intelligence Underpinnings of American Covert Radio Broadcasting in Germany during the Cold War. *Journal of Intelligence History* 1 (2) (Winter). http://www.intelligence-history.org/jih/previous.html.

Dagrón, Alfonso Gumucio, and Lupe Cajías, eds. 1989. *Las Radios Mineras de Bolivia*. La Paz: Cimca-Unesco.

Des Forges, Alison. 2007. Call to Genocide: Radio in Rwanda 1994. In Allan Thomson, ed., *The Media and the Rwanda Genocide*, 41–54. London: Pluto.

Desjarlais, Robert, and Jason Throop. 2011. Phenomenological Approaches in Anthropology. *Annual Review of Anthropology* 40.

Downing, John. 2001. *Radical Media: Rebellious Communication and Social Movements*. London: Sage.

———. 2007. Grassroots Media: Establishing Priorities for the Years Ahead. *Global Media Journal* 1 (1): 1–16.

Early, John D. 1973."Education via Radio among Guatemalan Highland Maya. *Human Organization* 32 (3): 221–229.

Eiselein E. B. 1976. Applied Anthropology in Broadcasting. *Human Organization* 35 (2): 165–172.

Eiselein, E. B., and Martin Topper. 1976. Media Anthropology—A Theoretical Framework. *Human Organization* 35 (2): 113–121.

Eisenlohr, Patrick. 2004. Language Revitalization and New Technologies: Cultures of Electronic Mediation and the Refiguring of Communities. *Annual Review of Anthropology* 33:21–45.

Erlman, Veit, ed. 2004. *Hearing Cultures: Essays on Sound, Listening and Modernity*. New York: Berg.

Escobar, Arturo. 1995. *Encountering Development: The Making and Unmaking of the Third World*. Princeton: Princeton University Press.

Fabian, Johannes. 1983. *Time and the Other*. New York: Columbia University Press.

Fanon, Frantz. 1959. *A Dying Colonialism*. Translated by Haakon Chavalier. New York: Grove.

Fardon, Richard, and Graham Furniss, eds. 2000. *African Broadcast Cultures: Radio in Transition*. Oxford, UK: James Currey.

Fava, Jorge de. 1989. Argentina: Radio as a Tool of Culture; The Impact of Communication Media on Indigenous Peoples. *IWGIA Newsletter* 57:27–32.

Feld, Steven. 1996. Waterfalls of Songs: An Acoustemology of Place Resounding in Bosavi, Papua New Guinea. In Steven Feld and Keith H. Basso, eds., *Senses of Place*, 91–136. Santa Fe: School of American Research Press.

Feld, Steven, Aaron A. Fox, Thomas Porcello, and David Samuels. 2004. Vocal Anthropology: From the Music of Language to the Language of Song. In Alessandro Duranti, ed., *A Companion to Linguistic Anthropology*, 322–345. Malden, MA: Blackwell.

Fink, Howard, John Jackson, Greg Nielsen, and Rosalind Zimmer. 1981. Literary and Sociological Approaches to the Analysis of CBC English Language Radio Dramas. *Culture* 1 (2): 73–87.

Fisher, Daniel. 2009. Mediating Kinship: Country, Family, and Radio in Northern Australia. *Cultural Anthropology* 24 (2): 280–312.

Fisher, H. A. 1990. Community Radio as a Tool for Development. *Media Development* 4:19–24.

Flueckiger, Joyce. 1991. Genre and Community in the Folklore System of Chhattisgarh. In Arjun Appadurai, Frank Korom, and Margaret Mills, eds., *Gender, Genre, and Power in South Asian Expressive Systems*, 181–200. Philadelphia: University of Pennsylvania Press.

Foucault, Michel. 1980. *Power/Knowledge: Selected Interviews and Other Writings*. Edited by C. Gordon. New York: Pantheon.

———. 1988. Technologies of the Self. In Luther H. Martin, Huck Gutman, and Patrick H. Hutton, eds., *Technologies of the Self*. Ann Arbor: University of Michigan Press.

Fox, Aaron. 1997. "Ain't It Funny How Time Slips Away?" Talk, Trash, and Technology in a Texas "Redneck" Bar. In B. Ching and G. W. Creed, eds., *Knowing Your Place: Rural Identity and Cultural Hierarchy*, 105–130. New York: Routledge.

Fraser, Colin, and Sonia Restrepo-Estrada. 1998. *Communicating for Development: Human Change for Survival*. London: Tauris.

———. 2001. *Community Radio Handbook*. Paris: UNESCO.

Fraser, Nancy. 1991. Rethinking the Public Sphere: A Contribution to the Critique of Actually Existing Democracy. In Craig Calhoun, ed., *Habermas and the Public Sphere*, 109–142. Cambridge: MIT Press.

Freire, Paolo. 1973. *Education for Critical Consciousness*. New York: Seabury.

Gaonkar, Dilip Parameshwar, and Elizabeth A. Povinelli. 2003. Technologies of Public Forms: Circulation, Transfiguration, Recognition. *Public Culture* 124 (3): 385–397.

Garnham, Nicolas. 2000. *Emancipation, the Media and Modernity: Arguments about the Media and Social Theory*. Oxford: Oxford University Press.

Gerdes, Marta Lucia de. 1998. Media, Politics and Artful Speech: Kuna Radio Programs. *Anthropological Linguistics* 40 (4): 596–616.

Gibson, James. 1979. *The Ecological Approach to Visual Perception*. Boston: Houghton Mifflin.

Ginsburg, Faye. 1991. Indigenous Media: Faustian Contract or Global Village? *Cultural Anthropology* 6:92–112.

———. 1994. Embedded Aesthetics: Creating a Discursive Space for Indigenous Media. *Cultural Anthropology* 9:365–382.

———. 1997. From Little Things Big Things Grow: Indigenous Media and Cultural Activism. In Richard Fox and Orin Starn, eds., *Between Resistance and Revolution: Cultural Politics and Social Activism*. New Brunswick: Rutgers University Press.

———. 2002. Screen Memories: Resignifying the Traditional in Indigenous Media. In Faye Ginsburg, Lila Abu-Lughod, and Brian Larkin, eds., *Media Worlds: Anthropology on New Terrain*. Berkeley: University of California Press.

Ginsburg, Faye, Lila Abu-Lughod, and Brian Larkin. 2002a. Introduction to Faye Ginsburg, Lila Abu-Lughod, and Brian Larkin, eds., *Media Worlds: Anthropology on New Terrain*, 1–36. Berkeley: University of California Press.

———. 2002b. *Media Worlds: Anthropology on New Terrain*. Berkeley: University of California Press.

Girard, Bruce. 1992. *A Passion for Radio: Radio Waves and Community*. Montreal: Black Rose Books.

Gitelman, Lisa. 1999. *Scripts, Grooves, and Writing Machines: Representing Technology in the Edison Era*. Stanford: Stanford University Press.

Gitelman, Lisa. 2006. *Always Already New: Media, History, and the Data of Culture*. Cambridge: MIT Press.

Goffman, Erving. 1981. Radio Talk: A Study in the Ways of Our Errors. In *Forms of Talk*, 197–327. Philadelphia: University of Pennsylvania Press.

Gray, Frank, and Eila Murphy. 2000. The Unlikely Missionary: Radio Rises to the Challenge of the Unreached People Groups. Posted on *MissionFrontiers*, November 1. http://www.missionfrontiers.org/issue/article/the-unlikely-missionary.

Greene, Paul, and Thomas Porcello. 2005. *Wired for Sound: Engineering and Technologies in Sonic Cultures*. Middletown, CT: Wesleyan University Press.

Grimson, Alejandro. 1999. *Relatos de la Diferencia y la Igualidad: Los Bolivianos en Buenos Aires*. Buenos Aires: Felafacs.

Guattari, Felix. 1978. Popular Free Radio. In *La Nouvelle Critique* 115 (296): 77–79.

Habermas, Jürgen. 1989. *The Structural Transformation of the Public Sphere*. Cambridge: MIT Press.

Hadlow, Martin. 2004. The Mosquito Network: American Military Radio in the Solomon Islands during World War II. *Journal of Radio and Audio Media* 11 (1): 73–86.

Hall, Stuart. 1980. *Encoding/Decoding*. In Stuart Hall, ed., *Culture, Media, Language*, 128–138. London: Hutchinson.

———. 1997. *Representation: Cultural Representations and Signifying Practices*. London: Sage.

Hartley, John. 2000. Radiocracy: Sound and Citizenship. *International Journal of Cultural Studies* 3 (2): 153–159.

Head, Sydney. 1979. British Colonial Broadcasting Policies: The Case of the Gold Coast. *African Studies Review* 22 (2): 39–47.

Helmreich, Stefan. 2007. An Anthropologist Underwater: Immersive Soundscapes, Submarine Cyborgs, and Transductive Ethnography. *American Ethnologist* 34 (4): 621–641.

Hendy, David. 2000. *Radio in the Global Age*. Cambridge, UK: Blackwell.

Hill, Marianne. 2003. Development as Empowerment. *Feminist Economics* 9 (2–3): 117–135.

Hilmes, Michele. 1997. *Radio Voices: American Broadcasting, 1922–1952*. Minneapolis: University of Minnesota Press.

———. 2002. Rethinking Radio. In Michele Hilmes and Jason Loviglio, eds., *Radio Reader: Essays in the Cultural History of Radio*, 1–19. New York: Routledge.

———. 2005. Is There a Field Called Sound Culture Studies? And Does It Matter? *American Quarterly* 57 (1): 249–259.

Hirschkind, Charles.. 2006. *The Ethical Soundscape: Cassette Sermons and Islamic Counterpublics*. New York: Columbia University Press.

Hopkinson, Tom, and Jo Tacchi. 2000. Behind Radiocracy: The Genesis of a Conference. *International Journal of Cultural Studies* 3 (2): 147–151.

Houdini, Harry. 1922. Ghosts That Talk, by Radio. *Popular Radio*, 100–107.

Howley, Kevin, ed. 2009. *Understanding Community Media*. London: Sage.

Huesca, Robert. 1995. A Procedural View of Participatory Communication: Lessons from Bolivian Tin Miners' Radio. *Media, Culture & Society* 17 (1): 101–119.

Hullot-Kentor, Robert. 2009. Editor's Introduction: Second Salvage: Polegomenon to a Reconstruction of *Current of Music*. In *Current of Music*, by Theodor Adorno, 1–39. Cambridge, UK: Polity.

Husserl, Edmund. 1999 [1919]. *The Idea of Phenomenology*. Dordrecht, Netherlands: Kluwer.

Hutchby, Ian. 1999. Frame Attunement and Footing in the Organisation of Talk Radio Openings. *Journal of Sociolinguistics* 3 (1): 41–64.

Imam, Ayesha. 1991. Ideology, the Mass Media, and Women: A Study from Radio Kaduna, Nigeria. In Catherine Coles and Beverly Mack, eds., *Hausa Women in the Twentieth Century*, 244–252. Madison: University of Wisconsin Press.

Inoue, Miyako. 2006. *Vicarious Language: The Political Economy of Gender and Speech in Japan*. Berkeley: University of California Press.

Jelavich, Peter. 2006. *Berlin Alexanderplatz: Radio, Film, and the Death of Weimar Culture*. Berkeley: University of California Press.

Kahn, Douglas. 1994. Radio Space. In Diana Augaitis and Dan Lander, eds., *Radio Rethink: Art, Sound and Transmission*. Banff, Canada: Water Phillips Gallery.

Kahn, Douglas, and Gregory Whitehead, eds. 1994. *Wireless Imagination: Sound, Radio, and the Avant-Garde*. Cambridge: MIT Press.

Kapchan, Deborah. 2008. The Promise of Sonic Translation: Performing the Festive Sacred in Morocco. *American Anthropologist* 110 (4): 467–483.

Kaplan, Danny. 2009. Songs of the Siren: Engineering National Time on Israeli Radio. *Cultural Anthropology* 24 (2): 313–345.

Katriel, Tamar. 2004. *Dialogic Moments: From Soul Talks to Talk Radio in Israeli Culture*. Detroit: Wayne State University Press.

Kellow, Christine L., and H. Leslie Steeves. 1998. The Role of Radio in the Rwandan Genocide. *Journal of Communication* 48 (3): 107–128.

Kittler, Friedrich. 1999. *Gramophone, Film, Typewriter*. Stanford: Stanford University Press.

Klain, Bennie, and Leighton Peterson. 2000. Native Media, Commercial Radio, and Language Maintenance: Defining Speech and Style for Navajo Broadcasters and Broadcast Navajo. *Texas Linguistic Forum* 43:117–127.

Kunreuther, Laura. 2006. Technologies of the Voice: FM Radio, Telephone, and the Nepali Diaspora in Kathmandu. *Cultural Anthropology* 21 (3): 323–353.

Larkin, Brian. 2008. *Signal and Noise: Media, Infrastructure, and Urban Culture in Nigeria*. Durham: Duke University Press.

———. 2009. Islamic Renewal, Radio, and the Surface of Things. In Brigit Meyer, ed., *Aesthetic Formations: Media, Religion, and the Senses*, 117–136. New York: Palgrave Macmillan.

Latour, Bruno. 1991. Technology Is Society Made Durable. In John Law, ed., *A Sociology of Monsters: Essays on Power, Technology, and Domination*, 103–131. London: Routledge.

———. 2005. *Reassembling the Social: An Introduction to Actor-Network Theory*. Oxford: Oxford University Press.

Latour, Bruno, and Peter Weibel. 2006. *Making Things Public: Atmospheres of Democracy*. Cambridge: MIT Press.

Lazarsfeld, Paul. 1940. *Radio and the Printed Page: An Introduction to the Study of Radio and Its Role in the Communication of Ideas*. New York: Duell, Sloan and Pearce.

Lazarsfeld, Paul, and Frank Stanton. 1941. *Radio Research*. New York: Arno.

Lerner, Daniel. 1958. *The Passing of Traditional Society: Moderning the Middle East*. New York: Free Press.

Levin, Thomas, and Michael von der Linn. 1994. Elements of a Radio Theory: Adorno and the Princeton Radio Research Project. *Musical Quarterly* 78 (2): 316–324.

Lewis, Peter. 1993. Alternative Media: Linking the Global and the Local. *Reports and Papers on Mass Communication* (UNESCO) 107.

Lind, Lars. 1950. UNESCOS's Work in Mass Communications. *Library Quarterly* 20 (4): 259–271.

Liu, Alan. 2004. Transcendental Data: Toward a Cultural History and Aesthetics of the New Encoded Discourse. *Critical Inquiry* 31:49–81.

Llorens, Jose. 1991. Andean Voices on Lima Airwaves: Highland Migrants and Radio Broadcasting in Peru. *Studies in Latin American Popular Culture* 10:177–189.

Luykx, Aurolyn. 2001. Across the Andean Airwaves: Satellite Radio Broadcasting in Quechua. In Christopher Moseley, Nicholas Ostler, and Hassan Ouzzate, eds., *Endangered Languages and the Media: Proceedings of the Fifth Foundation for Endangered Languages Conference, Agadir, Morocco, 20–23 September 2001*, 115–119. Bath, UK: FEL.

Lynd, Robert, and Helen Lynd. 1937. *Middletown in Transition: A Study in Cultural Conflicts.* London: Harcourt Brace.

Martín-Barbero, Jesús. 1988. Communication from Culture: The Crisis of the National and the Emergence of the Popular. *Media, Culture & Society* 10 (4): 447–465.

———. 1993. *Communication, Culture and Hegemony: From the Media to Mediations.* London: Sage.

Matza, Tomas. 2009. Moscow's Echo: Technologies of the Self, Publics and Politics on the Russian Talk Show. *Cultural Anthropology* 24 (3): 489–522.

Mazzarella, William. 2004. Culture, Globalization, Mediation. *Annual Review of Anthropology* 33:345–367.

Mbembe, Achille. 2001. *On the Postcolony.* Berkeley: University of California Press.

McLuhan, Marshall. 1964. *Understanding Media: The Extensions of Man.* Cambridge: MIT Press.

Meadows, Michael. 1992. Broadcasting in Aboriginal Australia: One Mob, One Voice, One Land. In Stephen Harold Riggins, ed., *Ethnic Minority Media: An International Perspective*, 82–101. Newbury Park, CA: Sage.

Meadows, Michael, Susan Forde, Jacqui Ewart, and Kerrie Foxwell. 2006. Creating an Australian Community Public Sphere: The Role of Community Radio. *Radio Journal: International Studies in Broadcast and Audio Media* 3 (3).

Mehlman, Jeffrey. 1993. *Walter Benjamin for Children: An Essay on His Radio Years.* Chicago: University of Chicago Press.

Meintjes, Louise. 2003. *Sound of Africa! Making Music Zulu in a South African Studio.* Durham: Duke University Press.

Melkote, Srinivas, and H. L. Steeves. 2001. *Communication for Development in the Third World.* 2d ed. London: Sage.

Merleau-Ponty, Maurice. 1962. *Phenomenology of Perception.* New York: Routledge.

Michaels, Eric. 1994. *Bad Aboriginal Art: Tradition, Media, and Technological Horizons.* Minneapolis: University of Minnesota Press.

Miller, Toby. 1992. An Introduction for Radio. In Radio-Sound, special issue, *Continuum* 6 (1): 5.

Mody, Bella. 1983. First World Technologies in Third World Contexts. In Everett M. Rogers and Francis Balle, eds., *Communication Technology in the United States and Western Europe.* Norwood, NJ: Ablex.

Morris, Rosalind. 2000. Modernity's Media and the End of Mediumship? On the Aesthetic Economy of Transparency in Thailand. *Public Culture* 12 (2): 457–475.

Mrázek, Rudolf. 2002. *Engineers of Happy Land: Technology and Nationalism in a Colony.* Princeton: Princeton University Press.

Murillo, Mario. 2008. Weaving a Communication Quilt in Columbia: Civil Conflict, Indigenous Resistance, and Community Radio in Northern Cauca. In Pamela Wilson and

Michelle Stewart, eds., *Global Indigenous Media: Cultures, Poetics, and Politics*, 145–159. Durham: Duke University Press.

Myers, Fred R., and Donald Brenneis. 1984. Introduction: Language and Politics in the Pacific. In Donald Brenneis and Fred R. Myers, eds., *Dangerous Words: Language and Politics in the Pacific*. New York: NYU Press.

Myers, Mary. 1998. The Promotion of Democracy at the Grassroots: The Example of Radio in Mali. *Democratization* 5 (2): 200–216.

Norman, Donald. 2002. *The Design of Everyday Things*. New York: Basic Books.

Norrish, Pat. 1999. Radio and Video for Development. In *SD Dimensions*. Geneva: Sustainable Development, Food and Agriculture Office of the United Nations.

O'Connor, Alan. 1990. The Miners' Radio Stations of Bolivia: A Culture of Resistance. *Journal of Communication* 40 (1): 102–110.

———. 2006. *The Voice of the Mountains: Radio and Anthropology*. Lanham, MD: University Press of America.

Ojebode, Ayobami, and Akin Akingbulu. 2009. Community Radio Advocacy in Nigeria: Lessons for Theory and Practice. *African Journalism Studies* 30 (2): 204–218.

Oosterbaan, Martijn. 2008. Spiritual Attunement: Pentecostal Radio in the Soundscape of a Favela in Rio de Janeiro. *Social Text* 26 (3): 123–145.

———. 2009. Purity and the Devil: Community, Media, and the Body; Pentecostal Adherents in a Favela in Rio de Janeiro. In Birgit Meyer, ed., *Aesthetic Formations: Media, Religion, and the Senses*, 53–70. New York: Palgrave Macmillan.

Palmer, Craig. 1990. Telling the Truth (Up to a Point): Radio Communication among Maine Lobstermen. *Human Organisation* 49:157–163.

Panos Institute. 2008. *Radio and ICT in West Africa: Connectivity and Use*. Paris: PIWA.

Pazderic, Nikola. 2004. Recovering True Selves in the Electro-Spiritual Field of Universal Love. *Cultural Anthropology* 19 (2): 196–225.

Peters, John Durham. 1999. *Speaking into the Air: A History of the Idea of Communication*. Chicago: University of Chicago Press.

Peterson, Leighton. 1997. Tuning In to Navajo: The Role of Radio in Native Language Maintenance. In Jon Reyhner, ed., *Teaching Indigenous Languages*, 214–221. Flagstaff: Northern Arizona University Press.

Peterson, Mark Allen. 2003. *Anthropology and Mass Communication: Myth and Media in the New Millennium*. London: Berghahn.

Pinch, Trevor, and Karen Bijsterveld. 2004. Sound Studies: New Technologies and Music. *Social Studies of Science* 34 (5): 635–648.

Pinch, Trevor, and Frank Trocco. 2004. *Analog Days: The Invention and Impact of the Moog Synthesizer*. Cambridge: Harvard University Press.

Posner, Daniel. 2001. The Colonial Origins of Ethnic Cleavages: The Case of Linguistic Divisions in Zambia. Paper presented at LiCEP, Harvard University.

Postill, John. 2003. Knowledge, Literacy and Media among the Iban of Sarawak. *Social Anthropology* 11:79–99.

———. 2008. Localizing the Internet beyond Communities and Networks. *New Media and Society* 10 (3): 413–431.

Powdermaker, Hortense. 1950. *Hollywood, the Dream Factory*. Boston: Little, Brown.

———. 1962. *Copper Town: Changing Africa*. New York: Harper and Row.

Power, Marcus. 2000. Aqui Lourenço Marques!! Radio Colonization and Cultural Identity in Colonial Mozambique, 1932–74. *Journal of Historical Geography* 26 (4): 605–628.

Price, David. 1998. Gregory Bateson and the OSS: WWII and Bateson's Assessment of Applied Anthropology. *Human Organization* 57 (4): 379–384.

Priestman, Chris. 2002. *Web Radio: Radio Production for Internet Streaming*. Oxford, UK: Focal.

Prins, Harald. 1997. The Paradox of Primitivism: Native Americans and the Problem of Imagery in Cultural Survival Films. *Visual Anthropology Review* 9: 243–266.

Prins, Harald, and John Bishop. 2007. A Trickster's Explorations of Culture and Media. In Beate Engelbrecht, ed., *Memories of the Origins of Ethnographic Film*, 207–246. Berlin: Peter Lang.

Querre, Francois. 1992. *A Thousand and One Worlds: A Rural Radio Handbook*. Rome: FAO.

Raboy, Marc. 1993. Radio as an Emancipatory Cultural Practice. *Semiotext(e)* 6 (1): 129–136.

Radway, Janice. 1984. *Reading the Romance*. Chapel Hill: University of North Carolina Press.

Rice, Tom. 2003. Soundselves: An Acoustemology of Sound and Self in the Edinburgh Royal Infirmary. *Anthropology Today* 19 (4): 4–10.

Rodriguez, Clemencia. 2001. *Fissures in the Mediascape: An International Study of Citizen's Media*. Cresskill, NJ: Hampton.

Rodriguez, Clemencia, and Jeanine El Gazi. 2007. The Poetics of Indigenous Radio in Colombia. *Media, Culture & Society* 29 (3): 449–468.

Rodríguez, Clemencia, and Patrick Murphy. 1997. The Study of Communication and Culture in Latin America: From Laggards and the Oppressed to Resistance and Hybrid Cultures. *Journal of International Communication* 4 (2): 24–45.

Roth, Lorna. 1993. Mohawk Airwaves and Cultural Challenges: Some Reflections on the Politics of Recognition and Cultural Appropriation after the Summer of 1990. *Canadian Journal of Communications* 18 (3): 315–331.

———. 2005. *Something New in the Air: The story of First Peoples Television in Canada*. Montreal: McGill University Press.

Rozario, Santi. 1997. Development and Rural Women in South Asia: The Limits of Empowerment and Conscientization. *Bulletin of Concerned Asian Scholars* 29 (4): 45–53.

Samuels, David. 2004. *Putting a Song on Top of It: Expression and Identity on the San Carlos Indian Reservation*. Tucson: University of Arizona Press.

Scannell, Paddy. 1995. For a Phenomenology of Radio and Television. *Journal of Communication* 45 (3): 4–19.

———. 1996. *Radio, Television and Modern Life*. Oxford, UK: Blackwell.

Schafer, R. Murray. 1977. *The Soundscape: Our Sonic Environment and the Tuning of the World*. Rochester, VT: Destiny Books.

Schiffer, Michael Brian. 1991. *The Portable Radio in American Life*. Tucson: University of Arizona Press.

Schramm, Wilbur. 1964. *Mass Media and National Development*. Stanford: Stanford University Press.

Sconce, Jeffrey. 2000. *Haunted Media: Electronic Presence from Telegraphy to Television*. Durham: Duke University Press.

Seremetakis, Nadia, ed. 1996. *The Senses Still: Perception and Memory as Material Culture in Modernity*. Chicago: University of Chicago Press.

Seward, Robert. 1999. *Radio Happy Isles: Media and Politics at Play in the Pacific*. Honolulu: University of Hawaii Press.

Shandler, Jeffrey. 2009. *Jews, God, and Videotape: Religion and Media in America*. New York: NYU Press.

Shanks, David. 1999. *Voices for the Voiceless: Report for the World Association for Christian Communication*. London: World Association for Christian Communication.

Shaul, David Leedom. 1988. Topic and Information Structure in a Hopi Radio Commercial. *International Journal of American Linguistics* 54 (1): 96–105.

Shields, Steven, and Robert Ogles. 1995. Black Liberation Radio: A Case Study of Free Radio Micro-Broadcasting. *Howard Journal of Communications* 5:173–183.

Silverstein, Brian. 2008. Disciplines of Presence in Modern Turkey: Discourse, Companionship and the Mass Mediation of Islamic Practice. *Cultural Anthropology* 23 (1): 118–153.

Skuse, Andrew. 2005. Voices of Freedom: Afghan Politics in Radio Soap Opera. *Ethnography* 6 (2): 159–181.

Smith, Bruce, and M. L. Cornette. 1998. Eyapaha for Today: American Indian Radio in the Dakotas. *Journal of Radio Studies* 5 (2).

Soley, Lawrence. 1989. *Radio Warfare: OSS and CIA Subversive Propaganda*. New York: Praeger.

Spinelli, Martin. 1996. Radio Lessons for the Internet. *Postmodern Culture* 6 (2).

———. 2000. Democratic Rhetoric and Emergent Media: The Marketing of Participatory Community on Radio and the Internet. *International Journal of Cultural Studies* 3 (2): 268–278.

———. 2006. Rhetorical Figures and the Digital Editing of Radio Speech. *Convergence* 12 (2): 199–212.

Spitulnik, Debra. 1993. Anthropology and Mass Media. *Annual Review of Anthropology* 22: 293–315.

———. 1994. Radio Culture in Zambia: Audiences, Public Words, and the Nation-State (Volumes I and II). Ph.D. diss., University of Chicago.

———. 1996. The Social Circulation of Media Discourse and the Mediation of Communities. *Journal of Linguistic Anthropology* 6 (2): 161–187.

———. 1998. Ideologies in Zambian Broadcasting. In B. B. Schieffelin, K. Woolard, and P. Kroskrity, eds., *Language Ideologies: Practice and Theory*, 163–188. Oxford: Oxford University Press.

———. 2002. Mobile Machines and Fluid Audiences: Rethinking Reception through Zambian Radio Culture. In Faye Ginsburg, Lila Abu-Lughod, and Brian Larkin, eds., *Media Worlds: Anthropology on New Terrain*, 337–354. Berkeley: University of California Press.

Stenbaek, Marianne. 1982. "Kalaa Uit-Nunaata Radioa—to Be Master of One's Own Media Is to Be the Master of One's Own Fate. *Etudes Inuit Studies* 6 (1): 39–47.

———. 1992. Mass Media in Greenland: The Politics of Survival. In Stephen Riggins, ed., *Ethnic Minority Media*, 44–62. Newbury Park, CA: Sage.

Sterling, Christopher, and John Kittross. 2002. *Stay Tuned: A History of American Broadcasting*. London: Erlbaum.

Stern, Nicholas, Jean-Jacques Delthier, and F. Halsey Rogers. 2005. *Growth and Empowerment: Making Development Happen*. Cambridge: MIT Press.

Sterne, Jonathan. 1997. Sounds like the Mall of America: Programmed Music and the Architectonics of Commercial Space. *Ethnomusicology* 41 (1): 22–50.

———. 2003. *The Audible Past: Cultural Origins of Sound Reproduction*. Durham: Duke University Press.

Stoler, Ann. 2002. *Carnal Knowledge and Imperial Power: Race and the Intimate in Colonial Rule*. Durham: Duke University Press.

Strauss, Neil, and Dave Mandl, eds. 1993. *Radiotext(e)*. New York: Semiotext(e).

Swinehart, Karl. 2009. Redemption Radio: Aymara Language Planning at Radio San Gabriel. *Working Papers in Educational Linguistics* 24 (2): 79–98.

Tabing, Louie. 1997. Villages Find Their Voice: Radio Brings Empowerment to Rural Communities in the Philippines. *UNESCO Courier*, February.

Tacchi, Jo. 1998. Radio Texture: Between Self and Others. In Daniel Miller, ed., *Material Cultures: Why Some Things Matter*, 25–46. Chicago: University of Chicago Press.

———. 2002. Transforming the Mediascape in South Africa: The Continuing Struggle to Develop Community Radio. *Media International Australia* 103:68–77.

Tamminga, Philip. 1997. Is Community Radio an Effective Tool for Grassroots Development? A Case Study of Two Honduran NGOs. PhD dissertation, Simon Fraser University.

Thompson, Emily. 2002. *The Soundscape of Modernity: Architectural Acoustics and the Culture of Listening in America, 1900–1933*. Cambridge: MIT Press.

Thomson, Allan, ed. 2007. *The Media and the Rwanda Genocide*. London: Pluto.

Tomlinson, John. 1991. *Cultural Imperialism: A Critical Introduction*. London: Continuum.

Tsing, Anna. 2003. The News in the Provinces. In Renato Rosaldo, ed., *Cultural Citizenship in Island Southeast Asia*, 192–222. Berkeley: University of California Press.

Tufte, Thomas, and Paolo Mefalopulos. 2009. *Participatory Communication: A Practical Guide*. World Bank Working Paper 170. Washington, DC: World Bank.

UNESCO. 1997. *World Communication Report: The Media and the Challenge of the New Technologies*. Paris: UNESCO.

Urla, Jacqueline. 1994. Outlaw Language: Creating Alternative Public Spheres in Basque Free Radio. *Pragmatics* 5 (2): 245–261.

Valaskakis, Gail. 1983. Communication and Control in the Canadian North: The Inuit Experience. In Benjamin D. Singer, ed., *Communications in Canadian Society*, 237–247. Menlo Park, CA: Addison-Wesley.

———. 1992. Communication, Culture and Technology: Satellites and Northern Native Broadcasting in Canada. In Stephen Riggins, ed., *Ethnic Minority Media*. Newbury Park, CA: Sage.

Vargas, Lucila. 1995. *Social Uses and Radio Practices: The Use of Participatory Radio by Ethnic Minorities in Mexico*. Boulder, CO: Westview.

Wall, Tim. 2004. The Political Economy of Internet Music Radio. *Radio Journal* 2 (1): 27–44.

Warner, Michael. 2002. *Publics and Counterpublics*. New York: Zone Books.

Warner, W. Lloyd, and William Henry. 1948. The Radio Daytime Serial: A Symbolic Analysis. *Genetic Psychology Monographs* 37:3–71.

Weidman, Amanda. 2006. *Singing the Classical, Voicing the Modern: The Postcolonial Politics of Music in South India*. Durham: Duke University Press.

Weill, Kurt. 1984 [1926]. Radio and the Restructuring of Musical Life. In Jost Hermand and James D. Steakley, eds., *Writings of German Composers*. New York: Continuum.

Weiss, Allen. 1995. *Phantasmic Radio*. Durham: Duke University Press.

Westerkamp, Hildegard. 1994. The Soundscape on Radio. In Daina Augaitis and Dan Lander, eds., *Radio Rethink, Art, Sound and Transmission*. Banff, Canada: Walter Philips Gallery.

———. 2002. Linking Soundscape Composition and Acoustic Ecology. *Organised Sound: An International Journal of Music and Technology* 7 (1).

Williams, Raymond. 1974. *Television, Technology, and Cultural Form*. Middletown, CT: Wesleyan University Press.

Winocur, Rosalia. 2003. Media and Participative Strategies: The Inclusion of Private Necessities in the Public Sphere. *Television and New Media* 4 (1): 25–42.

———. 2005. Radio and Everyday Life: Uses and Meanings in the Domestic Sphere. *Television and New Media* 6 (3): 319–332.

Zilm, Jeff. 1993. Nomad Radio. *Semiotext(e)* 6 (1): 189–192.

Zivin, Joselyn. 1998. The Imagined Reign of the Iron Lecturer: Village Broadcasting in Colonial India. *Journal of Modern Asian Studies* 32:717–738.

2

Aurality under Democracy

Cultural History of FM Radio and Ideologies of Voice in Nepal

LAURA KUNREUTHER

The beginnings of FM radio in Nepal coincided with the emergence of liberal democracy and a radical reimagining of the state from several different and often opposing perspectives.[1] Prior to the democratic watershed of the 1990 *jan āndolan* (People's Movement), the "prehistory" of the FM was closely related to currents of liberalization and emerging initiatives in urban media generally and privately owned or operated radio in particular. The success of the *jan āndolan* of 1990 enabled a host of previously suppressed political parties to voice their demands in public, and the very idea of free speech quickly acquired social currency in Kathmandu. Beginning in 1996, FM radio emerged as a product of the *jan āndolan*. Its cultural history traces the changing landscape of political discourse and subjectivities that marked the mid-1990s and early 2000s. During this tumultuous time, Nepalis lived through and participated in two national People's Movements (1990 and 2006), a decade-long Maoist civil war, an ongoing sequence of ethnic nationalist movements, and the final dissolution of the monarchy. Demands for transparency and participation, understood as necessary in order to sustain a healthy democracy, lay at the heart of discussions about post-1990 media and political culture. The commercial FM radio, with its novel emphasis on listener and consumer participation, quickly became a symbol of this new democratic moment.

Yet as a symbol of the larger moment, FM radio has signified both the possibilities and problems with the emergence of liberal democracy in Nepal. On the one hand, activists and community organizers saw early FM radio as the ultimate medium for enabling increased participation in public and political life. Media activists celebrated the possibility of giving "voice to the voiceless" (Dahal 2002, 39) and touted FM radio as the "most democratic medium, because it is cheap and localized" (Onta 2006, 118). But FM radio was also critiqued by those who felt the programs were too commercial and "ruining Nepali culture" (*sanskriti bigrinchha*) through their almost exclusive focus on personal stories, individual confessions, and intentionally provocative discussions about sex and romantic love. Many Nepalis with explicitly democratizing political agendas thought the programs on FM were overly sentimental, vulgar, and melodramatic and not grounded in the deeper problems that people in Kathmandu face every day.

Central to the discourse for and against FM radio have been ideas about voice—what kind of voice should be heard and the significance of voice to the democratic moment that FM radio represented. "Raising voice" (*åwåj uṭhåune*) was a key metaphor to describe activities that brought Nepalis onto the street in protest during the 1990s. "*Åwåj uṭhåune*" did not emerge whole cloth from these democracy movements, nor is it associated exclusively with broad-scale political movements. Rather, it characterizes forms of discourse that seek to gain the attention and persuade authorities to effect change. If a man beats his wife and others in the neighborhood or village protest against his actions, it is referred to as a form of *åwåj uṭhåune* on the wife's behalf. If a community wishes to maintain rights to a nearby forest that has been declared "forest preserve" by the government, they refer to the confrontation between the government and villagers as a form of *åwåj uṭhåune*. *Åwåj uṭhåune*, like its English equivalent, refers not only to one's own voice but also to those who speak on behalf of others or represent the collective interests of any group. Over the past fifteen years, *åwåj uṭhåune* has come to signify speech, political or otherwise, that is especially associated with political and social changes brought on by various democratic movements. As a local translation of a global discourse, *åwåj uṭhåune* is closely associated with political representation, agency, and public discourse, creating what might be called a "political voice."

While FM radio has become symbolic of a democratic moment, and the new relations democracy enabled, it also is a novel site where longstanding social relations are reproduced. The opening of the FM airwaves, for those with extra cash in their pockets, became a new form of property and investment. Large landowners saw the potential of FM radio for advertising and commercial enterprise. Though the new FM radio programs largely celebrated social relations of equality that were seen as more "democratic," those who invested in purchasing FM stations also maintained older forms of inequality that were central to their elevated social position. Large landowners who established FM stations often hired radio hosts at minimal wages, creating labor relations that eerily mimicked the landowner-tenant relations on their farms.

The figure of voice, as represented through FM radio, indicates not only a coming into political consciousness but also the process of learning to be a self-conscious individual with a complicated interior life (Kunreuther 2010). The expression of one's interior life is something that is associated, in Nepal, particularly with the world of international development (*bikas*). Indeed, many people's response to development-sponsored projects is that they suddenly learned something new about themselves, their desires, and their feelings. As Tatsuro Fujikura has argued, early development projects "aimed at creating in people a new sense of self, a self which could imagine oneself as a self with enormous potential (and feels, retrospectively, that such potential was there all along)" (2001, 303). This idea of a conscious and problem-solving individual is bound up with the ideal person of a much broader democratic and often neoliberal ideology within which development projects operate in Nepal: subjects who are self-sufficient, enabled to make their own choices such that their intimate and inner life becomes the main site of political transformation.[2] In this chapter, I link the cultural history of FM radio with the ideologies of voice that characterize this moment in Nepal.

Figure of Voice / Field of Radio

To speak of a figure of the voice is to draw attention to the varied meanings of voice that circulate during this moment in Kathmandu. On the one hand, the voice is a sign of personhood and individuality that is considered inherent in any human voice—a particularly intimate convention of identification that marks personal specificity, often considered to be as natural in its relationship to identity as the fingerprint or signature. In Nepalis' discussion of the radio voices on FM programs, the voices themselves often seem to be animate things, possessing a living agency inseparable from the dense materiality of embodied existence—the soft, soothing voice of one FM host versus the fast-paced, bubbly voice of another or the loud, pointed voice of a politician. In daily life, then, the voice appears as a physical medium of highly individualized transmission, at once physical and symbolic, material and disembodied, present and on the move, associated often with the most significant utterance and yet deeply affecting at levels beyond the meaning of the spoken word. Conceived of as a material sound uniquely generated within the human body, the voice has a social life associated with its role as the primary medium of human utterance. In this life, it is imbued with an irreducible authenticity yet is itself ubiquitously mediated through a range of technologies.

In Nepal, the connection between sound, presence, and voice is directly implied in the actual Nepali term for voice, *åwåj*, which signifies sound as well as the human voice.[3] Nepalis involved in the political protests also exploited this meaning of *åwåj*, particularly during the nineteen-day curfew in April 2006, by going to the top of their roofs and banging metal plates with spoons. The effect was an almost deafening noise that some explained as a way to humiliate King Gyanendra. It was as if to say to the king, "You say you will not hear or listen to us by declaring curfew, but we will, from within the confines of our houses, make sure that you literally *hear* the sound of our discontent." The beating of drums, pots, and pans was deployed by many different protesters, such as a group of Kamaiyas (bonded laborers) during their protests in Kathmandu, who sought to "wake up the conscience of the government officials" (Fujikura 2008, 343). In both these instances, as well as many others, an effective form of *åwåj uthåune* paradoxically took place without words.

And yet "voice" serves also as a figure of speech in daily discourse. In rhetorical speech, reference to "the voice"—finding it, having it, raising it—refers to something seemingly of the nature of a personal possession, a property of selfhood. This sense and use of a voice, the voice that can be "had" or lost, repressed or developed, is in fact a central figure circulating with ever-greater frequency and shifting significance in the daily speech and political discourse of contemporary Kathmandu. The phrase "the figure of the voice" refers to a nexus of metaphors associated with the voice as a sign of intimacy, selfhood, consciousness, and presence, associated, above all, with those modes of selfhood central to democratic political agency. I distinguish, but treat in tandem, the rhetorical figure of the voice, on the one hand, and the social life of those material sounds that are embodied and circulated human speech, on the other.[4]

The voice is such a powerful metaphor because of its capacity to embody specific qualities (its iconic properties) and to indicate particular subjectivities and ethnic, class, gender, racial, or other social identities (its indexical qualities) (Weidman 2006, 13).[5] "Modern subjectivity hinges on the notion of voice as a metaphor for self and authenticity," writes Amanda Weidman, "and on the various techniques—musical, linguistic, and literary—by which particular voices are made to seem authentic" (2006, 7–8). The seeming directness of the voice evokes a presence that many radio listeners in Nepal and around the world assume provides greater closeness and that often becomes an index of truth and authenticity. Here I argue that the figure of voice, as a cultural construct, has gained new significance in Nepal during this moment of neoliberal democratic reforms and an explosion of new media and technology. Radio, of course, is an ideal "field" to study both the rhetoric and soundscape of the voice.

One of the powerful effects of radio, like other forms of media, is its extension of the specific parts of the body into technological forms (McLuhan 1994 [1964]; Kittler 1999). The radio extends the voice and ears such that speaking and listening can be experienced across great distances in space. Often the appeal of speaking on the FM radio in Kathmandu was to have one's voice circulate throughout the city and, quite simply, to hear one's own voice. One thrill of speaking on the radio is that a person can be in two places at once, in what seemed like an almost disembodied experience. As one of the presenters explained to me, "It doesn't matter what you say. People just want to talk and to hear their voice broadcast next to them." At the same time, many people told me that the meaning of this talk was important: for this was a place where they could express their most real (bāsta-bik) thoughts.

The technology of radio alone does not determine its recognition as a medium of directness, transparency, or truth (pace Kittler). These semiotic properties of technology exist within a social world and historical genres of narratives that affect the media's significance. Jonathan Sterne (2003) has argued that the desires and concepts embedded in any technology must be understood from within a broader history of ideas. These desires set the stage for innovation in technology rather than deriving exclusively from the materiality of that new technology. In the case of FM radio, both its historical emergence during a moment of a transitioning democracy along with its material and technological features that incorporated other technologies of voice within its broadcasts—the phone and voice recorders—all contributed to its significance as a medium of directness and, often, a more credible source of information or truth.[6]

Ideologies about radio in many parts of the world also rely on ideas of directness, immediacy, and transparency that are assumed to inhere in the voice. Jo Tacchi writes of radio in England and more generally "as a medium [that] is immediate, intimate, and direct" (Tacchi 2002, 242). Daniel Fisher's work on Australian Aboriginal radio shows that the presumed immediacy of radio broadcasts enables a "linking up" of dispersed kin through request programs, such that "kinship itself comes to typify the kinds of immediacy, intimacy, and connection that radio enables" (Fisher 2009, 282). The media ideology of directness and transparency derives from the material technology of sound recording (its indexical features), the specific features of its broadcast (i.e., live versus recorded broadcasts), and the sociohistorical context in which these broadcasts take place (Kunreuther 2010). The world of international development, the emergence of new media and publics, neoliberal economic policies, and the democracy movements that have prevailed in Nepal, particularly since 1990, all contribute to the sense of directness and transparency associated with voice and FM radio. To situate these ideologies of voice and radio, I turn now to this cultural and political history.

Cultural History of FM

All FM broadcasts on the initial five semiprivate stations in Kathmandu first took place across the hall from the studios of Radio Nepal in Singha Durbar, a former Rana palace that became the official seat of the government in 1951. In addition to housing Radio Nepal, Singha Durbar is the site of Nepali Parliament, the state television (Nepal TV) studios, and other ministries and government offices. In 1996, I accompanied one of the FM managers to the Singha Durbar studios just after the government-sponsored FM station had opened. I recall the decrepit grandeur of the palace I had previously only seen from the street, as we were waved through the tall black, iron gates by a guard dressed in forest-green uniform with a felt beret. The inside studio had a faint smell of musty mildew that was offset by sounds of international pop music reverberating through the shiny glassed-in studio. The studio was brimming with chatter and youthful energy of the several "RJs" (radio jockeys) who occupied the space. All of them spoke rapid Nepali slang, with a smattering of English words, characteristic of middle-class Nepali youth. They were clearly distinguished from the more subdued, middle-aged, largely male civil servants across the hall, who hosted the government Radio Nepal programs.

Fig. 2.1. Singh Durbar, First Radio Nepal and FM Radio Studio (Photo: Cristeena Chitrakar)

When the first radios arrived in Nepal in the 1920s, access to technology and access to political power were synonymous. Like all other forms of technology, radios were the exclusive possession of the family oligarchy of Rana prime ministers and select Nepalis supporting their rule. For anyone else, listening to the radio was a capital crime against the state. All the broadcasts that the Rana elite could tune in to came from the colonial-supported All-India Radio (AIR), established in 1936. Despite the tight control on access to technology, some Nepalis did manage to smuggle in radios and listen to broadcasts from India. Though radios were not available to the general Nepali public, middle-class Nepalis began buying radios through agents who would purchase them in India at least five years before the Ranas were ousted from power. Satya Mohan Joshi remembers that he bought a radio set from an agent in v.s. 2003 (1946) that cost him 350 rupees, a price that was five times his monthly salary (Joshi 2005, 46). Prior to the opening of Radio Nepal in 1951, the Nepali Congress established the first radio station in Nepal in the Terai city of Birantnagar, dedicated to aiding their fight against the Ranas (Onta 2003).

With the dissolution of Rana rule in 1951, the new government created Radio Nepal and a national voice for all who had access to a radio set. Gradually, the ownership of radios increased and was encouraged across the country. As Devraj Humagain suggests, Radio Nepal modeled its initial programming and broadcasts on the Nepali Congress's first underground experiments with radio (2003, 39). Until 1955, all the programs were broadcast from live musicians or from the few gramophones used during World War II that England gave as a gift to Nepal (Mukarung v.s. 2056, cited in Humagain 2003, 55).

The FM radio was established in 1996, forty-five years after the creation of Radio Nepal and six years after the national People's Movement (*jan ándolan*) had transformed the decades-long monarchical oligarchy into a multiparty democracy. By 1996, approximately 51 percent of Nepali households owned radio sets, including 80 percent of the households in the Kathmandu Valley (Radio Nepal 1997, 24). The FM was the first nongovernmental electronic media in Nepal to be managed by private businesses. "Freedom of expression after 1990," writes Pratyoush Onta, "coincided with the expansion of the market (and the concomitant greater need to advertise)" (Onta 2002, 259). This move toward privatization in the radio medium had begun in the early 1980s, when the government pulled out most of its money from Radio Nepal and the radio station began to survive on advertisements (Humagain 2003, 57). The FM extended this privatizing trend and fundamentally transformed the nature of broadcasting.

The beginning of FM radio fit well into broader agendas of international development agencies and the Nepali business community, both of which sought to liberalize the public sphere, and the broader political economy, after the *jan ándolan* I. Just after the *jan ándolan* I, several FM managers told me, a group of Japanese development agents from UNESCO made a proposal to open the FM radio waves to the public. The proposal lay dormant until November 1995, when the Nepali government inaugurated an experimental government-run station on FM 100. Six months later, the government held an open auction to rent out blocks of airtime to private companies from seven a.m. to midnight. Six different companies, many already in the media or communication business, signed a yearlong contract with the government that gave them different slots of airtime throughout the day. For the first five years of broadcasting, then, the FM stations broadcast from a studio within the government quarters at Singha Durbar.

The beginning of FM was also clearly linked to the dramatic growth in mass media, particularly the press, during the 1980s and the 1990s, as well as changes in the new constitution of 1990, which established constitutional protections for all media from closures and some forms of government censorship. Indeed, the democratic constitution of 1990 provided legal measures to enforce freedom of expression, the right to establish organizations, and the right of assembly. Most important, the constitution emphasized the right to protection from what was colloquially known in media circles as the three black Cs of the press: government censorship, cancellation of registration, and closure.

However, censorship was built into the initial FM contract signed between entrepreneurs and the government. At the outset, private stations were prevented from broadcasting news, religion, or any political information. Most of the managers of the companies did not seem to be uncomfortable with these initial contractual restrictions, as sweeping as they may appear. "The government restrictions from Radio Nepal's point of view were quite liberal and fair, I would say," a manager of one of the largest FM companies told me. "Basically it was political: only entertainment, no political things, nothing 'antisocial,' that is, against the society. Your messages should not be revolutionary." "Strictly entertainment," many of the FM managers used to tell me, "that is our business—entertainment and fun."

The government gave its first private license not to a commercial enterprise but to a community radio station, Sagarmatha FM, in 1997. The station was owned by the NGO Nepal Forum for Environmental Journalists (NFEJ). Several commercial stations acquired their licenses from 1998 onward. By July 26, 2001, following a challenge to a government directive that required, among other things, that "independent radio stations could [only] broadcast news obtained from the official HMG sources" (Onta 2006, 101), stations were allowed to begin broadcasting their own news. This opened up a whole new set of prospects for FM radio, and many of the bigger stations began hiring their own reporters to begin producing the news.

Though the majority of initial licenses were given to stations within the Kathmandu Valley, now only a minority of stations are located in the Kathmandu Valley.[7] Many of the stations outside the Valley, however, buy programs or news produced in Kathmandu. Program-distribution groups such as Communication Corner, for example, produce national and local news about events in Kathmandu that are aired on FM stations outside the Valley, with the express purpose of bringing listeners from outside Kathmandu emotionally closer to the center (Onta 2002, 2003). Within Kathmandu, large mainstream stations such as Kantipur FM have acquired additional licenses to broadcast in other parts of the country, but the vast majority of their programming is conducted from Kathmandu and sent via satellite to their connected stations around the country. Thus, FM entertainment programs, despite advertising themselves as a local medium, often end up, directly or indirectly, reinforcing the centrality of Kathmandu Valley to national imaginings.

This sense is enhanced by the fact that many FM stations outside the Valley were established through the help of well-known radio personalities in Kathmandu. Several of the radio hosts in Kathmandu returned to the cities or villages from which they hailed, in various locales around the country, to set up FM stations themselves or to help others in such efforts. Even when Kathmandu radio hosts were not involved in the initial efforts, oftentimes they were hired as consultants to aid in programming for stations that had opened outside the Valley. It would be wrong, however, to suggest that there are no examples of local FM stations that began without the aid of Kathmandu programming or residents. One of the first FM stations to operate even before official government licenses, for example, was the FM radio in the midwestern bazaar town of Tansen in the Palpa district.

Over the course of the 1990s, the FM radio became a desired space for connection and public interaction in Kathmandu. Often contrasted to the state Radio Nepal, which many people describe as a "one-way" medium, the FM quickly became a symbol of the new participatory, democratic moment. Managers and radio hosts promoted the FM radio as a "catalyst for discussion" and a place for "questioning authority." One of the clear contrasts between Radio Nepal and FM radio hosts was in the distinct cultivation of radio personalities through the quality and tone of their voices, enhanced by the difference in equipment (see the contrast in figures 2.2 and 2.3).

Fig. 2.2. Radio Nepal studio (Photo: Cristeena Chitrakar)

Fig. 2.3. Image FM radio studio (Photo: Cristeena Chitrakar)

Unlike the monotone and Sanskritized speech of Radio Nepal hosts, present-ers on the FM address listeners using informal conversational speech. On the FM, a fast-paced, verbose, chatty speaker, who peppers his or her speech with new slang, laughter, several different tones, and English, immediately conjures up the image of a young, urban, middle-class hipster—the most common (but certainly not the only) host of FM programs. It is also this person who is regarded as a more direct speaker, someone who has learned to say what he or she wants and not to hide his or her intentions within po-etic, metaphorical, or literary words, language that Nepalis describe as going round and round instead of straight (*siddha*). The FM programs appeared to be so different from Radio Nepal that during FM's initial years, people in Kathmandu frequently referred to them as different media. "I don't listen to radio," people told me. "I listen to FM."

Politics on the FM

After February 1, 2005, when King Gyanendra assumed sole control of the government and private media in a royal coup, FM radio took on an explic-itly political function that had been largely ignored or intentionally censored during the early years of FM radio. Despite restrictions on producing the news after the royal coup, FM stations found creative ways to broadcast the news. Some began increasing the "information" programs, which served as disguised news updates. A Pokhara FM station, a few people told me, played the news through song. Kantipur FM started running its "bulletins" about local happenings in the area every hour and then increased them to every half hour. Several students told me that they would carry handheld FM radio sets with them at all times during the 2006 movement in order to learn where the next demonstration was, where the police were located, and where not to go. Nepal Radio was one of the few FM stations that, having won a supreme court case against the government's banning their news, unabashedly criticized political leaders and the king. "They would blow and blow [words], scold and scold, scold the king, and also scold the leaders," said Binod Shrestha, one of the leaders of the civil society movement that was particularly active during the v.s. 2062–2063 *jan āndolan* II (2006 People's Movement). Speaking specifically of the success of the movement, Binod stated, "Where should the credit go? It should go to FM radio. . . . Gyanendra thought of ruling in an autocracy, but it was too late to be an autocrat. . . . Gyanendra did not think of the network of media, and he didn't have anyone advising him on this."

These direct interventions into the political life of the nation paralleled the general sentiment among media activists and journalists that the FM had become a space to "hear people's voices." Here the notion of "voice" was decidedly linked to democratic ideas of *āwāj uṭhāune*, or "raising voice," as many of the Kathmandu media constituencies mobilized against the king. This notion certainly seemed to contrast with the general rejection of politics that was so prominent in mainstream FM stations in the medium's early years. I recall in the first year of FM broadcasting, the Kantipur FM office was plastered with eight-by-ten computer printouts, taped around the periphery of the walls, that bore slogans in English which spoke out defiantly against political expression or the expression of any discontent. "No Politics Please," "Silence is the great art of conversation," or "Accept pain and disappointment as part of life." Some echoed a distinctly Weberian Protestant ethic: "Discipline yourself to save money; it's essential to success," or "Arrive early to work and stay beyond quitting time." On the wall facing the door read the most prominent sign: "Say No to Politics, We prefer Love. Say Love, Not Politics."[8] When asked directly about these printouts many years after they were posted, one of the managers declared that it was not politics they were protesting; but rather, making a play on the word for politics, he declared, "a dysfunctional system (*arajniti*) has been made in the name of politics (*rajniti*)" (*rajnitiko nam ma arajniti bhyo*).

Politics of FM Radio

As we have seen, the FM radio helps constitute a political and democratic voice, with all the complexities inherent in such a project. There are also many ways in which the structure of FM management replicates nondemocratic political structures that are themselves obscured by the project of representing all "voices" on the radio. This became clear to me during a visit I made to a station in Nepalganj, in the southern plains (Terai) of Nepal, with a radio-host friend of mine who lives in Kathmandu. This RJ, Dinesh Bhattarai, was a well-known radio personality not only in Kathmandu but also throughout the country because his program had been syndicated on numerous stations inside and outside the Kathmandu Valley. He was traveling to visit this station because he was interested in making a film about one particular RJ there, Amira Chaudhary, whom he had heard about in Kathmandu. Amira was a young Tharu woman from a village thirty-five kilometers away, I was told, who had traveled to the radio station from her village by bicycle to host a one-hour FM program in Tharu language. Tharus are a dominant ethnic group in the Terai, and they have traditionally served as bonded laborers (*kamaiya*) for the large landowners of the south. The story of Amira, in a condensed form, seemed to speak of FM radio's powerful ability to attract people from all regions and backgrounds, including traditionally subaltern groups, and to provide them with the opportunity to have a "voice" on public media. And this was the story the urban RJ from Kathmandu wished to tell in his film—a story that resonated with multiple other forms of "raising voice" (*åwåj uṭhåune*) that proliferated over the course of the 1990s.

What became more and more intriguing to me during the visit was Dinesh's own interest in this particular story, given his own family history with the Tharus. Dinesh comes from a large landowning family in a western bazaar town relatively close to Nepalganj. As it turns out, his family had a number of Tharu *kamaiyas* who worked their fields in exchange for food until bonded labor was officially declared illegal in 2000, in one of the most publicized and significant legal-social movements of the period (see Fujikura 2008). Many of the children of these former *kamaiyas* are still employed on their farms, working now for pay. Before Dinesh left his village to seek his fortune and "earn his name" in the capital's urban media system, then, he had grown up surrounded by the children of *kamaiyas*, learning his position as son of a landlord, who counted *kamaiyas* as part of his property and patrimony (Rankin 1999). Now, however, he describes himself as genuinely concerned with and sympathetic to the plight of the *kamaiyas* who worked in his household for generations. "When I gave our *kamaiyas* rice to take home to their families," he told me, "I always added an extra handful or two, when no one was looking." His sense of sympathy, though clearly limited, seemed central to his interest in making a film about the Tharu FM radio host.

The career of Dinesh thus links the agriculture-based *kamaiya* system with the emergent media formations in contemporary Nepal, giving the proposed project of a narrative film about the laborer-turned-radio-host a broader significance within the cultural history of FM. The *kamaiya* liberation movement reached its culmination a full decade after the restoration of democracy in 1990 (Fujikura 2008). The Maoist civil war was at its height, ethnic nationalist movements had transformed ethnic identities, such as the Tharus, into political identities, and many people across the country were consumed with a profound disillusionment over the many perceived failures of democratic politics. But the new democratic society had, for *kamaiya* activists, provided the necessary political avenues and sources of funding for them to successfully pursue liberation from their landlords. Prior to 1990, the key organization devoted to the liberation of *kamaiyas*, BASE, had no official recognition as an NGO or adequate institutional funding (ibid., 331). By 1991, it was able to register as an NGO and received a grant from DANIDA, the Danish Agency for International Development (ibid., 332). Just as *kamaiya* liberation activists drew on the language of "freedom" and "human rights," they described their activities as successful attempts to "raise their voice" against the government and social structures that perpetuated their bondage. Tatsura Fujikura quotes one of the key activists of BASE, Yagyaraj Chaudhari, as thinking of ways to eradicate the whole *kamaiya* system while he was working as a *kamaiya*. "Yagyaraj recalls that he thought many times that, 'if only there were someone who would help and support me, I would have *raised my voice* against the system' (Tharu 2057, 40)" (Fujikura 2008, 339; emphasis added).

Amira was hired a few years after the liberation of *kamaiyas*. Though her family was very poor, they were not *kamaiyas*, at least not in Amira's parents' generation. Nevertheless, her entry into the public life of FM radio, hosting the first program in Tharu language on the biggest FM station of the region, must be situated in the context of increased public awareness of Tharu people, largely inspired by *kamaiya* activists. By the mid-1990s, aid money for *kamaiya* projects had become a "virtual industry" (Fujikura 2008, 338), and thus Tharus were well-known to the foreign donor community and to businesses, such as FM radio, that were seeking a viable advertising base.

Dinesh and I met the young Amira in Nepalganj—the place where she now resided and the city where Bagaswari FM is located, where she now worked. We discovered where she lived from one of the tea boys at the FM station, the same person, we later learned, who had convinced Amira to apply for the position. Amira greeted us ceremoniously at her one-room wooden shack, which she shared with her paternal aunt (*phu-phu*) and a young boy from her village thirty-five kilometers away. Putting her hands together in a namaste, she composed herself almost immediately, standing up straight, and announced formally, "I will give you my introduction [*parichar*]." In English, in a tone of practiced memorization, she spoke, "My name is Meera Chaudhari. I am from the village of Bansai in the Bardiya district. I attend campus in Nepalganj and work at Bagaswari FM." We sat down to talk on a woven bed outside the house, and she described how and why she went to work at the FM station. She originally had gone to the station during a trip with her grandmother to the nearby eye hospital. It was a Saturday, the weekly holiday, so she decided to take the time to explore the FM station around the corner. There she met another Tharu, the tea boy, who informed her that the station was looking for a Tharu girl to co-run a program in Tharu language and that she should apply. She told me that she did not think she could do it, but the *malik* (owner) encouraged her, since she had some education. Amira hosted several different Tharu-language programs after she was hired, and from the perspective of the owner of the station, they were all successful since the station needed a "Tharu voice" to speak to the many Tharu consumers who lived in the area. The particular sounds of Meera's voice were not stressed by the owner, yet it was clear that her accent and her language marked her as an authentic Tharu speaker, who had learned Nepali as her second tongue. Her peripheral status to the dominant Nepali speakers in the region was clearly delineated both by her female and Tharu-accented tone. Amira's voice on the radio, the owner explained to me, was a voice that spoke to and became a symbol of all Tharus. Through her voice, she created a sphere of intimacy and imagined connection among Tamangs of the area, who listened regularly to her program. As a product of FM broadcasting, then, Amira's speech was thus transformed from a sign of personal identity into a sign of ethnic authenticity, a "Tharu voice."

The ideology of voice, in its different registers, is caught up in Amira's own desire to pursue the FM, in the owner's wish for a Tharu program, and in Dinesh's interest in Amira for his film. The key reason Amira wished to be on the FM, she told me, was to "earn a name" (*nam kamaune*) and to create an "identity" (*paricar*). Having her voice circulate would allow many people to know her, far beyond her reach, and this would potentially be helpful for her in the future, Amira surmised. She laughed when she recounted how strangers had sometimes stopped her after hearing her speak and asked if she was indeed the Tharu radio host from Bagaswari FM. For the owner of the FM, Tharu identity was synonymous with the "Tharu voice" that Meera represents through her speech. This voice was a symbol of collective and authentic ethnic identity and one that had recently claimed a public platform.

After watching Amira present her program, Dinesh immediately commented on the quality of her voice. Though he did not understand the language of the program, he criticized the overall tone and said she needed to work on refining her "FM voice." She spoke slowly and in monotone, instead of the quick-paced speech of urban youth or singsong lyrical tones of sentimental programs, such as Dinesh's own program. Amira's accent and pace, by contrast, highlighted her marginality from the mainstream of FM stations in Kathmandu and, more generally, hegemonic Nepali culture as a young woman and a Tharu. This, interestingly, became a measure of her voice's authenticity, a Tharu voice that became the base on which Amira could "earn a name" in a wider public. Thus, for Dinesh, despite his criticisms, Amira's voice was a sign of a new self-in-the-making, one that had ostensibly been liberated from the ties of agricultural labor that had once defined her.

But there are other ways in which Amira's place in the FM station closely resembles those social relations presumably transformed in the liberal democratic moment through movements such as the *kamaiya* liberation movement. To begin with, there is the lack of genuine payment for work. Amira and others like her are compensated with a mere Rs. 100 (Rs. 70 = US$1) for a program, and indeed this was one reason Dinesh was drawn to the sentimental possibilities in her story: why would someone travel thirty-five kilometers by bicycle to perform a program for only Rs. 100? To him, the reason seemed to lie in the robust and preexisting narrative about FM as a medium of liberation and progress that enables previously disempowered people a public place, a "voice." Amira's story thus glorified the seemingly democratic potential of FM radio. Dinesh wished to make her story into his own narrative film, in which Amira, as heroine, would emerge as a paradigmatic Tharu woman who can "raise her voice." Of course, the ideal of democratic participation supposedly symbolized in the FM voice is complicated by the fact that Amira is barely paid for her program, and yet she believed that the circulation of her voice may provide her with a potential route out of her current state of financial instability. The ideal of democratic participation on the FM is also complicated by Dinesh's own fantasy that Amira's story of "coming to voice" on the FM might be made into a lucrative film (which he would make and profit from), thereby replicating in a new form Dinesh's childhood relation with other Tharus. This fascinating relationship between Dinesh's life trajectory and Amira's life, as well as the potential narration of her life in a lucrative film, raises interesting questions about selfhood, celebrity, and the status of the public sphere. Here the voice is both a dense metaphor used to explain transformations in self and the material means through which these transformations ostensibly take place on the FM radio.

Conclusions: Possibilities for Ethnography of Radio

What happens, the chapters in this volume ask, when radio becomes the anthropological field? As I have suggested here, radio provides a platform for considering concepts of what is real, mediated, unmediated, direct, or present, all of which are central to what many listeners think radio is and what it does. Ethnographic inquiries of radio might turn away from the work of opposing concepts such as real versus mediated relations or present versus absent participants, which suggest, explicitly or otherwise, reified forms of subjectivity, interpersonal expression, or social relations. Ethnographies that take the radio as their field encourage us to rethink such dichotomies and what they imply about changes in modes of social being situated before or after a watershed of a given technological innovation. Central to the reimagining that such ethnography offers is the figure of the voice. What does it mean when people describe the radio as a means to circulate an authentic Tharu voice, such as Amira's, or when people say they feel as if the radio host is "really there" or that radio is a form of media that allows subaltern subjects "to find their voice." Ethnographies of radio address the voice as generated and circulated on radio programs and pursue the figure of the voice as central to understanding how people imagine presence, directness, and mediation itself. These questions lead us, inevitably, to inquire into ideologies of voice beyond the radio field, to connecting us to other spaces, contexts, and practices.

Concepts of mediation, voice, directness, and presence cannot be separated from the cultural and political history in which they are at play. The histories of democracy and democratic movements as well as neoliberal privatization are key sites where ideologies of voice are being produced and put into practice. They are also the historical moments in which FM radio came into being in Nepal and emerged as a symbol of the new democratic movement. In these contexts, the formation of new identities has been repeatedly imagined as the emergence or creation of a new "voice" within public culture. The story of Meera articulates several aspects of this moment vis-à-vis the FM radio and several implications of the figure of voice. Her entry into the FM is made possible through—and perhaps necessitated by —her participation in the distinctive identity of the Tharus, publicized and politicized through the *kamaiya* movement and its analogues among other ethnic nationalist and separatist movements. Her role within the formation of a new provincial outpost of the FM radio network is determined by her being hired to provide the "Tharu voice," which is at once constituted in this moment of reproduction. Meera encounters ideologies of voice within and outside the FM that make it possible to imagine "earning a name" through the circulation of her voice.

Ethnography of radio, then, asks us to reconsider and unsettle a field of concepts related to presence, voice, and authenticity that are themselves built into traditional ethnography. In most ethnographies, speech and voice are thought of as the authentic, unmediated mode of communication (Axel 2006, 369). "In relation to [the] ethnographic present," writes Brian Axel, "what is produced is . . . a time before the advent of new technologies of communication, a time of the old, traditionally communicative practices that are limiting, constraining, confining or binding. 'Face-to-face' is an index of this time before, which is also glossed in terms of 'physical proximity,' 'contexts' in 'real time and real space'" (ibid., 368–369). Frequently, analyses of media by anthropologists and other media scholars end up effectively producing an anterior space, which appears more direct and immediate, one that is often termed "culture." Yet in my own ethnographic exploration of FM radio, Nepalis often describe the "realness" of FM radio conversations in contrast to face-to-face conversations. The most interesting feature of such an inversion of conceptual common sense may be the degree to which it highlights the social mediation that constitutes *face-to-face* encounters, that is to say, the whole range of practices and interactions that are generally referred to as "culture."

In a critical ethnography of radio, we cannot separate "media" from "culture" and might instead think of these two spheres of action as interpenetrating fields of a broader and fundamental process of mediation (Mazzarella 2004). While the voice is often considered within ethnography to embody all that is classically thought of as "culture," it has, like any other medium, specific and highly contextual social histories. Most generally, the analytic appeal of the voice as a figure lies precisely in the resilience with which it defies a separation between "culture" and "media."

NOTES

Research for this chapter was supported by Fulbright-Hays Dissertation Fellowship, SSRC South Asia Dissertation Fellowship, Fulbright-Hays Faculty Research Abroad, and Bard Faculty Research funds. I wish to thank Kalyan Gautum, Sanjeev Pokharel, and Bhoju Paudel for their generous help in conducting this research at different stages and Cristeena Chitrakar for her photographs. Danny Fisher and Lucas Bessire were a pleasure to work with, and I thank them for their editing skills and efforts in putting this volume together.

1. This chapter is based on more than a decade of research, from 1996 through 2007. Some of the findings presented here will appear in another form in my forthcoming book, *Voicing Subjects* (Berkeley: University of California Press).

2. As I argue in my forthcoming book, the political and the intimate voice are mutually constitutive, both being important aspects of modern subjectivity emerging in Kathmandu (see also Kunreuther 2006).

3. The other common word for voice is *swar*. I discuss the distinction between *âwâj* and *swar* in my forthcoming book.

4. The idea of *âwâj uṭhâune* bears close resemblance to the metaphor of voice used in Euro-American discourses to describe consciousness and empowerment, particularly among a group of people who have not been adequately represented in history or politics. See, for example, Guha 1996, Gilligan 1982, and the academic feminist journal *Voices*. In Gyatri Spivak's famous article (1988), she critiques the collusion of agency and voice common among subaltern historians.

5. Weidman, along with those who coined the term "vocal anthropology" (Feld et al. 2004), provides invaluable insights about the relation of vocalized sound, music, and language that influence my own study of voice. While this research draws on their insights, I depart from their interest on the relation between music and vocalized sound, turning my attention more squarely on voiced sound and the metaphor of voice used to describe political representation and consciousness.

6. See Papailias 2005 for a related discussion of how tape recorders reconfigured oral historians notions of historical truth.

7. The vast majority of licenses granted by the government in 2007–2008 were to community FM stations, the first in South Asia. During the civil war, the Maoists also ran an unlicensed FM station that could be heard outside of Kathmandu and in the far west and east of Nepal.

8. Such messages parallel other emerging media during the mid-1990s, such as the "happy magazine" *Attitudes*, as Pratyoush Onta describes it. The advertisement for its first issue, Onta reports, was remarkably similar to these computer printouts: "The Nepalese media—dominated by political, economic and other depressing issues. The question—are things really that bad? We at ADDITUDES think differently. Life is beautiful, it is to be celebrated" (quoted in Onta 2006, 70).

REFERENCES

Axel, Brian. 2006. Anthropology and the New Technologies of Communication. *Cultural Anthropology* 21 (3): 354–385.

Dahal, Dev Raj. 2002. Mass Media, Trust, and Governance. In *Media and Society*, ed. P. Kharel, Dev Raj Dahal, Sushil Raj Pandey, and Krishna B. Bhattachan, 19–48. Kathmandu: Supravaha.

Feld, Steven, Aaron Fox, Thomas Porcello, and David Samuels. 2004. Vocal Anthropology. In Alessandro Duranti, ed., *A Companion to Linguistic Anthropology*, 321–345. Malden, MA: Blackwell.

Fisher, Daniel. 2009. Mediating Kinship: Country, Family, and Radio in Northern Australia. *Cultural Anthropology* 24 (2): 280–312.

Fujikura, Tatsuro. 2001. Discourses of Awareness: Notes for a Criticism of Development. *Studies in Nepali History and Society* 6 (2): 271–313.

——. 2008. The Bonded Agricultural Labourers' Freedom Movement in Western Nepal. In *Nepalis Inside and Outside Nepal*, ed. David N. Gellner, Hiroshi Ishii and Katsuo Nawa. Delhi: Manohar.

Gilligan, Carol. 1982. *In a Different Voice: Psychological Theory and Women's Development*. Cambridge: Harvard University Press.

Guha, Ranjit. 1996. The Small Voice of History. In *Subaltern Studies 10: Writings on South Asian History and Society*, ed. Gautum Bhadra, Gyan Prakash, and Susie Tharu, 1–12. Delhi: Oxford University Press.

Humagain, Devraj. 2003. Radio Nepalka Karyakram: Adharshataabdiko Samiksha. (Radio Nepal's Programs: Overview Collection). *Studies in Nepali History and Society* 8 (1): 37–66.

Joshi, Satya Mohan. 2005. Jindagikaa Hunharumaa Radio (Radio's Rhythm of Life). In *Radiosanga Hurkandaa: Tinpuste Nepaliko Anubhab (Growing Up with Radio: Three Generations of Nepali's Experience)*, ed. Shekar Parajuli and Pratyoush Onta. Kathmandu: Martin Chauteri.

Kittler, Fredrich. 1999. *Gramophone, Film, Typewriter*. Translated by Geoffrey Winthrop-Young and Michael Wutz. Stanford: Stanford University Press.

Kunreuther, Laura. 2006. Technologies of the Voice: FM Radio, Telephone, and the Nepali Diaspora in Kathmandu. *Cultural Anthropology* 21 (3): 323–353.

——. 2010. Transparent Media: Radio, Voice, and Ideologies of Directness in Post-Democratic Nepal. In Media Ideologies, ed. Ilana Gershon, special issue, *Journal of Linguistic Anthropology* 20 (2): 334–351.

Mazzarella, William. 2004. Culture, Globalization, Mediation. *Annual Review of Anthropology* 33:345–367.

McLuhan, Marshall. 1994 [1964]. *Understanding Media: The Extensions of Man*. Cambridge: MIT Press.

Onta, Pratyoush. 2002. Critiquing the Media Boom. In *State of Nepal*, ed. Kanak Mani Dixit. Kathmandu: Himal Books.

——. 2003. Radio Nepalbhanda Pahileko Yugmaa Nepaliko Radio Anubhab (Nepali's Experience of Radio before the Era of Radio Nepal). In *Radio Nepalko Samajik Itihas (Radio Nepal's Social History)*, ed. Pratyoush Onta et al. Kathmandu: Martin Chauteri.

——. 2006. *Mass Media in Post-1990 Nepal*. Kathmandu: Martin Chauteri.

Papailias, Penelope. 2005. *Genres of Recollection: Archival Poetics and Modern Greece*. New York: Palgrave.

Radio Nepal. 1997. *Radio Ownership and Listening in Nepal: A National Study*. Kathmandu: Radio Nepal, Audience Research Section.

Rankin, Katherine. 1999. The Predicament of Labor: Kamaiya Practices and the Ideology of "Freedom." In *Nepal: Tharu and Tarai Neighbors*, ed. H. O. Skar. Kathmandu: EMR.

Spivak, Gyatri. 1988. Can the Subaltern Speak? In *Marxism and the Interpretation of Culture*, ed. Cary Nelson and Larry Grossberg, 271–313. Urbana: University of Illinois Press.

Sterne, Jonathan. 2003. *The Audible Past: Cultural Origins of Sound Reproduction*. Durham: Duke University Press.

Tacchi, Jo. 2002. Radio Texture: Between Self and Others. In *The Anthropology of Media: A Reader*, ed. Kelly Askew and Richard Wilk. Oxford, UK: Blackwell.

Weidman, Amanda. 2006. *Singing the Classical, Voicing the Modern: The Postcolonial Politics of Music in South India*. Durham: Duke University Press.

3

From the Studio to the Street

Producing the Voice in Indigenous Australia

DANIEL FISHER

To listen to Aboriginal radio in Australia is to hear a broad range of voices. Some speak Indigenous languages such as Anindilyakwa or Yolngu Mata in the Top End or Arrernte in the Central Desert. Many more speak in English, often refigured by Aboriginal English or Kriol syntax and peppered with Aboriginal English slang. And most also endeavor to move listeners, to make them laugh, to cajole, persuade, and inform. They may seek a phatic, affecting link between kin. Others work to establish a shared perspective with non-Indigenous listeners. Others still will ask listeners to watch what they eat, to see a general practitioner regularly, or to walk or catch a lift if they have been drinking. Radio's mediation of these many voices has also meant that many people, chief among them Indigenous radio producers but also commonwealth policymakers and advocates, think, talk, and argue about how indigeneity inhabits and animates particular voices. This is to say that Indigenous radio is a place where the voice is culturally produced—where particular voices are sites of cultural practice, governmental intervention, and social reflection.

Aboriginal Australians have been producing radio and building radio stations for just over thirty years. Today Indigenous Australian broadcasters include remote satellite networks, larger regional broadcasters, and more urban stations operating under community broadcasting legislation. Such institutions have a long history as sites of political activism, have encouraged the growth of a significant Indigenous music industry, and are arguably the most successful Aboriginal media in Australia, frequently addressing a national Aboriginal public (Fisher 2009). As institutions in which people reflexively attend to the voice both discursively and through practical work on wired sound, many Aboriginal radio stations also foster collective reflection on the voice as a social fact and also a technical one, amenable to extensive expressive manipulation, governmental development, and intra-Aboriginal reflection.

In this chapter I draw on research in 4AAA "Murri Country," a technology-rich, highly successful Aboriginal community radio station, in order to explore features of this institutional "voice consciousness" (Feld et al. 2004) and to address the relationship between a broad, transnational discourse of voice as an index of collective identity and the highly reflexive, maximally technical work of Aboriginal radio production. I demonstrate that while "voice" has become a paramount icon of Indigenous agency and political power, and occasionally a fetish of policy discourse (Batty 2003; Michaels 1994; Sterne 2003), it is also persistently denaturalized in forms of technical labor and vocal performance and in the discursive give and take of Aboriginal radio production and musical curation. Indeed, in the increasingly industrial, digitally mediated work of Indigenous radio, the voice can at times seem a material object, external to particular bodies, and an effect of technological intervention and manipulation. In the course of my fieldwork at 4AAA, people talked about the voice constantly both in their professional labor and as a more generalized preoccupation. And this interest seemed intense in proportion to the ways that people's voices were experienced as estranged, as uncannily different or other, at once of Aboriginal selves and other to them.

In seeking to understand this experience I describe the ways in which radio production asked my interlocutors to put in juxtaposition several different ideas of the voice. On one hand, there are actual voices as they exist in radio and recording practice. These voices are produced in a fundamental sense through microphone selection and positioning and through a whole range of signal-processing, mixing, and mastering techniques. But this voice as a technologically plastic artifact exists in tension with a range of discourses and commonsense ideas about voice familiar to anthropologists through tropes of representation and identity, of the voice as agency and authenticity and as a site of governmental interest and elicitation. The material I present here aims to suggest some ways that my interlocutors endeavor, with mixed success, to bring these different domains together. In framing radio as a site of cultural production, my discussion foregrounds how technological and social experiences *of* voice may unsettle discursive certainties or propositions *about* voice.

Analyses of Radio as a Vocal Technology

That radio may amplify the voice's social meaning as index of collective agency is an idea with a distinguished history. Frantz Fanon's writings on radio are prescient in their interest in the uncanny, social power of a "voice" that is heard never in its "calm objectivity" but rather in light of colonial social relations, violence, and new kinds of national subjectivity. Anticipating Marshall McLuhan, and preceding Benedict Anderson's *Imagined Communities* by twenty-five years, Fanon writes of the changing meaning of the radio voice in Algeria over the course of the revolution—from being a voice of colonial power to one of national subjectivity and a way to affectively participate in the revolution, in which owning a radio meant "buying the right of entry into the struggle of an assembled people" (1959, 84). Vocal sound occupies a paradoxical place in this important chapter in Fanon's writing, at once central to it but curiously absent. The more the French colonial forces sought to jam the insurgent broadcasts of *The Voice of Fighting Algeria* and the more difficult it was to actually hear its broadcasts, he argues, the more powerful it became as an icon of Algerian independence and national identity.[1]

In psychoanalytic and deconstructive writings that dwell on the voice, the voice also figures as excessive to language, foundational for all meaning, and yet meaning nothing in itself (Barthes 1977; Derrida 1977; Dolar 2006; Salecl and Žižek 1996).[2] That is, the voice is not language but rather is the materiality of what we hear, an excess to meaning. It exceeds semiosis and "means" more than it can say because in this work the voice is not simply speech but rather what is left over "after" language and efforts to pin down language through phonology, linguistics, and so on (see especially Dolar 2006). Similarly, Fanon describes a radio voice that exceeds linguistic or prosodic, poetic analysis. It is foundational for a sense of Algerian national subjectivity and yet, as one seeks to tune in to it, remains static and noise. In Fanon's analysis the radio voice emerges as a kind of social Rorschach, an aural instigation to a listener's historically primed psychic life. In describing the ways that media itself became a "voice of free Algeria," Fanon thus provides a psychoanalytically informed account of the voice's mediatization at midcentury, one in which electronic noise is heard as the voice and becomes a potent screen onto which Algerian desires for liberation are projected.

Powerful equations of media with voice continue to shape how we think about radios' sounds today—and are deeply embedded in longstanding discourses about the voice as a prime index of agency and collective identity (Bauman and Briggs 2003; Kunreuther, chap. 2 in this volume). These broader discourses have long been both explored and critiqued to illuminate their historicity, potency, and sociohistorical variability (Feld et al. 2004; Weidman 2006; cf. Derrida 1977; Spivak 1988). Gayatri Spivak, for instance, famously deconstructs the voice as straightforward index of agency by exploring the great degree of mediation between speech and collective subject and the heterogeneity of the "subaltern" itself (1988). More recently, anthropologists have explored the ready equation of media technologies, voice, and communication by exploring how ideologies of voice may attend the globalization of media's techniques and technologies (Kunreuther 2006; Morris 2000; cf. Axel 2006). In these frameworks the "voice" as a figure of agency may in fact obscure local ontologies of mediation and mask the heterogeneity within any subject, collective or individual. From endeavors to negate the self (Spivak 1988) to dramatic stagings of the voice's insufficiency in the face of broader ontologies of mediation (Morris 2000), this scholarship suggests, with Fanon, some startling moments in which discourses of vocal agency are troubled by local, social complications of speaking in one's "own" voice.

In Australia these complications are precisely what makes radio an exciting thing to hear for Aboriginal people as much as for anthropologists. Radio in Australia has been celebrated as a means by which Aboriginal people can become "a people"—culturally empowered in the face of transnational media commodities and an encompassing society's damaging representations. And indeed, radio has become a crucial site for Indigenous cultural reproduction and activism, and the broad publics and intra-Indigenous relationships that radio production entails have transformed people's sense of possibility and promise in Indigenous Australia (see Ginsburg 1994, 1997). But producers are also aware of the many voices that jostle for space on Indigenous radio. The forms of emergent public culture that radio fosters keep people listening even as they entail conflict and anxiety about what radio sound should index and a frequent disavowal of efforts to "speak for" a broader Indigenous domain. So while Indigenous radio stations are today at once places where Aboriginal people exercise forms of agency and autonomy vis-à-vis a broader population, the voice that comes into being on such stations is neither static nor homogeneous. The many different levels of mediation that voices receive —governmental, technical, and discursive—make voice in these stations a site of radical reflection and sustained interest.

This reflection takes part in the context of a longer history in Australia in which forms of autobiography, film, and video, have been powerful means by which Aboriginal people have unsettled normative constructions of settler-Australian history. Conceptualized as "telling one's story," and this storying itself understood as a therapeutic means to heal traumas both individual and collective in character, these expressive practices inform progressive, state-supported projects aiming to "give voice" (Attwood 2001; Batty 2003). For instance, several projects draw on hip hop's popularity and cultural prestige to encourage Indigenous self-esteem in remote communities, instrumental-izing the metaphor for agency and power that "voice" has long provided (cf. Peters 2004). The group Indigenous Hip Hop Projects (IHHP) visits remote and regional Indigenous communities using hip hop music and dance to ani-mate "confidence circles" and "expression sessions" in which IHHP provides musical backing for students to generate rap lyrics. The capacity-building emphasis of this culture work is captured by an IHHP video clip, in which a DJ elicits participation in a confidence circle: "Who's going to go first?!" he asks. "Come out and give it a go, come out and be leaders, come out and express yourself!"

Indigenous radio stations themselves embrace a broad range of institu-tional tactics for eliciting and encouraging vocal expressivity that bring to-gether radio and music production, storytelling, and vocational education. The Australian Music Radio Airplay Project (AMRAP) encourages young people's media production and has funded Aboriginal media students to take equipment into Queensland's prisons to record the hip hop performances of young incarcerated men and women for broadcast on the National In-digenous Radio Service and for distribution to Australia's broad network of community radio stations. In western Sydney the community arts group In-formation and Cultural Exchange (ICE) works to encourage arts, media, and music production with Indigenous and new Australian immigrants in west-ern Sydney and has sought to promote and represent Indigenous hip hop art-ists and to train Indigenous and young new immigrants in radio production.

While originating in Aboriginal media activism, today much cultural pro-duction in radio stations thus receives governmental support and operates within a developed institutional network focused on giving voice. Indeed,

Aboriginal broadcasting joined community radio activism in the 1970s and 1980s in drawing attention to the limitations of a single national broadcaster and its structural presuppositions of a singular national public at a time when Australia's public culture was undergoing an unprecedented shift toward the recognition and inclusion of a diverse population (Ang, Hawkins, and Dabboussy 2008; Fisher 2009; Inglis 2006).[3] Philip Batty (2003) further argues that Aboriginal media institutions were the products of a kind of complicity between Aboriginal activists and policymakers then in need of partners in Indigenous development. Here forms of Indigenous voice became new "technologies of the self" (Burchell 1993; Miller 1993), at once platforms for Indigenous self-fashioning and forms of governmental practice.

As this intersection of diverse interests and institutional efforts should suggest, the stakes of Indigenous Australian radio production are high and its forms of address complex. Many radio stations are sites of highly reflexive and collective self-fashioning, in which discourses about voice join a range of musical genres and practices, as well as a number of techniques and technologies geared toward the voice's industrialized production and governmental instrumentalization. They are also places where diverse interests in eliciting an Indigenous voice find institutional and programmatic expression. So while Indigenous radio production and vocal training may allow the voice to become an object of discursive reflection tied to a broader struggle for Indigenous cultural survival, it is also a site of technical work and governmental investment. Together, these at times competing interests in and ideas about voice impel producers to reflexively consider its contours, boundaries, and social ramifications.

Aboriginal Radio

The advent of Indigenous radio production can be located in the early 1980s in two, related developments: first, the efforts of Aboriginal activists to develop community radio in urban and town locations and, second, the growth of activism and subsequently cultural policy to promote remote Indigenous broadcasting—initially within a framework of cultural survival and language maintenance. In Australia's southeast, Aboriginal activists began broadcasting on non-Indigenous community radio stations, often at the invitation of DJs involved in the peace movements of the 1970s and 1980s, and themselves inspired by the anarchist, oppositional politics of European and particularly Italian free radio. In relatively remote areas of Australia's north and west, and in response to the advent of satellite broadcasting across the Northern Territory, activists, academics, and policymakers saw in radio and in then-new video technologies a means to intervene in the kinds of media to which Aboriginal people would be subject (Ginsburg 1991, 1994, 1997; Langton 1993; Michaels 1994).

Aboriginal radio's expansive spatial reach began with the networking of remote broadcasters in the 1990s and with the 1996 establishment of the National Indigenous Radio Service (NIRS). These technological developments led to the possibility of national broadcast programming and mark the relatively recent arrival of a national, electronically mediated Aboriginal domain. In this period many stations have come to acquire bureaucratically rationalized internal organization and an industrially polished, technologically "professional" sound. At 4AAA these moves are understood as supporting an effort to build as large an audience as possible and to bring Aboriginal voices and musics to as broad of an Australian audience as possible.

Efforts to produce polished radio do not contradict 4AAA's political history and activist mandate. From the suppression of demonstrations by the famously conservative and corrupt state government of Joh Bjelke-Petersen to the clandestine preparations and excitement of public protest, older Aboriginal activists in South East Queensland speak of their early experiences producing media in the same breath as activist performance, racism, and a deep anger at the social exclusion of Aboriginal people from public and political life. Stories of racial exclusion and segregation, of times when "rednecks" and "blackfellas" locked heads and when the grandparents, mothers, and uncles of today's media trainees were locked in jail for demonstrating, all have a marked place in the conference rooms and studios of 4AAA today. They are told and retold to trainees in seminars and weekend outings, where the eventual successes of Aboriginal broadcasters around Australia are narrated for a younger generation. Many of these younger people have grown up in an era in which Aboriginal media are a pervasive, even valued aspect of an Australian media landscape. And for 4AAA's managers and educators, such stories are an intrinsic aspect of media training and connect the political aims of 4AAA with histories of its family networks and individual biographies. For this older generation the power to speak and represent oneself to a black community did not come cheaply or without struggle, and remembering this political history is a crucial aspect of production training.

4AAA itself began life in 1984 as an hour-long program on another local community station, 4ZZZ, and by the early 1990s it was taking sixteen hours a week on that station as the *Murri Show*—"Murri" being the local ethnonym for Aboriginal people in/from Queensland and northern New South Wales. Incorporated in 1993 as part of the Brisbane Indigenous Media Association, today the station acts as a partner company to a National Indigenous

Satellite network (which is housed across town in Brisbane). While early programming on 4ZZZ and 4AAA focused on a confrontational style and "redneck bashing" that accompanied 4AAA's critiques of the structural and institutional conditions that made even nonviolent Aboriginal protests illegal, the successful application for a community license dedicated to an Indigenous station in Brisbane led 4AAA's founders to reach beyond the Murri community. 4AAA's manager emphasized to me and to others at the station that the choice of country music as 4AAA's market niche met three important criteria. It was popular with Indigenous Australians, was underplayed on Brisbane's radio spectrum, and as importantly gave 4AAA an enormous non-Indigenous audience.

4AAA's choice of genre thus was at once strategic and historically obvious. Country music is cherished by Aboriginal people in every corner of Australia, and this popularity has deep historical roots that go back to recording tours of the 1940s and the first Aboriginal pop stars of the 1940s and 1950s. Not only did this choice allow 4AAA to reach a large non-Indigenous audience; it also gave the station access to a great deal of Aboriginal music, provided a potential commercial base by filling a niche then underdeveloped in Brisbane's broadcast market, and opened onto a wide, potentially national, Aboriginal audience. Today 4AAA seeks to reach both Aboriginal and non-Indigenous audiences through a shared musical genre, avoiding confrontation in favor of bridging an intercultural chasm and historical point of conflict. It is in these complex social conditions that technologies of sound production intersect with a local politics of "giving voice." Here the voices cultivated at 4AAA seek a broad audience.

Programming and Digital Production

4AAA's country music programming is joined by broadcast projects ranging from public service announcements and audio "bulletin boards" (addressed specifically to Brisbane's Indigenous population) to request programs geared toward those who have been incarcerated in South East Queensland's prisons. And it also entails training Indigenous young people in the various skills involved in radio production, from presentation and journalism to telephone sales, marketing, and social networking. This inclusion of trainees in 4AAA's broad range of broadcasting projects meant that radio production was a frequent topic of technical discussion and manipulation at 4AAA.

The station also was an early adopter of digital programming technology. In 2003 and 2004 an Australian-authored software program, Maestro, allowed DJs to preselect songs from a digital library and to schedule pro-

Fig. 3.1. Maestro software and broadcast hardware, Radio Larrakia, 2004 (Photo by Daniel Fisher)

gramming, including the forward- and back-announcing of songs, commercial advertising, and public service announcements. Such production work is also highly visual, run through the digital interfaces of Microsoft Windows–based software such as CoolEdit or SoundForge, and has as its formal aim the construction of a "live" community and the experience of copresence. While a good number of Aboriginal stations had moved to digital libraries and to the Windows-based control panel of Maestro, few, if any, had so completely embraced the digitization of the DJ's audience address. This was understood as a professionalization of 4AAA's operation, and the extremes of digital manipulation this entailed informed the great extent to which broadcast technique and vocal technologies became sites of discursive and practical consciousness.

During the course of my fieldwork the sixth and eighth floors provided a home to 4AAA's broadcast work, and the sixth was most frequently dedicated to media training. A large conference room occupied the main center of the floor. Scattered around its edges were long tables and desks for PC workstations. This large room was flanked by smaller offices, each containing one or two PC workstations also networked into 4AAA's large server. 4AAA's three production studios were located on both the sixth and the eighth floor and brought together a traditional mixing console with a desktop PC wired to 4AAA's institutional server. Soundproofed and outfitted with a mixing console, microphones, and another digital workstation, these studios were often occupied by 4AAA staff producing training recordings, conducting interviews with guests for later broadcast, or putting the finishing touches on prerecorded programs. Indeed, all these areas were in constant use—at times for manipulating the sounds that make up 4AAA's broadcasts and at other times to search the web for mp3s, to look at hip hop and R&B fan sites, and to produce the beats and hip hop rhymes that were a constant focus of interest for the young men training at 4AAA.

Radio production at 4AAA thus exemplified what Paul Greene and Thomas Porcello have termed "wired sound" (2005). That is, the "object" of 4AAA labor and the manifest focus of much training exists as information and electricity, signals tonally shaped through a visual digital interface. Levels are manipulated through Windows software and mastered in a studio situation using a professional audio program that "normalizes" audio levels through the compression of signal peaks and audio dropout to achieve a signal even in amplitude and "polished" for a smooth, broadcast-friendly signal. In 4AAA's studios, the actual sounds of radio production emerged only sporadically from desktop speakers, wired into the Windows-based digital workstations, and 4AAA's broadcast signal itself was generally heard only in the background, coming through the small speakers of the telephone intercom system and quietly battling with the tinny sounds of headphones. But sound was always an object of talk. While was possible for a particular recording to be downloaded to the digital library, "normalized" visually through CoolEdit, and sent to air through the Maestro scheduler without ever actually "sounding" in the space of 4AAA, the form of that signal—its sound, shape, and substance—was always a topic of conversation.

For instance, the shift away from live programming to a largely prerecorded format received a good deal of discussion and also reoriented the production work of the station. While students were being trained in the conference room to prepare a community service announcement free of digital clipping and without sudden surges of volume, others were discussing how best to script an appeal for volunteers or were learning to insert a musical "bed" beneath a prerecorded interview, and still others were working to preprogram a four-hour radio show for later broadcast. In the context of this production work the significance of DJ and listener copresence became a frequent point of discussion among station managers and DJs. Several employees and trainees found this prerecording an affront to their sensibilities

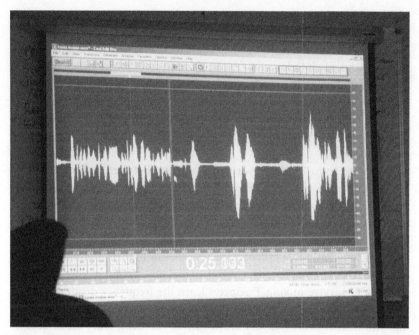

Fig. 3.2. Normalizing the voice in Cool Edit Pro, 4AAA's training studios, 2003 (Photo by Daniel Fisher)

as to what "radio" should entail. Although 4AAA did not advertise its digital disc jockey, some DJs felt that the lack of actual "liveness" was a liability for the station—"canned" programs were felt to be less dynamic, less able to draw in listeners. Perhaps in response to this pervasive sense that liveness was critical to the character of good radio, station management sought a more comfortable balance between "live to air" radio and digitally produced programming by including an overnight show geared toward "truckies" and live on-air DJs monitoring the signal throughout the day. Yet even these efforts seemed to encourage more discussion, rather than stemming a broad sense of anxiety that a mechanized voice was less compelling to listeners. "Liveness" was thus a frequent, though not the only, domain of debate and metapragmatic discussion.

These industrialized production practices draw attention to the more general status of radio's liveness and immediacy as semiotic and representational conventions as well as the object of a good deal of social labor. 4AAA works to produce this sense of liveness on the one hand with digital schedules and prerecorded programming technologies and on the other through the rebroadcasting of telephone requests and recorded "back-announcing," in which a DJ lists the songs just heard and perhaps comments on the material. The close interweaving of song, speech, and call sign are highly crafted, programmed streams that work to entail copresence and to grab the attention of listeners who, my interlocutors frequently remarked, might switch the channel at any moment.[4] The move to a prerecorded format also meant that much work was done in teams, prior to broadcast, much like studio music production. And this provided both the opportunity to involve more trainees in radio production and the focus of further discussion about the shape of the broadcast.

There are some further instructive overlaps between radio and music production techniques that emerged in the studios of 4AAA. While radio production training often emphasized clarity and the significance of maintaining a sense of copresence, its digital technologies also required producers to learn some rudiments of sound engineering. And learning to be a sound engineer frequently entails deconstructing sounds to their minimal constituents, bare slices of frequency spectrum, digital objects that require treatment and care to survive mixing. Engineers learn the frequency depth needed in order to lend the voice a body, to make it audible and aesthetically interesting within what is often a very crowded mix. Contemporary techniques of stereo mixing also entail a virtual spatialization of sound, allowing engineers to manipulate a perceptual space, creating "room" for voices, guitars, percussion, bass, all the sounds that one might mix together. A common technique, frequently termed "mirrored equalization" (see Case 2007; Hodgson 2010) involves distributing different ranges of a shared frequency to each sound and placing them at opposite sides of a horizontal stereo plane to lend them greater distinction. The use of panned, out-of-sync delay can also help to widen the perception of this lateral space and to lend a sense of depth to a stereo mix, allowing a wider audible space at the center for (typically) a voice to come clear.

Engineers also learn to listen to the voice as it emerges from a highly technologized signal path, training their ears to make audible those (often small) changes produced by techniques and technologies of production—that is, to hear the voice as produced and to hear qualities of sound that many listeners frequently place in the background. Instead of hearing the body in the voice, engineers learn to hear compression, delay, timbre, dynamic range, and virtual location as effects of analog and digital processing and other practical features of recording practice (see Hodgson 2010; Case 2007).

While most obviously about music production, these techniques and capacities are also cultivated in radio production—using compression, for instance, to boost the perception of signal and to even out peaks and troughs in the sound of an interview or using a large mixing desk to create radio-friendly sounds from a live music performance. And while all of my inter-locutors moved between radio desks and digital interfaces for audio produc-tion, a smaller subset also took their skills to analog, front-of-house mixing desks and into recording studios—going so far as to purchase their own mix-ing, sampling, and recording equipment. In sum, the young people I worked alongside in Brisbane were not just talking about how a radio voice should sound but were in fact involved in projects of varying intensity and sophisti-cation to actually manipulate sound.

Most days at 4AAA were thus filled with several kinds of ongoing radio and audio production. In the mornings one might find a DJ in the on-air studio, announcing country hits, sharing news and weather, conducting in-terviews, and occasionally bringing live performers in for brief on-air sets. Across the hallway, an evening presenter might be found prerecording and programming her Sunday-night request show, while in the news room spe-cial reports were written and taken into Studio B for production, prerecord-ing, downloading into the digital library, and adding to the scheduler for later broadcast. Meanwhile, trainee producers were producing beats, arguing over the sound of a vocal sample, and developing technical skills in audio mixing for radio broadcast.

From the Studio to the Street: Radio Sound and Social Mediation

If vocal sound is a constant focus of talk and technical practice at 4AAA, its politics and significance also emerged from the streets of Brisbane as much as from the studio. This was most apparent in the ways that the lives of my trainee friends trailed into production studios and conference rooms —spinning out from their anxieties about, interests in, and aspirations for the world outside.

The efforts by 4AAA trainers and Indigenous managers to cultivate a strong, professionally competent Aboriginal voice overlapped with the inter-ests of their younger trainees in hip hop performance and the cultivation of its particular vocal skill set. They also displayed a markedly greater interest in hip hop and R&B than the older trainers and station managers did. For many of the young men I knew at 4AAA, the technical skills provided by 4AAA's production training were thus put to service manufacturing "beats" —the rhythmic, musical foundation for the verbal contests and hip hop per-formances that spontaneously broke out in 4AAA's training studio—and my younger interlocutors at 4AAA sought skills in rhyming and the competitive poetics of hip hop improvisation. And these interests led them to pressure senior 4AAA staff to include more hip hop, more R&B, more "black" music in the station's broadcasting menu.

This advocacy, however, entailed some expressive dilemmas, as became clear to me in a relatively rare informal public performance I attended in 2003. In early March, I met 4AAA DJ and radio producer DK and several of his friends at Currie's, one of the many nightclubs and cafes located in Brisbane's Fortitude Valley. The performance venues for Aboriginal hip hop were then few, small, and informal—most often the performances occurred in homes, small parties, and radio studios. But something that everyone agreed was special happened when DK found Currie's lively open mic. Thursday nights featured "Bombshelter"—a weekly event dedicated to "freestylin," improvisatory rhyming battles. DK was coming down to take a second turn at the mic after a wild first visit several weeks before.

DK had earlier told me and another young Indigenous producer, TJ, how that previous battle had gone south when two rappers got too serious, "dissing" each other to the point where verbal boxing broke out into proper violence. Fists flew, he said, and then a large empty planter had found its way into the combatants' hands, breaking over a head and spilling blood.

> DK: When I got there, there's all these gammon rappers, hey.[5] So I walked in there, and I was about to grab it [the microphone], and I was thinking, "How many Australians are in here?" 'Cause they were all talking American accents, and all that talking about killing people and all this stuff, and "M-F this" and "M-F that." And I just heard that and I said, "Nah, I'm not going to rap, man. [And then] everybody started battling each other. I looked at 'em: "just let it go" [I thought to myself], and then the next minute, they started into it—they got into it, bruz![6]
>
> TJ: Started punching them?
>
> DK: Yeah, bruz, over a battle. And then one guy nearly got killed, bruz. . . . Hey, blood everywhere!

In recounting this outbreak of violence, DK provided a primer in what a proper Aboriginal performance should avoid, emphasizing the American accents put on by white Australian rappers, the frequent swearing of "gammon" rappers, and the aggressive, tense atmosphere that dissuaded him from picking up the microphone. DK's own overtly political music, in its express interest in valorizing Indigenous identity and in its formal aesthetics, resonates strongly with local critiques of American-based hip hop frequently voiced by an older generation at 4AAA. For these people the visual, verbal, and aural styles of global hip hop are worrying—both for the ways the genre threatens to supplant country music and more significantly for its racial iconicity— and they would frequently remind younger Murris that they were neither "gangstas" nor "African" but rather "Aboriginal." This is also the site at which many commonwealth-funded endeavors work to elicit Aboriginal expressivity—cultivating forms of blackness that to some can seem an institutionally driven imposition.

This older generation has its own distinct history of engagement with transnational black expressive cultural and politics, and "blackness" and "indigeneity" label longstanding forms of transnational identification that have been in at times conflicting and at other times complementary relationship in Australia. The historian Gary Foley, for instance, joined others to found the Black Panthers in Melbourne in 1968—an organization that overtly identified with the American movement (see Attwood 2003). More broadly, over the course of the 1960s, organizations advocating for Aboriginal civil rights debated the place of white Australians in their organization and increasingly figured their movement in racial terms. In 1969 the activist and Aboriginal poet Oodgeroo Nunnucal drafted "black commandments," which included number 7, "Thou shalt meet white violence with black violence," and ended with numbers 10, "Thou shalt think black and act black," and 11, "Thou shalt be black all the rest of thy days" (cf. Attwood 2003, 330).[7] But the inspiration drawn from a global black politics was leavened and mediated by the growing movement for land rights. In 1971 the loss of the high-profile Yolngu land-rights case in Arnhem Land and the Australian Black Panthers' move to establish the famous "tent embassy" on the lawn in front of parliament—a bristling declaration of Indigenous sovereignty—helped propel the rhetoric of Aboriginal rights toward issues of culture and belonging. When 4AAA managers and elders express ambivalence about the Aboriginal production of hip hop and underline the ways in which Aboriginal young people are Indigenous—heirs to land and law—they thus echo an older tension between a transnational identity as "black," antiracist activism, and a specific identity as "Aboriginal." The critique of hip hop's vocal style, then, is not elaborated as a critique of governmental imposition but as a racialization of Indigenous expressive practice. And these tensions enter into the production room, into people's relationship to a microphone and the ways they create a "mix."

Back in 4AAA's studio, DK, in describing his first experiences performing at the Bombshelter open mic, further suggested to me how he negotiates these tensions and underlined the significance of clear lyrics and constructive, noncombative battling. "When I started rapping, that's when people walking past started looking in. Because all them [other, non-Indigenous] guys, they just [*muffles his voice to imitate their rapping*]—you know, they're not clear. But I jumped on the microphone, and you could hear me word for word, you know, and I got a lot of respect for that." For DK, distinction depends on clear enunciation. And telling stories with clear rhymes makes the practice acceptable, even respectable to his elders and peers insofar as it successfully evades racialized markers of African American "gangstas." This prominence of vocals, out in front of the mix with their clarity unmarked by prosodic or timbral coloration, is a pervasive feature of Aboriginal hip hop, is central as well to the performance and production of country music, and was a constant point of explicit discourse in the studios at 4AAA. As a prolific white recording engineer and producer of Aboriginal country music stressed to me in 2008, the key to producing country music, whether live or in the studio, rests in foregrounding the voice—lending it clarity. "Mix it [the recording] like you do for the house at a live performance—with the voice up front and center. If you don't have a story, you don't move people," he said.

This practical and technical attention to engineering clear, understandable voices is also a feature of radio broadcasting and digital sound production as taught in 4AAA's studios. To get respect on the microphone, to sing an affecting story, or to sell an advertising spot, you need to put clarity front and center in the mix. In addition to teaching the rudiments of radio desk operation, 4AAA's Michael Scott drew trainees' attention to their own voices. Scott's efforts to train young Murri men and women in radio production thus frequently returned to several themes: "Avoid hard language; watch out for the pops and whistles where the microphone meets the body; hold your mouth slightly away from the mic; careful with your 'ahs' and 'ums'; if prerecording, edit these out for smoother diction." When DK himself rhymes, he also holds the mic at a distance, keeping its diaphragm from oversaturation and the distorted sounds of a clipped voice. This is in marked contrast with the non-Indigenous hip hop performers DK and I saw in Fortitude Valley, who cupped the microphone close up, making use of the microphone's "proximity effect" to maximize lower frequencies and also to greatly distort their vocal sound.[8]

One last, short instance from my fieldwork underlines the pervasive ways that audio media and their capacity to ventriloquize one's own voice may instigate social reflection. While my younger interlocutors were pressuring their elders to include more hip hop on the dial, the older managers and programmers were asking the younger to call around to remote Australia, to gather Christmas greetings in Indigenous languages, to import these into CoolEdit, and to create a compilation of "language" greetings from remote Australia. "When do whitefellas get to hear language?" one argued. "For that matter, when do we?" This observation led to robust discussion of what was lost with colonial settlement and to a valorization of the hybrid character of contemporary urban Aboriginal expressive culture. This was not solely directed toward urban or southeastern communities but also entailed a critique of "gammon" Aboriginal men who retain their language but not the will or capacity to look after their families (see Fisher 2010). There was, that is, momentarily a kind of technologically inspired deconstruction of language and voice as the grounds of cultural distinction. This was both a powerful instance of technology's capacity as vocal prosthesis and also a moment when the uncanny character of the "Aboriginal voice" became most explicit.

What Kind of Ethnographic Object Is the Mediatized Voice?

The remove from one's self that media may elicit has a rich history of problematization in media studies and anthropology. In addition to Fanon's discussion of Algeria's new national, radio-mediated self, Susan Buck-Morss (1996) argues that early cinema gave audiences a new sense of themselves as a mass public and an agent of history, going further to suggest that cinema provides a kind of technological *epoché* that makes perception available "to itself."[9] Friedrich Kittler (1999), attending to figures of transmission in psychoanalytic writings, has argued that the latter's varied figures of the unconscious might themselves be considered a "historical effect" of the 20th century's dominant media of telephone, film, and mechanized type. These different but provocative accounts of modernity's mediatized subject, placed at a remove from itself by media's prostheses, perhaps overvalue the power of media technologies (cf. Gitelman 2006). Yet they need not be taken whole to suggest a range of questions for how radio makes people's voices newly available to themselves. How does this vary from place to place, how does it intersect with a broader, transnational interest in "giving voice," and what are its consequences for local cultural politics?

In describing how the production of Indigenous radio entails diverse forms of vocal mediation, I have endeavored to suggest how the voice in such places may become denaturalized and opened to heightened forms of attention and contest. These forms of mediation include forms of governmental and institutional interests in eliciting Aboriginal expressive competence, the increasingly industrial and digital techniques by which voices are brought to air, and the broader cultural politics of black cultural production in southeast Australia. While taking voice may give shape to community, the forms that voice takes may be at once of a collective self and other to it—in a word, uncanny.[10] More than just a trope for representation, quite distinct voices emerged in my fieldwork as a matrix of desire, anxiety, and institutional labor.

NOTES

1. "Not hearing the Voice, the listener would sometimes leave the needle on a jammed wave length or one that simply produced static, and would announce that the voice of the combatants was here. For an hour the room would be filled with the piercing, excruciating din of the jamming. Behind each modulation, each active crackling, the Algerian would imagine not only words, but concrete battles" (Fanon 1959, 87–88).
2. In Barthes's well-known formula, the "grain" is "the body in the voice as it sings, the hand as it writes, the limb as it performs" (1977, 188). In more overtly psychoanalytic work the voice may figure as the paradigmatic *objet a*, the "object cause" of desire and the kernel of the real that ruptures or resists the narcissistic completion of a self. It is "returned as the other" and thus sets up the conditions for desire.
3. The broadest Australian response has been the Special Broadcasting Service, with a focus on multicultural broadcasting and, in Ang's terms, a mandate to make cultural diversity "a matter of public representation" (Ang, Hawkins, and Dabboussy 2008, 3).
4. Request programs are a staple of Aboriginal broadcasting, and elsewhere I analyze the significance of such programming for Aboriginal public culture and expressive practice more generally (Fisher 2009).
5. *Gammon* is an Aboriginal English term that can be variously glossed as "fake," "untrue," or "broken." For further discussion of this important term see Fisher 2010.
6. *Bruz* is a vocative pronoun conjoining both "cousin" and "brother"; it is frequently heard in the Aboriginal English of South East Queensland.
7. I am indebted to Hilary Emmett for transcribing the "black commandments" from the Papers of Oodgeroo Nunnucal, held by the University of Queensland's Fryer Library.
8. The "proximity effect" refers to the amplification of lower frequencies by placing a microphone closer to a sound source.
9. Buck-Morss makes an epistemological claim, suggesting that the camera as "prosthesis of perception" provides Husserl's phenomenological *epoché* with its unacknowledged prototype. "The objective, historically transient reality which he wants to bracket *out* of the cogitatio penetrates precisely into that realm of 'reduced' mental acts where he thought himself most secure" (1996, 48; italics in original).
10. Although I am drawn to this figure by moments at which individuals are unsettled by the forms their own voices take, this is not a psychoanalytic account. While in Freud's writings (2003 [1919]) the uncanny names a feeling of alterity within the self as a return of the repressed, I describe an alterity that owes more to the technologically plastic and socially reflexive character of mediatized speech than to an "originary violence" or repression (cf. Derrida 1977).

REFERENCES

Anderson, Benedict. 1993. *Imagined Communities: Reflections on the Origin and Spread of Nationalism*. New York: Verso.
Ang, Ien, Gay Hawkins, and Lamia Dabboussy. 2008. *The SBS Story: The Challenge of Diversity*. Sydney: University of New South Wales Press.
Attwood, Bain. 2001. "Learning about the Truth": The Stolen Generations Narrative. In Bain Attwood and Fiona Magowan, eds., *Telling Stories: Indigenous History and Memory in Australia and New Zealand*, 183–212. Crows Nest, Australia: Allen and Unwin.

———. 2003. *Rights for Aborigines*. Crows Nest, NSW: Allen and Unwin.

Axel, Brian Keith. 2006. Anthropology and the Technologies of Communication. *Cultural Anthropology* 21 (3): 354–384.

Barthes, Roland. 1977. The Grain of the Voice. In *Image, Music, Text*, 157. New York: Hill and Wang.

Batty, Philip. 2003. Governing Cultural Difference. Ph.D. dissertation, University of South Australia.

Bauman, Richard, and Charles L. Briggs. 2003. *Voices of Modernity: Language Ideologies and the Politics of Inequality*. New York: Cambridge University Press.

Buck-Morss, Susan. 1996. The Cinema Screen as a Prosthesis of Perception. In Nadia Seremetakis, ed., *The Senses Still Perception and Memory as Material Culture in Modernity*, 45–62. Chicago: University of Chicago Press.

Burchell, Graham. 1993. Liberal Government and Techniques of the Self. *Economy and Society* 22 (3): 267–282.

Case, Alex. 2007. *Sound FX: Unlocking the Creative Potential of Recording Studio Effects*. Boston: Focal.

Derrida, Jacques. 1977. *Of Grammatology*. Translated by Gayatri Spivak. Baltimore: Johns Hopkins University Press.

Dolar, Mladen. 2006. *A Voice and Nothing More*. Cambridge: MIT Press.

Fanon, Frantz. 1959. *A Dying Colonialism*. Translated by Haakon Chavalier. New York: Grove.

Feld, Steven, Aaron Fox, Thomas Porcello, and David Samuels. 2004. Vocal Anthropology. In Alessandro Duranti, ed., *A Companion to Linguistic Anthropology*, 321–345. Malden, MA: Blackwell.

Fisher, Daniel. 2009. Mediating Kinship: Country, Family, and Radio in Northern Australia. *Cultural Anthropology* 24 (2): 280–312.

———. 2010. On Gammon, Global Noise, and Indigenous Heterogeneity. *Critique of Anthropology* 30 (3): 265–286.

Freud, Sigmund. 2003 [1919]. *The Uncanny*. Translated by David McLintock. New York: Penguin.

Ginsburg, Faye. 1991. Indigenous Media: Faustian Contract or Global Village? *Cultural Anthropology* 6:92–112.

———. 1994. Embedded Aesthetics: Creating a Discursive Space for Indigenous Media. *Cultural Anthropology* 9:365–382.

———. 1997. From Little Things Big Things Grow: Indigenous Media and Cultural Activism. In Richard Fox and Orin Starn, eds., *Between Resistance and Revolution: Cultural Politics and Social Activism*. New Brunswick: Rutgers University Press.

Gitelman, Lisa. 2006. *Always Already New: Media, History, and the Data of Culture*. Cambridge: MIT Press.

Greene, Paul, and Thomas Porcello. 2005. *Wired for Sound: Engineering and Technologies in Sonic Cultures*. Middletown, CT: Wesleyan University Press.

Hodgson, Jay. 2010. *Understanding Records: A Field Guide to Recording Practice*. New York: Continuum.

Inglis, Kenneth Stanley. 2006. *Whose ABC? The Australian Broadcasting Corporation 1983–2006*. Melbourne: Black Inc Books.

Kittler, Friedrich. 1999. *Gramophone, Film, Typewriter*. Translated by Geoffrey Winthrop-Young and Michael Wutz. Stanford: Stanford University Press.

Kunreuther, Laura. 2006. Technologies of the Voice: FM Radio, Telephone, and the Nepali Diaspora. *Cultural Anthropology* 21 (3): 323–353.

Langton, Marcia. 1993. *"Well, I Heard It on the Radio and I Saw It on the Television . . .": An Essay for the Australian Film Commission on the Politics and Aesthetics of Filmmaking by and about Aboriginal People and Things.* Sydney: Australian Film Commission.

McLuhan, Marshall. 1964. *Understanding Media: The Extensions of Man.* London: Routledge and Kegan Paul.

Michaels, Eric. 1994. *Bad Aboriginal Art: Tradition, Media, and Technological Horizons.* Minneapolis: University of Minnesota Press.

Miller, Toby. 1993. *The Well-Tempered Self.* Baltimore. Johns Hopkins University Press.

Morris, Rosalind. 2000. Modernity's Media and the End of Mediumship? On the Aesthetic Economy of Transparency in Thailand. *Public Culture* 12 (2): 457–475.

Peters, John D. 2004. The Voice and Modern Media. In Doris Kolesch and Jenny Schrodl, eds., *Kunst-Stimmen*, 85–100. Berlin: Theater der Zeit Recherchen 21.

Salecl, Renata, and Slavoj Žižek, eds. 1996. *Gaze and Voice as Love Objects.* Durham: Duke University Press.

Spivak, Gayatri. 1988. Can the Subaltern Speak? In Cary Nelson and Lawrence Grossberg, eds., *Marxism and the Interpretation of Culture*, 271–313. Urbana: University of Illinois Press.

Sterne, Jonathan. 2003. *The Audible Past: Cultural Origins of Sound Reproduction.* Durham: Duke University Press.

Weidman, Amy. 2006. *Singing the Classical, Voicing the Modern: The Postcolonial Politics of Music in South India.* Durham: Duke University Press.

4

Editing the Nation

How Radio Engineers Encode Israeli National Imaginaries

DANNY KAPLAN

When I first started to write about Israeli radio and music broadcasting, I was not sure how to translate the Hebrew term *orech musikali* (literally, "music editor"). I noticed that most scholarly literature and general websites in English refer to the person who selects the songs to be aired by the radio station as "music programmer" rather than editor.[1] Following several years of studying the field, I came to realize that programming and editing reflect not only different models of music broadcasting but also different modes of engagement between radio music, the audience, and the national community. The concept of "music programming" emerged in the context of the US commercial radio, where marketing considerations encouraged standardization and required predetermined playlists and designated music "formats" (Lippmann 2007; Berland 1993). "Music editing," by contrast, connotes the specific task of designing the musical sequence in a radio broadcast. It downplays the broader organizational pressures and market considerations for choosing songs and gives closer attention to both "grammar" and "semantics" when editing a musical sequence. Because music editing is not committed to a clearly defined playlist, it offers more latitude to choose songs according to personal tastes, the nature of the intended radio show, and the wider social context of ongoing events that may concern the audience. This provides a fertile ground for assigning new meanings to music, including national meanings.

In this chapter I discuss music editing practices in Israeli radio, following an ethnographic study of Israeli public and commercial-regional radio during a decade of privatization reforms.[2] I describe how the key to editing lies in considering the right "cross" to make a smooth link between consecutive songs or between a song and concurrent external events. By deciding not just which songs to play but also how to link them with concurrent public events, music editors transform into engineers of the collective mood, actively forming new associations and interpretations of social and political life and investing them with national meanings.

Radio Engineers and the National Imaginary

Ever since Benedict Anderson's (1991 [1983]) discussion of the newspaper-reading community as a vehicle for imagining the nation, anthropologists have begun to explore the constitutive role of media technology in reproducing people's national identifications. Moving away from top-to-bottom, authoritative aspects of "nation building" (Hobsbawm 1982; Gellner 1983) toward a broader, civic understanding of "nation making" (Foster 1997), scholars have begun to ask how nationalism is conceived bottom-up through people's shared "social imaginary" (Taylor 2002) as they engage with variable representations of the nation, as in the use of technology, consumption, or popular culture. Contrary to the rich body of literature on the import of print media and television on national identity, there is relatively little research on the ways that radio evokes national meanings (Smith and Phillips 2006). Radio practices involved in nation making can produce a sense of collective identity but can also draw lines of exclusions. For instance, news reports broadcast from national capitals can acquire new meanings and implications as they reach audiences in remote and culturally distinct regions contained within the same state (Tsing 2003).

In this discussion I focus on the persons behind the radio broadcast—specifically deejays, music editors, and station directors—and ask how they make sense of music broadcasting, the audience, and the national community. Inspired by Rudolf Mrázek's (1997, 2002) historical work on nation making and technology in colonial Indonesia, I refer to this team of radio producers as "engineers." Mrázek shows how the attraction of technology was a constitutive metaphor for planning and dreaming about the nation among both the Dutch colonizers and the Indonesian nationalists, who at times considered themselves "radio mechanics" contributing to the creation of a common modern social space through the materialities of broadcast sound (Mrázek 1997, 32). At one level, radio engineering connotes the technical process of planning a broadcast, selecting its content, managing its transmission, and assessing its impact on the intended audience. But it also connotes the broader framework of social engineering, which has been used primarily to describe the pretentions of colonial ideologists and missionaries to educate local populations and to enact European notions of citizenship, perceiving the colonies as laboratories of modernity (Cooper and Stoler 1997, 5). Although the notion of engineering has not been employed systematically by radio scholars, it echoes key studies that have shown the explicit involvement of radio as a tool of modernization as well as socialization into the national culture (e.g., Scannell and Cardiff 1991; Hayes 1996; Spitulnik 1999; Douglas 2004). Like Mrázek's work, these studies often locate their analyses in historical moments when the presence of radio appears to have been more decisive and central to local society and its involvement in social engineering projects was executed mainly through the spoken word.

Israeli Radio and the National Setting

Historical studies of Israeli radio since state independence in 1948 suggest a similar picture of social engineering. Israel's socialist tradition favored a highly centralized structure with active government involvement in most areas of public culture (Ben-Ami 1996), including the electronic media.[3] The state-run radio Kol Israel and the military radio were instrumental in shaping the idea of a single national culture and disseminated a Zionist vision of progress and secular salvation to the various segments of the local Jewish and Arab population. Both stations spread for the first time the sounds of Hebrew as a modern, spoken language and advanced a European-oriented high culture in music and literature. They also produced educational programs through which new immigrants and first-generation Israeli Jews were socialized to national values such as the settlement of the homeland, agricultural activity, and military prowess (Liebes 2006; Penslar 2003).

The general operation of Kol Israel was borrowed from the British model of radio as a state apparatus committed to nation building (Scannell and Cardiff 1991), and a group of its founding members worked and trained in the radio service run by the British Mandate government prior to state independence (Penslar 2003). The state radio has played a particularly major role in transmitting national commemoration rituals as well as in covering emergency events. Israel's prolonged state of conflict with neighboring Arab countries and more recently with Hezbollah and Palestinian militias produced variable yet enduring episodes of violence ranging from full-fledged wars to border incidences to inner-city bombings. As the Israeli military continually engages in a combination of civil policing and low-intensity warfare in the Palestinian territories, the Israeli civil population undergoes repeated spells of indiscriminate missile attacks, shootings, and suicide bombings. Prior to the advances in televised and online news coverage, the radio's easy accessibility to events on the ground proved valuable for live reportage in these moments of emergency. Thus, state radio newsbreaks were the first to report of emergency events and provided the public with a sense of control.

In the 1990s new radio models appeared in the field. Decentralization and commercialization reforms led to the establishment of seventeen privately owned regional stations throughout the country. Although legislators authorized the new stations to provide new niches and to cater to distinctive needs of the residents within their designated regions, the stations mostly followed the public networks in presupposing and targeting a relatively homogeneous Jewish, secular or traditional audience.[4] Despite the growing competition from television and the Internet, contemporary Israeli radio attained a unique positioning in covering national events, not as a bearer of news reports but as an engineer of collective emotions, by way of music broadcasting. In what follows I describe how the practices involved in engineering Israel's national imaginary were rooted in the expertise of music editing, and I chart how both editing and national engineering endured through the commercial restructuring of the radio field.

Music Editing in the Face of Commercialization

In recent years radio stations across the world have increasingly concentrated on musical broadcasting, as television and the Internet have appropriated much of the verbal domain in mass media (Berland 1993). A similar trend has occurred in Israeli radio. In the face of the rising use of the Internet and the gradual decline in radio listening, recent audience surveys suggest that music has become a major source for securing and stabilizing audience exposure to radio (Doner 2004; BizPortal 2009). In the 1990s the military station established a substation, Galgalatz, specializing in nonstop mainstream pop music and traffic updates. It gradually became a key player in the music market (Lahav 2009) and by 2009 ranked as the most-listened-to radio station in the country next to Kol Israel's news station (Karmel 2008). Most new commercial-regional stations tried to compete with Galgalatz by offering a similar musical repertoire, with diversity between most stations narrowing down to their choice of balance between Hebrew and English mainstream pop songs. The field expanded in terms of music broadcasting but remained homogeneous.

How did commercialization affect the task of music editing? The success of Galgalatz lies in its implementation of a commercial radio format of easy listening known in the American radio market as "adult contemporary" (AC) (Greve 1996). It is based on a preprogrammed, restricted playlist of mainstream pop-rock songs, which reduces the ability of the broadcaster to engage with ongoing collective events shared by the audience. But none of the stations has adopted the full model of format radio with nonstop music. Because most regional stations cater to a nondifferentiated general audience in their designated area, most have opted to combine music with talk radio, competing not only with Galgalatz but also with news and talk radio offered nationwide by the public networks. This means that other than the noncommercial military station Galgalatz, paradoxically none of the new commercial stations has ever implemented a standardized commercial format. As a result, instead of a fully computerized playlist, much of their music content is still selected personally by the musical editor. Despite the success of Galgalatz and its playlist programming, the term music "programming" never entered local discourse, and the employment of music editors, sometimes renamed "music directors" in commercial stations, has remained the typical practice in Israeli radio.

Given the music revolution in Israeli radio, one might presume that its role in disseminating and consolidating a sense of national identity would diminish. For unlike the explicit content conveyed in news and talk programs, the meanings assigned to music and popular songs are vague and open to variable interpretations. Yet music could be as effective, if not more, in shaping the national imaginary by managing the collective mood. Dani Nishlis, director of Radio Haifa, a commercial-regional radio in northern Israel, explicitly described to me this standpoint:

> We have a file in the computer with some sad, melancholic songs. At the moment that something happens, they immediately go on the air. If I decide now that I want to cause a public panic, I just need to play these songs

> [*laughs*], which tell a story that something has happened. . . . If I want to
> raise the mood and make everyone happy, I play songs, and if I want to
> lower the mood, I use [these] songs, and people will ask what happened.

Israeli broadcasters repeatedly spelled out such explicit assumptions about
the power of radio to alter and manipulate public mood. Underlying these
arguments are distinct qualities of music editing that make it a valuable expertise for engineering the national imaginary.

Weaving Songs Together: The Logic of the "Cross"

The heart of music editing lies in the power to make new associations in the
listener's imagination by creatively linking between consecutive songs as
well as between a song and nonmusical items in the radio broadcast. This is
also where the divergence between editing and programming practices becomes most evident. The editor's prime task is to figure out the proper order
of songs in a musical sequence and particularly how to link between two
consecutive songs, a consideration termed in Israeli editing discourse as a
"cross." Interestingly, although this word is clearly borrowed from the English, I was unable to find similar references to it in discussions of radio in
English. The major criteria for forming a cross between songs are aesthetic,
attempting to maintain a smooth link in the musical sequence by taking into
account musical parameters such as the change of chords, groove, or music
arrangement as well as broader parameters of style such as the genre, era,
and language of the specified songs. Tal Hashiloni, a senior editor in Kol Israel, described how applying the cross logic is crucial to professional editing
and sets it apart from other ways to handle music:

> In terms of the sequence . . . I work by associations and by musical con-
> texts, melodic, rhythmic, and arrangement-wise. It's important to preserve
> something that I think is very important for music editing, which is the
> crosses, maintaining a link between the song currently on the air and the
> song that will follow it. Otherwise what you get is what I call editing from
> the shelf. Today everyone uses the Internet and can access their music li-
> brary and edit as they please, so we need to ask how the music editor is
> different from the average person who loves music.

Although Hashiloni did not say so explicitly, she was concerned that the
use of crosses is losing ground to the alternative practice of programming

that has partly permeated the local radio field. Programming aims to minimize human judgment and personal touch in the ordering of songs in a musical sequence. It does so by encouraging technical solutions that can help
create a smooth link between consecutive songs. The most common effect is
to insert a short jingle with the station's slogan or another brief message as
a separator between consecutive songs, relieving the programmer from the
need to consider the right crosses between songs. Ohad Raz, music director
at Radio Tel Aviv, a talk and music radio specializing in current pop music,
outlined some of these new principles. Having worked previously both in
Reshet Gimmel, the music station of Kol Israel, and in American and British
radio stations, Raz was able to identify some signs of change in the Israeli
field from editing to programming:

> During the era of Reshet Gimmel . . . you would see in their editing a mu-
> sical connection between songs, whether through a common chord or
> similar names. As soon as Galgalatz entered the picture, they broke this
> barrier, and today in Galgalatz there is no connection between one song
> and another. You could listen to a pop song from the '80s, and after that
> you suddenly hear the Yarkon Bridge Threesome [a Hebrew folk band
> from the '60s] with a totally different message. In the past this was not
> acceptable. . . . But for that reason you now have the connecting jingle [of
> the station] between songs. . . . This jingle has two functions. One function
> is to break the musical sequence, and the other is to tell the listener what
> station he's tuned to. . . . It's also very important how the deejay inserts the
> jingle. It has to be entered at the right timing, on the right intro; there are
> many factors involved.

The move from musical judgments to technical proficiency exemplifies
the changes from editing to programming. The former considers how to
form interesting associations between songs, while the latter applies predetermined effects precisely to untie unwarranted associations between songs.
These conflicting approaches for weaving songs together go beyond the
question of form and aesthetics. The significance of editing lies first and fore-
most in the attention to thematic associations. Editors address thematic associations between lyrics of consecutive songs as well as between a song and
the preceding or consecutive talk item on the show. This is precisely where
editors begin to exercise their faculty in generating new meanings to popular
music. Hashiloni from Kol Israel elaborated on the typical themes she may
pick up when editing for talk and music shows:

> When I edit the daily news show, I open the program with something that links in my view to what's happening around me. It could be the weather, the number of casualties in a car accident, Left and Right, returning land for peace or not, the relationship with America, Russia. I simply can't ignore the connection to current affairs . . . or if it's a holiday or back-to-school day, International Women's Day.

Notice how the logic of crossing treats different kinds of public events—from weather reports and car accidents to politics and the Israeli-Palestinian conflict—as equally suitable for this form of music editing.

Crossing between Music and the Nation

Under the commercial logic associated with music programming, the preoccupation of editing with thematic crosses is considered obsolete. For instance, Ofer Weinstein, a music director in regional radio Lev Hamedina who favored commercial programming, commented to me that selecting songs according to thematic links with talk items—or "winking on a topic," as he put it—was by now "sometimes regarded as a little pathetic." However, I argue that it is precisely this faculty of generating associations between sounds and events which may be still central to radio's mode of operation in contemporary Israel. In fact, facing growing competition from other media forms, radio's ability to cross between music and everyday life may provide a strategic vantage point, particularly when it generates recognizable cues for identifying with the nation.

Thus, similar to the way that Israeli broadcasters like to air special songs rich with rain imagery during spells of rainy days, which are not common in the Israeli climate, Israel's hectic political climate offers them numerous occasions to cross radio songs with public life. This involves an extension of the logic of crossing from the linear dimension of the musical sequence to the simultaneous dimension of the cross between the song and concurrently occurring external events. The faculty of simultaneity is central to national identification. As noted by Anderson (1991 [1983]), early modern print media linked in the readers' imagination unrelated yet concurrently occurring events so that they could imagine how they shared a strong sense of communion with fellow readers. Radio's continuous transmission imposes on its audience an even stronger sense of simultaneity than print media by setting a uniform pace to engage in the shared ritual of listening. In Israel in particular, newsflashes are broadcasted on most radio stations at hourly or even half-hourly intervals, generating a singular shared moment when people come to a standstill and jointly reflect on current events. On the face of it, playing popular music offers little direct engagement with national concerns. Yet against the backdrop of music radio during everyday life, editors can explicitly juxtapose songs with external events set in a widely shared, fixed, and ritualized context and invest the music with national meanings.

Editing National Narratives

Over the years Israeli radio has developed a particular logic of "mood shifting," adopted from state commemoration rituals and dramatizing a metanarrative of national liberation (Kaplan 2009). As part of the "bureaucratic logic" of the state (Handelman 2004), a classification system that invokes and formalizes preexisting cultural conceptions, mood shifting draws on a cultural code of climactic pulsation, a deep-seated Jewish conception of collective time as a unidirectional movement from the low and ordinary to the morally superior and extraordinary. In Zionist cosmology this cultural code translates into the metanarrative "from destruction to resurrection," used to characterize the establishment of the State of Israel. The climactic pulsation is dramatized in the deliberate sequencing of the three new national days of remembrance, Holocaust Memorial Day, followed a week later by Memorial Day for Fallen Soldiers and the immediately consecutive celebrations of Independence Day. The close proximity between these days encodes an annual movement from the catastrophe of the Holocaust through the sacrifice of lives in the struggles for liberating the nation and culminating with the resurrection of the State of Israel.

The bureaucratic logic of the state is implemented and engineered bottom-up by radio practices of mood shifting. State law forbids electronic media to broadcast commercials on Memorial Days (Second Authority for Television and Radio 1999) and directs them instead to "express the unique character of the day" (Knesset 1963), but beyond this vague regulation there are no binding guidelines. However, virtually all radio stations interpret this directive in a uniform manner, as in the case of Memorial Day for Fallen Soldiers. It begins in the preceding evening with a siren sounded throughout the country, intended to bring all the people to a standstill for a moment of silent communion with the war dead. Around this time all radio stations self-consciously orchestrate this mood shift by playing a selected canon of memorial songs, solemn Hebrew songs that originate from the heritage of Israel's wars and center on themes of fallen soldiers, sacrifice, and friendship.[5] The shift from the schedules of the stations' routine pop music to the sacred songs of national remembrance embodies the foundational narrative and

movement from the low and ordinary to the morally superior and extraordinary. This "commemorative mode" of nonstop music broadcasting (Kaplan
2009) is carried out for twenty-four hours on almost all stations (some combine it with talk programs on fallen soldiers). Editors repeatedly conveyed to
me that they get very enthusiastic feedback from their audience for playing
beautiful Hebrew songs in a nonstop commercial-free format.

The commemoration mode comes to a sudden end with a second mood
shift in the evening, indicating the beginning of Independence celebrations,
when all radio stations perform an abrupt switch from the genre of solemn
memorial songs to upbeat party and dance music, in both Hebrew and English. Whereas the first mood shift is enforced by a nationwide siren, the second follows the official state ceremony held in Jerusalem, which marks the
transition from the twenty-four-hour mourning to the celebrations of Independence. A brief selection of readings and Hebrew songs are performed
by a choir on the stage, and as the music becomes more tuneful and high
spirited, it acts as a mood shift between the two days, again embodying the
climactic pulsation from low to high (Handelman 2004, 129). Whereas only
a limited number of people participate in the official ceremony or attend to
it on some TV and radio stations, what is striking is how all other radio stations transmit the exact timing of this mood shift simultaneously through a
change in their music broadcasting. Against the relative diversity of music
programming before and after Memorial Day, this uniformity across stations
forms a singular twenty-four-hour period when all radio stations cross between their music and a shared public event and jointly create a powerful atmosphere of collective mourning followed by public celebration. In doing so,
radio engineers evoke the narrative cues which tell of the repeated sacrifices
and triumphs of the nation.

Editing the National Morale

From the perspective of the radio engineer the commemoration mode and
associated logic of mood shifting can be easily extended to other events of
national significance. Any unfolding of events on the ground can be accompanied by a shift in musical genres and rhythms in order to reflect, evoke,
or initiate an ideal change of mood. The following account by Yaniv Bin-
yamini, who worked as a deejay in Radio Haifa, provides the quintessence of
such emotional engineering, namely, choosing the right song that will function as a mood shifter in preparing for the siren during Memorial Day for
Fallen Soldiers:

There's a meaning in the song that gets aired just before the siren. I would choose a very heavy song, and for an obvious reason: to tell people, "OK, listen to this song, because in one minute you'll be in another world, closing your eyes and connecting to the memory of that soldier." I would deliberately choose a song that can bring them to that state, because there are people who are very tough and firm in their emotions and take it very easy. And so that song could connect them and make them concentrate. . . . As a deejay, I try to make them . . . do that switch, get out of the routine and connect together. I connect them in the hard way, because for me Memorial Day is sacred: all of my brothers lost their best friends. . . . So when I broadcast [on that day], I want the listener to . . . understand that in the next four minutes, first the song and then the siren, you're gonna be all there. And it works; its goes into the subconscious and delivers a hidden message. . . . So there's a reason for this song; other musical editors would ask to put the same song. I recall this incident when on my shift in the six-o'clock morning news they reported that two Israeli soldiers got killed. The [senior] editor had prepared the playlist that was to start with this [cheerful pop] song "I'm Crazy about Her," but I simply couldn't play it after such news. So I first put a sad song and then returned to the list. . . . The programmer scolded me for not sticking to the list. . . . Maybe he was harsh at me because I was new, but I stood my ground and said that if it happened again, I'd do the same. Because as far as I'm concerned, it's a soldier that was killed, one of us, and so you need a style of song that connects to a moment of sadness and then go on and put an upbeat song.

In the first part of Yaniv's story he reflects in detail how the strategic song immediately preceding the siren is expected to trigger an emotion of communion with the dead and indirectly a sense of communion among the living. But notice also how Yaniv intuitively extends this logic to another, unrelated event, when a news report of casualties among Israeli soldiers interrupted his routine morning broadcasting. The details of the second event remain rather vague in his account. Apparently Yaniv refers to Israeli soldiers killed in Lebanon during a clash with Hezbollah forces. Yet there is no explicit reference to an enemy in his account, an omission that is indicative of a wider cultural phenomenon in Zionist discourse, in which representations of Arabs are often confined to the status of the national other, an abstract entity with little attention to distinct cultural characteristics, specific group identities, and diverse ideologies (Kaplan 2000). For example, media reports refer to Arab adversaries (other than state militaries) under term *mehablim* (literally, "saboteurs"), applying this term in an undifferentiated manner both to Palestinian armed militants and to Hezbollah fighters. By the same token, any fatal attack carried out by *mehablim* on Jewish targets is indiscriminately termed "terror attack," regardless of whether the target was a civilian or a soldier.

Elsewhere I have discussed how this undifferentiated response to discrete sources of violence set in varying historical and political contexts is echoed in the unique manner through which Israeli radio places emergency events in a mythic time frame encoded by the commemorative mode (Kaplan 2009). Thus, Israeli radio stations respond to fatal attacks on civilians or soldiers by halting the ongoing musical broadcast and switching temporarily to a repertoire of nonstop downbeat solemn songs, an emergency broadcasting that follows the same editing practices employed during Memorial Days. Yaniv's spontaneous act of mood shifting immediately after hearing of the terror attack followed exactly the same logic. His response was reprimanded by his superior not because the commercial-regional station avoided such practices but because at that point in time the station decided to raise the "threshold" for switching to emergency broadcasting beyond the level of a few casualties, a decision which Yaniv ignored or was unaware of, being new at the job. Taken together, the two parts of Yaniv's account exemplify how the expertise of editing extends to questions of national morale. The editorial logic underlying the management of an emergent crisis on the ground is identical to the one which guides the editors in crossing between songs and events in everyday life. Just as rainy weather invokes a cross with songs that convey a rainy mood, disturbances in the national climate propel radio engineers to devise a cross with songs that reflect a change in the national spirit. Hence, engineering the national imaginary is made possible by combining the logic of music editing with the bureaucratic logic that invests mood shifting with national narratives. But this engineering is primarily dependent on the active participation of the music editors, many of whom consider managing the public mood as part of their duty both as media professionals and as citizens. Whereas weather conditions cannot be simply altered by encoding them in the musical broadcast, most music editors see it as a civic and patriotic responsibility to alter what they perceive as national morale in cases of commemoration or crisis. They make strategic broadcast decisions accordingly, as Eran Eliakim, music director of Galgalatz, explains: "The radio signifies the national mood. . . . X hours have passed since the terror attack, and we want to return the color to the cheeks, lift the spirit, and go back to normal life despite the pain. . . . The motivation to make a change is something we need to decide. We need to reach a decision and stick to it."

An occasion for such "editing" which may have direct impact on public morale materialized in Radio Haifa during the 2006 Lebanon War. The regional radio guided and consoled residents during their stay in shelters that came under rocket attacks from Hezbollah combatants across the northern border. The radio station self-consciously attempted to use music as a means to manage the mood and morale of the community. As soon as the war broke, the music repertoire switched almost exclusively to Hebrew music, not in the commemorative mode associated with heavy casualties but to spirited contemporary pop songs. Guy Bazak, the senior music director, recounted how after each spell of siren alarm and authorization to leave the shelters, they would start the broadcast with an upbeat Hebrew song: "We didn't air sad songs, because we are not depressed. We wanted to keep the morale high from the moment people left the shelters and returned to ordinary life."

Describing some of the station's schedules during the war, he laid out how hour by hour the station engineered and regulated the mood of its listeners: "In the morning we had this [news and talk] show where [the host] screamed, how come nothing was being done [by the government] and why hadn't they declared the city of Haifa as a warzone, . . . screams and interviews [with residents] whose small businesses were collapsing." This was followed at nine a.m. with another host, who switched to a more emotional and soothing tone: "She would calm down the people from the area, speak to them from the heart." And finally, "between ten a.m. and noon we broadcasted a retro party, the message being that we will go on dancing alongside the alarm sirens. We would play dance music, and the alarm interrupted. So we'd give a fifteen-minute update and went back to our party, until the next alarm."

Editing the Nation from Afar: The Case of Red Sea Radio

Given the prevalence of emergency situations in Israel, it is perhaps not surprising that many radio stations, not only the state and military radio but also the rising commercial stations, have adopted a common hegemonic position with regard to national engineering: maintaining the practices of editing and the associated skills of crossing music with public events in order to gain audience appreciation for their involvement in national concerns. To demonstrate this point further, it is intriguing to observe how these norms are embraced even in areas where emergency events are extremely rare and national concerns seem far away. Such is the case of Red Sea Radio, a regional station catering only to the residents of Eilat, Israel's southernmost town and its prime vacation resort.

Red Sea Radio emphasizes local content in its talk shows and is intimately involved in the mundane activities of the small local population of roughly fifty thousand residents. Indeed, of all regional stations Red Sea Radio is the only one to reflect the original charter and vision of the regional reform, which urged radios to reflect the needs and desires of local communities (Balint 2004). The station tries to reinforce its local appeal by producing a relatively high portion of self-made programs and avoids purchasing popular programs that are available through national syndication. One of its main shows is a daily noontime talk show combining national and local current affairs. Station director Guy Markman described the effort involved in catering to the local audience: "You may ask yourself, what's there to report every single day about Eilat? So today we host the chief of the police, listeners call up and ask questions. . . .Yesterday they talked about the city council and raised some debates. . . . So you got to sit down [with your staff] over a couple of croissants and a cup of coffee and to reinvent the wheel. It's hard but not impossible."

But appealing to the local audience does not preclude engagement with national concerns. On the contrary, Red Sea Radio systematically addresses themes related to Zionist identification. This has to do with the overall structure of the radio field. Whereas in central Israel the radio field is denser and regional stations compete with each other, secluded peripheral stations such as Red Sea Radio compete only with the nationwide public networks, which typically deal with national affairs and disseminate Zionist values. Peripheral stations respond to this challenge precisely by drawing on common national sentiments shared by their local audience and by following Zionist rituals in their broadcasting practices. For instance, in order for Red Sea Radio to better prepare its listeners for the solemn atmosphere of Memorial Days, it refrains from airing commercials already two hours prior to the onset of these days, earlier than most stations. Station director Markman explained, "We get amazing responses about Memorial Day [for Fallen Soldiers] and on Holocaust Day, I'm afraid to say. It's nonstop music with no commercials, and the listeners are simply happy, even though the music is of mourning."

Radio Eilat was also the first radio station to initiate a special jingle and designated song to commemorate Israel's missing soldiers, a ritualized gesture which was broadcast on a daily basis and was later adopted by other radio and television programs, as part of Israel's public infatuation with its missing soldiers (Kaplan 2008). Even more telling is an occasion when the radio decided to cover a major disaster that occurred not only beyond its area but thousands of kilometers beyond Israeli territory: in 2001 a Russian plane crashed in Siberia with dozens of Israeli-Russian immigrants among its casualties. Whereas most stations hardly covered the distant disaster or discussed its impact on the marginalized Russian immigrant population, Red Sea Radio made a point of suspending its regular programming and switching to the commercial-free mode of commemorative music for a few hours to commemorate the national disaster.

Radio stations lose profits from suspending commercials during Memorial Days and emergency events, but in abiding by the sanctity of these special days of national communion they gain in public relations all year long. Such national programming substitutes material capital for symbolic capital (Meyers, Zandberg, and Neiger 2009). Even if momentarily national constraints seem to contradict commercial needs, in the long run maintaining practices of radio engineering that reflect immediate response to national concerns seems to be an important market positioning for a commercial radio station in the Israeli context, even in the periphery.

Conclusion

Radio engineers can plan, select, and transmit live popular music in ways that can elicit collective identifications by placing music in a widely shared, ritualized, and performative context which provides recognizable cues for invoking the national imaginary. In news and talk programs such meanings and discourses of "the nation" are conveyed explicitly and independent of the broadcasting circumstances. In fact, news content can be accessed just as easily through other media sources such as the Internet and newspapers. In contrast, a musical broadcast may elicit national themes and particularly national sentiments such as grief, communion, or elevation only in juxtaposition to collective experiences shared by the audience at the time of transmission. It is precisely this irreplaceable and context-dependent quality of live music radio that makes it a powerful vehicle for identification with the nation.

Radio's potential in engineering national sentiments becomes apparent in the Israeli case. Despite pressures to adopt commercial programming based on a standardized, predetermined playlist with no relation to external events, most public and regional stations in Israel have opted to preserve a long-standing practice of music editing. Because the mechanisms of signification involved in listening to music often depend on implicit scripts and emotional cues, radio's entanglement with the national imaginary may be better understood as a bottom-up production of nation making (Foster 1997), yet one which coincides with official national discourses. Popular music on the air is like the flag hanging unnoticed in public buildings, a banal background for everyday life (Billig 1995). But it is against this backdrop that radio engineering can juxtapose music with collective events. The logic of the "cross" is central to this process and gives it material form. As music editors extend the linear associations between consecutive songs to the simultaneous associations between songs and external events—from spells of rain to spells of terror attacks—they weave songs to narratives of crisis and to discourses of a singular national community.

Since Israeli society is marked by frequent events of commemoration and emergency, radio stations across the country are encouraged to reflect and even shape the appropriate mood through their music broadcasting. Dependent on a popular discourse of "morale," this entails encoding radio sounds within well-rehearsed national narratives that explain how suffering and loss can transform into triumph or redemption. These days of national significance enjoy high public esteem so that even remote peripheral stations, as in the case of Red Sea Radio, have an incentive to cross music with Memorial Days or terror attacks. This self-conscious desire to intensify national identification using radio sound is so acute that even in the absence of immediate local crisis, radio engineers may invoke distant disasters instead.

In turn, the special music broadcasts during commemoration and emergency establish a framework for conceptualizing the work of radio stations all year long. They push station managers to apply the same logic of crossing in everyday life and to partly synchronize their daily music with concurrent public events shared by their community, a task which could only be accomplished by preserving the job of music editors. Furthermore, by favoring the tasks of live editing over radio models of predetermined programming, Israeli radio establishes a strategic market positioning in the face of growing competition from Internet music and media players. In a country that is perhaps poor in rain but rich in rocket strikes and the politics of collective memory, editing practices that facilitate national engineering may prove to be radio's last vantage point in the changing field of electronic media.

NOTES

1. A search in scholarly journals conducted in November 2009 yielded thirty abstracts related to radio in conjunction with music programming and virtually none that referred to music editing. A corresponding search in open-access websites yielded an estimated fifty thousand sites with the term "music programming" and twenty-two thousand sites mentioning "music editing."
2. Fieldwork on Israeli radio was conducted between 2004 and 2010. I held in-depth interviews with music editors, deejays, and station managers in public and commercial-regional stations specializing in popular music or in talk and music shows. I also carried out in-situ observations in four regional stations, among them Red

Sea Station in Eilat, kept diaries of live listening sessions during designated days of national commemoration, and carried out participant-observations with selected audiences during Memorial Days and periods of rocket strikes on the Israeli home front. Public discussion of radio practices and policies were examined through local journals and Internet forums. The fieldwork was conducted with the assistance of Orit Hirsh and Noa Bergman.

3. Whereas television established its cultural dominance over radio in most Western states by the 1950s and was the prevailing national medium in Third World states emerging in the 1960s (Katz and Wedell 1977), Israeli radio benefited from near exclusivity during its formative years, as television broadcasting was deliberately delayed by the government until 1968 (Liebes 2006).

4. Only five regional stations focus on differentiated audiences, such as the Palestinian community of northern Israel, the Sephardic ultra-Orthodox community, or the Russian-immigrant population.

5. For a cultural analysis of the national narrative associated with male friendship in some canonic Israeli songs of commemoration, see Kaplan 2006.

REFERENCES

Anderson, Benedict. 1991 [1983]. *Imagined Communities: Reflections on the Origins and Spread of Nationalism*. London: Verso.

Balint, Anat. 2004. Regional Radio: Traveling Far Away, Feeling Close. *Seventh Eye*, April 1. Retrieved October 21, 2009, from http://www.the7eye.org.il/articles/Pages/article3817.aspx?RetUrl=/WRITTERS/-Pages/anat_balint.aspx [Hebrew].

Ben-Ami, Ilan. 1996. Government Involvement in the Arts in Israel: Some Structural and Policy Characteristics. *Journal of Arts Management, Law and Society* 26 (3): 195–219.

Berland, Jody. 1993. Radio Space and Industrial Time: The Case of Music Formats. In Tony Bennett, Simon Frith, Lawrence Grossberg, John Shepard, and Graeme Turner, eds., *Rock and Popular Music: Politics, Policies, Institutions*, 104–118. New York: Routledge.

Billig, Michael. 1995. *Banal Nationalism*. London: Sage.

BizPortal. 2009. TGI Survey. July 29. Retrieved October 21, 2009, from http://www.bizportal.co.il/shukhahon/biznews02.shtml?mid=209153 [Hebrew]. OK

Cooper, Frederick, and Ann Laura Stoler. 1997. Between Metropole and Colony: Rethinking a Research Agenda. In Frederick Cooper and Ann Laura Stoler, eds., *Tensions of Empire: Colonial Cultures in a Bourgeois World*, 1–56. Berkeley: University of California Press.

Doner, Shlomi. 2004. TGI Survey: Rise in Exposure to Internet. *YNet*, July 19. Retrieved October 21, 2009, from http://www.ynet.co.il/articles/1,7340,L-2949582,00.html [Hebrew].

Douglas, Susan J. 2004. *Listening In: Radio and the American Imagination*. Minneapolis: University of Minnesota Press.

Foster, Robert J., ed. 1997. *Nation Making: Emergent Identities in Postcolonial Melanesia*. Ann Arbor: University of Michigan Press.

Gellner, Ernst. 1983. *Nations and Nationalism*. Oxford, UK: Blackwell.

Greve, Henrich R. 1996. Patterns of Competition: The Diffusion of a Market Position in Radio Broadcasting. *Administrative Science Quarterly* 41:29–60.

Handelman, Don. 2004. *Nationalism and the Israeli State: Bureaucratic Logic in Public Events*. Oxford, UK: Berg.

Hayes, Joy Elizabeth. 1996. Touching the Sentiments of Everyone: Nationalism and State Broadcasting in Thirties Mexico. *Communication Review* 1 (4): 411–439.

Hobsbawm, Eric. 1982. *Invention of Tradition*. Cambridge: Cambridge University Press.

Kaplan, Danny. 2000. The Military as a Second Bar Mitzvah: Combat Service as an Initiation-Rite to Zionist Masculinity. In Mai Ghoussoub and Emma Sinclair-Webb, eds., *Imagined Masculinities: Male Identity and Culture in the Modern Middle East*, 127–144. London: Saqi Books.

———. 2006. *The Men We Loved: Male Friendship and Nationalism in Israeli Culture*. New York: Berghahn Books.

———. 2008. Commemorating a "Suspended Death": Missing Soldiers and National Solidarity in Israel. *American Ethnologist* 35 (3): 413–427.

———. 2009. The Songs of the Siren: Engineering National Time on Israeli Radio. *Cultural Anthropology* 24 (2): 313–345.

Karmel, Asaf. 2008. Survey by Kol Israel: Galgalatz Is the Most Listened To Station in the Country. *Haaretz*, January 17. Retrieved October 21, 2009, from http://www.haaretz.com/hasite/spages/945385.html [Hebrew].

Katz, Elihu, and George Wedell. 1977. *Broadcasting in the Third World*. Cambridge: Harvard University Press.

Knesset. 1963. *Law of the Day of Remembrance for the Fallen of Israeli Wars—1963*. Retrieved October 21, 2009, from http://www.knesset.gov.il/laws/special/heb/chok_yom_hazikaron.htm [Hebrew].

Lahav, Sahi. 2009. *Play List: The Way Galgalatz Changed the Israeli Music* [Hebrew]. Tel Aviv: Am Oved.

Liebes, Tamar. 2006. Acoustic Space: The Role of Radio in Israeli Collective History. *Jewish History* 20:69–90.

Lippmann, Stephen. 2007. The Institutional Context of Industry Consolidation: Radio Broadcasting in the United States, 1920–1934. *Social Forces* 86 (2): 467–495.

Meyers, Oren, Eyal Zandberg, and Motti Neiger. 2009. Prime Time Commemoration: An Analysis of Television Broadcasts on Israel's Memorial Day for the Holocaust and the Heroism. *Journal of Communication* 59 (3): 456–480.

Mrázek, Rudolf. 1997. "Let Us Become Radio Mechanics": Technology and National Identity in Late-Colonial Netherlands East Indies. *Comparative Studies in Society and History* 39 (1): 3–33.

———. 2002. *Engineers of Happy Land: Technology and Nationalism in a Colony*. Princeton: Princeton University Press.

Penslar, Derek. 2003. Transmitting Jewish Culture: Radio in Israel. *Jewish Social Studies* 10 (11): 1–29.

Scannell, Paddy, and David Cardiff. 1991. *A Social History of British Broadcasting*, vol. 1, *1922–1939: Serving the Nation*. Cambridge, MA: Blackwell.

Second Authority for Television and Radio. 1999. *Rules of Authority for Television and Radio (Advertisements and Commercial References in Radio Broadcasting)—1999*. Retrieved October 21, 2009, from http://www.rashut2.org.il/editor%5CUpLoadLow%5CB-76.pdf [Hebrew].

Smith, Philip, and Tim Phillips. 2006. Collective Belonging and Mass Media Consumption: Unraveling How Technological Medium and Cultural Genre Shape the National Imaginings of Australians. *Sociological Review* 54 (4): 818–846.

Spitulnik, Debra. 1999. Mediated Modernities: Encounters with the Electronic in Zambia. *Visual Anthropology Review* 14 (2): 63–84.

Taylor, Charles. 2002. Modern Social Imaginaries. *Public Culture* 14 (1): 91–124.

Tsing, Anna Lowenhaupt. 2003. The News in the Provinces. In Renato Rosaldo, ed., *Cultural Citizenship in Island Southeast Asia: Nation and Belonging in the Hinterlands*, 192–222. Berkeley: University of California Press.

5

Reconsidering Muslim Authority

Female "Preachers" and the Ambiguities of
Radio-Mediated Sermonizing in Mali

DOROTHEA SCHULZ

Opening: A Radio Controversy

The political opening in Mali following the fall from power of President Moussa Traoré and his single-party rule in 1991 has generated unprecedented dynamics in the national media landscape. Following the granting of multiparty democracy and of attendant civil liberties, numerous private press organs were created along with more than 150 local radio stations that cover most of Mali's urban and semiurban environments.[1] The proliferation of private media has been accompanied by the emergence of a broad spectrum of interest groups that intervene in public debate. Among them are various Muslim activist associations that rely on local radio stations and audio- and videotaped sermons to extend their call for an Islamic renewal of society and self to broader constituencies and to articulate their divergent positions on matters of proper Muslim conduct and practice in public debates. The interventions of these Muslim activists generate new debates and struggles over radio-mediated sermonizing and, most conspicuously, over gender-specific forms of spiritual and moral authority.

Central issues of these debates among Muslims are captured in a controversy I followed in November 2003, while conducting research on Islamic moral renewal in San, a town in southwestern Mali, and in the capital, Bamako. At the center of the controversy was the immense popularity of a weekly religious program broadcast on one of Bamako's numerous private local radio stations. The radio program essentially consisted of weekly installments of the "moral instruction" offered by one particular "radio speaker" (whom I shall call Aminata), an elderly and very respectable leader of one of the Muslim women's neighborhood associations that have been mushrooming since the early 1990s. Aminata had started broadcasting her advice on matters of proper female conduct in 1999. Since then, numerous women, not only those who considered themselves supporters of the Islamic renewal movement, keenly awaited—and eagerly followed—each weekly installment of her lectures. Aminata herself emphasized, during her broadcast lectures and in off-stage conversations, that her role was not that of a "preacher." Yet many of her female—as well as some of her male—fans stressed that her "moral lessons" were equal in importance and quality to the sermons offered by male preachers on Malian national and local radio.

During my earlier research on Islamic revival in urban Mali, I had taken Aminata's popularity as a radio speaker as something unproblematic. I was therefore shocked to witness how, in November 2003, several male radio preachers reprimanded her and other women lecturing on local radio programs and denounced their "pretense" in "assuming the role of preachers while lacking the knowledge to do so." As one of these critics complained in his sermon broadcast on Radio Islamique, one of Mali's two private Islamic radio stations,

> There are people these days . . . who claim that God asked them to address wider audiences [jamaa], to speak to them about Islam. They think that having the means and opportunities to talk [baro] on radio endows them with the right to lecture in public, to give people moral lessons. But . . . these people lack propriety, they lack a sense of modesty. How can it be that someone who has little learning and understanding in the matters of Islam all of a sudden claims to be a teacher? With radio stations now popping up everywhere, anyone may claim the right to speak on radio. . . . Does a radio make you a teacher? Does owning a radio post turn you into

an erudite? No, I tell you, these women should keep in mind the teachings they received from their mothers and from [male] Muslim teachers [*kara-mogo*]: that a woman should know her proper place at home. (Author's translation of broadcast sermon)

This statement illustrates how controversial the appearance of female "preachers" on national and local radio has become in recent years. At stake is not only the validity of women's lectures and arguments but also the question as to who has the authority to speak in public and *as* an authority in religious matters. Clearly, the relatively recent proliferation of radio broadcasting technologies in various local settings generates new struggles over gender-specific realms of religious discourse and interpretive authority.

The divisiveness of these questions is, in itself, a reflection of the heterogeneous field of Muslim debate that emerged along with the diversification of the Malian media landscape since the early 1990s. Women who, like Aminata, lecture on "Islam" on local radio stations can be seen as the product of these developments. Aminata's new public audibility—as well as that of many other supporters of Islamic renewal—has spawned new controversies among these people themselves over what it means to be a proper Muslim (Schulz 2007, 2008c). Their associations and proselytizing (*da'wa*) activities tend to be associated by many Malians with "Arab Islam," that is, practices and interpretations of Islam that have drawn inspiration from Salafi-Sunni reformist trends in Egypt and Saudi Arabia since the early 20th century. Especially Malians who view themselves as defendants of the principle of *laïcité* against the onslaught of Islamic "fundamentalism" regard the activities of these Muslim activists with suspicion.

The diversification of national and local radio fields and the concomitant mushrooming of Muslim revivalist activism parallel developments elsewhere in Africa, yet the connection between these two developments has yet to receive sustained scholarly attention. Recent political liberalization, paired with longstanding processes of widening access to religious education, has significantly transformed the field of Muslim debate and the ways in which various Muslim actors engage institutions of the state to make their claims heard in public arenas. Supportive of these developments has been the simultaneous emergence of a competitive field of radio (and in some countries television) broadcasting in which new media and religious entrepreneurs insert themselves with aplomb (Schulz 2006; see Haenni 2002; Larkin and Meyer 2006).

Particularly remarkable about these developments is the new prominence of women who, in their efforts to convince others to "search for greater closeness to God," place a special weight on the public practice of piety. Although these women claim a key role in these reform-oriented Islamic movements and enjoy great—often iconic—visibility, their public role has received comparatively little scholarly attention.[2] This neglect is surprising. After all, as the introductory anecdote illustrates, these women's efforts to publicize their visions of an Islamic moral order are likely to generate new debates over religious authority, over authoritative radio preaching, and over the significance of religion to public order.

In southern Mali, "Muslim women"[3] who participate in the Islamic renewal movement organize themselves around female leaders to whom they refer as "group leaders" (singular, *tontigi*) or with the honorific title *hadja*. These leaders offer advice on proper conduct in ritual and daily settings and emphasize the key role of Muslim women in effecting moral transformation of Malian society. Some *hadjas* also disseminate their "moral lessons" (*ladili*)[4] on local radio programs and in audio recordings that circulate beyond the networks of their immediate followers.[5] Other women who lecture to female audiences on "the rules of Islam" belong to a group of younger married women who were trained at institutions of higher learning in North Africa; they are invited to lecture in the religious programs of national radio and television (ORTM).

Male leaders of the Islamic renewal movement often laud the role of women as guides of moral reform, yet some of them also voice the (contested) Muslim scholarly opinion that women should not be allowed to preach in public because the sensuality of their voices risks arousing male desire. This criticism is directed mostly at the group leaders, who, their critics maintain, should not be mistaken for Islamic "teachers" (singular, *karamògò*) because of their lack of religious erudition. This view is shared by men who work in administrative structures geared toward implementing what the state defines as "proper" Islam.[6] Those in charge of Muslim religious programs on national radio, for instance, speak condescendingly of "these 'radio *hadjas*' who talk on local radio without knowing much about Islam." Their scorn is echoed by some younger, highly educated women who, at the behest of the religious programs director of the ORTM, deliver lectures on "women's rights and duties in Islam" on national radio. While these critics dismiss the "radio *hadjas*" as women who lack religious erudition and propriety, followers of individual female leaders often stress their spiritual authority.

How can we explain the apparent tension between the religious authority that these listeners assign to their female leaders and the criticism these women encounter on the part of male preachers? Wherein consists the challenge that these *hadjas* pose to conventional forms of religious discourse and authority?

Radio Fields and Controversies over Female Authority: Framing the Terms of Analysis

The radio lectures by *hadjas* seem to support the argument that new media technologies undermine the foundations of traditional, text-based forms of authority and foster a "democratization" of religious interpretation (e.g., Turner 2007; see Eickelman and Anderson 1999). According to this view, broader access to religious knowledge allows women and other marginalized groups to "carve out" new spaces in a male-dominated field of religious interpretation.[7] This view of the instrumental role of new media in supporting women's "empowerment" vis-à-vis established (male) religious authority echoes a dominant trend in recent scholarship on radio broadcasting in African societies. Much of this scholarship focuses on political liberalization since the early 1990s and the concomitant emergence of a plural radio landscape, and it thus stresses the democratic and liberating potential of radio broadcasting (e.g., Karikari 1994; Fardon and Furniss 2000; Nyamnjoh 2005; Bosch 2006). Yet it is far from certain whether new media technologies have the liberating effects that these authors envisage. Stressing the progressive implications of radio technology for women is also in line with a tendency in studies of Muslim societies to conceive of gender relations in terms of oppression and struggle (but see Abu-Lughod 1998; Mahmood 2005).[8]

There are several shortcomings to the stress on radio's "empowering" effects. First, the argument starts from a largely instrumentalist view of the workings and effects of radio broadcasting technology, by positing that this medium simply transmits, rather than also affects, the "message" it carries (Schulz 2006). Second, a focus on the subversive effects of local radio broadcasting cannot explain why the *hadjas*, although "gaining a voice" in public, do not challenge the authority of male representatives of the movement, by articulating independent religious interpretations.[9] Finally, an emphasis on the "empowerment" of women (vis-à-vis male religious authority) does not account for the great resentment that these women's interventions on local radio stations generate among their female critics, particularly among the younger generation of women who are invited to lecture on national religious radio programs. These female critics of the *hadjas* owe their public recognition to the same set of media technologies, that is, radio broadcasting. Interpretations that highlight technological innovation as a central venue of transformations in gender and religious hierarchies fail to elucidate the heterogeneous composition of female Muslim activism.

A more promising perspective on these controversies is to examine how radio broadcasting, as a relatively new technology of "mediating religion" (de Vries and Weber 2001; Stolow 2005; de Witte 2008) inflects the message it publicizes, and circumscribes the ways in which listeners engage with it. Such dynamics reconfigure public debate by fostering new imaginations of religious community but also of moral difference.[10] We should take account of long-term continuities in the ways authority is asserted and attributed (Gaffney 1994), rather than remaining preoccupied with the changes purportedly introduced by audio recording and broadcasting technologies and the disruptions in the foundations of religious authority they engender.

Islamic Moral Renewal in Mali

Since the 1980s, social institutions of Islamic moral renewal, such as the Muslim women's neighborhood groups, have been thriving. Their success is partly attributable to the financial support they received from different countries in the Arab-speaking world. But their emergence also points to a longer process of Muslim educational reform that gradually led to the extension of ritual and religious instruction to broader segments of society, most notably to middle-aged, married women from the urban middle and lower-middle classes.[11] Throughout the colonial period and until the 1970s, religious learning remained largely the prerogative of older women from families of religious specialists and merchants. These elite women owed their erudition to the support of their fathers, brothers, and husbands. Their economically privileged position allowed them to lead a life devoted to religious study, withdrawn from public scrutiny. For the majority of Muslim women, however, religious instruction was limited to knowledge about proper ritual conduct.

A novel aspect of the present-day Muslim women's groups is that they attract many women from the middle and lower-middle classes. Some of these women have never been at school; others may have received Western school education but consider this kind of knowledge inadequate. Even if many participants in the Muslim women's learning groups acquire only basic knowledge in Arabic and of the teachings of Islam, they still feel that participation in the groups prepares them for the life of a proper believer.

Offering Moral Lessons: "Radio Hadjas'" Self-Understanding as Educators

Today, I will lecture to you . . . because this has always been the duty of an older woman: to offer moral lessons [ladili] to her younger sisters and daughters, and to teach them proper behavior. . . . Women, listen carefully, so that you will understand what God expects from you. . . . The role that God the Almighty assigned to you is unique. . . . It depends on you whether peace will reign in your home or whether your family will be disrupted by endless quarrels, between you and your husband, and between you and your co-wives. . . . Prayer makes a Muslim woman a true believer. But this is not enough. What counts is your right attitude which shows in your daily behavior. . . . The comportment required of a woman is patience [*munyu*, "endurance"]. . . . The second virtue you need to practice is modesty [*maloya*]. A true Muslim woman should work hard on these capabilities. Do not gossip or backbite. Do not spend your time pointing at others and saying "such-and-such did this-and-that."

This radio lecture of a *hadja*, recorded in August 2001 in Bamako, starts with a fairly typical justification of her radio appearance as a matter of the moral obligation that older women have toward other women who are ranked below them in terms of age and status. By providing this rationale for her radio lecture, the *hadja* alludes to a broader culture of moralizing in which women beyond menopause but also professional public speakers and praise singers, known as the *jeliw* (singular, *jeli*), conventionally engaged (Schulz 2001). Other *hadjas*, too, who appear on local radio legitimate their role as "educators" not by putting themselves on an equal footing with male preachers or "teachers" (singular, *karamògò*) but by reference to older women's "traditional duties." What this portrayal leaves out is the profoundly changed social conditions that enable, and constitute the subject of, their radio lectures. Conducive to this process has been the mass import of relatively affordable radio recorders (many of them with a cassette function) from Southeast Asia since the mid-1980s. The multiplication of local radio stations since the early 1990s, with the privileged broadcasting of local radio programs in Bamanakan (the lingua franca of southern Mali) and other national languages, created new motivations to purchase a radio recorder among more solvent listeners.

Although the female Muslim leaders understand—and present—their moral lessons as part of their return to more authentic modes of interpreting and living God's word,[12] their advice, such as the previously quoted cautioning against backbiting among co-wives, reveals their engagement with radically changing gender relations in town. Female leaders also advise their disciples on proper comportment in domestic and public settings and on their duty to invite others to embark on the path to God. True religiosity, the educators argue, should manifest itself not only in the performance of the conventional obligations of worship, such as the five daily prayers, but in the purposeful cultivation of certain emotional capabilities. Relatively novel

elements of their teachings consist in the stress on women's individual responsibility for salvation, on women's conscious decision to "become a better
Muslim," and on the necessity to become a "public" example of moral excel-
lence. The emphasis on individual responsibility and "choice" contrasts with
the times when Muslim identity formed part of a family or professional identity (see Launay 1992). Moreover, the self-conscious assertion of a public role
departs from the traditional relegation of female religiosity and devotional
practices to an intimate, secluded space within the domestic realm. Whereas
before, women's spiritual experiences were predicated on their withdrawal
from the area of worldly matters and mundane daily activities, Muslim wom-
en's public worship establishes a direct link between the practice of piety and
its public profession (Schulz 2008b).

Voice, Mediation, and Charismatic Authority

Given the fact that the moral lessons of the female leaders do not challenge
the interpretations and prerogatives of male radio preachers but resonate
with conventional norms of female propriety, the vitriolic reactions to their
radio appearances appear puzzling. What is so special about *hadjas'* radio
intervention that it increases their authority in the eyes of their followers?

One way to address this question is to look into the modes of perception
that radio broadcasting reinforces or generates, a perception that potentially
supports listeners' recognition of radio-mediated "moral lessons" as compelling "teachings." Furthermore, a historical perspective promises insight
into differences between the mass-mediated lectures of present-day "radio
hadjas" on one side and earlier modes of female sermonizing on the other.[13]
As noted earlier, historically the written traditions of Islam played a marginal
role in informing the evaluations by ordinary believers of the moralizing activities of older women and also in investing their own listening practices
with specific ethical significance. Still today, knowledge of the written traditions of Islam plays a minor role in informing female listeners' views of
how to conduct a life in accordance with Islamic norms. For this reason, it
would be misplaced to apply an analytical framework similar to the one proposed by Charles Hirschkind (2006) in his discussion of the personal, ethical significance of sermon listening practices. According to Hirschkind, male
participants in Islamic revival in contemporary Cairo frame their quest for
ethical self-improvement and their visions of the ethically constitutive role of
sermon listening practices by drawing on specific disciplinary, written traditions of Islam. In Mali, most believers lack the religious interpretive knowledge but also access to the institutional infrastructure that would enable

them to draw on textual knowledge in ways that Hirschkind describes for male supporters of Islamic renewal in Cairo. To understand the significance that Muslim women and other believers attribute to the "moral lessons" of female Muslim leaders as well as to the practice of listening itself, greater attention should be given to the ways in which people in Mali society speak in more general terms of the aesthetic and moving force of the spoken word and of its principal medium, the human voice.

Scholarship on oral performances and orality in Sahelian West Africa has noted the special significance attributed conventionally to speech. Regardless of discrepancies among regional cultures, there exists a pervasive, strong appreciation of the spoken word. Speech is widely considered to mobilize people's affective and agentive capabilities through the "touching" sound of voice (Schulz 2003). In Mali, the most prominent example of the view that speech not only represents but makes reality is the public speech and praise events during which specialists of the spoken word, the *jeliw, make* the reputation of their patrons by the very act of speaking about it. During these performances, one often witnesses how members of the audience spontaneously express their enthusiasm about a performer who, by virtue of his or her forceful speech, moves people to action even against their own will. Listeners frequently comment on "successful speech" in terms of its capacity to enlighten and edify people and to move them to exemplary action by molding and indeed creating in them the perceptive and cognitive potentialities necessary for these instances of extraordinary deeds. In this view, the human voice is at the origins of social action because it mediates the perceptive qualities that make hearing—and heeding—speech possible in the first place.

These culturally anchored perceptions of the agentive, action-inducing capacity of the voice, and of the irresistible nature of skillful speech, also become manifest in the embodied reactions by audiences, such as when people spontaneously jump up and perform the reputation that praise singers have just conferred on them through "dignified" and slow dance movements. All these reactions attest to the importance people attribute to the spoken word in making—and shaking—social and political realities.[14]

Yet as much as listeners appreciate speech and voice as media essential to the making of everyday social relations, they also feel ambivalent toward the spoken word. Indeed, it is very much in acknowledgment of the enormous potential of human speech to move a person's senses and emotions that speech is also highly distrusted. Speech is considered—and, if possible, controlled—as a process that sets free the damaging forces of delusion, of distortion of true events, and thus ultimately of betrayal (Camara 1976; Kendall 1982; Diawara 2003).

The equivocal views on the force and dangers of speech and voice are reflected in the controversial appreciation of the lecturing activities of the female Muslim leaders. The positive, ethically formative effects of speech are highlighted by female followers and other listeners who are supportive of the Islamic renewal movement whenever they comment on the *hadjas'* radio lectures. Those who are critical of the radio-mediated interventions of the *hadjas*, on the other hand, are well aware of their potential of affecting the hearts and minds of listeners, yet they frame their resentment as a critique of these women's want of propriety. But their followers show themselves immune to these allegations by insisting on the edifying effects not only of their leaders' speech but of their own practices of listening. "Oumou," a member of a Muslim women's association in the popular neighborhood of Bamako, in which I lived during my research in 2001, succinctly summarized her understanding of the edifying effects of listening to a radio lecture:

> People's ways of hearing [*mèn*] a lecture are quite different. Listening to a *hadja*'s moral advice may affect you very differently. If you only hear it with your ears, then it will not move you to action. Only if you listen to a lecture in a way that reaches the depths of your heart can you be truly moved. Then you will be carried away. . . . A sermon that you understood in all its deep truth will open your heart; it will reach your soul. It will awaken in you the desire to move forward and submit to God's demands.

Oumou explains that she, similar to others who regularly listen to the radio lectures by preachers and *hadjas*, views a person's *potential* to feel touched by sound as an essential prerequisite for moral being and action (see Hirschkind 2006, 70–72). Hearing and speaking thus go together with validating an educator's "moral lesson"; being touched or "captivated" (*mine*, literally "apprehended") by the (sound of a) voice is the principal marker of "truthful" and compelling speech (Schulz 1999). The emphasis on the moving capacities of voice and speech is important in order to grasp why the moralizing activities of the radio *hadjas* are so highly appreciated by their followers. The authority that these followers assign to their *hadja* in the course of their radio-mediated interactions is grounded in culturally anchored understandings of voice as an essential medium for facilitating spiritual experience and moral subjectivity (Schulz 2008a, 2011b, chap. 7). Spontaneous responses to the "moral lessons" often highlight the "gripping" effects of the timbre of a *hadja*'s voice. These responses suggest that women experience audition as an at-once aural and tactile sensation, a tactility that, if we follow their spontaneous reactions, tends to be heightened by radio broadcasts. The sensation of tactile intimacy reinforces the experience of commonality and the emotional identification that *hadjas* evoke in their "moral lessons." Radio broadcasting thus grants additional possibilities to women leaders to establish themselves as figures of ethical guidance. It allows female leaders to assert a form of leadership for which textual knowledge is of lesser importance because it draws on the sensation of empathy and commonality. Voice, by virtue of the perceptive modes it facilitates, forms the cornerstone of an interactive generation of spiritual leadership. By fusing established notions of forceful speech and of a "heartfelt" hearing experience with new technologies of mediating these experiences, the followers of the radio *hadjas* contribute to the ongoing relevance of these understandings to Muslim religious practice and to the making of religious authority.

Disagreements about mass-mediated religious sermonizing, and over the "preaching" activities of Muslim women in particular, should be read in the light of listeners' general ambivalences toward speech. Because the authority of the *hadjas* and their mass-mediated lectures is grounded importantly in—what their followers identify as—the "moving" force of their voice, the criticism the *hadjas* face seems to originate in the challenge these female "preachers" pose to text-based forms of religious (interpretive) authority. Radio broadcasting reinforces this challenge by multiplying and inflating opportunities for experiencing the Janus-faced qualities of the voice, especially its capacities to move the heart against one's own will. People's equivocal feelings about this process come out in gender-specific evaluations of the acceptability of radio preaching. Whereas the authority of certain male radio preachers may be challenged by casting doubt on their erudition (Schulz 2006), anxieties about women who moralize on local radio are articulated differently. The validity of their interventions is challenged through a moralizing judgment, that is, by questioning their modesty and propriety. In this fashion, deeply anchored ambivalences about the voice and its "uncontrollable" nature, ambivalences that are reinforced through radio broadcasting technology, are translated into a moralizing discourse that contrasts the validity and authoritative nature of male preaching to the illegitimate and improper nature of female preaching.

Conclusion

The controversial appearance of female Muslim "preachers" on local radio stations in Mali cannot be understood in their complexity if examined primarily as a struggle over correct interpretive practice and authority that opposes women to men. Rather, these controversies reflect on a complex remapping of fields and experiences of religious authority. To grasp the authority that the radio *hadjas* hold in the eyes of their followers and other listeners, their broadcast lectures need to be analyzed with reference to the conventions and technologies through which religious leadership has been commonly attributed in this area of West Africa. Radio broadcasting technologies are adopted into conventional forms of sermonizing in ways that continue to privilege sound as a primary medium for genuine religious experience. Contemporary understandings draw on, and partly reproduce, long-standing techniques that established effective forms of "touching" speech and make it available to ordinary believers and religious specialists.

Conceiving of the relationship between the moralizing activities of *hadjas* and their radio-mediated lectures not in terms of contrast and rupture but as drawing on a common genealogy of "touching speech" allows scholars to expand the analytical perspective that studies of Islam—in Africa and beyond—have often applied to the relationship between religious authority and mass media (e.g., Anderson 1999; Eickelman and Anderson 1999; Mandaville 2007; Turner 2007; Volpi and Turner 2007). The adoption of radio broadcasting technologies by supporters of Islamic moral renewal in Mali does not engender a radical break between conventional understandings of religious authority and mass-mediated experiences of "God's compelling truth." These technologies and the attendant social and material practices of spiritual mediation allow some religious leaders to cross this conventional divide and to expand the "touching" effects of their discursive interventions into new domains of spiritual experience. Listeners who embrace similar ideas about the capacity of voice to pass on the powers of God's word may establish these media engagements as part of commonsensical religious practice (Schulz 2008a). Still, given the considerable resistance these believers encounter, on the part of various other religious actors, the result of this process remains unpredictable.

NOTES

1. The majority of these radio stations cover towns and their immediate surroundings in Mali's southern triangle. Of these local radio stations, about 65 percent are commercial radio stations; others are either local relay stations of national radio or community radio. In spite of nominal differences in statute and funding modalities, commercial and community radio stations do not differ significantly with regard to their organizational structure, their programming, and the financial and technical constraints they face (Schulz 1999).

2. Notable exceptions are Alidou (2005) and Kleiner-Bosaller and Loimeier (1994). Miran (1998, 2005), LeBlanc (1999), and Augis (2002) deal primarily with the disciples of these female "teachers." Other scholarship on female religiosity in Muslim

West Africa tends to focus on Sufi-related practices and understandings of authority (e.g., Coulon and Reveyrand 1990; Reveyrand-Coulon 1993; Evers Rosander 1997, 2003; see also Dunbar 2000).

3. The women refer to themselves simply as "Muslim women" " (*silame musow*) and thereby distance themselves from "other women" (*musow to*), who, in their eyes, are not "true believers" because of their lax attitude toward the Islamic duties of worship. See Schulz, 2011b.

4. *Ladili* refers to a category of edifying speech associated conventionally with older women and with professional specialists of the spoken word, the *jeliw* (Schulz 2001).

5. The "moral lessons" that a *hadja* has initially offered in a live radio program are often later circulated as audiotapes among her followers and their friends.

6. Among these structures are the national Muslim association, AMUPI (Association Malienne pour le Progres et l'Unite de l'Islam), the Bureau des Ulemas, the section of the national broadcast station that supervises (Muslim) religious programming, and the Haut Conseil Islamique, a subdivision of the Ministry of Interior Affairs.

7. E.g., Eickelman and Anderson 1999.

8. Numerous anthropological studies on Muslim women's educational activities, for instance, continue to study them in terms of a struggle between men and women over "gaining a voice" and "carving out new spaces" in a male-dominated religious field, for instance, with respect to authoritative interpretation (e.g., Weix 1998; Nageeb 2004; also see Alidou 2005; Masquelier 2009).

9. Interpretations of women's public interventions as indications of their "empowerment" also ignore the longstanding importance of elite women's educational and organizational activities in Muslim West Africa (Boyd 2001).

10. See Meyer 2005; Meyer and Moors 2006; Schulz 2006, 2007; Stolow 2006.

11. Instrumental for this development were the activities of a younger generation of Muslims who, after prolonged stays in Saudi Arabia, Egypt, and sometimes North Africa, initiated educational and other reforms to respond to the new situation established under French colonial rule (Brenner 1993).

12. Many female group leaders owe their influential position to a combination of credentials and economically privileged backgrounds. Nevertheless, the controversies among Muslims cannot be explained merely as a competition over access to state institutions and resources or as a reflection of "identity politics."

13. The following discussion is based mostly on oral historical sources collected in the period between 1998 and 2006.

14. Elsewhere I show that similar ambivalences toward the Janus-faced potential of speech also underlie the unease with which critics of the radio *hadjas* comment on the separation of voice from body and authorship that audio recording technologies enable (Schulz 2011a).

REFERENCES

Abu-Lughod, Lila. 1998. Feminist Longings and Postcolonial Conditions. In Lila Abu-Lughod, ed., *Remaking Women: Feminism and Modernity in the Middle East*, 3–31. Princeton: Princeton University Press.

Alidou, Ousseina. 2005. *Engaging Modernity: Muslim Women and the Politics of Agency in Postcolonial Niger*. Madison: University of Wisconsin Press.

Anderson, Jon. 1999. The Internet and Islam's New Interpreters. In Dale Eickelman and Jon Anderson, eds., *New Media in the Muslim World*, 41–56. Bloomington: Indiana University Press.

Augis, Erin. 2002. Dakar's Sunnite Women: The Politics of Person. Ph.D. diss., University of Chicago.

Bosch, Tanja E. 2006. Radio as an Instrument of Protest: The History of Bush Radio. *Journal of Radio & Audio Media* 13 (2): 249–265.

Boyd, Jean. 1989. *The Caliph's Sister: Nana Asma'u (1793–1865), Teacher, Poet, and Islamic Leader*. London: Cass.

———. 2001. Distance Learning from Purdah in Nineteenth-Century Northern Nigeria: The Work of Asma'u Fodio. *Journal of African Cultural Studies* 14 (1): 7–22.

Brenner, Louis. 1993. Constructing Muslim Identities in Mali. In Louis Brenner, ed., *Muslim Identity and Social Change in Sub-Saharan Africa*, 59–78. Bloomington: Indiana University Press.

Camara, Sory. 1976. *Gens de la Parole: Essai sur la condition et le rôle dans la société Malinké*. Paris: La Haye.

Coulon, Christian, and Odile Reveyrand. 1990. L'Islam au féminin: Sokhna Magat Diop Cheikh de la Confrérie Mouride (Senegal). *Travaux et Documents* (Centre d'Étude d'Afrique Noire) 25.

de Vries, Hent, and Samuel Weber, eds. 2001. *Religion and Media*. Stanford: Stanford University Press.

de Witte, Marleen. 2008. Spirit Media: Charismatics, Traditionalists, and Mediation Practices in Ghana. Ph.D. diss., Department of Anthropology, University of Amsterdam.

Diawara, Mamadou. 2003. *Empire du verbe et l'éloquence du silence: Vers une anthropologie du discours dans les groupes dits domines au Sahel*. Cologne: Rüdiger Köppe.

Dunbar, Roberta Ann. 2000. Muslim Women in African History. In Nehemia Levtzion and Randall Pouwels, eds., *The History of Islam in Africa*, 397–417. Athens: Ohio University Press.

Eickelman, Dale, and Jon Anderson. 1999. *New Media in the Muslim World*. Bloomington: Indiana University Press.

Evers Rosander, Eva. 1997. Le dahira de Mam Diarra Bousso de Mbacké. In Eva Evers Rosander, ed., *Transforming Female Identities: Women's Organizational Forms in West Africa*, 160–174. Uppsala: Nordiska Afrikainstitutet.

———. 2003. Mam Diarra Bousso: The Good Mother in Porokhane. Paper presented at the Workshop "Modern Adaptations in Sufi-Based Islam." Berlin, Centre for Modern Oriental Studies, April.

Fardon, Richard, and Graham Furniss, eds. 2000. *African Broadcast Cultures: Radio and Public Life*. Oxford, UK: James Currey.

Gaffney, Patrick. 1994. *The Prophet's Pulpit: Islamic Preaching in Contemporary Egypt*. Berkeley: University of California Press.

Haenni, Patrick. 2002. *Au-del'a du repli identitaire: Les nouveaux prêcheurs Egpytiens et la modernisation paradoxale de l'islam*. Religio-Scope, Analyse, November. Electronic document, http://www.cedej.org.eg/ (accessed September 30, 2005).

Harrison, Christopher. 1988. *France and Islam in West Africa, 1860–1960*. Cambridge: Cambridge University Press.

Hirschkind, Charles. 2006. *The Ethical Soundscape*. New York: Columbia University Press.

Karikari, Kwame, ed. 1994. *Independent Broadcasting in Ghana: Implications and Challenges*. Accra: Ghana Universities Press.

Kendall, Martha. 1982. Getting to Know You. In David Parkin, ed., *Semantic Anthropology*. London: Academic Press.

Kleiner-Bosaller, Anke, and Roman Loimeier. 1994. Radical Muslim Women and Male Politics in Nigeria. In Mechthild Reh and Gudrun Ludwar-Ene, eds., *Gender and Identity in Africa*, 61–69. Münster: LIT Verlag.

Larkin, Brian, and Birgit Meyer. 2006. Pentecostalism, Islam and Culture: New Religious Movements in West Africa. In Emmanuel Akyeampong, ed., *Themes in West African History*, 286–311. London: James Currey.

Launay, Robert. 1992. *Beyond the Stream: Islam and Society in a West African Town*. Berkeley: University of California Press.

LeBlanc, Marie Nathalie. 1999. The Production of Islamic Identities through Knowledge Claims in Bouaké, Côte d'Ivoire. *African Affairs* 98 (393): 485–509.

Mahmood, Saba. 2005. *Politics of Piety: The Islamic Revival and the Feminist Subject*. Princeton: Princeton University Press.

Mandaville, Peter. 2007. Globalization and the Politics of Religious Knowledge: Pluralizing Authority in the Muslim World. *Theory, Culture & Society* 24 (2): 101–115.

Masquelier, Adeline. 2009. *Women and Islamic Revival in a West African Town*. Bloomington: Indiana University Press.

Meyer, Birgit. 2005. Religious Remediations: Pentecostal Views in Ghanaian Video-Movies. In Mediating Film and Religion, guest ed. Stephen Hughes and Birgit Meyer, special issue, *Postscripts* 1 (2–3): 155–181.

Meyer, Birgit, and Annelies Moors, eds. 2006. Introduction. In Birgit Meyer and Annelies Moors, eds., *Religion, Media, and the Public Sphere*, 1–28. Bloomington: Indiana University Press.

Miran, Marie. 1998. Le Wahhabisme à Abidjan: Dynamisme urbain d'un islam reformiste en Côte d'Ivoire contemporaine (1960–1996). *Islam et Sociétés au Sud du Sahara* 12:5–74.

———. 2005. D'Abidjan à Porto Novo: Associations islamiques et culture religieuse réformiste sur la Côte de Guinée. In Laurent Fourchard, André Mary, and René Otayek, eds., *Entreprises religieuses transnationales en Afrique de l'Ouest*, 43–72. Ibadan, Nigeria: IFRA, Karthala.

Nageeb, Salma Ahmed. 2004. *New Spaces and Old Frontiers: Women, Social Space, and Islamization in Sudan*. Lanham, MD: Lexington Books.

Nyamnjoh, Francis. 2005. *Africa's Media: Democracy and the Politics of Belonging*. London: Zed Books.

Reveyrand-Coulon, Odile. 1993. Les énoncés féminins de l'islam. In J.-F. Bayart, ed., *Religion et modernité politique en Afrique Noire: Dieu pour tous et chacun pour soi*, 63–100. Paris: Karthala.

Schulz, Dorothea. 1999. In Pursuit of Publicity: Talk Radio and the Imagination of a Moral Public in Mali. *Africa Spectrum* 99 (2): 161–185.

———. 2001. *Perpetuating the Politics of Praise: Jeli Praise Singers, Radios and Political Mediation in Mali*. Köln: Rüdiger Köppe.

———. 2003. "Charisma and Brotherhood" Revisited: Mass-Mediated Forms of Spirituality in Urban Mali. *Journal of Religion in Africa* 33 (2): 146–171.

——. 2006. Promises of (Im)mediate Salvation: Islam, Broadcast Media, and the Remaking of Religious Experience in Mali. *American Ethnologist* 33 (2): 210–229.

——. 2007. Evoking Moral Community, Fragmenting Muslim Discourse: Sermon Audio-Recordings and the Reconfiguration of Public Debate in Mali. *Journal for Islamic Studies* 27:39–72.

——. 2008a. "Channeling" the Powers of God's Word: Audio-Recordings as Scriptures in Mali. *Postscripts* 4 (2): 135–156.

——. 2008b. Piety's Manifold Embodiments: Muslim Women's Quest for Moral Renewal in Urban Mali. In Reconfigurations of Gender Relations in Africa, guest ed. Marloes Janson and Dorothea Schulz, special issue, *Journal for Islamic Studies* 28:26–93.

——. 2008c. (Re)Turning to Proper Muslim Practice: Islamic Moral Renewal and Women's Conflicting Constructions of Sunni Identity in Urban Mali. *Africa Today* 54 (4): 21–43.

——. 2011a. Equivocal Resonances: Islamic Revival and Female Radio "Preachers" in Urban Mali. In Liz Gunner, Dina Ligaga, and Dumisani Moyo, eds., *Radio in Africa: Publics, Cultures, Communities.* Johannesburg: University of Witwatersrand.

——. 2011b. *Muslims and New Media in West Africa: Pathways to God.* Bloomington: Indiana University Press.

Stolow, Jeremy. 2005. Religion and/as Media. *Theory, Culture & Society* 22 (4): 119–145.

——. 2006. Communicating Authority, Consuming Tradition: Jewish Orthodox Outreach Literature and Its Reading Public. In Birgit Meyer and Annelies Moors, eds., *Religion, Media, and the Public Sphere*, 73–90. Bloomington: Indiana University Press.

Turner, Bryan. 2007. Religious Authority and the New Media. *Theory, Culture & Society* 24 (2): 117–134.

Volpi, Frederic, and Bryan Turner. 2007. Introduction: Making Islamic Authority Matter. *Theory, Culture & Society* 24 (2): 1–19.

Weix, Gretchen G. 1998. Islamic Prayer Groups in Indonesia: Local Forums and Gendered Responses. *Critique of Anthropology* 18 (4): 405–420.

6

Community and Indigenous Radio in Oaxaca

Testimony and Participatory Democracy

LYNN STEPHEN

In 2006, hundreds of women in Oaxaca, Mexico, took over state-owned public radio and television stations as part of a larger social movement driven by
Local 22 (Sección 22) of the National Union for Educational Workers (Sin-
dicato Nacional de Trabajadores de la Educación, SNTE) and the Popular
Assembly of the Peoples of Oaxaca (Asamblea Popular de los Pueblos de Oaxaca, APPO). The takeovers proved to be the tactical lifeline of the movement at the time and have since emerged as some of the most enduring
legacies of the 2006 mobilization. After and partly because of the events of
2006, the reach of community radio networks has broadened considerably in
southern Mexico. New community and indigenous radio stations have been
created and existing ones strengthened by a growing corps of young radio
practitioners. Radio stations occupied by the APPO in 2006 subsequently

served as widely accessible public forums where long-term social relations of inequality were challenged and alternative visions for more equitable systems of political participation were imagined. During and after the 2006 movement, indigenous and grassroots radio stations became important arenas for a transformative cultural politics that determines "the meanings of social practices, and moreover, which groups and individuals have the power to define these meanings" (Jordan and Weedon 1995, 5–6).[1]

This chapter uses an in-depth ethnographic analysis of the 2006 Oaxaca radio-station takeovers and subsequent endeavors of indigenous community radio stations to explore the relation of radio practices, and in particular the testimonials they broadcast, to the enactment of participatory democracy. While such testimonials are often inaudible within the cultures of ruling political parties, the halls of state assemblies, and in mainstream Mexican media, they are central to models of decision-making in local social movements in Mexico. When political discussion hit the airwaves following the occupation of radio stations in Oaxaca, testimonials were widely broadcast. Today, they continue to be programmed on indigenous community radio broadcasts in Oaxaca.

I explore how the dynamics of deliberation in community radio programming and in indigenous community assemblies are facilitated by testimonial speech acts on the air and in face-to-face gatherings (Brodkin 2007; Polletta 2002; Stephen 2005). I link the format of indigenous and grassroots radio programming to this speech genre and suggest what this implies for participatory democracy. I argue that indigenous radio has flourished in Oaxaca partly because listeners are accustomed to and comfortable with the testimonial format these stations often feature. I also describe how radio broadcasts amplify and intensify this communicative genre's popular appeal.

The testimonial genre is deeply rooted in the decision-making processes of community assemblies, in which formalized interactional styles are self-consciously used to solicit and emphasize shared opinions while accommodating divergent ones. I will show that the role of testimony in such local deliberative processes provides a model for radio programming through describing the case of women's takeover of the Corporación Oaxaqueña de Radio y Televisión, or COR-TV (Oaxacan Radio and Television Corporation), in Oaxaca and the subsequent experience of indigenous radio stations nearby. Oaxaca is a state with sixteen different indigenous languages and a population that largely receives news through nonprint media such as radio and television. In the following, I sketch the links between the orality of radio, the increasingly audible presence of radio testimonials in Oaxaca, and the continuity between radio formats and the decision-making forms of community assemblies. I argue that efforts to explain the widespread adoption of radio within many indigenous communities, or to understand how such radio practices relate to discourses of community autonomy, must begin by taking seriously this intersection of technology, political history, and cultural style.

Testimonial Formats on the Radio and in Community Assemblies

At the most basic level, testimony refers to a person's account of an event or experience as delivered from the lips of a person through a speech act. It is an oral telling of a person's perception of an event through seeing, hearing, smelling, and other sensory information. It signifies witnessing. Testimonials are also performative. Testimony is a crucial element of rights claiming and public politics in many contemporary indigenous communities and social movement assemblies in Oaxaca, Mexico. Oral testimony allows people to stand witness and archive their feelings, experiences, wrongs committed, and visions of hope. This happens most effectively in a public space through creating a shared community of speakers who "have the right to speak" and listeners who sanctify the speakers through "hearing" the speakers and granting them "the right to be heard" through constituting an audience (see Maier and Dulfano 2004; Poole 2007; Spivak 1988). Giving public voice through testimony legitimates those who have been previously silenced. Testimony is considered capable of healing social and political wounds and/or opening new ones, as reflected in the literature on the role of truth commissions in places such as South Africa, Guatemala, El Salvador, and Peru (Ross 2002; Theidon 2007).

Rights in Oaxaca are often grounded in claims to indigeneity, gender, or a universal humanity. In each case, they are held to depend first on the right to speak. And in Oaxaca, as elsewhere, the right to speak begins with *actually speaking*, with thinking of yourself as someone who can speak about experiences of injustices. It depends on a sense of membership within a larger community of people of similar speakers with similar rights. *Being heard* involves having access to public space and channels of communication that cut across different social sectors, cultural worlds, and venues. The rights to speak and to be heard are foundational rights.

In the context of the Oaxaca social movement, the merging of appropriated notions of universal human rights with particular, local injustices suggests a kind of rights talk in which "actors gesture towards aspects of human rights, [but] talk with very little specificity or actual content" (Wilson 2007, 358; cf. Goodale 2007, 160) in relation to specific laws, regulations, or treaties.

In order even to articulate these more specific, institutionally defined ideas of human rights in distinct local domains, the rights to speak and to be heard must first be established and collectively embodied.

Here I discuss the public deliberative space created through radio call-in and on-air testimonies that occurred during the takeover of COR-TV in 2006 by women in Oaxaca City and compare it to the testimonial dynamics in an indigenous community assembly. I then further develop this comparison by looking at the way contemporary indigenous community radio stations have drawn from the 2006 radio takeovers to make a similar testimonial format central to their programming.

The August 1, 2006, takeover of COR-TV—equivalent to state-run public broadcasting systems in the United States—was seen by many of the women who participated as part of an effort to democratize the state and its public institutions. The takeover of COR-TV was also partly a response to programming shifts at the station. In the early 1990s, COR-TV had a director who was well-known for his support for public media and was also a reporter. Under his direction, people in Oaxaca became accustomed to having the programming content reflect a wide range of concerns from across the state. This included programming in indigenous languages that represented all the different ethnic groups in Oaxaca—although always mediated through a semicorporate media model with an undertone of "folklore." In the 2000s, this somewhat progressive stance of COR-TV changed. By 2006, COR-TV and radio were widely considered as a propaganda outlet for a deeply unpopular governor, and there was little indigenous presence on the state television or radio stations (Stephen 2011). Many observers thought radio stations had abandoned their earlier role as an effective and inclusive public station.

Within days of the 2006 station occupations, however, COR-TV became the strategic center for the APPO, Local 22, and the broader social movement that was flourishing in Oaxaca City. Women who took over the station state that they did so originally to make their voices publicly audible after being ignored by mainstream media. The takeover of the station also served as a key tactic for broadening the movement to include many people in the city through their participation in on-air broadcasts and their ability to listen around the clock. After taking over the radio station of COR-TV, the women renamed it "Radio Caserola," or "Casserole Radio," after the preceding march, in which they banged on casserole pots and pans.

The two hundred women who took over the station decided to engage in this action after radio- and TV-station personnel refused to let them have an hour on the air to share their perspectives (see Stephen 2011). They wanted to report on human rights violations and the unacceptable governing practices of Governor Ulises Ruiz Ortiz. Six weeks earlier, Ruiz Ortiz had sent police to force some fifty thousand teachers out of the historic center of Oaxaca, where they had been protesting. Poorly trained police supported by helicopters tear-gassed teachers and their families; beat teachers; broke into the teachers' radio station, Radio Plantón, and destroyed equipment; and arrested leaders of the teachers' movement. While the eviction strategy was unsuccessful in removing the teachers, the police action did enrage many people who lived in the center of the city, who were also tear-gassed and some of whom were beaten. In response three days later, a coalition of over two hundred organizations came together, calling itself the Popular Assembly of the Peoples of Oaxaca (APPO), built around a common aim to have the state of Oaxaca declared "ungovernable" by the national congress and thus forcing Governor Ruiz Ortiz out of office. The APPO coalition held together many groups that had historically disagreed with one another (and subsequently found it increasingly difficult to work together; see Stephen 2010).[2]

Just prior to the takeover of the public radio and TV stations, the APPO movement had a very solid presence in the city and was in control of significant parts of the city as well as key buildings and public squares (see Gibler 2009, 139–189; Osornio 2007; Martínez Vásquez 2007). Many cultural activities were attached to the movement, including concerts and video and music productions that documented the movement and that were subsequently aired on the taken radio and TV station. Murals, stenciling, and a wide range of street art in support of the movement also proliferated (see Magaña 2008).

On August 10, 2006, the road leading up to the occupied TV and radio station was lined with several public buses and cars that had been commandeered by the movement and were spray painted with references to the APPO, Local 22, and the inevitable fall of the governor Ulises Ruiz Ortiz (e.g., "Ya cayó," "he has already fallen"). A crowd of about one hundred people from the neighboring community of Telixtlahuaca gathered outside the station. Other small delegations lined up as well. The women occupying the station had decided to open up the airwaves to on-air testimony speaking to the injustices suffered and to different visions for how to improve the state of Oaxaca. Speakers came not only from Oaxaca City but increasingly from more distant communities. Individuals or groups would come to the station, register with the women, and receive a time to come and speak. There were often long lines of people waiting for a chance to speak on air and preparing statements for the radio. Testimonies included a wide range of topics but were often related to the themes of racism, discrimination, victimization by state officials or police forces, charges of corruption on the part of local or state officials, statements about human rights violations, and the sharing of ideas for how the state could be made better.

On August 10, 2006, while I was waiting to clear security to go inside the station, the members of the delegation of the Organization of Mototaxis of the State of Oaxaca (Organización de Mototaxis de Oaxaca) were practicing their testimonial outside before later going on the air. Arguing that they were "victims of indifference" and concerned with the safety of their drivers who were in taxis bearing the APPO logo, they sought to publicly document corruption on the part of state officials who they argued favored another taxi union over theirs because it was associated with the PRI, the Institutional Revolutionary Party, which was the party of the governor. Their testimony of corruption and favoritism was a genre repeated many times by a variety of groups on the renamed Radio Caserola.

After I secured permission to enter, we were ushered in through a court-yard where many women were sorting food, clothing, and blankets that were provided to those who spent long days and nights occupying the station. We were escorted upstairs past the television studios and into the radio station. Two young women were serving as engineers, and another was emceeing a call-in show receiving cell-phone updates about a large march winding its way to the center of the city. In the studio, two women were preparing to begin a testimonial segment about the current social movement and how it had affected them as women. Pilar Montenegro began to speak about her experience of the attempt to force the teachers from the center of the city, as viewed from inside her home.

> I think I first opened my eyes early that morning hearing someone saying, "Fuck your mother." I heard someone else screaming from the street about what was going on. I was able to go down to the street in that moment in my pajamas. I got to the corner of Avenida Morelos and Avenida Juárez, and there was a group of heavily armed police. I was terrified, and I ran back to my house because I couldn't believe the level of aggression that was going on at this point.
>
> So we lived through the attempted *desalojo* [eviction] from our home. The teachers began to leave, and my family went down the street. We went down to be with the teachers because not only was it an invasion against democracy and the right to freely demonstrate, as the teachers were doing with their sit-in, but it was also an invasion into our homes. We went out because we didn't want to permit this violence. . . .
>
> You are never prepared for this kind of violation, and that is what we mothers felt in the historic center. . . . It felt like the city was raped.

The center was pulled apart, beaten, wounded. It was this sensation you would feel walking downtown. We walked on Morelos Street past the store called the Gem Palace, and we saw little blankets, baby shoes, and a sheet. I took a picture there because I had such a strong feeling about that spot where a small child had been. It made me feel really sad. We saw a lot of things like that in the historic center on that day that we will not forget for decades.

Pilar's graphic imagery of the pillage of downtown Oaxaca by state police captures the fear and sense of violation and invasion felt by many residents. The power of the images she paints through her personal testimony resulted in many callers contacting the radio station during the broadcast, identifying with and echoing her feelings.

Through Pilar's testimony about her experience, she places herself physically in the center of the city as a resident and then as someone who experienced the repression of June 14. She then goes on to identify her solidarity with the group of teachers occupying the city center and herself as physically present and interacting with them through offering them coffee and food. The last part of her testimony then grounds her as a part of the larger entity of "the city," which she characterizes as being oppressed and victimized—raped, pulled apart, wounded, beaten—a metaphoric woman who has been violated. By using this metaphor to include not only herself but a much broader group of people who live in the city, Pilar emphasizes a shared sense of suffering and community. People who called in identified with both the physical and social suffering outlined in Pilar's call and underlined the connections between the individual suffering of teachers and their families and the structural violence that was all around them, both in the past and in the present. Pilar's testimony and the shared community expressed through the callers on the air connected such experiences of violence to "a language of dismay, disappointment, bereavement and alarm" (Kleinman, Das, and Lock 1997). After she finished giving her testimonial and listening to those who called in, Pilar stated that she felt a great sense of connection to all the women who had called in to share their stories. She said, "I don't feel alone. We are all here together." Through the testimonial experience, she felt connected to a larger community.

Pilar's airing of her testimonial legitimates her as someone with the right to speak and the right to be heard. Those who are listening are her shared speech community, as are those who are present in the station. This genre of radio broadcast places and legitimates the speaker in much the same ways as community assemblies. Consider the following description of such an assembly in the Zapotec community of Teotitlán del Valle (where the author has worked since 1983; Stephen 2005).

Inside the building labeled "Salon de usos multiples, Xa Guiea"—Hall for Multiple Uses (in Spanish) of Teotitlán del Valle (in Zapotec)—about two hundred people have assembled. The crowd is primarily men, with perhaps ten to fifteen women present, all speaking in Zapotec. There are also men standing in the back of the room. This community assembly has been called to elect slates of new officials to various civil cargo[3] positions in the civil government. The meeting begins with a roll call in which each of six different neighborhoods of the community (Secciónes) are called out and people stand, state their name, and report "I am present." In this way, all the people in the meeting publicly identify themselves and where they live physically in the community. After the official agenda items are read in Spanish by the *síndico*, who serves as the chief fiscal officer for the community, discussion rapidly switches into *Didxsaj* [didʒ'saʰ], or Zapotec. People begin their statements in third-person formal Zapotec and include ceremonial forms of address, which connote humility before the public assembly and great respect for all present.

Point number three on the agenda is the naming of new municipal *policía*, or police. The *síndico* begins to call out names of people proposed to be *policías* from different neighborhoods, and people begin to raise their hands to speak. A microphone is passed around, and one by one people begin to testify about their personal senses of increased danger and a lack of security in the community, often speaking for five to ten minutes at a time. While this apparently disrupts the process of naming the individuals who are to assume the positions of municipal police, no one seems to mind. Instead the process opens up a broad conversation about crime, safety, and what the police actually are able or required to do. It continues for more than an hour. When no more testimonials seem to be forthcoming, the *síndico* moves back to the process of naming new police. The assembly continues until well after midnight. Such testimonials are repeated throughout the meeting whenever an urgent topic is discussed. This style of interaction produces an assembly that often lasts for three, four, or five hours or sometimes longer.

In this community assembly and through Pilar's on-air testimony with call-in respondents, speakers anchor themselves as legitimate members of a shared community through locating themselves in a specific place (in the community assembly as part of a particular neighborhood in Teotitlán del Valle and on Radio Caserola as a resident of the historic center of Oaxaca City), through identifying themselves with their names, and through their shared experience with those to whom they are speaking. Once testimonial speakers are located, they proceed to deploy their rights to speak and be heard by a larger public.

Not only do decisions about whether or not to have a radio station begin in a community assembly, but the community radios in indigenous communities can take on some of the functions of community assemblies in terms of creating shared spaces for public discussion and the forging of agreement across different perspectives, usually expressed through personal testimonials. Juan José García, a Zapotec videographer and radio producer who works for the Oaxacan NGO Ojo de Agua Comunicación and who provided technical assistance during the radio takeovers,[4] explicitly notes the centrality of testimonials not only in community assemblies but also in the broadcasts of Radio Cacerola in 2006.

> During the process [in Radio Cacerola], people could express themselves freely and a lot of people responded to this—not everyone, but the radio did open things up to a certain point. People called in from all over on their phones. They sang on the radio. They raised their voices against the government and the rich. There was a whole oppositional discourse and an attitude of challenging the status quo. But there were also many people detained and it was hard to even go out on the street. In response to this, a lot of people were interviewed. They gave their testimony on audio and on video. There were a lot of testimonies about aggressions of the state against the people.

During 2007 and 2008, Juan José and others logged and edited hundreds of hours of video and audio testimonials about government repression and human rights violations that occurred during the radio takeovers to submit to the Mexican Supreme Court for a hearing on Oaxaca. The audio testimonials broadcast on the radio as well as video collected by Mal de Ojo TV have become key evidence for claiming and documenting human rights violations by the Oaxacan state government and associated institutions during the political upheavals of 2006.

Testimony and the Multiplicity of Identities

As a speech form, testimonials are hybrid, interstitial, and flexible discursive spaces that reflect political and linguistic complexity (Beverley 2004; Maier and Dulfano 2004). When testimonials are deployed to claim rights in a specific political and cultural context, they are a part of real political practices that can literally let "the subaltern speak" and confer legitimacy (see Spivak

1988). For the twenty-one days that women controlled the state TV and radio station and subsequently other radio stations, the subaltern was literally speaking in ways that had never been heard or seen before.

The kind of subaltern speaking which women initiated in 2006 bears a direct lineage to the programming, structure, and organizational forms and practices associated with indigenous and community radio. The 2006 broadcasts, as in indigenous and community radio more broadly, offered a striking example of the complex identities and subject positions of such media practitioners. As such, they challenged and unsettled the conventional categories of homogeneous ethnic or racial types that commonly circulate within the Mexican public sphere. Such types are often believed to define media audiences and producers, as well. For example, state television stations such as COR-TV and commercial radio and television tend to use self-contained, hierarchical categories to distinguish "indigenous," "Spanish," or "mestizo" people.

Broadcasts on Radio Cacerola, however, belied such categories. They were often multilingual, in a range of indigenous languages and in Spanish, featured different kinds of Oaxacans, and challenged the hegemony of language, ideas, and the racial heritage of "the Spanish." By demonstrating the multiple cultural and technological fluencies of the participants, radio broadcasts unsettled the boundaries of the indigenous, as well. The Oaxaca social movement included many participants who identify wholly or partially as indigenous either in nearby communities or as a part of their urban location. In some cases, such identifications are glossed as color terms such as "brown" or "not white." Slogans painted on walls, shouted at rallies, and broadcast on the radio, such as "Spanish get out" and "Gauchupines [Spanish] leave," provide an entry into the racialized and anticolonial narratives that circulated during the movement and on the air. In order to describe these complex senses of identity expressed in the movement and on the radio, it is necessary to invoke a more complex frame that transcends linear or additive formulations of race, gender, class, and ethnicity and instead embraces subjective multiplicity (see Hames-García 2011; Lugones 2007).

Arguing that it is impossible to perceive human experience at the intersection of discrete, separate categories within colonial realities, Maria Lugones (2007) proposes that we use the concept of a "fractured locus" as a lens for understanding the politically agentive identifications of subjects such as the actors in the Oaxaca social movement. In the city of Oaxaca, for example, urban, working-class women of Zapotec and Mixtec descent are not easily located within conventional local categories of race, class, and gender (see Stephen 2007). Rather, they simultaneously occupy multiple subject positions in relation to various interlocutors. Through radio testimonials, such contested subjectivities were asserted as politically legitimate. The complexity of the identities invoked by those who participated in the Oaxaca social movement and broadcast on Radio Cacerola requires an effective form of subaltern speech capable of accommodating such multiplicity. Testimonials are ideal for such aspirations. They offer a space to synthesize personal lived histories and to ground claims to certain subject positions within appeals to popular discourses of race, gender, ethnicity, and class (Latina Feminist Group 2001). Consider the following testimonial recorded in August 2006 from Fidelia Velasquez (a pseudonym) after the women's takeover of COR-TV.

> I am a woman born in Oaxaca of Zapotec and Mixtec blood. We Oaxa-can women ask that a woman be treated with the same rights as a man. Our mission as women is to create, educate, communicate, and partici-pate. That is why we are here occupying the state radio and TV station. . . . We are like a lot of the humble, sincere, working people of my state. From the countryside to the city, we Oaxacan women are tired of bearing this burden alone of the repression we are experiencing from the long line of people who have governed us and from our current governor, Ulises Ruiz.

In this excerpt, we can see the ways Fidelia locates herself in relation to mul-tiple categories of the person and political subject: "born in Oaxaca" (urban), "of Zapotec and Mixtec blood" (indigenous), "we Oaxacan women" (female), "we are humble, sincere, working people" (working class). In the speech act of her testimony, she asserts herself as an active subject whose entanglement in social realms that are often considered distinct enhances, rather than erases, her political agency. Radio broadcasts amplify such words. When broadcast, testimonial speech and speakers are embedded in a larger com-munity of listeners who become additional witnesses to the theme of the testimonial, which often resonates with some aspect of their lives and ex-perience. This mediatized resonance can put new formulations of political agency into motion. It can also move people to action, as often happened through radio broadcasts in 2006 in Oaxaca. In such ways, community radio broadcasts can inspire concrete actions and become catalysts for a transfor-mative cultural politics.

Community Radio and Participatory Democracy

The legitimizing of those who do not have a voice in formal, electoral po-litical systems through testimonials is also connected to the larger project of creating a public, political culture of participatory democracy—something which does not exist in much of contemporary Oaxaca. Both the format and the content of broadcasting seen on Radio Cacerola in 2006 and subsequently on other community radio stations contribute to the building of a new understanding of how politics should be defined in Oaxaca and what kinds of participatory processes publicly matter. The Zapatista movement publicly launched in Chiapas, Mexico, in 1994 has provided a pioneering model of participatory, public political culture that has influenced other parts of Mexico.

The Zapatista political model of good-governance councils expands the structure of the community assembly described earlier to a networked regional seat of governance which operates outside the political party system. In August 2003, the Zapatistas announced the creation of five *caracoles* (literally "spiral shells" but meaning points of communication) that are the seats for five Juntas de Buen Gobierno (Good Governance Councils). Each of the five Juntas includes one to three delegates from each of the already-existing Autonomous Councils in each zone. There are approximately thirty Zapatista Autonomous Municipalities in Rebellion with their own autonomous councils that feed into the five Juntas. Autonomous councils are charged with governing Zapatista territory in rebellion under the logic of *mandar obedeciendo* (rule by obeying).

What is relevant to our discussion here is the Zapatista model of public decision-making. A keystone of "good" governance holds that authorities are to carry out decisions that are arrived at consensually, not to make them. Decisions are to come through a careful deliberative process that does not involve a strict consensus but bears some resemblance to what Francesca Polletta describes as the deliberative and experimental model of decision-making she encountered in a range of social movement organizations she studied from the 1960s to the present in the United States (2002, 209). The central shared element in cultures of participatory democracy is acknowledgment that unity in decision-making comes through "recognizing the legitimacy of different opinions as well as shared ones" (ibid., 210). Polletta suggests insightfully that what distinguishes this model of decision-making from majoritarian voting is "its emphasis on having participants make their reasoning accessible and legitimate to each other. Solidarity is re-created through the process of decision-making, not its endpoint" (ibid.). In this deliberative model of reasoning that is a part of the political culture of indigenous community assemblies and in some social movements in Oaxaca, the speech act of the testimony plays an important role.

The testimonial positions the speaker as speaking from a personal perspective but in the context of larger shared structural political, economic, and cultural circumstances. Its synthetic ability to profile a distinct perspective and opinion, but also within a larger context of some shared circumstances, makes it a natural vehicle of expression in cultures of participatory democracy. Indigenous community radio—which often mirrors the process of decision-making and culture of participation described earlier—provides one of the important forums for realizing local aspirations for a public culture of participatory democracy. Organizations such as Ojo de Agua have built on some of the ideas of Zapatista governance and incorporated them into indigenous and community radio in Oaxaca.

The Struggle to Make Indigenous Radio Autonomous in Mexico

Since 1998, Ojo de Agua has provided a production facility and space for indigenous and other media producers of radio, video, and television to carry on their work without depending on state sponsorship for their existence (Wortham 2004, 365). The establishment of Ojo de Agua in Oaxaca is connected to efforts made by the Zapatistas in the 1990s to establish indigenous community radio as a collective right of indigenous communities that could be used to fortify the agenda of indigenous autonomy through the arena of cultural rights. As a part of the peace-accord process negotiated between the Zapatista Army of National Liberation (EZLN) and the Mexican government, the 1996 San Andrés Accords on Indigenous Rights and Cultures dealt specifically with communications media. The document made explicit reference to turning over control of state-run radio stations administered by the National Indigenous Institution (INI) to indigenous communities. The accords also laid out further specifics for empowering indigenous communities with rights within the area of communications. These efforts, however, ended in disappointment when, in 2001, the Mexican Congress passed a greatly watered-down version of the original accords that omitted many of the concrete proposals, such as that for media. While the national legislation that was passed on indigenous rights in 2001 states that it aims "to establish conditions for villages and indigenous communities to acquire, operate, and administer mass media," indigenous access to media was to be granted "in accordance with existing laws" (McElmurry 2009, 4).

The limitations of the legislation's phrasing, in terms of creating significant reforms to facilitate better access and control of media for indigenous communities, became evident in 2006. In 2006, the ruling party (PAN) passed a modification to Mexico's Federal Telecommunications Law and Federal Radio and Television Law that clearly favored corporate media and severely disadvantaged community radio and other forms of grassroots media. The law established that radio and television enterprises that hoped to gain access to new parts of the TV and radio spectrum would be granted licenses through a process of competitive public bidding. While this was supposed to facilitate much-needed transparency in the granting of media licenses, it placed poorer community radio stations at a clear disadvantage. Since there is no consideration of cultural reasons for granting licenses in the bidding process, few indigenous radio stations outside the INI-controlled network of stations currently have licenses, and they are thus technically illegal. Eugenio Bermejillo, coordinator for Boca de Polen—a network-building organization that supports community radio stations—estimates that there are 150 to 200 community radio stations in Mexico and only 15–20 percent of them are licensed by the Mexican government (McElmurry 2009, 4). This leaves the majority as unlicensed "pirate" radio stations. Such stations are seen by the Mexican government as operating outside the law and vulnerable to government seizure of equipment under the General Law of National Goods; that law considers radiophonic space a public good possessed by the nation, which is thus being used by the stations without legal permission (Prieto Beguiristáin 2009, 2).

Conclusions: Expanding a Culture of Participatory Democracy through Indigenous Radio in Oaxaca

I have shown that the takeover of commercial and state-run TV and radio in the Oaxaca social movement of 2006 is related to the ongoing history and expansion of indigenous and community-based radio. Since 2006, there have been minimally ten new community-based radio stations formed in Oaxaca, in addition to those already in existence at the time.[5] Through direct social action, the "right to speak" and the "right to be heard" that anchor face-to-face testimonials have come to define an emergent set of regional radio practices. I have argued that such community media practices are guided by indigenous political cultures that often are self-consciously aimed at building consensus capable of accommodating different perspectives. This overlap of radio technology and local political culture has made Oaxacan community radio particularly suitable for expressing the complex and multiple subject positions of its practitioners. Moreover, I suggest that the common usage of testimonials in both radio and local politics illuminates how grassroots social movements gain greater public traction through their entanglements with radio technology.

The emergence of community radio networks has indelibly shaped the form of political participation in Oaxaca. Community radio stations provide important roles in communication, community building, and promoting local cultural forms. These roles range from providing a call-in forum where indigenous migrants in the United States can communicate with relatives to broadcasting local dance or music performances, as well as programs discussing health, education, and human rights. Often, as in the case of Radio Jen Poj, these community radios are considered by their participants to be sources of cultural revitalization (Díaz 2007).

In addition, there are more than twenty radio stations in the Zapotec Isthmus of Tehuantepec. Some, like Radio Totopo[6] and Didhza Kieru (Our Words),[7] broadcast in the Zapotec language.[8] The continuity and proliferation of community radio, particularly in indigenous communities, illuminates the changing political cultures and spaces of participatory democracy in Oaxaca. Moreover, this has provoked ongoing efforts by the government to control and eliminate community-based radio. In 2008, the Assembly of Free and Community Radio Stations (Asamblea de Radios Libres y Comunitarias de Oaxaca) was formed in response to such repression (ARLC 2008). Composed of twenty-two Oaxacan community radio stations, along with three international radio stations, representatives from eight universities, and a wide range of NGOs, this assembly was constituted just one day after federal and local police ransacked the community radio station known as La Rabiosa, a Mixtec radio station based in the town of Huahupan de León. Despite a concerted effort by the regional government to raid radio stations and harass radio practitioners, community radio in Oaxaca continues to grow.

While there is a tendency in the analysis of social movements and politics to focus much attention on marches, control of physical space and buildings, and ultimately the ability of movements to cohere through time and to influence the outcome of electoral politics, the cultural spaces of community-based media such as television, grassroots-produced videos, and radio are equally informative for such analyses. The maintenance and proliferation of community-based radio, particularly in indigenous communities in the state of Oaxaca and elsewhere, have proven to be fertile grounds through which nonmainstream political processes, strategies, and ideas have continued to exist and grow. I have suggested that a longer view of the antecedents and legacies of the Oaxaca social movement of 2006 reveals that community-based radio is a vital technology for shaping the form and content of political agency in Oaxaca.

NOTES

1. Following Alvarez, Dagnino, and Escobar (1998), I define cultural politics here as "the processes enacted when sets of social actors shaped by, and embodying, different cultural meanings and practices come into conflict with each other" (7).

2. Throughout the remainder of June and in July, the APPO and Local 22 of the National Union for Education Workers (SNTE) (which is also part of a dissident federation of locals within the SNTE called the National Coordinator of Education Workers, or CNTE) organized several large marches known as Megamarches that mobilized between one hundred thousand and five hundred thousand people. In addition, the APPO took over many state and some federal buildings, such as the state legislature, the governor's office, offices for social services and tax collection, and more.

3. This is a local system of governance based on community assemblies that assign more than 250 unpaid jobs, ranging from mayor, judges, police, and school committees to irrigation committees, fire fighters, and committees regulating land use and caring for the local church. Agreeing to serve in civil cargo positions throughout one's adult life is a part of the citizenship requirements for living in many indigenous communities in Oaxaca (see Stephen 2005).

4. Ojo de Agua offers media production and training to indigenous communities in Oaxaca. During the 2006 takeovers, it provided technical assistance to the women.

5. This estimate was given by Roberto Olivares in an interview on December 3, 2009, at Ojo de Agua Comunicación.

6. First on the airwaves in 2005, Radio Totopo is located in a neighborhood known as the "barrio de Pescador" (fisherman's neighborhood), one of the oldest and most marginal neighborhoods of Juchitán. Local residents who volunteer there receive support from others in the form of food and small donations. The station includes musical programming from a group of young people, broadcasts Alcoholics Anonymous programs in Zapotec, promotes local events, and also has an ongoing project to use words in Zapotec that people have forgotten and replaced with Spanish.

7. This collective is recognized and supported by the local authorities in the municipality and by the assembly of communal land holders (see Ojo de Agua Comunicación 2009a). The station is acknowledged as part of the structure of local governance and recognized within the same political and cultural structure that houses community assemblies. The radio station exists in parallel with the assembly, and working in the station is recognized as a form of contributing service to the community as part of a civil cargo.

8. Interview with Juan José García on December 4, 2009. See also Ojo de Agua Comunicación 2009b.

REFERENCES

Alvarez, Sonia, Evelina Dagnino, and Arturo Escobar. 1998. Introduction: The Cultural and the Political in Latin American Social Movements. In *Cultures of Politics/Politics of Culture: Re-visioning Latin American Social Movements*, ed. Sonia Alvarez, Evelina Dagnino, and Arturo Escobar, 1–32. Boulder, CO: Westview.

Asamblea de Radios Libres y Comunitarias. 2008. Declaration of the Assembly of Free and Community Radio Stations of Oaxaca 2008. Villa de Zachilla, Oaxaca. Available

at http://www.radio-utopie.de/2008/09/05/declaration-of-the-assembly-of-free-and
-community-radio-stations-of-oaxaca/ (accessed January 20, 2010).

Beverley, John. 2004. *Testimonio: On the Politics of Truth.* Minneapolis: University of Minnesota Press.

Brígido-Corachán, Anna. 2004. An Interview with Juan José García, President of Ojo de Agua Comunicación. *American Anthropologist* 106 (2): 368–373.

Brodkin, Karen. 2007. *Making Democracy Matter: Identity Making and Activism in Los Angeles.* New Brunswick: Rutgers University Press.

Díaz, José Guadalupe. 2007. Historia: La Energía del Viento. Tlahuitoltepec, Oaxaca: Radioxhjpfm. http://www.radiojenpoj.org/index.php?option=com_content&task=view&id=5&Itemid=26 (accessed January 20, 2010).

Gamio, Manuel. 1916. *Forjando Patria.* México, D.F.: Porrúa.

Gibler, John. 2009. *Mexico Unconquered: Chronicles of Power and Revolt.* San Francisco: City Lights Books.

Goodale, Mark. 2007. The Power of Right(s): Tracking Empires of Law and New Modes of Social Resistance in Bolivia (and Elsewhere). In *The Practice of Human Rights: Tracking Law between the Global and the Local,* ed. Mark Goodale and Sally Engle Merry, 130–162. Cambridge: Cambridge University Press.

Hames-García, Michael. 2011. *Identity Complex: Making the Case for Multiplicity.* Minneapolis: University of Minnesota Press.

Jordan, Glenn, and Chris Weedon. 1995. *Cultural Politics: Class, Gender, Race and the Postmodern World.* Oxford, UK: Blackwell.

Kleinman, Arthur, Venna Das, and Margaret Lock. 1997. *Social Suffering.* Berkeley: University of California Press.

Latina Feminist Group. 2001. *Telling to Live: Latina Feminist Testimonios.* Durham: Duke University Press.

Lugones, María. 2007. Heterosexualism and the Colonial/Modern Gender System. *Hypatia* 22 (1): 186–209.

Magaña, Maurice. 2008. Articulating Social Networks in a Mexican Social Movement: The Case of the Asamblea Popular de los Pueblos de Oaxaca (APPO) in Oaxaca. Master's paper, Department of Anthropology, University of Oregon, June.

Maier, Linda S., and Isabel Dulfano. 2004. *Woman as Witness: Essays on Testimonial Literature by Latin American Women.* New York: Peter Lang.

Martínez Vásquez, Victor Raúl. 2007. *Autoritarismo, Movimiento Popular y Crisis Política: Oaxaca 2006.* Oaxaca: Universidad Autónoma "Benito Juárez" de Oaxaca, Instituto de Investigaciones Sociológicas, Centro de Apoyo al Movimiento Popular Oaxaqueño, A.C., Servicios para la Educación Alternativa (EDUCA), Consorcio para el Diálogo Parlamentario y la Equidad, A.C.

McElmurry, Sara. 2009. *Indigenous Community Radio in Mexico.* Washington, DC: Americas Policy Program. http://americas.irc-online.org/am/5977 (accessed January 20, 2010).

Ojo de Agua Comunicación. 2009a. *Didhza Kieru.* Oaxaca: Ojos de Agua Comunicación. http://www.ojodeaguacomunicacion.org/programas-de-ojo-de-agua/espacios-de-comnicacion-comunitaria/didhza-kieru (accessed January 20, 2010).

———. 2009b. *Radio Totopo.* Oaxaca: Ojos de Agua Comunicación. http://www.ojodeaguacomunicacion.org/programas-de-ojo-de-agua/espacios-de-comnicacion-comunitaria/espacio-de-comunicacion-del-istmo/radio-totopo (accessed January 20, 2010).

Osornio, Diego Enrique. 2007. *Oaxaca Sitiada: La Primera Insurrección del Siglo XXI.* Mexico City: Grihalba.

Polletta, Francesca. 2002. *Freedom Is an Endless Meeting: Democracy in American Social Movements.* Chicago: University of Chicago Press.

Poole, Deborah. 2007. The Right to Be Heard. *Socialism and Democracy* 21 (2): 113–116.

Prieto Beruiristáin, Iñigo. 2009. *Radio Ñomndaa: The Word of Water.* Washington, DC: Americas Policy Program. http://americas.irc-online.org/am/6164 (accessed January 20, 2010).

Quijano, Aníbal. 2007. Coloniality and Modernity/Rationality. *Cultural Studies* 21 (2): 168–178. http://dx.doi.org/10.1080/09502380601164353.

Ross, Fiona. 2002. *Bearing Witness; Women and the Truth and Reconciliation Commission in South Africa.* London: Pluto.

Rylko-Bauer, Barbara, Linda Whiteford, and Paul Farmer, eds. 2009. *Global Health in Times of Violence.* Santa Fe, NM: School for Advanced Research Press. ??

Spivak, Gayatri. 1988. Can the Subaltern Speak? In *Marxism and the Interpretation of Culture*, ed. Cary Nelson and Lawrence Grossberg, 271–313. London: Macmillan.

Stephen, Lynn. 2005. Negotiating Global, National, and Local "Rights" in a Zapotec Community. *Political and Legal Anthropology Review* 28 (1): 13–150.

———. 2007. *Transborder Lives: Indigenous Oaxacans in Mexico, California, and Oregon.* Durham: Duke University Press.

———. 2010. Karen Brodkin and the Study of Social Movements: Lessons for the Social Movement of Oaxaca, Mexico. *Critique of Anthropology* 30 (1): 1–27.

———. 2011. The Rights to Speak and to Be Heard: Women's Interpretations of Rights Discourses in the Oaxaca Social Movement. In *Gender at the Limits of Rights*, ed. Dorothy Hodgson, 161–179. Philadelphia: University of Pennsylvania Press.

Theidon, Kimberly. 2007. Gender in Transition: Common Sense, Women, and War. *Journal of Human Rights* 6:453–478.

Wilson, Richard Ashby. 2007. Tyrannosaurus Lex: The Anthropology of Human Rights and Transnational Law. In *The Practice of Human Rights: Tracking Law between the Global and the Local*, ed. Mark Goodale and Sally Engle Merry, 342–369. Cambridge: Cambridge University Press.

Wortham, Erica Cusi. 2004. Between the State and Indigenous Autonomy: Unpacking Video Indígena in Mexico. *American Anthropologist* 106 (2): 363–368.

7

The Cultural Politics of Radio

Two Views from the Warlpiri Public Sphere

MELINDA HINKSON

Warlpiri people residing at the town of Yuendumu, central Australia, have been involved in a range of audiovisual media projects over the past three decades, from radio broadcasting through to film and television production and videoconferencing. In this chapter I consider two moments in this recent history with a specific focus on radio, as a way to reflect on the shifting relations between Warlpiri people and the Australian state. Warlpiri radio broadcasting reveals the distinctive cultural imperatives that may be observed more broadly in Warlpiri social interaction, but simultaneously broadcasting activity occurs against/in response to the demands of the Australian state. Increasingly these demands call out a new kind of Warlpiri subject, the responsible individual worker who would reorder his or her social obligations so as to bring them inline with those of "mainstream" Australia.

In the first case considered here we glimpse the contradictory nature of the emergent community-based mediated public sphere and the ongoing challenges that Warlpiri social imperatives pose to the realization of a Warlpiri "community." In the second case, the time of a neoliberal intensification of state "intervention," we hear senior Warlpiri voices reflecting on the similarities and differences of the colonized past and present. These voices, carried by radio waves and the Internet, are directed both to the local community and to more distant listeners. In attending to these two moments, this chapter considers what radio activity reflects on Warlpiri people's sense of who they are in turbulent times and on the increasingly complex parameters of their public sphere.

Beginnings

The town of Yuendumu originated as a ration depot on the edge of the Tanami Desert in 1946. The establishment of such depots, which were subsequently gazetted as Aboriginal reserves, was a cornerstone of "protection"-era policy in Australia, wherein nomadic Aborigines of the continent's interior were sedentarized and segregated from rural towns.[1] Warlpiri people remember the early days of the settlement in terms of clear demarcations between themselves and the state agents who oversaw the town's operations. Their camps were physically set outside the town perimeter. Adults worked as domestics, cleaners, gardeners, and laborers. All were fed in a central dining room. Yet one of the features of this early period of settlement, which in state terms was a focused exercise in the training of citizens, was that Warlpiri people retained a degree of autonomy from Europeans that enabled them to continue organizing their social world according to long-held cultural imperatives. They were subject to a strict authoritarian regime and regulated work routines during weekdays but then left to themselves after hours and on weekends. Warlpiri language was banned from the school classroom but continued as the lingua franca of the camps. Boys continued to be made into men through circumcision ceremonies, customary marriages and polygyny continued to be practiced, the extended kin relationships that organized land tenure and enacted cosmology continued to be fostered. In short, a kind of domain separation ensured that two forms of authority co-resided, probably for about the first fifteen years of settlement (see Trigger 1986). The children who were schooled during this period grew up with a distinctly bicultural orientation to their social world.

In 1967 more than 90 percent of Australians voted in favor of a national referendum to amend two clauses of the constitution to enable the

Commonwealth government to make policy for the benefit of Aboriginal people (see Attwood and Markus 1997). The referendum symbolized an important, albeit somewhat indeterminate, shift in public sentiment regarding the place of Aboriginal people in Australian society, and a series of significant governmental moves followed. Warlpiri people experienced a radical shift in the nature of settlement life with the end of assimilation and the introduction of the approach of self-determination or self-management following the election of the Whitlam Labor government in 1971 and the commencement of welfare payments from the same period. Increased mobility followed as the newly available cash allowed people to purchase motor vehicles, and the passing of the Aboriginal Land Rights (Northern Territory) Act 1976 encouraged them, along with the anthropologists and linguists who were documenting their customary land tenure laws, out of the settlement and back onto their lands. Small outstation communities were established on land newly recognized under Aboriginal freehold title. A kind of cultural renaissance followed the newly established connections to customary lands and was fostered further with the creation of new community-controlled organizations: an art center, a bilingual resource agency, an outstation resource agency, and from the early 1980s, the Warlpiri Media Association.

While self-determination is often characterized as supporting Aboriginal autonomy, in Australia the shift in policy drew Aboriginal people into closer involvement in the workings of the state (see Batty 2005). Life at Yuendumu could no longer be characterized in terms of a clear separation of Warlpiri and European domains. The old government superintendent was replaced by a new process of community governance in which Warlpiri people would be drawn more directly into service delivery and the running of their own town through community councils, organizational committees, and boards of management. In this period Warlpiri people came to speak of themselves doing things "two ways," working alongside the non-Aboriginal advisers and coordinators of the new organizations. Educated Warlpiri moved to take up newly created positions as teachers' aids to help deliver the school's new bilingual education program. Media activity, in the first instance video production, was initiated under the auspices of an Adult Education program, then with the support of an Australian Institute of Aboriginal Studies research fellowship undertaken by American researcher Eric Michaels, to explore the effects of introducing national television into remote Aboriginal Australia (see Michaels 1986, 1994). All this activity aimed at generating new forms of work and enterprise that were supportive of Warlpiri aspirations to continue living a life that was distinctively Warlpiri.

Early media activity in the town both exemplified and recorded the flavor of social activity in this dynamic period—video records were made of culturally engaged school-based activities, as well as trips to country outside the settlement by people reestablishing connections to places not visited for many years, old people reminiscing, and meetings between residents and visiting bureaucrats about all manner of community development issues. Undertaken in a period prior to the launch of the first national satellite and before the development of legislative guidelines for remote broadcasting, the activity at Yuendumu was indeed relatively independent.[2]

Community-based media activity shifted onto a new footing after the federal government responded to calls to recognize the distinctive issues posed by the launch of national media, especially television, for remote-living Aboriginal people, by introducing the Broadcasting for Remote Aboriginal Communities Scheme (BRACS). BRACS equipment delivered to small towns across remote Australia enabled residents of these places to receive and rebroadcast to a local area of approximately one kilometer in diameter two television and two radio stations. Built into this equipment was a capacity to interrupt the incoming satellite signal and insert locally produced material. However, the equipment came without the necessary training and other financial support that would enable local production, and as a result, only a small number of towns established their own media associations and their own locally produced content.

Radio broadcasting has historically been overshadowed by the relative excitement of visual media, yet it is the mode of mediated communication that Warlpiri people are most straightforwardly able to undertake on their own terms. At Yuendumu the early burst of video production and local television broadcasting soon gave way, in a period of dwindling resources and support, to radio-based work. Radio broadcasting that utilizes the first and subsequent generations of BRACS equipment is technologically straightforward, is the least demanding of financial support, and requires very little training. So throughout the mid-1990s, in a period when the Warlpiri Media Association was relatively underresourced and a succession of non-Aboriginal managers came and went, Warlpiri media workers went about their business, broadcasting music and messages to the local community with very little support or encouragement of non-Aboriginal managers.

There is a sense in which radio work is particularly well suited to the dynamics of Warlpiri daily life. Radio workers can simply walk into the studio, flick a switch to override the incoming signal, and start broadcasting material of their own selection, which will be immediately heard by people listening. On completion of a session they simply switch over to the incoming signal and walk out of the studio. This was the informal and low-key approach to radio work throughout much of the 1990s by the small number of radio workers attached to the media association, with an average of about six hours of local broadcasting per week.

Case 1. Mediated Relations: Women Broadcasters and the PAW Radio Network

Part of the story of Warlpiri people's interactions with radio is about the changing government policies that have variously constrained and enabled new areas of activity. Warlpiri Media's expansion and eventual evolution into the regional Pintupi Anmatyerre Warlpiri Media Association reflects the response of its coordinating non-Aboriginal staff to diverse governmental pressures and local and regional needs and interests. What started as an entirely local project established in the early 1980s was regionalized by 1995, when the organization became training provider for seven neighboring towns. This expanded focus was partly driven by demand from residents of the towns in question and partly by the organization's need to generate new forms of revenue in order to sustain activity locally.

In 2001, following the appointment of an enthusiastic radio trainer with experience in the community-radio sector, the Warlpiri Media Association established the Pintupi Anmatyerre Warlpiri Radio Network (PAW Radio), which would create networked radio links between eleven towns spread across 480,000 square kilometers of the central and western deserts northwest of Alice Springs. The residents of these towns share close familial and ceremonial ties, and there are high levels of mobility as people travel to attend to the demands of these relationships. The radio network was integral to the emergence of a new kind of public sphere—not local, not national, not even regional in the conventional sense, but rather specifically drawing together the residents of these predominantly Aboriginal towns in a shared aural orientation to each other and the wider nation. Its launch heralded a new era in the mediated engagements of central Australian Aboriginal people and, with it, a new approach to broadcasting.

The radio network utilizes digital equipment whose operation requires radio workers to have reasonable levels of literacy. The first group of young adults who presented themselves as interested to take up the work of radio broadcasting were, notably, women. Throughout the 1990s one Warlpiri woman, Valerie Napaljarri Martin, had provided the stable point of reference in a workplace that turned over both Warlpiri and non-Aboriginal staff with great frequency. At the time of PAW's establishment Napaljarri had moved

into Alice Springs, but before leaving she recruited her niece to take up a position as media worker. This woman was followed by her own niece and Napaljarri's daughter, as well as her daughter's close classificatory sister. Two of
these women were also closely related to the radio trainee at nearby Mount
Allan, as well as to a highly mobile male radio worker who broadcasted variously from three different towns. Although not all Warlpiri people employed
by the media association are related, as this brief survey suggests, relatedness
is a significant consideration.

Importantly, the women working at Yuendumu also shared the distinc-
tion of having completed unusually high levels of education through their
enrollment in a senior girls class at the Yuendumu school in the mid-1990s.
The class utilized the community's videoconferencing equipment—the Tanami Network—in a Northern Territory–sponsored trial of the delivery to
Yuendumu of secondary-school-level curriculum (see Hinkson 2005, 2007.
Classes were taught via videoconference by teachers based at the Northern
Territory Correspondence School in Darwin, with tutors working alongside
students in the classroom at Yuendumu. In the course of this trial a number of students graduated to work at year ten and eleven levels, an unprecedented achievement in a town whose school was then only teaching to
postprimary (year seven to eight) level. The trial meant that for the first time
young women (a number of them mothers to infant children) were able to
gain a partial secondary education without leaving their hometown. Prior
to the trial, students had to attend boarding schools hundreds of kilometers
away if they were to complete secondary education. The outcomes of the
trial were considered by local educators to be quite remarkable. The women
received a new kind of affirmation as a result of completing their studies,
and the effects of this were widely observable at a broader social relational
level. In the period following their completion of various stages of the trial,
members of the class secured most of the jobs on offer to Warlpiri people
in Yuendumu's community organizations. Their higher levels of numeracy
and literacy, computer proficiency, and all-round confidence made them desirable employees and enthusiastic workers. Their education experience also
encouraged these women to consider a wider horizon of possible futures
than they might have otherwise. It is notable in this respect that while one
broadcaster's mother had relocated to Alice Springs, she herself had elected
to stay and work at Yuendumu.

The establishment of PAW Radio sparked unprecedented radio activity
and a major increase in the number of young people approaching the organization looking for work. There was a dramatic increase in the number

of hours of local radio broadcasting across the networked towns, with radio workers from at least two locations broadcasting regularly for six to eight hours a day, five days a week.

Requests and the Politics of Dedicated Listening

> BROADCASTER: Yuwai, nat that one, Cold Chisel, "Forever Now," ngulaju. Umpuku Pukarac, Ingrid, Wakku, Nana, Minu, Jampijin, Derek, Warwick, Japangard, and . . . Yah, jinta kari, 'nother one, Spinifex Band and Rising Wind; double play nyampuju. Spinifex "Pina Yantarni" and Rising Wind "Karnta-kangku pantirli." Double play ngulaju. Tiffany, Olivia, Edith, W, Leanne, Sharmane, and kurdu-k. Nyambpu now, double play, umpuj.
>
> [TRANSLATION: Yes, that was Cold Chisel with "Forever Now," going out for Pukarac, Ingrid, Wakku, Nana, Minu, Jampijin, Derek, Warwick, Japangard. . . . And now here's another one, two songs from Spinifex Band and Rising Wind. Spinifex's "Come Back" and Rising Wind's "The Woman Is Waiting." This one's a double play for Olivia, Edith, W, Leanne, Sharmane, and the kids. Here it is now.][3]

The women radio broadcasters take a distinctive approach to their on-air work. When they are broadcasting, the radio room is abuzz with excitement. The telephone rings incessantly, with listeners calling in requests and dedications. Announcers follow the same procedure for each song played: they announce not just the name of the caller but a list of names for whom a requested song is to be played. On the completion of a song the same announcement is made, the same list of names carefully recited. Rarely do these women play a song without an accompanying dedication. Rarely is a song announced as having been requested by a single individual.

Music is a major dimension of life in the central and western deserts. From Warlpiri's own ceremonial music that enacts the fundamental relations between persons, country, and spirit through to country-and-western, gospel, hip-hop, and their own innovative rock and roll, a passion for music is an observable intergenerational phenomena. Many popular genres of music are represented in the PAW computerized database, and most broadcasting sessions run by the women are likely to include an even sprinkling of most styles. The songs of Warlpiri and other desert bands are interspersed with the latest Top 40 hits, 1970s American classics, Australian pop, reggae, and dance, as well as songs by Aboriginal bands from across the country. The most recently released popular songs are repeated often during the one on-air session. Choice of material may be influenced by many factors, but the most significant in the case of the young women broadcasters are requests and dedications.

The women broadcasters estimate that about half the calls they receive while broadcasting are from people they refer to as "family," the other half from "anybody." In the course of a broadcasting slot phone calls are likely to be received from across many of the networked towns. But it is also common for radio workers to receive several calls from the same destination, as it is for the same song to be requested and played several times. Significantly, calls are also received from Aboriginal people locally related but living outside the networked towns.

As suggested by the lists of names, caller's requests tend to be made on behalf of some kind of social grouping associated with the caller. But what kind of social grouping? During two sessions I spent in the radio room in November 2002, I noted a variety of relationships being invoked. For example, Marlette Napurrurla, a close classificatory sister of one of the broadcasters, has ready access to a telephone at the childcare center where she works. She calls the radio room a number of times during the broadcast session to request "gospel songs." The dedication announced by the broadcasters is for all the Warlpiri women working alongside Marlette at the childcare center, as well as a number of named children, including Marlette's grandson.

The radio workers explained to me that the playing of requests takes precedence over the playing of their own choice of song. But when one listens to PAW Radio, things do not appear to be so clear-cut. For there is a third approach these women regularly take: they dedicate songs to relatives and friends who do not ring in. During the session I sat in on, one of the two women broadcasting sent a dedication to her sister and others, currently living in the large regional center Alice Springs. The song was Marvin Gaye's "Sexual Healing." Alice Springs lies well outside the station's range, as the broadcaster is fully aware, and so her sister would not hear the dedication being made. But dedications can travel via alternative routes to radio waves. The intensity of Warlpiri mobility means that someone who knows the broadcaster's sister and has heard the dedication is likely to meet her in coming days and tell her that she had been named by her sister on the radio.

During the broadcasting session of the woman in question, she made two other unsolicited dedications, one to her close classificatory mother and to other Warlpiri and some non-Aboriginal staff with whom she works at the local Warlukurlangu Artists Association. This was followed by yet another unsolicited dedication to "everyone in South Camp," among whom a close classificatory brother was named.

What is revealed in the "groups" named in these requests and dedications is the inherent dynamism of Warlpiri social relations in the postcolonial present. The assemblages of people listed are in many cases kin but more often members of highly dynamic residential groups whose constitution changes frequently.[4] They are also "friendship" groups and workplace groups, but they are rarely inclusive of all members of a workplace. None of these groups may be considered permanent or bounded; they are networks of individuals that reflect the crosscutting layers of allegiance and association that constitute contemporary Warlpiri life. The articulation of these networks, the public naming of oneself in association with particular others, reflects a core moral principle of Warlpiri sociality: one should move with, camp with, and look after others, not simply oneself. As the parameters of the Warlpiri universe strain against and transcend the local, new communications media such as radio provide the mechanisms both for such expansion and for its possible accommodation.

As suggested by the tendency to make unsolicited dedications on behalf of kin, the radio workers are by no means neutral points of mediation in the public invocation of on-air relationships. The status of the relationship between the broadcaster and people calling in is highly significant, as is reflected in the criticisms of the women's approach to their work by some residents. "They only play for their own family," one man complained to me, an accusation that was repeated by others whose views I sought on the women's broadcasting style. One Yuendumu resident told me she got frustrated with the radio workers because they never played her family's requests. Now she waits until one of her own relatives is broadcasting from nearby Nyirripi before calling in, because she knows he will always play her songs. When confronted with the accusations of family bias, the women smile and tell me, "Sometimes we *forget* other people's requests and get growled."

This political context of broadcasting renders complex any idea that Aboriginal media can be simply understood as community owned and driven and indeed constituted in something called "community."[5] The question of whether the women consider their activity to be work on behalf of a wider community is also implicitly raised by some of the criticisms of their approach. "They don't run the show smoothly. They just walk in and out as they like. There should be proper training for them," remarked one senior man. He continued, "You've got to remember, we've listened to a lot of radio for a long time. We know what good radio is." Criticisms such as these reflect intergenerational tensions around understandings of the relative importance of work.

People make work meaningful by grounding it in their existing social networks wherever possible. But as suggested in the friction surrounding the women's approach to broadcasting, the demands of family are not necessarily compatible with those of community-based work. Indeed the question of whether the women regard their on-air activity as "work" is interesting to consider. Two of the broadcasters are undertaking further study at Batchelor College as part of their training; they received "top up" wages as well as their fortnightly Community Development Employment Program (CDEP) scheme, otherwise known as "work for the dole," payments. A third refuses to take a wage, preferring to receive unemployment benefits and the family allowance payment she is eligible for as a single mother of two. Through this kind of arrangement she feels she is "not really working" and retains flexibility to come and go from broadcasting as she pleases.

There is some reluctance on the part of the women to undertake the kind of on-air tasks that would give their programs a more formal structure: accepting paid advertisements, conducting interviews, playing prerecorded programs such as locally produced oral histories and biographies. In 2002 they needed active encouragement of non-Aboriginal coordinators to carry out these tasks.

This case study reveals the significance of radio as a medium for exploring what it is to be Warlpiri in the present. Networked broadcasting has been embraced by young women because it mimics and indeed supports the kind of intensive sociality displayed in other contexts of daily life. While the PAW network extends well beyond Warlpiri territory, there is a sense in which it functions as a communication mechanism primarily oriented to the local. The case we shall now move on to consider deals with radio's mediation of Warlpiri experience of events directed at them, originating elsewhere.

Case 2. Yapa Patu Wangkami: Remembering Interventions

The period in which PAW Radio was established coincided with a highly productive set of collaborative relations between Warlpiri and non-Warlpiri staff of the media association. Other television, film, and video productions completed in this period produced something of a financial buffer for the organization, enabling the new network to be established and the spike of enthusiastic broadcasters to be supported and paid.

In 2007 the federal government launched the Northern Territory "Emergency Response" Intervention, ostensibly in response to the findings of the Little Children Are Sacred Inquiry, which reported widespread child sexual abuse across remote Aboriginal communities. Enabled with the rapid passing of complex legislation and the suspension of the Racial Discrimination

Act, the Intervention mobilized the army into remote towns, followed by increased permanent police presence to help "stabilize" these places. It introduced mandatory quarantining of half the income of all welfare recipients to ensure money would be spent on food and care of children, promised to deliver improved housing, and imposed tougher restrictions on alcohol and pornography, along with a raft of other measures (Hinkson 2007). After initial hope as well as fear as to what the Intervention might actually mean on the ground, Warlpiri people became increasingly disappointed at the lack of any significant changes to their circumstances and also angry and apprehensive at government rhetoric and shifts in policy discourse that Warlpiri interpret as a direct threat to their existing way of life (Hinkson 2010).

While the announcement of the Intervention was dramatic, the shift in policy it represented had in fact been unfolding in Australia over the past decade and a half. Over that same period a shift in the national politics of representation could also be observed, as one set of images that oriented the general public to remote Aboriginal Australia—culture, community, self-determination—were displaced by ideas of failure, suffering, abuse.[6] Warlpiri people have been observing this shift in discourse and sentiment with a growing sense of alarm. Coupled with the coercive Intervention measures and heightened government attention to those aspects of their lives that the state identifies as dysfunctional, they sense echoes of the civilizing experiments of the early settlement days. Yuendumu's residents have been outspoken critics of the Intervention and have utilized every opportunity to make their views known to wider Australia via whatever media interest has come their way.[7]

Working with and against the Neoliberal State

By mid-2007 the radio studio had undergone considerable change. The group of women who had been the major drivers of broadcasting five years earlier were no longer working for PAW. One of them had died suddenly of heart-related problems in 2004, and her female relatives stopped working there soon after. The studio had subsequently become a predominantly male domain, although in mid-2009 a project was under way to build a second studio which would function as a separate women's space, as a way to encourage further young women into radio.

Broadcasting appeared more technically demanding and complicated than ever before. PAW had recently begun to record everything that goes to air to ensure compliance with the Community Broadcasting Associations Act. The organization had a commitment to broadcast twenty hours per

week but was finding it hard to maintain these hours. Broadcasters continued to come and go.

The Intervention influenced people working in radio in three main ways:
first, it brought increased government revenue into PAW through the place-
ment of paid radio advertisements to advise residents of the PAW member
communities of the stream of changes being introduced. In other words,
radio became a primary carrier of government discourse about the shifting
policy landscape to its remote Aboriginal subjects. Up to twenty government
advertisements were played on air per day.

Second, one of the measures associated with the Intervention was the
canceling of the CDEP scheme and the replacement of a limited number
of positions with government-sponsored places in "real jobs," funded for
three years. This was a significant development for the organization, which
had previously found the flexibility of CDEP suitable in accommodating
its highly mobile workforce. The change brought with it an unprecedented
distinction between a small number of "professional" workers, who receive
intensive training with the aim of producing new levels of sophistication in
their media skills, and the larger casual pool of workers who would continue
to come and go according to other pressures and stimuli in their lives. In an
associated development a code of conduct was developed that the professional trainees are required to sign prior to taking up a position with the
media association. The code of conduct is aimed at fostering both individual
and public understanding of the responsibilities of workers and the recognition of a need for some degree of division between responsibility to the
workplace and to one's family. Through these developments, which echo debates in the wider Australian public sphere about the need to foster in remote-living Aboriginal people a greater sense of individual responsibility,[8]
there is a clear sense that the way work is understood and experienced by
Warlpiri people is in the process of undergoing considerable change.

Third, the Intervention provoked more radio use as residents sought information about what was going on, as well as avenues to express their be-
wilderment, concern, and anger at the new governmental approach. In response to the heightened public discussion among residents attempting to
make sense of the turbulent experiences of the present, a series of oral history interviews were recorded with senior women and men, specifically to be
played on the radio for both local and wider audiences.

Yapa patu wangkami[9] is an oral history program structured around Warlpiri memory and opinion in relation to three historical moments: presettlement, early postsettlement, and the post-Intervention present. It draws perspectives from men and women of different generations, thus conveying a

sense not only of historical transformation in the Warlpiri world but also of diverse subjective experience across time. The interviews and translations are conducted by Warlpiri media workers—women interviewing and translating the accounts of women, men working with men. In many cases the interviewers are related to those whose stories they have recorded. This is important as it enables the younger questioner to pose issues for discussion, or raise points of clarification, without being "shamed." The relational context of the interviews also characterizes these testimonies as something other than simply "stories" for a "public"—the recordings point to a kin-based process of intergenerational knowledge transfer, which is recognized as a crucial conduit for the activity of the media association. In other words, media work is undertaken in a distinctively Warlpiri way and shaped by particular kin-based social imperatives.

Yapa patu wangkami can be downloaded as podcast in a series of six programs structured around individual accounts or as a one-hour compilation. Here my focus is on the compilation program. The program opens with the testimony of Johnny Japangardi Miller, speaking of his memories of living in the bush in his grandfather's country, prior to Yuendumu's establishment. What is particularly striking about Japangardi's account is the way it is explicitly framed against an articulated fear that "government" will "take away this land." In a forceful, animated voice filled with urgency, he recounts his intergenerational inheritance and responsibility to look after the land: "We can't just give our land away easily. We have ceremonial ties, we've got to hold onto it. This land has lots of Dreaming stories. No government can take this land. All these kids were born here. The white people brought us here. . . . I would not give this land away. It has too many precious stories." Japangardi's translated account conveys something of the rhythm of nomadic life, but it continuously circles back to focus on the concerns of the present. His story illustrates the ways in which memory is powerfully animated and shaped in and against contemporary experience.

The next account, by Dennis Japangardi Williams, a man in his fifties, recalls a constantly mobile life, even in the supposedly sedentary postsettlement era. Here we are given an evocative sense of the voluntary and forced movement that structured experience for some Warlpiri people through the 1950s and 1960s, as they were forcibly removed into Alice Springs by state agents to attend school, from station to station accompanying parents in paid work, and out to bush camps to be initiated or to attend other ritual events.

Senior women recount the depth of knowledge of country that saw their parents and grandparents move from soakage to soakage following scarce water resources and the bush-based expertise that treated the sick, the elderly, and the frail. These women emphasize the physical strength and health of Aboriginal people in the presettlement period, in contrast with the widespread and debilitating influence of diabetes, substance abuse, and malnutrition in the present.

Listeners learn from two generations of men and women of the harsh treatment they experienced at the hands of schoolteachers, the constant attention of missionaries, and the routinized physical education and feeding regimes. Many Warlpiri people recall those days in largely positive terms. While decrying the physical abuse of their teachers, older Warlpiri people regard the relative order of life under the superintendent as "really good." Memories of the past are a foil for thinking about the present, and vice versa. In these recollections the present is cause for concern on two fronts: speakers reflect not simply on government action and inaction but also on the trouble caused by young people today—and interestingly, those who reflect on the "problems" of today's teenagers are not so old themselves: in one case a man in his early twenties passes critical comment on today's kids "who think they're already adults." There is also a sense in which the current governmental changes are being felt so intensively that transformations in experience between the generations are also intensified. In this way a man in his twenties can speak confidently about Yuendumu being "a really strong place" when he was a child and a "big mess" in the wake of the Intervention.

The final two reflections in the compilation program are from senior women Peggy Nampijinpa Brown and Tess Napaljarri Ross. Nampijinpa speaks of the distinction between Warlpiri law, which never changes, and government law, which changes every year: "Government mob make different rules every year. They write it down in the newspaper. We see it nearly every day. . . . It hurts our feelings." And she goes on to say that Warlpiri people would not treat others in the way they are being treated by the government, as they would "get shamed." Referring to the government's refusal on a number of occasions to take on board Warlpiri people's expressed desires regarding their future, Nampijinpa tells her interviewer, "We can't listen to *kardiya's* [whitefella's] message only. They need to listen to our story as well. Can't they look at what we do and think about supporting us? . . . They should be supporting us because we do lots of good things for the community and its people. . . . But they keep threatening to take our land away."

Tess Ross similarly reflects on the present: "In these Intervention years we are going backwards. It really hurts us. White people don't even know our law." And then she moves to illustrate the extent to which Warlpiri people have embraced their complex and troubled relationship with wider Australia: "We didn't ever know God. But now we know God exists. We know these political people in Canberra. We know Queen Elizabeth in England. We know where the famous places are in the cities, and we know who we are. We know where our families live in the other communities, and we know where our *kardiya* friends are."

These women appeal to two distinct but related ways in which Warlpiri morality is affronted in the present: by the lack of reciprocity they experience in their encounters with representatives of the Australian state and by the suggestion that they have conducted themselves in such a way as to require government intervention. At the root of both issues is the suggestion that the government does not understand Warlpiri people or the cultural impera-tives that characterize Warlpiri ways of doing things or indeed the cultural distance that Warlpiri have traveled in committing themselves to an intercul-tural imaginary.

Significantly, this case illustrates ways in which the earlier-observed Warl-piri atomism, or "lack" of community, is largely overcome in turbulent times. Warlpiri are adept at mobilizing a strong, unified front when actions identi-fied as originating from "outside" are felt to threaten the moral order of their social universe.

Conclusion

Why make a radio program about such issues? For a community of people who continue to privilege face-to-face communication over that which is technologically mediated, it might be suggested that the process of local dis-cussion and expression of opinion around these issues may be more highly valued than the finished product or its broadcast to a wider audience. But the testimonies considered here suggest a more complex situation. Tess Ross appeals to the thoroughly intercultural parameters of contemporary Warl-piri experience. In the post-Intervention period Warlpiri people have trav-eled regularly between Yuendumu and Canberra and further afield to put their views on the new policy landscape directly to politicians and bureau-crats in face-to-face encounters. They have also taken every opportunity to share their opinions with the wider Australian public via interviews with journalists and in contributing to a major six-part series "Voices from the Heart," publishing Warlpiri perspectives on a range of topics in the country's only national newspaper, the *Australian*. This commitment to a form of me-diated political activism belies Warlpiri people's longstanding experience as both subjects and producers of a variety of media—they understand what is at stake in the contemporary politics of representation, in which negative stereotypes of culture as cause of dysfunction and suffering are becoming increasingly dominant (see for example Hughes 2007; Windschuttle 2009; Sutton 2009).

Warlpiri people make a distinction between presence and distance as modes of communication and knowing and make clear their privileging of the former when they appeal to politicians, journalists, and researchers to come and "sit down" at Yuendumu to get to "really know" Warlpiri people. Yet in seeing themselves simultaneously as Warlpiri and Australian, they are committed to participating in a public sphere that transcends the local and the regional. Consequently they embrace those modes of interaction that enable them to do so. When Tess Ross states, "We know Queen Elizabeth in England. We know where the famous places are in the cities, and we know who we are," she is making clear the impossibility of disentangling the contemporary Warlpiri worldview from both colonial experience and contemporary Australian society. The kind of public sphere being enacted here is more complicated than that which we might infer from the work of either Habermas (1989) or Appadurai (1990). Thoroughly constituted in the production of a global imaginary on the one hand, Warlpiri motivation to perform as global citizens derives from their ongoing attention to the local and specific. Yet significantly, these spheres are now understood as thoroughly entangled. In this sense Warlpiri face the same distinctly modern challenge as the rest of us, to coherently integrate the two modes of engagement that characterize contemporary social experience and to order them according to their distinctive moral imperatives (Thompson 1995). In this sense the activity around the Yuendumu radio room might be understood as a microcosm of wider Warlpiri experience.

NOTES

1. "Protection" was established as the policy approach to remote-living Aboriginal people in 1911 and ran to the early 1950s, when it was replaced by "assimilation." See Rowse 1998.
2. However, the media project was dependent on the skills and resources that Eric Michaels brought with him as part of his research project.
3. This section of the chapter draws from material published in Hinkson 2004.
4. For a detailed account of Warlpiri residential mobility see Musharbash 2008.
5. This debate has been a central theme in the writings on Aboriginal media; see for example Michaels 1989; Molnar 1999; Meadows 1993; Ginsburg 1995; Hinkson 2005.
6. While there is a clear lineage to this discursive shift, it is beyond the scope of this chapter to attend to it in any detail. See McCallum 2009; Hinkson 2010.
7. See for example "Voices from the Heart," a six-part series from Yuendumu published in the Australian newspaper fortnightly in mid-2007, available at http://www.reconcile.org.au/getsmart/pages/get-the-basics/whats-it-really-like/voices-from-the-heart-of-the-nation.php; Price 2009; Trofimov 2009.

8. Such debates have been fueled most particularly by the writings and public commentary of Cape York Aboriginal leader and intellectual Noel Pearson. See especially Pearson 2001.

9. The program is available to download as a podcast at http://www.pawmedia.com. au/audiopodcast/?p=103. It won the awards for Best Oral History (Radio) and Best Documentary (Radio) at the 11th Annual Remote Indigenous Media Festival in 2009.

REFERENCES

Appadurai, Arjun. 1990. Disjuncture and difference in the global cultural economy. *Public Culture* 2 (2): 1–24.

Attwood, Bain, and Andrew Markus. 1997. *The 1967 Referendum, or, When Aborigines Didn't Get the Vote*. Canberra: Aboriginal Studies Press.

Batty, Philip. 2005. Recruiting the Aboriginal voice: The state development of Aboriginal broadcasting. In Luke Taylor, Graeme K. Ward, Graham Henderson, Richard David, and Lynley A. Wallis, eds., *The Power of Knowledge, the Resonance of Tradition*, 169–181. Canberra: Aboriginal Studies Press.

Ginsburg, Faye. 1995. Production values: Indigenous media and the rhetoric of self-determination. In Deborah Battaglia, ed., *Rhetorics of Self-Making*, 12–138. Berkeley: University of California Press.

Habermas, Jürgen. 1989. *The Structural Transformation of the Public Sphere: An Inquiry into a Category of Bourgeois Society*. Cambridge, UK: Polity.

Hinkson, Melinda. 2004. What's in a dedication? On being a Warlpiri DJ. *Australian Journal of Anthropology* 15 (2): 143–162.

———. 2005. New media projects at Yuendumu: Towards a history and analysis of intercultural engagement. In Luke Taylor, Graeme K. Ward, Graham Henderson, Richard David, and Lynley A. Wallis, eds., *The Power of Knowledge, the Resonance of Tradition*, 157–168. Canberra: Aboriginal Studies Press.

———. 2007. In the name of the child. In Jon Altman and Melinda Hinkson, eds., *Coercive Reconciliation: Stabilise, Normalise, Exit Aboriginal Australia*, 1–12. Carlton North, Australia: Arena.

———. 2010. Media images and the politics of hope. In Jon Altman and Melinda Hinkson, eds., *Culture Crisis: Anthropology, Politics and Remote Aboriginal Australia*. Sydney: UNSW Press.

Hughes, Helen. 2007. *Lands of Shame*. Sydney: Centre for Independent Studies.

McCallum, Kerry. 2009. News and local talk: Conversations about the "crisis of Indigenous violence" in Australia. In S. Elizabeth Bird, ed., *The Anthropology of News and Journalism*, 151–167. Bloomington: Indiana University Press.

Meadows, Michael. 1993. Reclaiming a cultural identity: Indigenous media production in Australia and Canada. *Continuum* 8 (2): 270–292.

Michaels, Eric. 1986. *The Invention of Aboriginal Television, Central Australia 1982–96*. Institute Report Series. Canberra: Aboriginal Studies Press, 1986.

———. 1989. *For a Cultural Future: Francis Jupurrurla Makes TV at Yuendumu*. Sydney and Melbourne: Art and Text.

———. 1994. *Bad Aboriginal Art: Tradition, Media and Technological Horizons*. St. Leonards: Allen and Unwin.

Molnar, Helen. 1999. The Broadcasting for Remote Aboriginal Communities Scheme: Small versus big. *Media Information Australia* 1999:147–154.

Pearson, Noel. 2001. *Our Right to Take Responsibility*. Cairns, Australia: Cape York Institute.

Price, Bess. 2009. "Outsiders beat the drum against change for wrong reasons." *Australian*, 27 August.

Rowse, Tim. 1998. *White Flour, White Power: From Rations to Citizenship in Central Australia*. Cambridge: Cambridge University Press.

Sutton, Peter. 2009. *The Politics of Suffering*. Carlton: Melbourne University Press.

Thompson, John. 1995. *The Media and Modernity: A Social Theory of the Media*. Stanford: Stanford University Press.

Trigger, David. 1986. Blackfellas and whitefellas: The concepts of domain and social closure in the analysis of race-relations. *Mankind* 16 (2): 99–117.

Trofimov, Yaroslav 2009. "'Tough love' in the outback." *Wall Street Journal*, 17 January. http://online.wsj.com/article/SB123214753161791813.html (accessed 20 February 2009).

Windschuttle. Keith. 2009. Bill Stanner and the end of the Aboriginal high culture. *Quadrant* 5. http://www.quadrant.org.au/magazine/issue/2009/5/bill-stanner-and-the-end-of-aboriginal-high-culture (accessed 9 September 2009).

8

Frequencies of Transgression

Notes on the Politics of Excess and Constraint among Mexican Free Radios

JEFFREY S. JURIS

I headed out on a chilly, gray afternoon through the overflowing streets of Mexico City, making my way to the studio where my new radio show was set to kick off later that day. I had recently arrived in this massive Latin American capital to study the links between media activism and autonomy and had eventually come across Radio Autónoma,[1] part of the city's burgeoning free radio scene. As a free or pirate radio, Radio Autónoma eschews permits, operating outside the law. Nikita and Simón, two regular voices on the radio, had agreed to cohost a program with me, called *Caminos Autónomos*, about the meaning and practice of autonomy among social movements in Mexico and beyond.[2] The show, I hoped, would provide a strategic location from which to explore the dynamics of autonomy among free radios in Mexico.[3]

I arrived at the studio a few minutes early and took some time to observe the murals, posters, and stickers on the walls from free media projects around Mexico and the world, as well as grassroots autonomous struggles including the Zapatistas, the teachers' rebellion in Oaxaca, and the movement in defense of the land in Atenco. As usual, the show would start late, reflecting the informal, improvisational style of the radio. When Nikita and Simón finally got to the studio, they decided to give an impromptu lesson to another new DJ who had been waiting for them, going over key DOS commands as well as critical functions such as shifting between playlists, adjusting the volume, and initiating cross fades. Once the lesson concluded, we ran into trouble with the recording system. Fifteen minutes later, the program finally began. As I explained on the air, "*Caminos Autónomos* is a laboratory for learning about contemporary struggles, creating critical analysis, and developing proposals for the construction of autonomy in our territories and social spaces." Nikita added that the program would be a mix of live and taped interviews, music, and commentary and that "we want the program to be a space of participation and collaboration."

We then shifted to a musical track by a Venezuelan artist living in San Diego that mixed Latin rhythms and *electronica*, an example of the non-commercial fusion styles popular at the radio station. Meanwhile, Simón explained that we were doing okay but that the conversation should be more loose and freewheeling. We needed to be more spontaneous and interactive, to interrupt each other once in a while. Above all, we should try to speak like "regular" people, not like radio professionals, and we should express ourselves freely. When the track—which was called "Rhythm of the Phoenix"—ended, we began talking about the image of the phoenix rising up from the ashes and whether autonomy required such a violent foundational event:

NIKITA: It's important to realize that society is changing constantly and to think about autonomy as a project under permanent construction. We don't know if it's a particular moment that starts the process, or if we can start moving that way little by . . .

LOBO:[4] I think we can, but the question is whether it also helps to have an event that clears the field and opens the space for autonomy. In other words, to what extent do we need spaces that are outside the dominant society, or to what extent can we take advantage of little cracks within . . .

SIMÓN: This is an extremely interesting and productive question because it brings us to the issue of whether autonomy is a rupture, like the classic

concept of revolution, or simply a foundational moment in which new
relations are constituted. . . .

NIKITA: But we also need to remember that all societies create institutions
constantly. There is no society that does not create its own spaces.
The question is whether creating these institutions has to pass through
the legal or institutional sphere of the state, or whether there is another way.

The title of the song we had aired sparked a dynamic exchange about the nature of autonomy at Radio Autónoma that echoed a key principle articulated
by Cornelius Castoriadis (1987), namely, that autonomous societies are both
instituted and instituting, existing as self-reflexive processes of creative self-
alteration powered by the "radical imagination" (369–373). Nikita and Simón
were very much influenced by this idea, emphasizing a vision of autonomy
as a collaborative process of self-construction. Others at the radio saw autonomy more as a radical separation from dominant institutions, social relations, and cultural practices. Nikita and Simón thought that such a separation
was neither possible nor desirable. Instead, the goal was to collectively control the terms of such interactions. For Castoriadis, and this is consistent with
my own view, as an ideal, the project of autonomy is not about closing oneself off but is rather an open process of building new "social-historical forms"
through ongoing practices of self-constitution and self-reflection (1991, 162–
163). Zapatista communities in Chiapas, the Popular People's Assembly of
Oaxaca (APPO), and decentralized networks of squats, collectives, and free
media projects represent concrete manifestations of autonomy in action. Our
new radio program, *Caminos Autónomos*, would provide a space to reflect on
these and other movements, including their goals, prospects, and contradic-
tions, as well as debates about the meaning and practice of autonomy within
and beyond Radio Autónoma. It would also allow me to reflect ethnographically on the show and its articulation with Radio Autónoma and the wider
world of free media in Mexico by becoming an active program participant.

Mexican free radios operate in one of the most highly concentrated media
markets in the world. Televisa and TeleAzteca run the majority of television
outlets, while radio is controlled by fourteen conglomerates, or "families"
(Soria Arenas 2007, 11), leaving little room for noncommercial outlets. Despite the existence of assimilationist "*indigenista*" radios as well as govern-
ment- and university-run "cultural" stations, independent community radios
have been few and far between. The rise of Ke Huelga Radio during the 1999
student strike at the National Autonomous University of Mexico (UNAM)
ushered in the recent Mexican free radio boom (ibid., 56–57). Many of

the founders of Ke Huelga went on to help create and/or provide material and technical assistance to newly emerging free radios in Mexico City and other regions, including the southern, largely indigenous states of Chiapas, Guerrero, and Oaxaca. Some of these stations continue to operate without a license, while others have gone on to secure permits (often after suffering violent state repression) with the help of the Mexican branch of the World Association of Community Radio Broadcasters (AMARC). Urban free radios such as Radio Autónoma are immersed in youth-oriented countercultures, but they also link up with rural indigenous free radios through wider free media networks and autonomy movements such as the Zapatista-inspired "Other Campaign."[5]

Given the critical role of free and other alternative media in promoting self-managed communication, information sharing, and reflection among grassroots social movements, they are privileged institutional arenas for the construction of autonomy as a discourse, ideal, and mode of social practice. What follows is my initial attempt to begin making sense of the infrastructures, practices, logics, and forms that underlie free radio in Mexico. With respect to the former, radio is inescapably material, built out of complex networks of machines, electronic devices, software, wires, and electromagnetic waves. What distinguishes *free* radio is a self-conscious commitment to autonomous and democratic uses of technology beyond the constraints imposed by external forces or codes imposed by states and corporations. However, as I quickly learned, technology can also be disruptive, and the frequent technological breakdowns that free radio activists confront often mean that seemingly mundane, material concerns overshadow their more idealistic goals (cf. Larkin 2008).

Moreover, as the vignette of my visit to Radio Autónoma suggests, free radio involves the production of particular modes of sound and communication, entailing a unique approach to audio aesthetics and style, which I analyze in this chapter using Steven Feld's (1988) metaphor of "lift-up-over sounding." Finally, free radio projects also have a unique relation to (il)legality and the state. Indeed, one of the defining characteristics of "free" as opposed to other forms of noncommercial radio is the practice of unlicensed broadcasting as a strategic component of an overall project of asserting and promoting autonomy. Underlying the cultural practices and logics in each of the spheres just outlined is a tendency toward excess and transgression. Excess in the sociocultural field, or the transgression of the bounds of a prevailing institutional or normative order, can represent a powerful means of challenging that order while shining a critical light on the relations, practices, forms, and representations through which it is constituted. It is in this sense that we can speak of a "politics of excess" tied to a process of critical reflection regarding received institutions and significations. Free radio activists thus employ excess and transgression as practices to symbolically challenge dominant technological, media, and political-legal orders, particularly in the context of media consolidation under neoliberal globalization. In so doing, they enact a collective subjectivity through alternative modes of autonomous, self-reflexive communication and organization.

However, autonomy as an ideal does not mean anything goes.[6] Rather, the project of autonomy espoused by free radio activists invariably involves the setting of rules and limits, even if they are presumed to derive from a collective process of self-reflexive negotiation rather than symbolic recourse to a transcendent sovereign. Nevertheless, despite this claim, autonomous projects may have contradictory effects, often reproducing dominant modes of power, hierarchy, and governmentality, further constraining the creative, transgressive activity of particular subjects in materially specific ways. External instances of authority, such as the state, may also intrude on autonomous projects, more or less violently. In what follows, I examine how the cultural politics of free radio are constituted through a complex interplay between excess and constraint in wider entanglements of technology, aesthetics, and state regulation. As we shall see, ethnographically tracing free radio discourse and practice also raises salient issues with respect to the anthropology of radio and media anthropology more generally.

The Materiality of Free Radio

Much of the recent anthropological work on radio has emphasized the medium's material qualities: its underlying technologies, its insertion into broader networked infrastructures (Fisher 2009; Larkin 2008; Spitulnik 1998–1999, 2002), and the materiality of sound itself (Tacchi 2002; Weidman 2003). Brian Larkin (2008) suggests that in colonial Nigeria the particular material shape of broadcast radio emerged through a complex process of negotiation. More generally, radio was an information order designed to support the colonial regime. At the same time, he notes that technologies are mutable and unruly, having the "capacity to create possibilities in excess of their expected use" (47). This is precisely the power of free radio as an oppositional materiality, transforming an assemblage of technologies initially developed in the service of order and profit into a potent tool of dissent (cf. Buddle 2008; Murillo 2008; O'Connor 2004).

When joining a free radio project such as Radio Autónoma, one immediately confronts the need to become familiar with and use a bewildering series of technical instruments: computer programs, microphones, mixers, recording devices, and editing software. For the non-technically-minded, this can be disorienting. Licensed radios avoid this problem through a division of labor between technicians, producers, broadcasters, and other workers, but free radio projects lack sufficient material and human resources for such a solution, while their ideology directly challenges logics of specialization.

Upon walking into a free radio, one immediately notices the recycled computers, hand-me-down microphones, scratched mixers with missing buttons, cables held down with duct tape, and dirty walls covered with political propaganda. The material aesthetic is cyberpunk, a romantic rebel expression of the "recycled modernity" (Sundaram 1999; cf. Larkin 2008) that characterizes popular technological cultures in developing countries such as Mexico. These recycled technologies allow free radios to achieve a modicum of material autonomy. However, like the postcolonial technological infrastructures examined by Larkin (2008), they are also prone to failure. The everyday experience of free radio is thus shaped by hard drive crashes, software problems, light and Internet outages, server breakdowns, signal shifts, and antenna malfunctions.

For example, *Caminos Autónomos* frequently began with frantic attempts to restart the server, replace malfunctioning mikes, or troubleshoot a software glitch. We were often forced to call for help, despite the emphasis on solving our own technical problems. The "culture of repair" (Larkin 2008, 236) reproduced by the more technically proficient members of the radio allowed the project to exceed the technological constraints posed by resource poverty, yet the frequency of breakdown signaled a limit in the speed and fluidity of the autonomous functionality to which the radio aspired. Meanwhile, the constant need for repair reinscribed hierarchies of technical experience, constraining the free radio vision of technological egalitarianism and autonomy.

Another important dimension of free radio materiality is the use of free and pirated software for tasks such as audio editing, storage and transmission, and Internet streaming. Free radio activists generally view free software — that is, software produced with a license requiring the distribution of the source code along with the software itself (Kelty 2008) — as a strategic aspect of their commitment to autonomy with respect to technological infrastructure. Radio Autónoma uses its own Linux-based archive and broadcast software, for example, while many free radio activists use free audio-editing software such as Audacity. As Pancho from Radio Revolución explained during an interview, "Capitalism turns everything into a question of profit. Free software breaks this by building community around technology and software."

Free software is widely viewed as a way to reinforce autonomy by breaking dependence on proprietary, corporate-driven software. At the same time, limitations may emerge, particularly with respect to nonproprietary operating systems such as Linux. Sandra, from the Mexico City–based Free Media Network, put it this way: "We agree with the principle of Linux, but it makes me dependent: now I can't edit the video I recorded, and it will take a month to learn." Efficacy is another concern. With respect to audio editing, for example, some activists felt the available free software was inferior to the proprietary alternatives. In these cases, piracy becomes the preferred mode of transgression, particularly given the widespread practice of unregulated media circulation in developing countries such as Mexico (cf. Larkin 2008). Many activists understand piracy as a latent political practice. As Pancho explained, "Piracy is a form of resistance, even if it isn't conscious. . . . We have to continue using, distributing, and pirating proprietary programs and using free software where possible." However, piracy fails to build the autonomous community of technology users that free software does. Piracy and free software thus represent alternative modes of excess and transgression, yet each comes along with its own particular constraints.

Free Radio Aesthetics

Given the diversity among Mexican free radio projects with respect to music, politics, participants, audience, and style, it is difficult to talk about an overarching free radio aesthetics. In particular, there is a significant gap between indigenous free radios—which tend to emphasize cultural identity, language, traditional music, and community politics and relations—and the urban, youth-oriented free radios that exhibit a more alternative, eclectic, and self-consciously rebellious style. The former approximate the kind of content and approach that characterize the indigenous, aboriginal, and other community radios that have drawn attention by anthropologists, particularly with respect to themes such as cultural identity and activism, diasporic relations, and kinship ties (Buddle 2008; Fisher 2009; Kunreuther 2006; O'Connor 2006). The latter are more in line with the countercultural free radio traditions of Europe, North America, and other Latin American urban centers (Downing 2001; Soley 1999; Urla 1997). However, this distinction should not be exaggerated; indigenous free radios in Mexico, like their counterparts elsewhere (O'Connor 1990, 2004; Murillo 2008), have cultivated a strong culture and discourse of resistance, while urban free radios also provide spaces for expressing culture and identity.

Still, it is among urban free radios where a more freewheeling, excessive style is most apparent. Here autonomy means, in part, the freedom to play different, often wildly divergent genres—punk, hip hop, hard core, *electronica*, reggae, folk, alternative rock (almost always noncommercial, and with a strong preference for fusion styles)—to mix radical politics with music and cultural commentary, to exhibit a playful, nonscripted, often irreverent mode of speech, and, above all, to break out of the highly regimented formats of commercial radio. There is also an emphasis on nonstructured interactive communicational styles, often with background sounds and rhythms, announcers talking over one another, frequent voice-overs, and audios and promos mixing heterogeneous voices, sounds, and musical clips.

The idea of "lift-up-over sounding" employed by Steven Feld (1998) provides a useful metaphor for grasping the unique aesthetic quality of free radio. Lift-up-over sounding is characterized by continuous layers, sequential but not linear; nongapped multiple presences and densities; overlapping chunks without internal breaks; and a spiraling, arching motion tumbling slightly forward, thinning and thickening back again (78–79). Given the popularity of politically conscious hip-hop and the proliferation of fusion and *electronica* beats, this cut 'n' mix style is highly popular at free radios such as Radio Autónoma. Lift-up-over sounding is not restricted to music; it also encompasses the "egalitarian interactional style" (83) that is so appealing to free radio hosts.

The program *Mezclando Sonidos* from Radio Autónoma provides a nice illustration of these aesthetic qualities. The show, hosted by members of a local radical band that plays a fusion of hip-hop, reggae, and world beat, features a complex amalgam of music, live performances, political commentary, and recorded tracks. The overall style is lively, creative, eclectic, and self-consciously rebellious, involving the kind of mixing, blending, and constant voice-over reflected in the idea lift-up-over sounding. For example, one particular *Mezclando Sonidos* episode during my time in the field combined analysis of the ten-year anniversary of the 1999 UNAM strike, which successfully defeated a plan to begin charging tuition (which striking students saw as the start of privatization), with a live studio performance by a percussion troupe, discussion of West African drumming, recorded music, and political audios. The show began with a track mixing techno, reggae, and drum 'n' bass, interrupted by a live voice-over: "104.1, *Mezclando Sonidos* starts now!" As the song continued, live percussion kicked in, and the hosts conducted sound tests: "*Sí, sí, sí.*" That kicked off a round of high-energy dialogue with drumming in the background:

TRUCHA: Welcome to *Mezclando Sonidos*! We're starting late, but now we're ready to go. We're in the mood to party tonight because we have some great kids here with us—

VIENTO [*interrupts with a yelp*]: Yoo, yoo, hey, guys!

BAND MEMBER: What's going on, guys, yee, hee, hee! [*The DJs and two band members then let out a collective primal scream.*]

TRUCHA: These guys are gonna accompany us tonight. They're gonna share their vibrations. We also have some issues to discuss. We're gonna talk about the ten-year anniversary of the strike. . . .

VIENTO: That's right, man; we're also gonna be playing some tunes with the band and talking to them and also talking a little about the origin of their drums. . . .

TRUCHA: They also have some lyrics [*Viento starts screaming again in the background*: "ha, ha, roo, roo, ratata"]: their urban poetry, their rap. Stay with us. We're gonna start at any moment. . . .

LEO [*who just arrived, with the drummers in the background*]: Hey, *sí, sí,* greetings to everyone celebrating the strike against the privatization of education. Greetings to everyone at the concert. Want to let everyone know there were two marches today . . .

Leo continues to discuss the strike, as one of the drummers starts to rap about war and violence. Trucha then goes into a segment about the history of African drums, with the band playing in the background. The rest of the program continues in the same vein: fusion tracks mixed with live percussion and rapping, discussion of the sociocultural context of drumming along with analysis of the student strike (always with faint music and drum beats in the background), occasional political audios, and frequent hollering. The program is chaotic, reflecting a self-consciously employed lift-up-over aesthetics, including a creative mix of content, genres, and musical/verbal styles, with frequent dubs, voice-overs, interruptions, and rapid-fire informal interactions.

The emphasis on expression unconstrained by commercial strictures and intentionally distinct from the styles or genres believed to constitute mainstream or regulated broadcast media also resonates with rural indigenous free media. Here the musical tastes are different, less oriented toward urban youth and more directed toward traditional indigenous sounds, but a similar logic of expression is at work. Although indigenous free radios are not as freewheeling as their urban counterparts, they provide critical spaces beyond the bounds of commercial and *indigenista* radio where local community members can speak their own language; play their own music; talk about traditional culture and medicine; send greetings to friends and family in the community, other parts of Mexico, and the United States; or request their favorite songs. These are immediate forms of expression by people who lack a voice in other media outlets (cf. Salazar 2009).

Other free radio activists stressed the more political dimension of free radio aesthetics. For them, free radio style is about unrestricted freedom of political expression, giving voice to popular struggles, and transcending the problematic notion of objectivity. When I asked Pancho, from Radio Revolución, how he would characterize free radio aesthetics, he replied, "We try to highlight our anticapitalist social movements. There is great diversity: free radios in Oaxaca or Veracruz play the music from their communities; we play more urban music. There is a different worldview. But we are all highlighting grassroots struggles." Urban and rural free radios thus aspire to exceed established political, cultural, and stylistic bounds and to highlight voices that are otherwise silenced within the mainstream commercial media. However, it is important to point out that although the enhanced circulation of marginalized voices may expand the sphere of democratic communication, it does not *necessarily* lead to more democratic social relations.

There are also important limitations on free radio expression, including the self-imposed guidelines, both formal and informal, prevailing at most Mexican free radio stations. Radio Autónoma, for its part, had internally agreed upon rules against speech that could be construed as sexist, racist, inciting violence, or hateful in any way. It proved difficult, however, to interpret when rules had been violated or what to do in the case of infringement. For example, El Zapo, of another free radio project, Radio Subversión, used to have a program at Radio Autónoma, but he and his collective left the radio after one of them was accused of using sexist language on the air. El Zapo described the situation in this way: "We had a problem with our friend because he used to say crazy things. They called him a misogynist, but that was unfair. He just says things as they come. . . . When we got to the studio one day, there were some folks from the collective, and they wanted to throw our friend out. But we said, 'No, he's part of our collective. If he goes, we all go.'" Free radio expression is excessive and unbounded, but only to a point—reflecting the limits of the ideal of autonomy espoused by free radio activists. Norms constrain the kinds of things that can be said, while there are often implicit guidelines with respect to style, as different radios are known for distinct musical, political, and aesthetic tastes. In this sense, Zapo's friend's behavior reflected the excessiveness of free radio expression, yet it was also a sign of the dangers of communicative excess.

Legality, Excess, and Transgression

Perhaps the most transgressive dimension of free radio is the unlicensed use of an FM frequency.[7] There are many reasons for the decision to broadcast without a permit, including practical considerations such as the high cost of acquiring the approved equipment, the difficulty of meeting the stringent technical guidelines, the need to create a formal civil society association, and the sheer difficulty of winning approval for a broadcast permit. Although the Secretary of Communications and Transportation (SCT) issued a string of permits in the mid-2000s to a series of formerly free radios that had begun to work with AMARC, many of them indigenous, Mexico still has one of the most restrictive media environments in the world (Calleja and Solís 2007).

For many Mexican free radios, however, the decision to broadcast without a permit is an expressly political act linked to their commitment to a broader politics of autonomy. Whereas the radios associated with AMARC are dedicated to the promotion of "communication rights" via the legalization and proliferation of community radios, the free radio movement encourages "communicational autonomy" by taking the airwaves through illegal broadcasts. In this sense, communicational autonomy is based on an explicit policy of transgressing the laws, practices, and institutions of the state. For many free radios, illegality is seen as central to a wider strategy of resisting the neoliberal state's role as a guarantor of rights (cf. Speed 2008).[8]

Many free radios activists view their commitment to unlicensed broadcasting in precisely such terms. Illegality is seen as a source of political identity and an important tool of liberation. When I asked Pancho from Radio Revolución about the significance of illegality, he replied,

> The laws in Mexico are constructed and administered by those who have economic and political power. . . . In this country, radios can only be managed by businesses. . . . The law requires that you have a certain amount of resources to broadcast. We say . . . the air belongs to everyone, like the land and water. . . . If we are going to build another world, we have to do it now without respecting the laws that benefit a certain class. As Magón said, to be a revolutionary means being an illegal because whoever abides by the law is just a protester.[9]

For Pancho, the role of a free radio is not simply to provide a space for free expression but also to serve as a tool for revolutionary transformation, which is not possible within the confines of the law. Specifically, the goal is to appropriate and collectively manage the air, along with other resources such as the land and water, for the benefit of the community. On this view, illegality is a political practice intricately tied to the construction of autonomy beyond the market and state.

This discourse of the airwaves as a communal resource to be appropriated and managed collectively in excess of the regulatory techniques and apparatus of the state is also widespread among indigenous free radios, particularly those linked to the "Other Campaign." As Ricardo, from Radio Mundo, an indigenous free radio in the hills of the Costa Chica in Guerrero, put it, "The airspace above is also part of the territory of a *pueblo*, and we as a *pueblo* have decided to use the airwaves to speak, to transmit our voice through our frequency." This is a kind of subversive twist on the international law principle that the airspace above a territory is part of that territory and is thus subject to state regulation. The claim to autonomous control of the airwaves is thus constructed as analogous to the broader claim for autonomous control of the community's physical territory, both of which are seen as exceeding claims of state sovereignty.

Indigenous radios such as Radio Mundo further base this claim in what they perceive to be the rights of indigenous people encoded in international treaties and in Mexico in the San Andrés Accords, signed by the Zapatistas and the Mexican government yet never implemented by the latter (Speed 2008). Nonetheless, urban free radios make a similar claim about their right to collectively use the airwaves, much like any natural resource. The major limitation here, beyond the real and perceived omnipresent threat of state repression, is that the airwaves, like physical territory, are not in unlimited supply, and without regulation, they would become saturated by signal interference, particularly in the major cities. Against the argument for state regulation, however, free radio activists hold that community-based radios should be able to autonomously coordinate their signals without the need for intervention by an external authority. Both rural-indigenous and urban free radios express the broader logic of an ideal autonomy with respect to control of territory, law making, and self-regulation.

However, there are important differences between indigenous free radios and their urban counterparts with respect to the conception of illegality as political practice. This can be seen in Radio Mundo's response to an offer of a permit by the Mexican government following the government's failed effort to physically dismantle the radio. Two hours into an assembly of free radios at Radio Mundo's fourth-anniversary celebration, which I attended along with dozens of Mexico City–based activists, Miguel, from the radio's coordinating committee, read the following:

> Given that for many years we have tried to become an integral part of our country, to be recognized as an indigenous people, yes, we would like a permit. . . . We would like it as part of the recognition of our collective rights. . . . [But] as long as the conditions do not exist in this country [for] a full recognition of our rights, we are going to continue broadcasting . . . with the permission of our people.

This text is extremely ambiguous, lacking a clear rejection of the *idea* of a permit, in contrast to the more oppositional stance of many urban free radio activists. For the latter, breaking the law is an end in itself, an expression of autonomy that directly challenges the state, whereas for indigenous radio stations such as Radio Mundo, illegality is a means to a related yet different goal: full recognition of indigenous autonomy and rights *within* a transformed pluricultural state.

In this sense, Radio Mundo does not view itself as engaged in illegal activity, as Ricardo explains: "The radio is not breaking any laws. Why? Because we are transmitting our voice on the airwaves. . . This is a recognized part of our rights as indigenous people. We are not harming anyone; we are simply speaking in our own language to strengthen our identity as an indigenous people." Ricardo is referring to a higher law and a set of "natural" rights that are prior to and exceed the state (Speed 2008). Radio Mundo is struggling together with a larger indigenous movement for a reconfiguration of the state along pluricultural lines so that the collective rights and autonomy of indigenous peoples will be fully recognized. There is nothing inherently wrong with a permit, but it would have to be issued from a state that is viewed as legitimate, and it would have to allow for a full expression of autonomy. Radio Mundo posits a sphere of autonomous authority transcending the state, as do its urban free radio counterparts, who reject the very idea of the state and its right to issue permits. In both cases, unlicensed broadcasting represents a communal politics of excess.

This same transgression provokes a key external constraint to free radio practice reflected in the legal and repressive apparatus of the state itself. For many practitioners, particularly those who perceive autonomy as *necessarily* in opposition to the law and the state, free radio autonomy *requires* illegality. Autonomy in this sense *intends* to provoke and contest the authority of the state to police its own boundaries and laws as a way to articulate alternative definitions of politics, citizenship, and belonging. In doing so, however, such provocations may endanger the very project of autonomous free radio by unleashing the full force of repression and co-optation on the part of the state, reflecting a key contradiction of free radio practice.

For example, the Mexican state had attempted to close down Radio Mundo during a violent raid meant to arrest participants and seize the transmitter. It was the rapid, determined response by community members that prevented the arrests and seizures. Only after the failed raid did the Mexican government offer a legal permit as an alternative strategy of bringing the radio under the direct control of the state. Beyond the question of state legitimacy, Radio Mundo also rejected the permit due to the associated regulations that effectively discipline neoliberal subjects with respect to particular kinds of citizenship and participation (cf. Ong 2003; Postero 2006; Speed 2008). These include requirements, many of which are beyond the financial reach of grassroots communities and/or contradict the idea and practice of autonomy, such as the creation of a civil society association, the use of authorized equipment, and the broadcast of certain programming including campaign ads, the national hour, and the national anthem.

Whereas transmitting without a permit had previously been treated as a civil violation, the Mexican state has recently begun to prosecute unlicensed radio broadcasters for violating "national patrimony," a federal offense that carries heavy fines and jail sentences. The Mexican state is thus beginning to criminalize free radio to justify raids and crackdowns, while holding out the olive branch of legal permits—a form of neoliberal governmentality that shapes political subjects in particular ways—to projects that have been able to resist repression. The main limitation is that many free radios lack either the capacity or the level of community support needed to effectively resist state crackdowns. It was in this context that many formerly free indigenous radios decided to seek legal permits. The most long-lasting free radio projects, such as Radio Mundo or Radio Autónoma, have depended on the support of the community, in the former case, and the protection afforded by the autonomous status of the wider university from which the radio broadcasts, in the latter. Many other free radios have been shut down, have decided to seek legal status, or have turned to Internet transmissions. Meanwhile, free radios that have been able to continue broadcasting on the air have been forced to expend increasing time and resources on security issues and less on developing their projects of autonomous expression.

Conclusion

This chapter has explored the dynamics of autonomy within Mexican free radios in terms of three areas of concern to the anthropology of radio and media anthropology: technology, aesthetics, and state regulation. I have suggested that autonomy, as an ideal, does not mean complete separation from dominant institutional spheres. Rather, as Cornelius Castoriadis (1991) maintains, autonomy has more to do with the generation of new social practices, subjects, and representations that always exist in relation to received institutional boundaries. It is in this sense that autonomy as a set of guiding values and subjectivities among free radio activists can be viewed as a politics of excess and transgression. However, the notion of autonomy deployed in free radio practice also entails constraints. This involves both self-imposed limits and complex dynamics of power that surround the stations, which we saw in the conflicts over style and aesthetics at Radio Autónoma. There are also important external limitations, including periodic technological breakdowns or the strategies of co-optation and repression enacted by the state. In the context of free radio practice, autonomy, as I have argued, thus involves a complex interplay between the politics of excess and constraint.

Given the critical role of the media in producing and circulating representations of social, cultural, and political reality, free media are seen as a key dimension of the wider project of autonomy. On the one hand, like other forms of alternative media, free radio provides a space for informing about, analyzing, and communicating movements for autonomy, such as the Zapatista struggle in Chiapas, the popular rebellion in Oaxaca, or the UNAM strike in Mexico City. Free radios have played key roles as command and control centers during conflicts (Stephen, chap. 6 in this volume), as well as spaces for representing and circulating those struggles to a wider audience. On the other hand, free radio projects also represent concrete projects for realizing local visions of autonomy in their own right, small-scale experiments in generating new cultural practices, social relations, and institutional forms that attempt to move beyond dominant institutional spheres.

At the same time, free radio also raises issues that are relevant to the anthropology of radio and media anthropology. A key theme has to do with the use and appropriation of new media and digital technologies. The emphasis on technological autonomy among free radio activists, albeit contradictory, points to some interesting dynamics with respect to emerging patterns of interaction between subjects and new technologies. For example, given the emphasis on collaborative organization and opposition to formal hierarchies and divisions of labor within many Mexican free radios, all participants are expected to become proficient in the operation of the radio's technological infrastructure. However, many participants remain dependent on their more technologically savvy counterparts, while technological breakdown is common with older, recycled, or pirated systems. Free radio technical infrastructures thus exceed the bounds of professional corporate systems, yet they pose significant limitations in terms of their operation, their quality, and the reproduction of hierarchies of knowledge and expertise.

Another relevant domain of inquiry with respect to media anthropology has to do with aesthetics and style, where free radio terrains involve a tension between the drive to transcend the bounds of commercial and licensed public radio formats and the reinscription of alternative constraints. Both rural-indigenous and urban free radios emphasize distinct norms of expression, interactive, nonprofessional communication, and the foregrounding of traditionally marginalized "everyday" voices. The eclectic, freewheeling, "lift-up-over" aesthetics of urban free radios, in particular, combines diverse sounds and voices while interspersing music, news, and commentary. However, free radio styles are limited by internal codes, cultural particularities, and stylistic conventions, often giving rise to internal tensions that problematize the universal applicability of the category itself.

A final contribution of free radio to the anthropology of radio and media anthropology more broadly has to do with the political implications of radio broadcasting for subaltern groups. Much of the literature on indigenous media emphasizes the democratizing effect of the production and inclusion of marginalized images and voices within dominant and alternative media spheres, reflecting an underlying liberal bias. Free radio shifts the focus from the simple expansion of democratic public spheres to the issue of who controls and manages the underlying technologies, infrastructures, and resources on which media production and transmission are based. As we have seen, for many free radio activists, unlicensed broadcasting is a part of a wider social project that views the airwaves as a common resource to be managed collectively like the land or the water. However, whereas for many urban free radio activists, illegality is seen as a critical dimension of their opposition to the state, many indigenous free radio activists have a more complex position, viewing unlicensed broadcasting as a legitimate form of social, cultural, and political expression authorized by the community and enshrined in international accords. Nevertheless, both rural-indigenous and urban free radios intentionally exceed the regulatory bounds of the state, provoking state responses ranging from efforts to legalize free radios in order to produce acceptable modes of neoliberal participation to direct, sometimes violent repression.

In light of the preceding analysis, what can we make of the future prospects for free radio in Mexico? On one level, the situation looks grim, given the growing criminalization of free radio, on the one hand, and the increasing willingness of existing free radio projects, particularly in the most vulnerable urban areas and indigenous communities, to enter into a process of legalization, on the other. Whether or not a critical mass of free radios will be able to survive in the current climate of repression remains to be seen. On another level, though, the continued strength and vitality of long-running projects such as Radio Autónoma, Radio Revolución, and Radio Mundo suggests that a small number of free radios with strong institutional cover and/ or community support may be able to withstand the current onslaught. Such projects continue to circulate and communicate diverse grassroots struggles in Mexico and abroad, while serving as autonomous laboratories for the generation of new sociohistorical practices, representations, and forms. At the same time, the politics of excess tell us as much about the dominant institutional orders transcended as about the alternatives themselves. In this sense, free radios and other autonomous media shine a light on the increasing commercialization and consolidation of mass-media spheres in an age of neoliberal globalization, signaling the need for alternative regulatory frameworks to ensure space for innovative, free-form, politically engaged, and truly community-based media.

NOTES

1. I have used pseudonyms to protect the anonymity of particular free radio projects, except for historical passages when I provide information that is publicly available.
2. The names of individuals that appear in this chapter are pseudonyms as well, replacing the nicknames used by most free radio and other radical activists in Mexico.
3. This chapter is based on fourteen months of ethnographic research, funded, in part, by a postdoctoral research grant from the National Autonomous University of Mexico from September 1, 2008, to August 31, 2009 (the grant was administered by the Coordinator of Humanities, and I was affiliated with the Institute for Social Research).
4. *Lobo*, meaning "wolf," is a pseudonym for my own nickname at the radio.
5. The Other Campaign is an alliance of anticapitalist movements in Mexico struggling for autonomy. It was convened by the Zapatistas as an alternative to the electoral Left and the PRD's candidate, Manuel López Obrador, during the 2006 presidential campaign.
6. On the contrary, the term *autonomy* comes from the root *autos-nomos*: to give oneself laws (Castoriadis 1991, 164).
7. In Mexico, this means broadcasting without a *permiso* (permit) from the Federal Commission of Telecommunications (COFETEL) and formerly from the Secretary of Communications and Transportation (SCT). Commercial broadcasters are licensed through a *concesión* (concession), which allows them to sell commercial air time, which is prohibited for radios operating with a permit (Soria Arenas 2007, 20–35).
8. In much recent anthropological writing (see, for example, De Genova 2002, 2003), illegality is conceived in Foucauldian terms as a kind of excess produced by the state to construct certain groups and practices as criminal, delinquent, or deviant. In contrast, for Heyman and Smart (1999), illegality should also be seen as "an option, a

resource, that diverse groups use at varied times" (13; see also De Genova 2002, 430). In this sense, illegality can be viewed as a tool of resistance actively appropriated by grassroots actors struggling for autonomy and social justice.

9. Pancho is referring here to Ricardo Flores Magón, the Mexican anarchist and revolutionary who was one of the major intellectuals of the Mexican Revolution.

REFERENCES

Buddle, Kathleen. 2008. Transistor resistors. In *Global indigenous media*, edited by Pamela Wilson and Michelle Stewart, 128–144. Durham: Duke University Press.

Calleja, Aleida, and Beatriz Solís. 2007. *Con permiso*. Mexico City: Fundación Freidrich Ebert–México.

Castoriadis, Cornelius. 1987. *The imaginary institution of society*. Cambridge: MIT Press.

——. 1991. *Philosophy, politics, autonomy*. Oxford: Oxford University Press.

De Genova, Nicholas. 2002. Migrant "illegality" and deportability in everyday life. *Annual Review of Anthropology* 31:419–447.

——. 2003. *Working the boundaries*. Durham: Duke University Press.

Downing, John D. H. 2001. *Radical media*. Thousand Oaks, CA: Sage.

Feld, Steven. 1988. Aesthetics as iconicity of style, or "lift-up-over sounding." *Yearbook for Traditional Music* 20:74–113.

Fisher, Daniel. 2009. Mediating kinship: Country, family and radio in northern Australia. *Cultural Anthropology* 24 (2): 280–312.

Heyman, Josiah McC., and Alan Smart. 1999. States and illegal practices. In *States and illegal practices*, edited by Josiah McC. Heyman, 1–24. Oxford, UK: Berg.

Kelty, Christopher. 2008. *Two bits*. Durham: Duke University Press.

Kunreuther, Laura. 2006. Technologies of the voice. *Cultural Anthropology* 21 (3): 323–353.

Larkin, Brian. 2008. *Signal and noise*. Durham: Duke University Press.

Murillo, Mario A. 2008. Weaving a communication quilt in Colombia. In *Global indigenous media*, edited by Pamela Wilson and Michelle Stewart, 145–159. Durham: Duke University Press.

O'Connor, Alan. 1990. The minders' radio stations in Bolivia. *Journal of Communication* 40 (1): 102–110.

——. 2004. *Community radio in Bolivia*. Lewiston, NY: Edwin Mellen.

——, ed. 2006. *The voice of the mountains*. Lanham, MD: University Press of America.

Ong, Aihwa. 2003. *Buddha is hiding*. Berkeley: University of California Press.

Postero, Nancy. 2006. *Now we are citizens*. Stanford: Stanford University Press.

Salazar, Juan Francisco. 2009. Self-determination in practice: The critical making of indigenous media. *Development in Practice* 19 (4–5): 504–513.

Soley, Lawrence. 1999. *Free radio*. Boulder, CO: Westview.

Soria Arenas, Estrella C. 2007. Las radios libres en la Ciudad de Mexico. Honors thesis, National Autonomous University of Mexico.

Speed, Shannon. 2008. *Rights in rebellion*. Stanford: Stanford University Press.

Spitulnik, Debra. 1998–1999. Mediated modernities. *Visual Anthropology Review* 14 (2): 63–84.

——. 2002. Mobile machines and fluid audiences. In *Media worlds*, edited by Faye D. Ginsburg, Lila Abu-Lughod, and Brian Larkin, 337–354. Berkeley: University of California Press.

Sundaram, Ravi. 1999. Recycling modernity. *Third Text* 47:59–65.

Tacchi, Jo. 2002. Radio texture. In *The anthropology of media*, edited by Kelly Askew and Richard R. Wilk, 241–257. Malden, MA: Blackwell.

Urla, Jacqueline. 1997. Outlaw language. In *The politics of culture in the shadow of capital*, edited by Lisa Lowe and David Lloyd, 280–300. Durham: Duke University Press.

Weidman, Amanda. 2003. Guru and gramophone. *Public Culture* 15 (3): 453–476.

9

"Foreign Voices"

Multicultural Broadcasting and Immigrant Representation at Germany's Radio MultiKulti

KIRA KOSNICK

In the wake of labor migration that brought large numbers of migrants from the Mediterranean region to Germany during the 1960s and '70s, radio broadcasting emerged as the most important media technology to supply so-called guest workers with media contents in their native languages. During a period in which the development of information and communication technology did not yet allow for the transnational circulation of media contents, German public service broadcasters developed special foreign-language radio programs to service labor migrants as both orientation help and a "bridge to home" (Kosnick 2000). Over time, the purpose of this programming changed: with labor migration increasingly recognized as an immigration process rather than a temporary sojourn, public service broadcasters sought to provide integration-oriented programs and developed new formats to encourage "intercultural dialogue" and promote tolerance among a nonimmigrant German target audience. By the early 1990s, the paradigm of multiculturalism was increasingly significant for thinking about ethnic minorities' access to a mass-mediated public sphere (Kosnick 2007). The Berlin-based public service radio station Radio MultiKulti, opened in 1994 in response to an upsurge of racist violence in Germany, was the most ambitious effort to translate multiculturalist integration aims into concrete radio programming. Between 1994 and 2008, the station provided daytime German-language content, switching in the late afternoon to specialized foreign-language programs which targeted the city's largest immigrant minorities in their native languages. Claiming to "give a voice" to immigrant minorities rather than just targeting them as an audience, the station presents a case study in a politics of aural representation that is both based on and stabilizes multiculturalist integration paradigms. The analysis of radio programming and production reveals the deeper layers of the claims to minority empowerment in the public sphere, as migrant voices are shown to be carefully constructed in order to conform to majority expectations.

This chapter presents ethnographic material gathered in the context of working as an intern and freelance journalist at Radio MultiKulti in the course of fieldwork that was carried out between 1998 and 2000.[1] Driven by a mission to give a voice to ethnic minorities on its airwaves, the station has had to face numerous problems associated with rendering ethnocultural diversity audible on its airwaves. Contrasting the station's claims to inclusiveness with the day-to-day processes of constructing audible representations of ethnic difference, the chapter demonstrates the strengths of participant observation in being able to reveal the actual power dynamics that inform practices of audio representation. Aspects such as Radio MultiKulti's use of accents in its German-language programs in order to denote a "foreign view," questions of editorial control in the backrooms, and the construction of an imagined "native" target audience are analyzed and shown to practically undermine the station's claims to give a voice to immigrants and to contribute to minority empowerment.

It is my fourth week of working as an intern for Radio MultiKulti, and one of the editors for the German-language programming has given me an assignment typically given to newcomers: go out and do a quick survey, asking "young ethnic Berliners" about the Loveparade and what it means to them. What do young people have to say about the Loveparade in Berlin, an event that (at the time) moves millions of them to dance on the streets to earsplitting techno music? "Get some foreign [*ausländische*] voices," the editor tells me. My piece is to be run as a trailer in the morning program, with the moderator giving more specific information about the parade. The voices in my trailer have to speak for themselves; no names or special context will be given that could indicate immigrant origin and the like. So, the editor says, "get some accents!"

I spend a hot summer day out on the streets with my microphone. First, I go to a neighborhood in Wedding, an inner-city district with a high percentage of Turkish residents. I walk up to young people on the street whom I identify as potentially "ethnic," of immigrant background based on their looks, and I ask in German, "What do you think of the Loveparade? Will you go?" Most are eager to answer and have a lot to say. It is only after having talked to about five people that I come to realize my predicament: who on earth will identify their authentic and appropriate "ethnic difference," given that almost all the answers have been produced in the local Berlin dialect? Second- and third-generation migrants do not, of course, speak German with a foreign accent. I decide to shelve the project for the day and talk it over with the editor. When I report back on my dilemma the following day, she does not respond immediately but just looks at me with an expression of slight annoyance and amusement. Then she offers a single piece of advice: "But you do know what it is that we're looking for, don't you? So just go get it." I am dismissed and take to the streets once more.

I get lucky with a few people in front of a shopping center, though they are not particularly young. Opinions about the Loveparade are forthcoming in accented voices. Not enough, though. Eventually, I end up in front of the language-instruction center in my own neighborhood, where a friend of mine is attending a "German for foreigners" course. During breaks, the students assemble to smoke in front of the building. There is no danger of not finding accents there, and my friend and her classmates are eager to help me out. The problem is, most of the students are tourists rather than immigrants, and thus not exactly the people the trailer is claiming to represent. But the trailer needs to get done, and so I collect a beautiful-sounding assortment of accents and statements ranging from "I hate the whole thing" to "oh, yes, I'll definitely go," just as the editor has requested, in the interest of "balanced objectivity." My friend wants to be included: after all, being young and Italian and planning to stay in the city, she actually qualifies! I hand her the microphone, and she rehearses a sentence she herself has come up with: "Oh, no, I don't like the music at the Loveparade. I'd much rather listen to Radio MultiKulti!" Eventually, she has a laughing fit. In the afternoon, I return to the station and cut the trailer, including her statement and subsequent laughter at the very end. One and a half minutes. I inform the editor of where it has been saved in the database and expect to hear no more about it. The next day, though, I receive praise: the editors had really liked it, especially the laughter at the end.

Learning to produce contributions for the German-language programs of Radio MultiKulti involved internalizing a certain set of standards that made MultiKulti both similar and different with regard to other public service stations under the common roof of the public service corporation Rundfunk Berlin-Brandenburg (RBB). The ways in which an assignment was composed —how much interview material and sound to use; how to give background information, choose the right statements, and come to a particular conclusion—were quite similar across different stations. In fact, Radio MultiKulti entered its own productions into a database shared by all public service stations in Germany, and productions were often picked up and rebroadcast by other stations. The difference lies in the "multicultural" orientation of the station, the very reason and justification for its existence.

"We Speak with an Accent"

Radio programming entails quite distinctive challenges for the production of identifiably "multicultural" broadcasts. As an audio medium, radio cannot rely on visual appearances that are usually central to processes of categorization along ethnic and racial stereotypes. There are no images which could function as indicators of ethnic belonging in the context of radio broadcasting, and so language has to play a central role in signaling ethnic otherness. "We speak with an accent" was a prominent slogan the station used in its promotional material (Vertovec 1996).

Radio MultiKulti not only wanted to represent immigrants in the sense of broadcasting *about* them; the station claimed also to give them a voice by involving them directly in production. And it unquestionably did so as far as the foreign-language programs were concerned: the editorial and journalistic staff of all the different foreign-language programs was entirely composed of immigrants. However, these programs targeted only specific immigrant groups in the city and were not directly tied into the second mission of the station, which was to contribute to intercultural understanding among *all* inhabitants of the city. German was the lingua franca of the station, and necessarily so, given that MultiKulti wanted to counter racist and xenophobic attitudes among the German nonimmigrant population. The potential to

counter such attitudes was a central legitimizing factor in the political decision to establish the station in the first place and was continuously mobilized
in the station's ultimately futile efforts to secure permanent funding.

It was after the racist murders in the cities of Solingen and Mölln in 1993
that the often-voiced demand for multicultural broadcasting finally found
sufficient political support in the Berlin state parliament. A station that
could serve as "a forum of integration and communication among ethnic
minorities and Germans in the city" (Holler 1997, 15) was seen as an appropriate response to increasing anti-immigrant sentiments and racist violence.
"Speaking with an accent" contains an important claim which pertains to
the nature of such intercultural dialogue: At MultiKulti, immigrants were
to present their own views on all kinds of topics, instead of just being the
topic of discussion themselves. The first director of the station, Friedrich
Voß, highlighted the aim as a central aspect of MultiKulti's broadcasting philosophy: "The magazine parts in the lingua franca German are dedicated to
comprehensive information but also to the idea of integration. Above all, the
program wants to let foreign moderators and commentators have their say,
so that the programmatic stance of a 'different viewing angle' is rendered audible as well" (Voß 1996, 6; author's translation from German). "Speaking
with an accent" thus denotes the entry of immigrants as active participants
into the public domain. MultiKulti not only aimed to reflect multicultural
diversity in the city but wanted to act as a forum of intercultural dialogue.
Challenging the widespread assumption that cultural differences are private
or communal matters, whereas public space should remain the domain of
the majority culture (Rex 1991), MultiKulti wanted to give immigrants a public voice on the airwaves. The "different viewing angle" suggested that the
substance of what was focused on was similar to other public service stations: matters of common and public concern, but now seen and discussed
from a different, "foreign" perspective.

Creating a shared public space in which different ethnic communities are
able to interact, represent themselves, and engage in dialogue was a major
concern of "progressive" western European multiculturalist policies in the
1990s (Frachon and Vargaftig 1995). The public spheres created through public service broadcasting in western European nation-states were always implicitly linked to "a whole way of life" (in Raymond Williams's term) in the
sense of national majority cultures. Giving a voice to immigrants in public
service broadcasts potentially "denaturalizes" the link between public space
and this dominant "way of life." An article on Radio MultiKulti published
in the German UNESCO journal described the benefits for members of the
dominant majority culture in Germany:

> Listeners should learn to relativize their own German standpoint, gain a foreign perspective on themselves and accept that their own attitudes and behavior have only limited importance. The German-language part is produced with the strong participation of foreign, German-speaking staff. . . . This leads to the questioning of judgments and prejudices, and to the acceptance of different perspectives. (N.N. 1995, 177)

It was taken as a given that immigrants will provide a perspective that represents a "different viewing angle" or "foreign view." At Radio MultiKulti, this was rendered audible through the accented voice which inevitably denotes foreignness, approaching the German language and majority culture from elsewhere. The accent—as opposed to "making mistakes," in the sense of grammatical errors, lacking vocabulary, and so on—is a subtle indication of ineradicable difference, one that has come as close to linguistic and cultural mastery as it can but remains always a bit off the mark in its sentence melody and pronunciation of words. Ethnic-minority moderators in the German-language programs of Radio MultiKulti tended to have an excellent command of German, but the preference was for immigrants whose German retains a "foreign flavor," so to speak.[2]

It is instructive to draw a parallel between "unmarked German," German spoken without accent, and the "unmarked ethnicity" that differentiates those who pass as Germans from stereotypical "foreigners" in everyday life contexts. Even though explicitly racialized categories have disappeared from mainstream public discourses since World War II, the general concept of "foreigner" and more recently "migrant" as used in policy discourses and mainstream German media implicitly produces and stabilizes a form of German Whiteness.[3]

Whiteness has been brought forth as an analytical concept and object of study in order to investigate how structural positions of privilege and power between racialized groups are simultaneously constructed and masked (Frankenberg 1993). Noting that the study of "race" had been by and large focused on people of color, scholars have focused on the question of how whiteness could become an implicit norm against which racial "otherness" is represented (Dyer 1993, 1997). In the context of radio broadcasting, racial and ethnic difference cannot be seen; it must be heard. In the absence of visual markers, it was the accent that denotes "marked" ethnic and racial difference on Radio MultiKulti. However, as is to be expected in the course of immigration history, second- and third-generation immigrants are no longer speaking with an accent.[4] It was thus predominantly people who had indeed come from another country, first-generation immigrants, who were mobilized to represent the "multicultural normality" of the city in the broadcasts of MultiKulti.

One reason this was not much of an issue for the station might have been that the term for foreigner (*Ausländer*) was still widely used to describe immigrants and their descendants in Germany. The term, literally referring to people (from) outside the country, functions to exclude immigrants from symbolic belonging to the nation and has increasingly become a racialized category (Mandel 1994; Räthzel 1990; Stolcke 1995). As such, the term now somewhat paradoxically also refers to descendants of particular immigrant groups who in the course of their lives might have never set foot outside Germany. While the descendants of certain immigrant groups become assimilated to the "unmarked" category of majority Germans, other groups remain outside this category. Prior histories of migration, such as the incorporation of eastern Europeans into Prussia and the early German nation-state, have been erased from public memory. The fact that a considerable part of the German population has Polish and other eastern European surnames has for half a century not been taken as an indicator of ethnic difference or "foreignness." The concept of being a foreigner veils the process of racialization that defines certain ethnic groups as inferior "others" and as people who cannot claim symbolic belonging, regardless of their length of residence in the country.

Radio MultiKulti's use of accents to denote a "foreign view" reinforced the problematic functioning of the foreigner concept instead of questioning it. The ethnic-minority viewpoint was a view from outside, a "foreign perspective" which at the same time had to be represented as "normality." As the head of the German-language programming section stated in an interview, "Just to be here, we are changing minds. Just to be on air, just that German listeners are listening to people with an accent and are getting used to it. And they're seeing: hey, it's normal" (Wolfgang Holler, quoted in Vertovec 1996, 22). Getting used to people with an accent refers to the station's effort both to reflect the "normality" of multicultural life in the city where German is spoken with manifold accents and to "normalize foreignness" for German nonimmigrant listeners. But what is it exactly that ethnic-majority listeners were getting used to? The performance of voices with an accent can emphasize that Germany is indeed a country of immigration, a fact that for a long time remained unacknowledged in the country's postwar history. But what it did not reveal was the fact that immigrant groups had been inserted into a racialized system of ethnic classification that is anything but foreign, but is very much an indigenous classificatory process of "differential incorporation" (Smith 1969). Whereas the large-scale migration of about nine million

ethnic Germans from different parts of eastern Europe after the World War
II was not even acknowledged as a migration process in postwar Germany,
the so-called guest workers who were recruited from Mediterranean countries in the late 1950s, as well as their descendants, have until recently been
considered to be foreigners instead of immigrants and thus to be irrevocably
alien (Räthzel 1990). While large parts of the liberal and left political spectrum denounced the much-debated *Ausländerfeindlichkeit* (hostility toward
foreigners) which took increasingly violent forms in the 1990s, the racist implications of considering certain migrants and their descendants perennial
foreigners were ignored. The fact that black Germans up until this day are
routinely asked in interactions with unmarked members of the white majority "where they are from" points to the persistence of racialized othering
that denies them national belonging (see also Oguntoye, Opitz, and Schultz
1986). To maintain that ethnic diversity can best be represented through
"foreign voices" at Radio MultiKulti therefore means to reinforce rather than
interrogate the process of "othering" which turns all racialized ethnic minorities into people who have just crossed the border.

It is only with regard to the German-language productions that the slogan
"We speak with an accent" made sense. In the Turkish-language broadcasts
of Radio MultiKulti, accents were in fact deemed completely inappropriate.
But speaking with an accent did not imply editorial control over program
contents. While about half of the moderators of the German-language programs had immigrant backgrounds, the reality in the editorial backrooms
was radically different. The following section examines how typical contents
of programs came to be produced and under what conditions.

At the time of my research, five of the eight German-language moderators for the crucial time slot from early morning until early afternoon were
of immigrant background. This period is most important for ratings, since
radio cannot compete with television during late afternoons and evenings.
Of the editorial staff, however, only one out of eleven fully employed staff
members had an immigrant background. This ratio had important consequences, since moderators mostly had very little influence over what actually
went on in the course of a program. They presented it, but they did not plan
it. It is the editorial staff that had control over the contents. On the airwaves,
however, moderators appeared to be in charge of the program.

"Giving a voice" to ethnic minorities thus often meant merely to perform
through an accented voice contents that had been decided on by nonethnic
producers. The consequences for the much-acclaimed project of renegotiat-
ing the political culture of the public domain are evident. Represented as a
different viewing angle, the accented voice conveyed the illusion of partici-

pation and dialogue, but it did so only by capitalizing on a particular form of cultural essentialism that equated the accent with a "foreign view" and remained ignorant as to the actual production process of statements. It is tempting to draw a parallel: just as the MultiKulti accent did not challenge the dominant consensus of how German should be spoken—it combined "correct" German with a "foreign flavor"—what immigrant moderators say does not necessarily challenge the dominant political culture of the public domain. Accents can much more easily be normalized than can substantively different perspectives which would denaturalize the dominant political culture, in the sense of revealing its link to a particular imagined national community (Anderson 1983) and thus marking—in the sense of rendering discernable—cultural "Germanness."

It has to be said that the lack of ethnic-minority journalists (as opposed to moderators) was quite early on acknowledged as a problem to be rectified by the station. Radio MultiKulti's management lamented the lack of qualified journalists who could meet the high standards of public service broadcasting. The station therefore aimed to train ethnic-minority journalists, but due to budgetary and institutional constraints, such training was very limited.

Formal Standards

The difficulties of not being able to attract enough foreign colleagues, as the director of the station put it, seem closely related not simply to a lack of so-called foreign journalists in Germany but also to the standards of public service broadcasting that the station was not willing to compromise. Newcomers had to quickly adapt to these standards; they could not challenge them. The standards appeared to be merely formal: knowing how to write a particular kind of prose for a feature, how to conduct interviews and select appropriate statements from it, how to structure a feature and make it "interesting to the audience," and how to record one's composition during the tightly allotted half-hour production time in the studio. Yet these formal requirements also functioned to regulate the "different viewing angles" that the station claimed to introduce, and thus to strongly affect the intended "content" of radio broadcasts.

The nonaccented majority listeners who formed the imagined audience of the German-language programs could not only count on "proper German," though spoken with an accent; they could also count on the features produced by immigrant journalists to comply with the very same standards guiding production in general. While the length of a feature and the balance between interview material and spoken text (within a span of three to three and a half minutes, about half of it allotted to interview material and sounds) might have still left some room for "difference," things got more problematic when it came to the particular "message" of a feature and how it was conveyed. Every manuscript had to pass the desk of an editor, who discussed it with the author and suggested changes before the feature could be produced in the studio. Whether of immigrant background or not, the editor was going to ensure that the manuscript was turned into an appropriate product for a particular program and its audience. When it comes to particular concepts, expressions, and details, apparently formal issues directly affected the content of broadcasts.

The guiding principle in these decisions was that only one idea and main argument can be presented during a feature, in order not to create confusion. Judging the clarity and complexity of arguments, however, implied a firm understanding of who was going to listen to a particular broadcast (non-immigrant Germans) and how these listeners would make sense of it. These assumptions had grave consequences for what needed to be said and what could not be said in a feature production.

Berlin had a number of Turkish theater groups and one exclusively Turkish theater, the Tiyatrom. Once a year, the Tiyatrom organized a festival in which different groups participated, some of them invited from Turkey. The event was advertised locally in both Turkish-language and German media. In the fall of 1998, it included a panel discussion in German on the topic "What kind of Turkish theater does Berlin need?" Radio MultiKulti asked me to cover the event and produce a feature for the following morning. Late at night, I faxed the following manuscript to the editor:

Feature: What Kind of Turkish Theater Does Berlin Need?

Intro for the moderator:
    What kind of Turkish theater does Berlin need? Last night, Turkish theater producers and their guests debated this question at the Tiyatrom theater in Kreuzberg. The panel discussion opened this year's Turkish theater festival, which focuses on the Borderless-Culture program between Berlin and Turkey. Does the city need more theater imports from Turkey or rather Turkish-language theater made in Berlin? The issue was hotly debated. Kira Kosnick was there.

Text:
    "One shouldn't argue like that in front of the Germans," a Turkish woman said to her partner after the event last night. There was general disappointment with the panel discussion, which was meant to debate

new perspectives for a Turkish theater in Berlin. But instead of new perspectives, the panel gave an insight into the conflicts among Turkish theater groups in the city. About one hundred guests had found their way to the Tiyatrom. Many of them were themselves part of the Turkish theater scene, and some did not miss the chance to criticize it severely.

Sound bite: (27 Sec.)

"It is really important for me to have at least some kind of theater here that we can call Turkish, but it needs to have its own voice. I want to state very clearly that we do not have such a theater right now. That is a fact. This theater [the Tiyatrom] does not have its own voice. It also doesn't have any perspective." (Tape 2, 4)

Text:

In the tumult that ensued, the speaker did not have a chance to elaborate on what could be the voice of Turkish theater in Berlin. The actor Ilse Scheer, who moderated the discussion, announced a break for tempers to cool off. Other panel participants included Barbara Esser from the Senate Administration, İsmail Koşan from the Green Party, and Joachim Preuss, theater expert from the SFB. The Turkish theater world was represented by Metin Tekin, Yüksel Yolcu, and Yalçın Baykul, directors of different theater groups in the city. But the panel did not have much to offer on the issue of voice. Instead, it was the audience which tried to describe what kind of Turkish theater is needed in Berlin.

Sound bite: (28 Sec.)

"Turkish theater and Turkish-language theater, these are two completely different things. The second of course includes the first. But it is a lot more. Turkish-language theater is theater in general. In the Turkish language. I want to be able to also see Brecht in Turkish in Berlin. I don't want an ethno-theater." (Tape 2, 2)

Text:

But what the needs of a Turkish audience in Berlin might actually be remained an open question. Instead, professionalism and money was at issue in the debate. Many charged that the local Turkish theater scene is dominated by amateurs who have managed to monopolize much-coveted funding from the Berlin Senate. Thus, all of the local producers came under attack. Only one of the producers present was met with approval by the audience, and he was flown in from Turkey. Müşfik Kenter will present his famous work on the poet Orhan Veli this coming Friday and Saturday. Ethno-theater yes or no, the Berlin audience needs to have access to quality theater productions from Turkey—this was the one fact that every-body was able to agree upon.

Soundtrack from Müşfik Kenter's work:
   "Ben Orhan Veliyim . . ."

For the moderator:
   The Turkish theater festival continues with German and Turkish contri-butions until the first of October at different locations throughout the city.

The manuscript moves uneasily between the topic the MultiKulti editors had been interested in—the question of whether Turkish theater should be ethno-theater—and the actual debate that had taken place. This debate was also interesting, but it addressed a very different issue, namely, the competi-tion among different Turkish theater groups and their relationship to Ger-man funding agencies and institutions. To a Turkish-German audience, this is an issue of great importance, since the question of how public funds ex-plicitly designated for "ethnic" purposes can be mobilized for competing cul-tural and social projects is relevant to other realms as well. The discussion also revealed that the German funding structure was directly involved in shaping what kind of Turkish theater could and should exist in the city. But for the MultiKulti editor, the "infighting" of Turkish theater groups was not something that could be turned into anything close to the expected focus of the feature. As we talked on the phone late that night, after I had written the manuscript and faxed it, she decided to cancel the feature. The issue was too complex, presupposing too much knowledge of the lines of conflict in the Turkish theater world and its implication in German funding schemes, lead-ing away from the artistic question of what Turkish theater in Berlin should look like.

In a sense, the editor's conclusion was similar to what the Turkish woman, a friend of mine and herself an actor, had said to her partner after the de-bate: one should not argue like that in front of the Germans. Asking her what she meant by that statement, she explained that the podium discussion had been an opportunity for Turkish theater groups to present themselves to a German audience in a positive light, given the presence of many journal-ists working for German media in the audience, and to voice shared con-cerns instead of revealing conflicts and saying bad things about each other. For the German editor of MultiKulti, there was simply nothing to report on: the expected discussion had not really taken place. People fighting over public funds was not what the audience expected and wanted to hear about with regard to Turkish theater in Berlin, she felt. To explain how and why the discussion had taken a different turn would have introduced too much "irrelevant" information.

Beyond the obvious editorial decision about what kinds of topics should be addressed in a feature, complexity and clarity functioned as standards that influenced content in more subtle ways. Linked to the needs and interests of a particular imagined audience—which might not even know that Turkish theater exists in Berlin—these standards were more than formal ones, and all the more powerful because they were hardly ever contested. While free-lance journalists could try to convince editors at MultiKulti to commission a feature on a particular topic, they had to "sell" it to the editor by appealing to the very same standards of what was interesting and "digestible," and they had to accept revisions of their manuscripts based on formal criteria that implicitly invoked these standards and the imagined audience they were tied to.

The particular insights and points of view that ethnic-minority journalists could bring to a topic were thus often inconflict with such standards. The "foreign view" that MultiKulti was aiming for in its German-language programs had to explain "foreignness" in "indigenous" terms. Ethnic-minority journalists had to be able to anticipate a certain cultural horizon of meaning within which the imagined audience would make sense of their statements. The "insider" perspective—sharing a particular background and horizon of meaning with the people one reports on—always had to be confronted with what counts as intelligible and interesting reporting for an audience of "outsiders" and reworked accordingly. The reverse process did not take place in the German-language programs. Such reversal could have meant to anticipate the horizons of meaning shared by immigrant groups listening to Radio MultiKulti and to actively question what might be called a German-majority horizon of commonsense and taken-for-granted understandings. But "being German" was not one ethnicity or culture among others; it was the implicit, unmarked referent toward which German-language programs were geared. In editors' decisions regarding what kind of information could and could not be taken for granted, they marked out minority cultural practices as those that needed specific contextualization in order to become intelligible, thereby reinforcing the unquestioned and unquestionable intelligibility of an assumed majority position of listeners.

In three and a half minutes, which was at the time the maximum length for a freelance feature production, there is no time to explore complexities. An acceptable feature production at Radio MultiKulti had to get its point straight across without creating possible confusion, and it had to introduce its topic in a way that required no prior familiarity. Of course, some background of understanding and knowledge is necessarily assumed in any kind of broadcasting, forming a baseline of taken-for-granted meanings that no longer appear as questionable or culturally specific. But, as has been shown earlier, what is assumed as self-evident or common knowledge in the German-language productions for Radio MultiKulti was geared toward a non-immigrant German audience that was introduced to migrant issues in particular ways—in ways that inevitably highlighted ethnic difference.

Essentializing Culture

The station's claim to give a "voice" to immigrant minorities, and thereby to contribute to minority empowerment, received an enthusiastic echo. There is a strong consensus across European policy discourses and academic studies of ethnic and indigenous media that access to mass media will allow disadvantaged minorities to "speak for themselves." As a consequence, Radio MultiKulti was praised both by academic researchers and by political institutions such as UNESCO, without a serious investigation into how "foreign voices" actually came to be constructed at the station. For many analysts, the very presence of immigrant voices in the media has seemed to guarantee minority representation and participation. Subaltern ethnic groups are assumed to "speak," if given the chance, and what is voiced, particularly in a native tongue to the members of the native group, consequently has to be an authentic expression of minority culture. It is this assumption which informs statements such as that by German academic Jörg Becker, who has described the emergence of a Turkish media sphere in Germany as an "ethnicization process": "Ethnicization of media means, from a cultural perspective, the primacy of including that which is one's own over the exclusion of that which is not. Ethnicization of media allows the members of one's own group to see themselves, one's own fates, one's own problems, one's own bodies" (Becker 2001, 16; author's translation from German). In the contrast between ethnic minority and majority society, the possible heterogeneity of the ethnic-minority population is effaced. Media produced by migrants for migrants appear by necessity to reflect that "which is one's own" (*das Eigene*) and to represent "themselves." In such an understanding of ethnic-minority media, two basic meanings of the concept of representation are collapsed: representation in the sense of *darstellen*, as a form of subject-predication in which the community is invoked as a given entity, and representation in the sense of *vertreten*, as a form of "speaking-for" as in political representation. Gayatri Spivak has argued in her influential essay "Can the Subaltern Speak?" for the importance of keeping the two meanings conceptually distinct. To collapse them, she challenges, means to (re)introduce a constitutive subject of the oppressed who can unproblematically "know and speak for themselves" (Spivak 1988). Both dimensions of representation are problematic when it comes to media invocations of the Turkish immigrant community: the stipulation that such community can be represented as an objectively existing entity and the further assumption that members of this community will "voice" its innermost interests.

While respect for diversity as *ethnische Vielfalt* (ethnic diversity) is a basic premise of multicultural policies and projects such as Radio MultiKulti, the enthusiasm for difference comes to a sudden halt when the "internal" composition of ethnic groups is concerned. In the conceptual slide that turns immigrants from Turkey into the equivalent of a "Turkish community," the possible heterogeneity of Turkish life in Germany is effaced. The concept of community signals a homogeneous, clearly delineated entity, with definite criteria for membership and belonging (Amit and Rapport 2002). The relative "sameness" that is attributed to its members becomes an implicit precondition for migrant media representations not only to depict or "talk about" migrants (in the sense of *darstellen*) but simultaneously to "speak for" them (in the sense of *vertreten*). Appearing to speak from the "inside" of a community, migrant voices are thus imbued with an inescapable authority that could also be described as a representational burden: rarely challenged with regard to the authority of their representational claims but simultaneously forced to represent the ethno-cultural "Other."

To regard migrant media as a form of collective self-representation is to accept broadcasters' claims to represent "the community" in this double sense, of being authorized not just to speak or produce images of it but to also be its political voice. Radio MultiKulti received praise on the widespread assumption that its "foreign voices" could represent immigrant groups in this second sense of the term. Many among Berlin's complex scene of Turkish migrant media activists begged to differ. Yet almost all of them similarly claimed to "speak for" migrants and represent their true qualities and concerns. Needing to legitimate their own productions within then-dominant frameworks of multiculturalism that tended to reduce culture to a marker of ethnic-group identity, many migrant producers had to take recourse to arguments of ethno-cultural membership to authorize their work.

Conclusion

Radio MultiKulti ceased its broadcasts on the last day of the year 2008. Hit by financial cutbacks and increasing ratings pressures, the public service broadcaster RBB, of which it formed part, decided to pull the plug. Low audience ratings and high costs were named as factors contributing to the decision, but the closure also needs to be placed within the context of changing integration debates in Germany. The idea and ideal of a multicultural society has increasingly eroded in a post-9/11 climate, in which fears concerning Islamism and talk of the alleged failure of Muslim migrants to integrate have come to dominate public discussions in the country. At the same time, however, the growth of Internet- and satellite-based media has led to a situation in which migrants and ethnic minorities (among others) can use and contribute to a huge range of information and communication offers operating at different geographical and geopolitical scales (Deuze 2006). The closure of Radio MultiKulti in this sense signals not only the erosion of multicultural paradigms of integration but also the demise of a public service ideal of an inclusive public sphere that lets different kinds of citizens engage in mutual conversation so as to influence democratic decision-making. This conversation, as has been shown by critics of the public sphere concept, was mostly a fictitious construct with manifold exclusions operating at different levels (Calhoun 1992; Robbins 1993; Warner 2002). Yet it is far from clear how the proliferation and complex new scaling of opportunities for mediated public debate is impacting processes of democratic legitimation. Can and should denizens of a geopolitical unit in which governance is democratically legitimated participate in a shared, inclusive forum of public debate? Can processes of democratic legitimation do without the fiction or reality of such a forum? And if the ideal of a single, inclusive public sphere is a hegemonic fiction, is the lowering of digital access thresholds, the possibilities for evading centralized control and censorship, the relative ease with which people in different locations around the globe can now engage in potentially limitless mutual conversations a cause for celebration and/or an opportunity to rethink the foundations of democracy itself?

Radio MultiKulti has a digital successor, the Internet radio station multicult2.0, its staff by and large working on a volunteer basis. Few of the old staff members have remained—interestingly, those who have are mostly migrants. Analyzing how the new station's digital broadcasting practices might now unfold in a context no longer shaped by public service broadcasting and state-endorsed multiculturalist paradigms would go beyond the scope of this chapter. However, it is significant to note that forms of audio representation that are confined to the Internet have a very different relationship to public space, compared to the terrestrial radio broadcasts which can form part of the soundscapes of public life. The connections between public spheres, usually understood as mass mediated, and public spaces as contexts of stranger relationality that are facilitating face-to-face encounters have been hinted at but remain severely undertheorized in the public sphere literature (Kosnick 2010). In debates that tend to use space in a metaphorical sense, discussing discursive publics with little reference to geographically locatable space, the question of how public stranger sociality is tied to the use and production of concrete spaces rarely arises. Yet by radio sounds no longer emanating from cars stopping at urban traffic lights, no longer providing a background noise to sales transactions in neighborhood stores, no longer offering a soundscape for a summer afternoon spent at the park, radio broadcasts cease to articulate the city as an essentially public social location. However multicult2.0 might manage to transform the multiculturalist agenda and move toward new forms of minority representation in the Berlin region, its link to the city as a diverse public has been significantly weakened.

NOTES

1. The chapter was published in a different, longer version in my book *Migrant Media: Turkish Broadcasting and Multicultural Politics in Berlin* (Bloomington: Indiana University Press, 2007).
2. There were exceptions, such as the two second-generation moderators of Turkish pop-music programs on Radio MultiKulti, Erci E. and Aziza A., who both achieved moderate celebrity status as hip hop stars in the 1990s.
3. I thank Charlotte L. Sever for drawing my attention to this important question.
4. This is not to subscribe to an "assimilationist view" of language change, presuming that migration backgrounds will leave no linguistic trace. There is ample evidence to suggest that postmigrant youths develop mixed codes and forms of slang (Dirim and Hieronymus 2003). However, such codes are at present too subaltern and fluid to have fully functioned as signifiers for Radio MultiKulti's target audience.

REFERENCES

Amit, Vered, and Nigel Rapport. 2002. *The Trouble with Community: Anthropological Reflections on Movement, Identity and Collectivity*. London: Pluto.

Anderson, Benedict. 1983. *Imagined Communities: Reflections on the Origin and Spread of Nationalism*. London: Verso.

Becker, Jörg. 2001. Zwischen Integration und Abgrenzung: Anmerkungen zur Ethnisierung der türkischen Medienkultur. In *Zwischen Abgrenzung und Integration: Türkische Medienkultur in Deutschland*, ed. Jörg Becker and Reinhard Benisch, 9–24. Loccum, Germany: Evangelische Akademie Loccum.

Calhoun, Craig, ed. 1992. *Habermas and the Public Sphere*. Cambridge: MIT Press.

Deuze, Mark. 2006. Ethnic media, community media and participatory culture. *Journalism* 7 (3): 262–80.

Dirim, Inci, and Andreas Hieronymus. 2003. Cultural orientation and language use among multilingual youth groups: "For me it is like we all speak one language." *Journal of Multilingual and Multicultural Development* 24 (1–2): 42–55.

Dyer, Richard. 1993. *The Matter of Images: Essays on Representation*. London: Routledge.

Dyer, Richard. 1997. *White*. London: Routledge.

Frachon, Claire, and Marion Vargaftig. 1995. *European Television: Immigrants and Ethnic Minorities*. London: John Libbey.

Frankenberg, Ruth. 1993. *White Women, Race Matters: The Social Construction of Whiteness*. Minneapolis: University of Minnesota Press.

Holler, Wolfgang. 1997. Radio MultiKulti gefährdet? *UNESCO Heute* 1–2:15–16.

Kosnick, Kira. 2000. Building bridges—media for migrants and the public-service mission in Germany. *European Journal of Cultural Studies* 3 (3): 321–44.

———. 2007. *Migrant Media: Turkish Broadcasting and Multicultural Politics in Berlin*. Bloomington: Indiana University Press.

———. 2010. Migrant publics: Mass media and stranger-relationality in urban space. *Revue Européenne des Migrations Internationales* 16 (1): 37–55.

Mandel, Ruth. 1994. "Fortress Europe" and the foreigners within: Germany's Turks. In *The Anthropology of Europe: Identity and Boundaries in Conflict*, ed. Victoria A. Goddard, Josep R. Llobera, and Cris Shore, 113–24. Oxford, UK: Berg.

N.N. 1995. SFB 4—Radio MultiKulti. *UNESCO Heute* 3:176–77.

Oguntoye, Katharina, May Opitz, and Dagmar Schultz, eds. 1986. *Farbe bekennen: Afro-deutsche Frauen auf den Spuren ihrer Geschichte*. Berlin: Orlanda Frauenverlag.

Räthzel, Nora. 1990. Germany: One race, one nation? *Race and Class* 32 (3): 31–48.

Rex, John. 1991. The political sociology of a multi-cultural society. *Journal of Intercultural Studies* 2 (1): 7–19.

Robbins, Bruce, ed. 1993. *The Phantom Public Sphere*. Minneapolis: University of Minnesota Press.

Smith, M. G. 1969. Some developments in the analytical framework of pluralism. In *Pluralism in Africa*, ed. Leo Kuper and M. G. Smith, 415–58. Berkeley: University of California Press.

Spivak, Gayatri, 1998. Can the subaltern speak? In *Marxism and the Interpretation of Culture*, ed. Larry Grossberg and Cary Nelson, 271–313. Urbana: University of Illinois Press.

Stolcke, Verena. 1995. Talking culture: New boundaries, new rhetorics of exclusion in Europe. *Current Anthropology* 36 (1): 1–24.

Vertovec, Steven. 1996. Berlin Multikulti: Germany, "foreigners" and "world-openness." *New Community* 22 (3): 381–399.

Voß, Friedrich. 1996. Low budget and high level. *Wort, Bild u Ton* 1:6.

Warner, Michael. 2002. Publics and counterpublics. *Public Culture* 14 (1): 49–90.

10

"We Go Above"

Media Metaphysics and Making Moral Life on Ayoreo Two-Way Radio

LUCAS BESSIRE

One of radio's main effects is the promotion of pure spirit. No
dream experience, no ancient religion ever separated spirit from
flesh more effectively than the electronic media.
—Edmund Carpenter

When dawn breaks or night falls over a village of Ayoreo-speaking people of
the Gran Chaco, the arrival and departure of the day are accompanied by a
series of iconic sounds: chopping wood, coughing people, chattering parrots,
the changing rhythms of the forest. Now, this includes crackling static and
voices coming over the two-way radio.

The stream of voices in the unwritten Ayoreo language is constant, the use
of these small, solar-powered shortwave community radios ubiquitous. Each
of the three dozen Ayoreo settlements on both sides of the Bolivia-Paraguay
border has a radio, as do the three Ayoreo tribal organizations, most NGOs,
and some missionaries working with these formerly seminomadic foraging
people, who entered into direct contact with outsiders between 1947 and
2004. Speaking over high-frequency transceivers allows any individual operator to contribute to the conversational polyphony, and anyone near a radio

set to listen in on any particular thread. Each community on both sides of the border has agreed to open its radio daily at eight a.m., noon, and five p.m. In the case of an exceptional event or crisis, the radio is used continuously.

During my long-term months of fieldwork among Ayoreo-speaking people, I never spent a day in any village where a working radio remained silent; it was not unusual for a rotating cast of villagers to spend as many as seven hours per day listening to and talking on these radios. People considered the radio to be a critically important element of any Ayoreo village; plans to establish new settlements had been abandoned due to the lack of a radio set. Ayoreo practitioners turned to this two-way radio technology to meet within an expansive "acoustic space" (Carpenter and McLuhan 1960). This chapter explores how, in doing so, Ayoreo-speaking people create a transcendent plane of sociality that is largely inaudible to outsiders and opaque to their interpretations, even as the forms of belonging it evokes and intensifies are central to contemporary Ayoreo life-projects.

This marked appropriation of electronic media technologies is not new for Ayoreo-speaking people. Individuals from different groups and Christian missions began sending cassettes to one another in the late 1960s, and ten years later an international circuit of homemade Ayoreo-language tapes between settlements had been firmly established. By 1977, cassette recorders were in such demand that evangelical New Tribes missionaries at El Faro Moro, in the heart of the Paraguayan Gran Chaco, noted that Ayoreo wage laborers were disposed to spend most of their meager cash earnings on blank tapes (see New Tribes Mission 1977). These multivocal cassettes, filled with stories, songs, and messages from many individuals, were mailed and sent with anthropologists, aid workers, and missionaries who traveled between far-flung settlements and across the Bolivia-Paraguay border (see Escobar 1988, 233). At the time of my fieldwork, even the smallest village had hundreds of such cassettes. One powerful leader in a prominent settlement had two one-hundred-gallon oil drums full of these homemade tapes in his house.

Cassette exchanges predated and accompanied an enthusiastic appropriation of two-way radio. Early missionary attempts to contact Ayoreo-speaking bands relied on shortwave radio sets, which were even carried in by Direquednejnaigosode-Ayoreo porters for live contact broadcasts during American evangelical missionary Bill Pencille's expedition to locate Guidaigosode-Ayoreo bands on the Bolivian-Paraguayan border in 1960 (Wagner 1967). Taught to operate this equipment, Ayoreo individuals in Bolivia soon borrowed the radio to communicate with relatives on affiliated Protestant missions, and the NGO Apoyo Para el Campesino del Oriente Boliviano (APCOB) gave radios directly to Bolivian Ayoreo villages in the 1970s. In Paraguay, the Norwegian foreign development service and the NGO Asociación Indigenista del Paraguay (AIP) gave radio sets and solar panels to seven communities in the late 1990s. After this date, most established Ayoreo settlements in Bolivia and Paraguay had access to solar-powered two-way transceivers, and the radio became a centrally important way to connect with relatives, clan kin, and acquaintances scattered in settlements often separated by hundreds of roadless miles.

Scholars have largely ignored the centrality of two-way radio technology within the everyday lives of Ayoreo-speaking peoples and neighboring Chacoan groups, despite its widespread use (but see mention of radio in Bartolomé 2000, 290). Most have dismissed such practices as static concealing or corrupting the more authentic essences of Native culture. The ethnomusicologist Jean-Pierre Estival (2006) is the only scholar to address Ayoreo radio practices, in which he finds the opposite: an expression of "cultural resistance" that reproduces past values and symbols in the present. Here, I argue that both approaches mistakenly reduce the analysis of indigenous media practices to a dichotomous opposition of cultural continuity and rupture. Such approaches risk overlooking the unique entanglements of dialogic radio sound and (post)colonial predicaments in the region. What might be heard if, rather than blocking out the noise of such media practices, we ethnographically tune in to Ayoreo frequencies?

Tuning In

This essay describes the form and content of two-way radio practices among Ayoreo-speaking people in order to craft a larger argument about the ways nonbroadcast radio technology may shape emergent forms of subjectivity and governance in a complex field of indigeneity. Specifically, I relate the social force of aural media to Ayoreo metaphysical theories which presume that radio circuitry both accelerates and regulates the movement of a soul-matter intrinsic to all forms of moral agency, particularly sympathetic speech, healing, and prayer. Because most Ayoreo-speaking people believe that this soul-matter has been fundamentally changed by contact and conversion to Christianity, these radio metaphysics are aimed at transcending, rather than preserving, the practices and selves associated with a past "tradition" that is now considered dangerously immoral. Through radio mediatization, this new moral soul-matter and the domains of the past it negates are rendered manageable in a culturally standardized way. Thus, I argue that Ayoreo aural media practices may be predicated on the refusal of what is politically intelligible as "culture," even as they profoundly assert Ayoreo capacities to control the terms of self-objectification and, thus, the moral reproduction of modern humanity (Turner 1991, 2009).

Ayoreo radio sociality is a case in which restricting analysis to a dichotomy of formal rupture versus cultural continuity is not sufficient to account for its contemporary appeal and efficacy. This also means that the ethnography of Ayoreo radio contributes to scholarship on indigenous media, often defined as a set of practices in which "cultural material is used and strategically deployed as part of a broader project of political empowerment," advocacy, or antihegemonic resistance to states and markets (Ginsburg, Abu-Lughod, and Larkin 2002, 7). Much of this scholarship focuses on how such practices shape public affects, realign social distinctions, or reorganize collectives, most frequently as crucial technologies for cultural activism, collective memory, or the revitalization of traditional practices and language (see especially Browne 1998; Buddle 2008; Ginsburg 1994, 1997, 2002; Prins 1997; Wilson and Stewart 2008). While Ayoreo electronic-media practices may create similar effects, their form and content are distinct. For instance, they are not a response to the homogenizing effects of mass media imposed from elsewhere but one venue in which Ayoreo-speaking people are negotiating the subjective meanings of the violence and ontological disturbances occasioned by internal colonialism. Ayoreo electronic-media practices are not sites of intercultural advocacy but are almost entirely inaudible to those who do not speak the Ayoreo language. Such media practices may be intrinsic to processes of identity formation and autonomous self-representation, but the unruly projects of becoming they create and evoke are not intelligible in the terms of an objectified Native culture.

These differences are partly attributable to the specific sensorial features of nonbroadcast, dialogic two-way radio technology, an understudied media form that implies conversational multiplicity and practitioners who are prosumers (producer and consumer at the same time).[1] Unlike the introduction of mass-media forms or the phonetic alphabet elsewhere, such conversational radio technology is amenable to preferred styles of face-to-face interaction and the social norms that govern vocal address. This also applies to media content: two-way radio does not entail orthographic, visual, or programmed quantification but, rather, an ephemeral vocality in which morally significant phatic content is constantly exchanged and debated with a wider public. It is this emotional register that allows for the organizational effects of Ayoreo radio. In such ways, Ayoreo radio resembles an aural indigenous intranet or horizontal participation platform in which users are authorized through language and moral personhood. The particular convergence of co-lonial violence, relational ontologies, and Ayoreo language ideologies makes two-way radio an ideal technology for contemporary Ayoreo life-projects of interpreting and transforming moral human life.

Forms of Ayoreo Media Practice

Today, it is possible to point out a dizzying array of factors that divide Ayoreo-speaking people in one settlement from those of another. Seventy years ago, they were not a recognizable "tribe" but, rather, divided into sev-eral fluid, politically autonomous, and mutually suspicious band confedera-tions, crosscut by ties of language, kinship, and seven patrilineal exogamous clans. Today, the descendants of these confederations are further divided by memories of past internecine violence, distinct histories of contact, affilia-tion with one of six competing Christian denominations, collaboration with several mutually hostile NGOs, divergent economic opportunities, frequent migration as wage laborers, vast distances, and the Bolivia-Paraguay border.

Despite such pressures, Ayoreo-speaking people on both sides of the border are actively bridging these divides. Radio networks and cassette ex-changes mean that Ayoreo individuals in theory are able to cross any of these divides at will. It is now possible, for instance, to pick up the radio handset in a remote Catholic mission settlement in Paraguay and carry on a con-versation with an evangelical preacher in an urban encampment in Bolivia. Ayoreo people often told me that media exchanges between distant groups —and cassette greetings especially—resembled the form and content of face-to-face interactions in the past, particularly during annual intraethnic gath-erings at the centrally located salt pans along the Bolivia-Paraguay border.

Ayoreo cassette and radio practices may haptically evoke a public space that is accessible to all Ayoreo-speaking groups, but Ayoreo individuals also use media to create more restricted acoustic spheres that often cite older Ayoreo political or kin collectives.[2] Radio exchanges are not evenly distrib-uted among all communities but, rather, are informally concentrated be-tween groups with higher numbers of related individuals. This creates, in effect, various spatial clusters where active radio exchanges are denser and others where direct radio contacts are less frequent or perhaps nonexistent. During my fieldwork among the Totobiegosode-Ayoreo subgroup, for in-stance, the vast majority of radio conversation was limited to people in other

Totobiegosode or neighboring Guidaigosode communities: those with whom they had established personal face-to-face relationships, close kinship ties, a common Christian denomination, or shared affiliations with traditional *gage* band confederacies. Similar patterns exist in other settlements.

The technological capacities of two-way radio allow Ayoreo people to accommodate and cite older boundaries of social inclusion within public radiophonic space. This happens on a formal level through the manipulation of radio channels. All Ayoreo radio occupies the shortwave or high-frequency section of the electromagnetic spectrum, spanning 3,000 to 30,000 kHz. Ayoreo operators have agreed to use twenty-five radio frequencies between 5,100 and 9,000 kHz. These frequencies are almost exclusively the domain of Ayoreo people; outsiders who attempt to communicate on them are typically harangued in Ayoreo language until they switch to another.

In order to talk on the radio, the usual procedure is first to "meet" on the main channel before moving to one of the other twenty-four possibilities depending on sound clarity and availability. These common channels span a wide range of frequencies (useful for different distances and times of day). Because these are difficult to locate manually, Ayoreo-speaking people have programmed the same frequencies into their transceiver channel presets. Thus, when a person from Paraguay says to a person from Bolivia, "Lets go to 4," they both move to the preset channel 4 and end up on the same frequency.

However, some Ayoreo villages have developed alternative frequencies that they say are "hidden" from other Ayoreo communities. Villages that desire to make a hidden frequency will arrange with one another to alter one or two of the preset channels to a different frequency that only they know. Because this channel is nearly impossible to find, using it allows only select groups to listen and participate. Totobiegosode, for instance, have created three such hidden frequencies known only to their communities, and most of their conversations occur on these channels. In such ways, Ayoreo people have made the electromagnetic spectrum of radio frequencies a new kind of social boundary, complete with its own particular forms of etiquette, constituency, and language practices (cf. Hutchby 1999). Although such Ayoreo media practices cite older communicative and social forms (particularly those associated with face-to-face encounters at the salt pans), radio use does more than reproduce traditional visual or symbolic practices in the present.

Sympathy and Spirit

My Ayoreo teachers told me that radio use entails strict rules: it should ideally strengthen harmonious relations and minimize conflict. Ayoreo media practitioners usually strive to avoid discussing potentially conflictive topics on the radio or cassettes. One village leader, for instance, would secretly edit any tape sent from his village by erasing potentially incendiary comments before it was sent.

> You cannot erase the words of radio like you could erase a cassette. They speak there, and it arrives to you. Everyone can hear it. Radio can make problems worse. With cassettes it was better because we could erase any bad words so no one could hear them. We were told before that the radio is not intended to express anger or have a problem with another person. It is only to share stories and songs and hear if someone is sick. That is what it is good for.

I was initially drawn to Ayoreo radio because I naively imagined that these dialogues represented an unfiltered Ayoreo response to modernity. As I noted in my journal during an early visit to the field, "Note to self: something *big* must be happening on those damn radios!" Once I learned enough of the Ayoreo language to participate in radio conversations, however, I discovered that the content is strikingly devoid of the "big" things I had expected. Rather, Ayoreo radio dialogues are typically phatic, that is, aimed at sharing feelings rather than tactical information. In contrast to other forms of print or televisual media, two-way radio is considered an appropriate venue for discussing the intimate details of daily life; conversations over it are constrained to widely recognized sentimental scripts that aim to provoke a response of sympathy, outrage, sorrow, or joy. The airwaves are filled with people crying, complaining, worrying, soothing, and reassuring. The most discussed topics are those most likely to generate a predictable emotional reply from listeners. The ethnography of Ayoreo two-way radio draws attention to the generative labor of such phatic media content.

The idea of expressing sympathy over the radio evokes and extends a theory of speaking and listening that was common at the time of my field-work.[3] Ayoreo-speaking people often linked hearing a spoken voice to the intimacy of physical proximity. It was commonly said that listening to someone's words is the source for pleasurable sensations of nearness, as in the expression *uneja becejode,* or "being near you all is sweet." This language ideology is extended by media operators, who also apply such characterizations to the acoustic presence of words spoken on the radio and recorded on cassettes. Ayoreo people used the same phrases to refer to physical presence and presence on the radio, such as *jene bagusi yejoi e,* or "now you are near me," which indicates clear reception. I was told that hearing someone's voice invokes the same subjective feelings as a face-to-face encounter.

The relation between physical and acoustic proximity is possible because of *ayipie* soul-matter. This fluid concept may encompass parts of what we call memory, soul, personality, conscience, intelligence, willpower, emotion, and thought—in sum, the constitutive elements associated with health and agency. Through this concept, Ayoreo-speaking people reconcile certain forms of affect and rationality and set fluid boundaries between body, mind, and larger moral ecologies. A person's *ayipie* is capable of transcending time and space. It is commonly said that one's *ayipie* may "go out" (*jno*) when one is dreaming, angry, frightened, concerned, agitated, or particularly focused. On such journeys, the soul-matter can cause real-world effects. The integrity, health, or agentive capacities of *ayipie*, in turn, depend on and index an individual's relation to an encompassing ecology of moral forces. A weak or compromised *ayipie* reflects a lack of individual agency or moral failing and commonly results in sickness. *Ayipie* is particularly associated with the moving breath of spoken words. Thus, someone with a strong *ayipie* is said to have "heavy words" that are capable of causing the effects they purportedly describe.

Certain forms of speech, and particularly that which is mediatized by cassettes or two-way radio, catalyze the movement of *ayipie*. "When I hear someone's words on the radio or a cassette, my *ayipie* goes near them," I was told. "And when they hear my words, I know that their *ayipiedie* are near me." In such statements, Ayoreo media practitioners hypothesize that radio technology allows for a double transference of linguistic content and potent disembodied matter. This capacity to haptically extend *ayipie* is the fundamental source of radio's appeal, traction, and power. Such entanglements of metaphysical content and technological form find maximum expression in discourses of healing, helping, and concern. Likewise, one can use the radio to reject contact with someone from another village and, thus, limit the circulation of his or her *ayipie*, as in the phrase *je yayipie d'ore* (My *ayipie* will not arrive to them).

When *ayipie* is mobilized through radio circuitry, the proximity of mediatized voice becomes the proximity of a forceful nonvisible substance. Such substances are shaped by dual processes of transduction, not only as they move from mouths to wires to ears but also as they move from lungs to words to radio waves and, potentially, into bodies and souls on the other end. The moral metaphysics by which *ayipie* becomes an agentive force is extended through aural media technology. This may explain why the standard content of Ayoreo radio is largely restricted to two central themes: illness and Christianity.[4]

Afflicted Bodies

Sick or ill bodies are the most common topic of radio discourse. Health is one of the first things addressed between any two people on the radio and may be the only topic discussed in an entire conversation. As one village leader put it, "Our land is being taken from us, but we won't talk about this on the radio. We want to know if anyone is sick." Ayoreo media practitioners also reiterated this ideal to each other in radio exchanges. A common expression used to end a conversation is "I have nothing more to tell you because we are all healthy here." The following is a typical exchange between two high-status, unrelated adult women on the hidden Totobiegosode frequency.

1: That's right, tell me your stories.

2: That's right, we are all okay here, we are healthy, we don't have many things to tell you because we are like rocks here [i.e., strong, healthy] in our community. It is a wonderful noon because we are hearing from you all. Cambio.

1: That's how it is, that's how it is. Some of us still have colds, but some are healthy here. I think that we are better because no one has slept yet. Cambio.

2: That's how it is. I understand that there is cough among you all. We are like stones here, and I am happy that we are healthy here in our little ugly community. Cambio.

1: That's how it is, that's how it is. Some of us have coughs, but these coughs don't kill anyone. Juan also had one, but it didn't enter him; it is staying in their throats.

2: That's how it is. I understand that Juan has a cough. I am happy that we are healthy here because we are very far from any hospital. God is who cares for us. Cambio.

1: That's how it is, that's how it is, that's how it really is. God is he who cares for us. He cares for us because he knows that we are people who are very poor. Cambio.

2: That's right. That is really right. I am happy that they are giving you all the word of God there. Your uncle already made the word of God this morning with Juan and with your other uncle, Pedro. Your brother has gone to Pai Puku. Cambio.

1: I understand, I understand, I understand. That's how it is. Cambio.

2: That's how it is, that's how it is. Can you tell your grandfather there that Iride has a cough, but it is okay because he is the Abode of Cough. The rest of us are healthy. Cambio.

1: That's right, that's right. It's his way. He is like your aunt here who also always has a cough, but sometimes she has a cough that isn't normal. Cambio.

2: That's how it is. I understand that it is her way. I say that I am happy that Iride is okay. He isn't very strong, but he is a little bit better. I say he is better because he doesn't have a new cough, but he is the Abode of Cough. Paquide is feeling better, and so is Dani'date, but sometimes things come out of her body. I don't know what else I have to tell you. Cambio.

1: That's how it is. I understand that some things are coming out of her body, but tell me if it itches her, too. Cambio.

2: That's how it is, that is exactly right. Her body itches. I looked at her yesterday, and I told her that first it wants to come out of her body, that she should heat water and bathe well.

1: That's how it is, what you told her. I have nothing else to tell you. Here my words end.

In such radio dialogues, particular relationships with individuals in the other community are often glossed as inquiries into their health. Detailed discussions of bodily sensations and symptoms are not restricted to the intimate talk between two women in neighboring communities. Illness is also a common topic in conversations between people of both genders who have never met in person and who hail from widely separated communities. A description of a healthy, strong, and resistant body does not necessarily evoke an emotional response of contentment or joy. However, discussing an ill or vulnerable body on the radio usually causes a burst of intense sociality in which people from other communities express their grief or sorrow for the ill person, often during sessions extending for several hours in which the same information is repeated again and again. Consider how both people use concern to mark their ties to a third person in the following exchange:

1: I got up very early, at four, because I was too worried about our clan relative. I couldn't sleep because I was worried. I heard that he was sick yesterday. I came to the radio early thinking they would turn it on because of this important news, but no one was there. I didn't even want to drink water before I went to the radio. But no one was there. Cambio.

2: I understand your words, and I am very content that I can hear what you are saying, too. I also got up early at four. Neither my wife nor I could sleep because we were worried about my uncle. I am happy that you are on the radio now and can tell us about what has happened to him. We want to know here because he is our relative and we are very worried. We could not sleep at all either. Cambio.

Such expressions of sympathy may express attachment to a person from whom the speakers are physically separated. They may also be a way to mark hierarchy as well as feelings of belonging. Crying is particularly marked in radio exchanges as evidence of sincerity and, thus, indicates a closer relationship with the family of the afflicted person than those who do not cry. Sympathy may also be a way to claim a closer degree of relatedness than others who may be listening.

Listening to one such exchange, I was told by my Ayoreo companions that the two participants were trying to outdo each other with increasingly exaggerated accounts of their own grief for a sick person. One young man, named Asi, said that if he wanted to beat both of them, he would go on the radio and say that the sick man is not his relative, that he has never visited their village before, and that he has never received any gift from the man in question. If he did so, Asi reasoned, they would surely respond that the sick man was so good that he would give gifts anyway if Asi happened to arrive. "But then I would just say that in fact I had arrived once before, but [the sick man] did not give me anything at all. If I said this, I would beat them both, and they would be angry." By first denying a relation and then asserting a counterexample, he would force the women into a trap which contests the moral purity of the sick man. Doing so allows for another diagnosis and morally appropriate response to the news of his affliction besides that of sympathy.

The slippage between expressing sympathy and asserting vertical relations of hierarchy has become a central part of the cultural and emotional scripts expressed on the radio. It is possible because Ayoreo-speaking people do not generally semantically distinguish between physical health, individual agency, and moral well-being. Expressions of concern for a physical body, then, may well imply doubts about one's moral and hence social standing. This makes it particularly easy for one to claim a superior moral ground over another through expressions of sympathy or compassion. Opening spaces for a harmonious encounter on the radio are further complicated by the fact that expressions of sympathy and dominance are themselves considered to be two distinct and oppositional moral values.

Radio Prayer

Because radio scripts are focused on moral and emotional attachments, it is not surprising that Christianity was the other defining content of radio speech at the time of my fieldwork. Common radio expressions include "Don't worry about us. God helps us here," "We know that God is the one who gives us everything," "I am happy because God gives us strength and health," and "God will help us all." People frequently use the radio to ask others to pray for them. Such requests are usually directed at people who are believed to have relatively more powerful prayers, often recognized authorities on the word of God. Because direct requests are considered rude, advice is solicited by offering up one's personal moral dilemma on the radio. High-status individuals also regularly "give" Bible verses or sermons to one another on the radio. This emphasis is so pervasive that a shared Christian faith is often a precondition for radio sociality, as in the following exchange between a man from Bolivia and a woman from Paraguay.

> 1: That is how it is, that is how it is. I cannot hear you well, and I do not know who you are. I understand that you are a clan relative of mine, but I want to know what your name is. Cambio.
> 2: That is right. I am Yahoge, who you met before in Campo Loro. Cambio.
> 1: That is right, Yahoge. I am happy that I am hearing your words. I am happy that God makes it so that although someone is far away, they can still talk. If people who are far away pray for one another, they can still help each other. I send many greetings to you all there. It does not matter who you are or where your community is, because it appears as though we all believe in the same God. We are the same people. God's people. Cambio.

Ayoreo media practitioners routinely evoke a contemporary moral ecology controlled by the Christian God. The space of the present is referred to as *Cojñone-Gari*, or "that which belongs to non-Ayoreo." It is considered to be the space of modernity itself, and so it has become. Within *Cojnone-Gari*, the only viable moral human is one whose *ayipie* has been evacuated and reconstituted by contact in ways that are pleasing to Jesus (Bessire 2011a). For such "new people," the *ayipie* of their past selves is a constant source of danger, contagion, and shame. This sense is routinely invoked in radio dialogues, as in the following "advice" sent from a man in Bolivia to a man in Paraguay.

We didn't think correctly when we lived in the forest before. That is why we had to know Jesus. And now we know him. Before, we didn't know who God was. God knows how to change our *ayipiedie*. He wanted us to give him thanks. Also, he wants us to thank people like me and to thank him for "touching" [capturing and converting] so many Ayoreo before. To this day, we are together, all of us, living in *Cojnone-Gari* as God's people [*Dupade-urasade*]. And today, we are looking for the Ayoreo still in the forest so they will join us as God's people. We have left behind the war with other Ayoreo that we always had before. I am always thinking that this life is fair because the work that we did saved all of our souls. We are together now with the word of God and with our faith, all the Ayoreo and the new people and the *cojñone* too.

Two-way radio and cassette technologies allow Ayoreo-speaking people to create a supralocal sense of belonging around shared membership in an ethnically inclusive Christianity and a collective transcendence of past practices and selves (Oosterbaan 2008). Aural media practices thereby can be understood as an assertion of Ayoreo control over the processes of self-objectification entailed by the transformation into viable modern, indigenous subjects. In doing so, they cite a longstanding Ayoreo theory that such capacities to control self-production are the defining traits of moral humanity and its originary differentiations from nature or nonhuman elements (Bessire 2011b; Turner 2009, 24).

The Moral Metaphysics of Ayoreo Sound Media

Electronic aural media may be appealing technologies for Ayoreo projects of becoming to the degree they allow for the cultural standardization and management of morally significant emotional expression. The restriction of phatic media content to formulaic sentimental scripts around illness and Christianity, in turn, was aimed at provoking an extended circulation of *ayipiedie*, a substance that is uniquely able to mediate the relationships between moral forces, physical bodies, and individual agency. Thus, the efficacy of Ayoreo media practices arises from two overlapping regimes of aural mediation: one that electronically collapses time and space and another that ideally reconstitutes the moral foundations of viable human life. This is possible because specific acoustemologies and language ideologies—which relate the breath and sound of spoken words to the circulation of *ayipie* soul-matter—may be extended to and through dialogic radio technology. Through this accelerated circulation, Ayoreo radio can be considered a technology of practical "help" or "assistance" as well as metaphysical transference.

> We listen to the radio to hear the stories of people in other communities. We can help them if we know what happened, by sending our *ayipiedie* to them. If something happens there, that day we will find out. If someone is sick, we want to know. We can be sad too. We would be disappointed if something happened and we didn't have our radio turned on. If someone gets angry at us here, we want to share our feelings with the others. If they don't have their radio on, we can't talk to them. They won't know what happened to us, and we won't know what happened to them. We can't help each other.

In certain cases, this help or assistance is explicitly rooted in the power of prayer. Like sympathy, prayer is believed to operate through the movement of one's *ayipie*.

> The radio helps us find out about other people, like those living in Puesto Paz. We heard recently that the *cojnone* had bothered one of them, and they asked us to pray for them. We can pray for them. We prayed a lot, and the situation in Puesto Paz improved. God helped them through the radio. Without the radio, we wouldn't have known, and the strength of our prayers and *ayipiedie* would not have reached them.

Such mediatized *ayipie* ideally intervenes in a situation of moral failing or individual weakness by influencing the relationships between its recipient and a larger ecology of exogenous forces controlled by the Christian God. These concrete effects are only possible when the *ayipie* that is sent resembles the receiving *ayipie*. *Ayipiedie* are said to be supportive of one another only when they are similar, and this power is cumulative. Thus, groups of people who possess "one *ayipie*" are considered to be stronger than individuals and more likely to achieve their goal. This notion of belonging explains why Ayoreo radio practices may effectively provide help for ill or suffering people, only to the degree they circulate a radically changed soul-matter that is now ideally shared by all Ayoreo-speaking people.

Ayoreo radio and cassette practices thus evoke and create what can be considered a transcendent Ayoreo soundscape that undergirds Ayoreo self-fashioning as modern subjects (Hirschkind 2006). Such media practices allow for a wide consensus to arise around the moral foundations of contemporary Ayoreo life and threats to it. Although Ayoreo aural media practices do not conform to most descriptions of the form and content of indigenous media, they are effectively transforming an unruly acoustic space into a zone of autonomy and claims to processes of self-production. They also create and evoke particular senses of being in the world that may be extended as interpretive regimes or a situated form of moral reasoning to other aspects of everyday life.

These haptic encounters shape face-to-face relations between Ayoreo-speaking people. Although these remain conflictive and fraught, Ayoreo people are increasingly translating the peaceful relations intensified over radio talk back into face-to-face meetings, visits, and cross-border political alliances. Even media contacts can become an occasion to give other kinds of gifts. Cassettes moving north are accompanied by thermoses and *garabata* fiber twine, while those moving south come with blankets and clothing. Radio exchanges may articulate a fluid field of standardized identifications, but this is held in tension with different modes of subjectivity and sentiment introduced through histories of violence and domination. In such ways, radio practices articulate the defining tensions of contemporary indigeneity in the Gran Chaco.

Conclusion

Scholars have either ignored electronic-media use by Ayoreo-speaking people and other Chaco peoples or struggled to interpret them as evidence of cultural continuity and a "medium of cultural resistance" (Estival 2006, 112). This chapter has argued that neither approach is sufficient to attend to Ayoreo media practices in all their complexity, contradiction, and consequence. Rather, it describes an indigenous media practice that is effective precisely to the degree it overlaps with other regimes of mediation, moral agency, and culturally specific language ideologies. Through this convergence of acoustic space and moral metaphysics, radio practices enable Ayoreo-speaking people to formulate a powerful response to the violent ontological disturbances implied by becoming internally colonized indigenous subjects. While some of the generative effects of Ayoreo radio practices resemble those of indigenous media elsewhere, they are uniquely predicated on the unruly sonic sensibilities enabled by dialogic radio and the notion that viable moral life is opposed to continuity with the limited set of practices that politically count as Native culture in Latin America. This does not mean, however, that Ayoreo media practices reveal the loss or lack of a defining essence of humanity. Rather,

Ayoreo-speaking people are using aural media technologies to assert their capacity to manage the reproduction of moral humanity in the present and the processes of self-objectification and self-transformation this entails.

Reducing the ethnographic analysis of such media practices to a dichotomy of continuity or rupture with "traditional culture" implies a denial of the Ayoreo capacity to control the terms of their self-objectification if these do not easily fit within liberal projects of intercultural activism or antihegemonic resistance. Ayoreo aural media practices are not only autonomous from national borders, state regulation, and outside surveillance; they are also autonomous from the frameworks through which indigenous media is often constructed as a site for political advocacy. In this case, the continuity of certain culturally specific ontological principles requires a drastic discontinuity of semantic or technological form. Culture here is not an evenly spread or a priori substrate of Ayoreo media practice but a technique by which such media practices may be intelligible and politically authorized by outsiders or not. The common misrecognition of Ayoreo media practices is attributable not only to such reductive frameworks but also to the particular qualities of two-way radio technology, an understudied indigenous media form. The efficacy of Ayoreo two-way radio and its metaphysics is based on repetitive, phatic content that is not available to other forms of broadcast mediation or the ethnographic analysis of cultural essences. Instead, it allows for distinct relationships between sound and embodied knowledge, or acoustemologies, that are also politically consequential in unexpected, socially vibrant ways (Feld 1996, 97).

In sum, Ayoreo aural media practices reflect a politics of indigenous media that is based not on externally authorized notions of culture but, rather, on the fluid cultural meanings of what constitutes media sound, moral life, and the range of human capacities. Imagining a public anthropology in this case means attending to the divergent mediations through which processes of self-transformation and self-objectification are envisioned or managed, collide or coalesce. This chapter has suggested several starting points for such a project. It remains to be seen how these aural media practices relate to ongoing Ayoreo struggles for decolonization, survival, and political agency.

NOTES

Research funding for this chapter was provided by Fulbright-Hays, Wenner-Gren, and an ACLS/Mellon Early Career Fellowship. Special thanks to Faye Ginsburg and Harald Prins.

1. Despite the widespread historical attention to this technology and its prevalent use by hobbyists and educators, media scholars have rarely distinguished the particular

forms of sociality associated with such technologies from "talk radio" or the social potentials of dialogic communication in general (i.e., Armstrong and Rubin 1989; Bucy and Gregson 2001; Hochheimer 1993; Talking into Your Radio 1947; Xu 1998; but see Palmer 1990 for a notable exception). As developed by Ayoreo practitioners, two-way radio technology seems to actualize on a small scale the early hopes of intellectuals like Bertolt Brecht and Walter Benjamin that radio could transform social relations by offering a "truly two-way form of communication" (see Cassirer 1977; Hochheimer 1993).

2. Although radio sets are considered to be communal property, access to them is often controlled by politically influential families. Each village has a customary radio operator, frequently a senior woman from an important family.

3. It should be noted that such language ideologies are undergoing rapid changes. This argument is only meant to reflect the social context of Ayoreo radio as observed between 2001 and 2008.

4. This emphasis on morality may be why expressing other emotions, such as romantic love, jealousy, or anger, is not considered appropriate for radio conversation.

REFERENCES

Armstrong, Cameron, and Alan Rubin. 1989. Talk Radio as Interpersonal Communication. *Journal of Communication* 39 (2): 84–94.

Bartolomé, Miguel. 2000. *El Encuentro de la Gente con los Insensatos: La Sedentarización de los Cazadores Ayoreo en el Chaco Paraguayo.* Asunción: CEADUC.

Bessire, Lucas. 2011a. Apocalyptic Futures: The Violent Transformation of Moral Human Life among Ayoreo-Speaking People in the Paraguayan Gran Chaco. *American Ethnologist* 38 (4): 743–757.

———. 2011b. Ujnarone Chosite: Ritual Poesis, Curing Chants and Becoming Ayoreo in the Gran Chaco. *Journal de la Société des Américanistes* 97 (1).

Browne, Donald. 1998. Talking the Talk on Indigenous Radio. *Cultural Survival Quarterly* 22 (2).

Bucy, Erik, and Kimberly Gregson. 2001. Media Participation: A Legitimizing Mechanism of Mass Democracy. *New Media & Society* 3 (3): 357–380.

Buddle, Kathy. 2008. Transistor Resistors: Native Women's Radio in Canada and the Social Organization of Political Space from Below. In *Global Indigenous Media: Cultures, Poetics, and Politics,* ed. Pamela Wilson and Michelle Stewart, 128–144. Durham: Duke University Press.

Carpenter, Edmund. 1972. *Oh What a Blow That Phantom Gave Me!* New York: Holt, Rinehart and Winston.

Carpenter, Edmund, and Marshall McLuhan. 1960. Acoustic Space. In *Explorations in Media: An Anthology,* ed. Edmund Carpenter and Marshall McLuhan, 65–70. Boston: Beacon.

Cassirer, Henry. 1977. Radio as the People's Medium. *Journal of Communication* 27 (2): 154–157.

Escobar, Ticio. 1988. *Misión Etnocidio.* Asunción: Comisión de Solidaridad con los Pueblos Indígenas.

Estival, Jean-Pierre. 2006. Os Casadores e o Radio: Sobre o Novo Uso Dos Meios De Comunicaçao entre os Ayoreo do Chaco Boreal. *Revista Anthropologicas* 17 (1): 103–114.

Feld, Steven. 1996. Waterfalls of Song: An Acoustemology of Place Resounding in Bosavi, Papua New Guinea. In *Senses of Place*, ed. Steven Feld and Keith Basso, 91–136. Santa Fe, NM: School of American Research Press.

Ginsburg, Faye. 1994. Embedded Aesthetics: Creating a Discursive Space for Indigenous Media. *Cultural Anthropology* 9:365–382.

———. 1997. From Little Things Big Things Grow: Indigenous Media and Cultural Activism. In *Between Resistance and Revolution: Cultural Politics and Social Activism*, ed. Richard Fox and Orin Starn. New Brunswick: Rutgers University Press.

———. 2002. Screen Memories: Resignifying the Traditional in Indigenous Media. In *Media Worlds: Anthropology on New Terrain*, ed. Faye Ginsburg, Lila Abu-Lughod, and Brian Larkin, 39–57. Berkeley: University of California Press.

Ginsburg, Faye, Lila Abu-Lughod, and Brian Larkin. 2002. Introduction to *Media Worlds*, ed. Faye Ginsburg, Lila Abu-Lughod, and Brian Larkin, 1–36. Berkeley: University of California Press.

Hirschkind, Charles. 2006. *The Ethical Soundscape: Cassette Sermons and Islamic Counter-publics*. New York: Columbia University Press.

Hochheimer, John. 1993. Organizing Democratic Radio: Issues in Praxis. *Media, Culture & Society* 15 (3): 473–486.

Hutchby, Ian. 1999. Frame Attunement and Footing in the Organization of Talk Radio Openings. *Journal of Sociolinguistics* 3 (1): 41–63.

New Tribes Mission. 1977. Report of Actual Conditions on the Mission of El Faro Moro. Unpublished report. Filadelfia.

Oosterbaan, Martijn. 2008. Spiritual Attunement: Pentecostal Radio in the Soundscape of a Favela in Rio de Janeiro. *Social Text* 26 (3): 123–145.

Palmer, Craig. 1990. Telling the Truth (Up to a Point): Radio Communication among Maine Lobstermen. *Human Organization* 49 (2): 157–163.

Prins, Harald. 1997. The Paradox of Primitivism: Native Rights and the Problem of Imagery in Cultural Survival Films. *Visual Anthropology* 9:243–266.

Talking into Your Radio. 1947. *Science News Letter* 52 (4): 51.

Turner, Terence. 1991. Representing, Resisting, Rethinking: Historical Transformation of Kayapo Culture and Anthropological Consciousness. In *Colonial Situations: Essays on the Contextualization of Ethnographic Knowledge*, History of Anthropology 7, ed. George Stocking, 285–313, Madison: University of Wisconsin Press.

———. 2009. The Crisis of Late Structuralism, Perspectivism and Animism: Rethinking Culture, Nature, Spirit and Bodiliness. *Tipiti* 7 (1): 3–42.

Wagner, Chuck. 1967. *Defeat of the Bird God*. Grand Rapids, MI: Zondervan.

Wilson, Pamela, and Michelle Stewart, eds. 2008. *Global Indigenous Media: Cultures, Poetics, and Politics*. Durham: Duke University Press.

Xu, Hua. 1998. Talk Radio in Urban China: Implications for the Public Sphere. In *Communication and Culture: China and the World Entering the 21st Century*, ed. D. R. Heisey and Wenxiang Gong, 329–347. Amsterdam: Editions Rodopi.

11

Appalachian Radio Prayers

The Prosthesis of the Holy Ghost and the Drive to Tactility

ANDERSON BLANTON

Academic accounts on the phenomenon of charismatic Christian radio in Appalachia often have approached radio as a passive technological medium for the transmission of a discrete, self-contained religious content (Baker 2005; Clements 1974; Dean 1998; Dorgan 1993; Rosenberg 1970; Titon 1988).[1] These scholarly accounts are governed by an imagined transparency of the technologies or instrumentality of the radio broadcast itself, understanding the effect and meaning of the religious message they carry as a mere epiphenomenon of its content and as not inflected in any essential way by the apparatuses through which it is transmitted. This chapter has a different point of departure and explores the unanticipated centrality of tactile experience within what is usually understood as an exclusively auditory phenomenon, namely, listening to prayer over the radio. In the following, I suggest that the force of radio as a specific communicative technology fundamentally affects how crucial charismatic ritual practices of intercessory prayer and faith healing are experienced and understood. This intertwined relation between haptic sensation, prayer, and the radio apparatus suggests new ways to describe and theorize "faith" within Pentecostal and charismatic healing traditions.

Scanning the airwaves of southern Appalachia on any given Sunday, the radio loudspeaker is certain to voice the importunate communal prayers, energetic singing, and "anointed" preaching styles that characterize the ecstatic performances of so-called folk religion in Appalachia. Unlike the highly produced, syndicated evangelical programs that also retain a daily place within the Appalachian ether, these charismatic broadcasts are recognizable by their spontaneous and improvisatory style. The guiding principle of these live broadcasts, repeated time and again during each worship service, is "Just obey the Lord." Implicit in this phrase is a profound sense of expectation and anticipation that the miraculous power of the Holy Ghost will instantiate itself within the ritual milieu, taking possession of the faculties of speech and bodily control for the purposes of healing physical ailments and blessing the listening faithful.

These charismatic radio broadcasts maintain a vague liturgical structure, yet this form is often deferred, interrupted, or completely derailed according to the precarious contingencies introduced into the worship context by the miraculous power of the Holy Ghost. When the "power falls," it often "anoints" the preacher with a particular poetic style characterized by a rhythmic delivery of sentences punctuated by guttural grunts and gasps for breath, while at other times the spirit is "quenched" and withholds the charismata of rhetorical inspiration. When the Holy Ghost power reaches ecstatic intensity, the anointing becomes so excessive as to completely enrapture the body of the speaker, initiating a "fallin' out in the spirit" that renders speechless the mouth of the preacher. This evocative phrase describes the sudden and precipitous collapse of the body into an inanimate mass whose only sign of life is the gentle, silent undulation of respiration. To people not present but listening on the radio, the abrupt silencing of an anointed voice usually signals that an in-studio congregate has fallen out, as if his or her consciousness were suspended in that nebulous space between transmission and reception. The power of the spirit can take on myriad manifestations and self-effacing intensities, and the structure of the broadcast must be flexible enough to accommodate these precarious potentials of the Holy Ghost.

Centrally located within the southern Appalachians, radio station 105.5 FM WGTH, "The Sheep," provides a good example of the small independent radio stations located throughout this region.[2] Transmitting from southwestern Virginia, the signal of this station is capable of reaching the listening faithful throughout portions of southern West Virginia, eastern Kentucky, western North Carolina, and eastern Tennessee. As if to mimic the improvised spontaneity of the charismatic worship services that take place within the live studio of this station, this structure was originally constructed as a domestic residence but has been converted with minimal alteration into a radio station. The space of the "live" studio clearly suggests its earlier domestic organization with its brick fireplace, now usurped by a wooden podium that functions as both a support for the single studio microphone and an altar for the participants of the worship service. A large window in this room reveals a dilapidated storage shed and an outmoded satellite dish resting wirily in the backyard, its rusted face still gazing expectantly toward the heavens. Abutting from the wall opposite the window, a bare incandescent bulb mounted in a porcelain housing looks strangely out of place. The sudden muted glow of this bulb signals to the live studio congregation that the sounds within this converted space are now being broadcast to the listening audience out in what is referred to as "radioland," a nondescript space where the totality of the dispersed listening audience is imagined as a single community. Two reclaimed church pews, well worn and stained from years of use, and fifteen mismatched chairs provide seating for the members of the live studio congregation. Though sometimes young children are present in the studio, the congregation is primarily made up of white working-class individuals (truck drivers, miners, service-industry employees, mechanics, etc.) generally ranging in age from forty-five to seventy. Women have a slight majority in terms of attendance and participation within the live studio. Underneath the naked bulb sits a piano that often gives instrumental accompaniment to the lively singing of hymns.

During the week, live charismatic worship services are interspersed with local news, obituaries, church announcements, and syndicated evangelical programming such as the *Back to the Bible Broadcast*. In addition, local businesses such as funeral homes, banks, restaurants, and farming-supply stores advertise on this station. On the weekend, however, the programming features a higher concentration of charismatic worship services and preaching. On Saturday and Sunday, the radio station is bustling with energy as preachers, instrument-toting musicians, and faithful congregants pass in and out of the studio in slots of airtime ranging from thirty minutes to an hour. One of the most popular weekend broadcasts is the *Jackson Memorial Hour*, airing during the prime Sunday listening time from eleven a.m. until noon. The main organizers of this worship service, Brother Alide Allen and Sister Dorothy Allen, have been preaching on the radio for over forty-three years.

Moreover, the Allens took the program over from Dorothy's father, Brother George Jackson, who began broadcasting in the mid-1950s on a radio program called *The Little Mountain Preacher*. Brother Aldie, the main preacher during this broadcast, had his conversion experience while listening to the voice of Brother George issuing from the radio loudspeaker.

As these brief historical details suggest, many of the self-proclaimed "old-time Gospel" worship practices in Appalachia are significantly related to the technology of radio. A significant amount of the charismatic faithful in this region grew up listening to worship services mediated over this apparatus. The prominent practice of radio listening, in combination with the aurally saturated metaphors of early Christianity ("Faith cometh by hearing," etc.), significantly influences how many of the charismatic faithful, both broadcasters and radio auditors alike, experience and understand practices such as intercessory prayer, faith healing, and glossolalia.

Like many of the charismatic broadcasts in this region, the *Jackson Memorial Hour* is oriented around the healing of physical illness. The key ritual performance and climax of emotional intensity in such radio programs is organized around the practice of faith healing. In order to create an efficacious milieu for miraculous cures, the force of the Holy Ghost must be instantiated into the worship context. Various theurgical apparati are set in motion in a *precarious* attempt to "get a prayer through" to the divine ear. As noted by Max Muller in his series of Oxford lectures "On Ancient Prayers," the word *prayer* has an important etymological similarity with the word *precarious* (1901). This analysis is helpful within the context of this study because it suggests the emergence of faith as a kind of burden or threat to the automatic efficacy of the magical incantation. An elementary contingency and potential breakdown, therefore, resides within the performance of prayer. Moreover, this supposed burden of faith gets to the core of significant debates within the emergent disciplines of comparative religion and ethnology. These debates have described how the automatic efficacy of the magical and materialized incantation undergoes a gradual process of abstraction, spiritualization, and interiorization through an ever-increasing technological control of the contingencies of the natural environment. Through this process of abstraction, the materialized and automatic efficacy of incantation becomes the precarious practice of prayer directed toward autonomous spiritual agents. Despite these earlier forecasts, however, material conduits always seem to insinuate themselves into the contemporary worship context in a tactile attempt to mitigate the precariousness of prayer. Thus, a panoply of charismatic techniques of the body, material objects, and media technologies are simultaneously engaged to make manifest the presence of the Holy Ghost.

Moreover, such material and ideational entanglements summon a physicality shared by both the spirit and the radio voice, a commonality that is necessary for successful faith healing.

Several times during the course of the *Jackson Memorial Hour*, the members of the studio congregation, referred to as "prayer warriors," are called to circle around the microphone and pray for the sick listeners out in "radioland." The altar mentioned during such healing prayers refers to the microphone and microphone stand as well as the wooden table they rest on. Congregants of the radio church occasionally kneel down in front of the microphone during moments of conversion and supplication. As the prayer warriors approach and place their hands on the wooden platform, the sensitive microphone crisply perceives brisk pops, cracks, creaks, and thuds as hands are placed near the microphone and as the microphone is adjusted. This call for participation in the healing prayer also includes the listening audience. Both the isolated sick in need of a cure and the distant worshiper who wishes to contribute to the theurgical efficacy are importuned to "lay your hand on the radio as a point of contact and pray with us." As if to mimic the early radio sets that had the capacity both to transmit and to receive, the radio loudspeaker becomes a two-way conduit for divine communication (Hill 1978; Schiffer 1991). For listeners out in radioland, it is as if the radio loudspeaker can simultaneously amplify or extend prayers from the everyday to that sacred space somewhere else *and* receive the miraculous transmission of healing force from the sacred to the everyday.

While these preparations for healing prayer are taking place, Brother Aldie further organizes the prayer by assigning "stand-ins" and arranging the most efficacious manual positioning for the communication of Holy Ghost power. Once again, the level of spontaneity and creative improvisation that characterizes these ritual preparations is worth noting. While observing these preparations, one is reminded of the creative informality of rural farmers who use whatever improvised materials at hand (garden hoses, tin cans, bailing twine, rusted washing machine parts, etc.) to get a tractor up and running again before the rain falls on the hay. "Standin' in" the gap between the everyday and the sacred, poetic techniques of prayer and material conduits of the spirit are mobilized through a consecrated performance of what Kathleen Stewart calls, in describing a local cultural poetics, "foolin' with thangs" (1996, 44).

Among charismatic practices in Appalachia, one member of the congregation who is present in the studio becomes the bodily substitute for a patient who is to be prayed for yet is not physically present. Blood relations usually provide the most efficacious "stand-ins" or conduits for the prayer, though some members of the congregation are believed to possess particular elective affinities for certain categories of illness and patients and may be employed as stand-ins in these cases. For example, one older sister was believed to have a special gift as an embodied conduit for sick children; therefore, when the congregation prayed for a distant child who had no kinship bond in the studio, this woman was often called on to stand in and thus become a physical medium for healing power on behalf of the ailing child.

Radiating outward like spokes around the hub of the microphone/altar, the outstretched arms and downward-facing palms of the studio worshipers demarcate a sacred circle for the communication of Holy Ghost power. As if to amplify the efficacious connectivity of the spirit through tactile contact, the body in communication with divine powers and the material mediations of the radio apparatus mimic each other almost without distinction. In this way, the haptic and proprioceptive sensations of the outstretched or uplifted "holy hand" seem to amplify the technical capacities of the microphone (Csordas 2004, 1994). Speaking forcefully toward the center of this sacred wheel, Brother Aldie begins the prayer: "Father God we call . . ." Like the sudden illumination of the exposed electric bulb protruding from a wall in the makeshift studio, his short invocation signals all the prayer warriors to commence praying their own specific prayer out loud.

What follows is a technique of prayer that is practiced in charismatic worship services throughout Appalachia and elsewhere. Because of the striking entanglement of articulated words created in this communal performance of divine communication, I have termed this practice *skein prayer*. Borrowed from the terminology of weaving and textiles, the word *skein* denotes both a bundle of yarn and the act of tangling or coiling thread. Thus, the phrase *skein prayer* suggests that there are elements of manual technique and haptic sensation intertwined with the oral performance of prayer.

As the prayer progresses, this atmosphere of language grows dense like the haze of coal dust: the bituminous unction of industrial modernity. As these atmospheres thicken, so does the explosive potential. In this entanglement, the possibility of articulation is immersed in a seething skein of noise.

As if this vociferous entanglement of dismembered words was not enough to secure the attention of the divine ear, the noise of the skein prayer is further affected and augmented by vocal exercises such as wailing, crying, and the most prominent and practiced form of these vocalizations, the undulating "Whooo." As if to further thematize the disarticulation of langue and immersion into the buzz of noise, the mouth cedes its function of *articulous* and simply cries out, voicing a basic capacity of the vocal organs. Skein prayer, according to many charismatic practitioners in Appalachia, is one of the most efficacious theurgical techniques to "get a prayer through" to the divine ear. Suddenly, this pulsating flow of skein prayer is cut through with the only clearly discernable sound, the percussive *pop* of hands rapidly clapped together in disjointed bursts of five to fifteen beats. If only for an instant, these percussive cracks pierce through the entangled thickness of noise. There is an important structural similarity between the overall aural effect of the communal skein prayer and the practice of speaking in tongues, or glossolalia. In both cases, the most efficacious forms of prayer are those which can be registered by the human ear but whose plentitude of meaning remains unavailable. To observe this performance of skein prayer in the space of the live studio, one is moved, perhaps even threatened, by the emotionally charged, ecstatic space that is produced. However, the translation of this performance through the radio apparatus produces a significantly different experience—an experience, moreover, that seems particularly apt for the ecstatic moment of skein prayer.

The performance of skein prayer in the live studio differs subtly from the way that this efficacious prayer is "traditionally" practiced. Whereas the ritual of skein prayer within the space of the church or revival tent is usually performed by each congregation member either where he or she is already positioned within the space (in the rows of chairs or pews, for instance) or perhaps concentrated around the body of the sick patient, the performance of this type of entangled prayer within the space of the live studio is specifically organized and oriented around the artificial ear of the microphone. As if to utilize the artificial amplifications of the electro-mechanical ear/mouth to enhance the efficacy of this theurgical technique, the prayer warriors gather around the microphone/altar.

Once again, this particularity of skein prayer oriented around the microphone suggests yet another entanglement: an intertwining between the technological infrastructure of the apparatus and the precarious hearing capacities of the divine ear. Early Christian anxieties around the potential for the divine ear to become "heavy," "dull," or "deaf" and thus unable to register "the cries of the people" suggests the historically and technologically contingent modes for understanding and experiencing divine hearing capacities, angelic messengers, divinatory speech, sacred postal economies, disruptive demons, oracular noise, and so on (Blanton 2009; Peters 1999; Schmidt 2000). Charismatic practitioners self-consciously utilize the radio apparatus to amplify "the cries of the people." Yet this amplification reacts back on the pious subject with unanticipated consequences and attunes particular modes of religious sensation. Within this particular charismatic context, the radio apparatus is an important component in what Birgit Meyer has recently termed the "sensational form" (2009). Senses of transcendence are inflected, attuned, and augmented in particular ways by the religious mediations within the worship context. Embodied techniques and pious training combine with material mediations of the divine to produce the ecstatic sensation of what de Vries, emphasizing the intimate relation between instrumental artifice and the miraculous, calls the "special effect" (2001).

It is as if the theurgical orientation around the microphone simultaneously facilitates a benediction on the ears of the listening faithful out in radioland and an amplification of the importunate intercessory cry toward heaven. In this way, the prayer warriors in the radio station anticipate the simultaneous voicing of their prayer somewhere else in the nebulous and nondescript space of radioland. Thus, the very organization of the prayer, even before the tongues have tangled and the percussive pops cut through the skein, prefigures a peculiar experience of simultaneity or doubling somewhere else. This basic detail concerning the different orientation and conception of the charismatic skein prayer offers an example of the way the radio apparatus inflects or augments experiences and performances of divine communication. Skein prayer voiced into the artificial ear of the microphone, therefore, is not merely the replication of "normal" charismatic worship practices "over" the radio but a profound alteration, reconceptualization, and reembodiment through the transforming process of technological mediation.

As the skein prayer is translated from the space of the live studio to the mouth of the loudspeaker, the listener, whose capacity for hearing is extended by the artificial ear of the microphone, experiences this moment in a condition of "blindness" (cf. Arnheim 1972 [1936]). The technical capacities of the radio do not convey any visual information about the prayer. There is no visual grounding to help orient and locate the voice issuing forth from the loudspeaker. Alternatively, when this type of prayer is experienced within the space of the studio or church, for example, the participant is able to differentiate and organize this otherwise cacophonous tangle of noise by visually identifying the positions of other congregants' bodies. Likewise, if the congregant has his or her eyes closed and hands raised in a posture of prayer, he or she is able to differentiate these voices by differing proximity and intensity of sound, reverberations created by architecture or surroundings, physical contact with other church members, and so on. Rather than detracting from the somatic and emotional power of prayer in the presence of a church space, this distinction may be useful to emphasize the different sensory registers and sense ratios that are invoked, attuned, and trained in what may seem to be the same practice. In comparison to the architectural space of the church, worship through the radio invokes, attunes, and trains significantly different sensory registers and sense ratios.

As if issuing from nowhere, this compelling force of sacred noise gains a new quality and intensity of disorientation through the radio. This vertiginous "special effect" of the radio apparatus foregrounds and attunes the sense of hearing at the expense of other perceptual capacities. Of course, this is not to say that the body of the listener loses all perceptual and embodied orientations in the private domestic space. Listeners are still experiencing this "canny" environment through the embodied orientation of the senses (seeing the table on which the radio sits, feeling the fabric of the couch, smelling the food cooking, etc.). This feeling of embodied familiarity, we might add, could further contribute to the strange sensation of aural disjuncture between the noise issuing from that peculiar elsewhere of the apparatus and the privacy of the everyday domestic space. The sacred noise of skein prayer rends the mundane and habituated "radio texture" that is usually associated with practices of radio listening within the domestic space (Tacchi 1998). Uncanny in the strict sense of the term, the ecstatic noise of skein prayer demarcates a numinous space within the intimate interior of the home.

One could add to the disorienting force of the "disembodied" skein prayer the technical failure of the microphone that is voiced by the loudspeaker. At moments, the noise of the prayer reaches such sonic intensities that the sensitivities of the microphone are unable to clearly register the sound. This inability to "hear" creates strange distorted sounds and thus adds to the efficacious noise mouthed by the loudspeaker. Like the stones in the book of Luke, the technical capacities of the apparatus themselves cry out, adding to the efficacy and sensorial impact of the prayer. This technological failure is voiced by the loudspeaker as a violent hiss of wind, static, and a bending or distortion of the skein voices.

Just as there are moments during the performance of prayer when the technological media fail to "faithfully" register the boisterous noise within the studio, there are many instances following the gradual lull and decrescendo of the skein prayer when the pastor declares, "That prayer ain't gone through yet. Keep prayin'!" When a member of the congregation senses that the prayer has not "gone through," the prayer warriors resume the prayer until everyone is satisfied that the theurgical transmission has reached the divine ear. Communication breakdown between the divine and the everyday is often attributed to the obstructing influences of the devil and his "dark principalities," as well as the burden of unbelief among the radio congregation and the listening audience. Likewise, the negative force of unbelief is said to "quench" the Holy Ghost, preventing the anointing power from entering the space of worship. Though many times the skein prayer is performed with no tangible manifestations of the spirit within the studio, there are occasional moments of ecstatic irruption when the numbing buzz of prayer unleashes the miraculous power of the Holy Ghost.

Many faithful listeners in radioland claim to have been miraculously healed as a result of hearing the skein prayer mediated through the radio apparatus. Take for example the cure of Sister Violet, a faithful listener to charismatic broadcasts and occasional participant in the space of the live studio, who gave a testimony to the miraculous cure of her severely infected index finger while listening to the radio:

> When my fanger was in bad shape,
> you know, Sister Dorothy was a-prayin'.
> She was a-prayin' one Sunday mornin' on there [the radio] for me.
> And I felta-sucha par a-shakin' my radio.
> And I just lifted my hands up, and then I realized that I had my fanger
>   on the radio,
> and my fanger began ta straighten out.
> And, you know, somebody's gotta pray the prayer of faith for ye.
> And I felt her, and then I realized my fanger was straight . . .
> You know, we need to tell, and stand up and tell what God does for us.
> And may God bless ya—I don't wonna take up no more time.

As Sister Violet testifies into the microphone for an unseen audience, her performance completes a circuitry of efficacious prayer. It is as if the healed body of the patient tracks back to the mechanical origin of the prayer. Recounting the miraculous event and thus tracing the infrastructure of the radio broadcast, the healed patient returns to the material source of transmission. Her "live" in-studio appearance in the technological space of transmission is voiced into the self-same microphone that once registered a prayer on her behalf. The anointed body of Sister Violet embodies a forgotten technical potentiality of the radio apparatus; the magnetic interface of the radio's transducer is not only capable of reception but transmission as well (cf. Sterne 2003).

Sister Violet's experience of "presence" entails sensations that are in excess of the merely instrumental capacities of the medium. Thus, the haptic and kinesthetic descriptions given by Sister Violet point to a specific effect of radio listening that transcends the informational content of the broadcast.

Not only are the sounds of Sister Dorothy's praying voice translated by the apparatus; Sister Violet *feels* the physical proximity of Sister Dorothy, and this specifically in relation to the somatic awareness of bodily disfigurement and proprioceptive sensations of elevated extremities.

Likewise, faithful listeners out in radioland also respond to radios' production of presence by actively participating with the broadcast. During interviews, for instance, listeners often described how they interact with the worship service by clapping their hands and singing along with the studio congregation. Several listeners claimed to actively encourage the radio preacher with exhortations such as "Preach it, Brother!" and "Come on!" Finally, this type of participation with the radio broadcast is accompanied by ecstatic manifestations such as the listener who called into the broadcast to testify that she received the anointing while doing house chores and suddenly began "just a-jumpin' and a-shoutin' all over the kitchen." Once again, the sound issuing from the radio loudspeaker produces an experience of calling or demand on the listener that is in excess of the informational content of the broadcast.

As Adorno notes, a basic characteristic of the radio apparatus is that during the experience of listening, the instrumental/material aspects of the radio apparatus (studio microphones, transmitters, receivers, electrical grids, etc.) are forgotten or repressed (2006). Through habitual use and a longing for the unmediated, the machinations and material details of the instrument fade into the background. This inability to actively conceptualize the infrastructure of broadcasting, therefore, creates a sensation of actuality—that an unmediated voice is present in the space of listening directly addressing the listener in his or her singularity. As I have suggested, this sensation is also described as the experience of the isolated radio listener suddenly singled out by a speaker who seems to be actually present in the space of listening. Using archival material such as letters, historian Tona Hangen has also demonstrated that the mediated voice of 20th-century evangelical preaching made it seem as if the preacher were actually present inside the privacy of the home (2002).

And yet it is not merely this capacity to forget that produces the most profound sensations of presence but a kind of doubled awareness that recognizes simultaneously the instrumental machinations of the apparatus and a vague sensation of something else at work behind the apparatus. This rupture or special effect that is produced when sensory capacities are augmented and extended by media such as radio brings us closer to understanding the moment when Sister Violet's radio trembled with divine power.

To be sure, the charismatic faith-healing tradition is saturated with metaphors and practices of touch. Throughout many charismatic radio broadcasts, for instance, phrases such as "he needs a touch from the Lord" and "touch her, Lord," are employed as metaphors of divine healing and miraculous intervention. Moreover, accounts within the New Testament of "laying on of hands" and various instances of efficacious communication of divine healing virtue through tactile contact are literally interpreted and translated into a plethora of tactile practices within the worship context. The performance of healing prayer is thus intimately and crucially linked to a frenetic drive to tactility.

In this way, the contagious potentiality of the Holy Spirit could be communicated through tactile contact with the radio loudspeaker. The specificities of charismatic radio tactility, however, cannot be merely collapsed into a more general charismatic drive to healing touch. As previously described, the act of touching the radio receiver in order to facilitate both the efficacious reception and transmission of Holy Ghost power is generally referred to as a "point of contact." Though this crucial theologico-technical term has spread out—a propensity of all sacred force—to encompass a significant inventory within the charismatic reliquary (anointing oil, photographs, letters, television sets, prayer stamps, prayer cloths, etc.), the concept of "point of contact" itself was formulated within the context of healing prayer mediated over the radio apparatus. Oral Roberts, arguably the most significant proponent of both the charismatic healing revival and Pentecostal faith-healing movements during the 20th century, coined this preeminent phrase as a theologico-technical term that helped to mitigate the distance from both the ear of the faithful radio listener and the efficacious healing virtue of the Holy Ghost. The term *theologico-technical* suggests that the point of contact is both a specific theurgical technique that augments or amplifies the efficacy of the prayer and a theological claim on the nature of divine communication and faith. According to Roberts (1950, 35), God institutes certain "instrumentalities" into the world to provide efficacious material conduits for divine force, allowing the patient to "turn faith loose" through an act of tactile contact.

Though most of the faithful must employ material and technological instrumentalities to unleash their faith and thus instantiate healing virtue, Roberts himself claimed to have been given as one of his *charismata* a specific "sense of discernment" in his right hand that allowed him to "detect" the presence of illness-causing demons. This presence was discerned through tactile sensations of pressure that were exerted on his healing hand by the malignant force of the illness-demon (1950, 35). For the isolated listener, tactile contact with the radio loudspeaker became a prosthetic extension of Roberts's gift of discernment and detection. Thus, as Roberts laid his hand on the microphone or a physical stand-in within the studio during the "prayer-time" of his famous *Healing Waters Broadcast*, the ailing patient placed hands on the radio loudspeaker to achieve access to Roberts's manual sense of detection. This tactile/objectile exercise of faith, in turn, "loosed their faith" and created a physical conduit for the communication of healing virtue.

In Roberts's famous treatise *If You Need Healing, Do These Things*, he emphasizes the radio as an important point of contact. Of course, Roberts's use of radio contact as a technique of immediacy, "liveness," and audience participation was not new. Early Pentecostal radio pioneers of the late 1920s, such as Sister Aimee McPherson, also encouraged listeners to make tactile contact with the loudspeaker during the prayer (Hangen 2002, 74). Roberts, however, made radio tactility a centerpiece of his *Healing Waters Broadcast* and explicitly formulated the theologico-technical phrase "radio as a point of contact." Moreover, his how-to manual of faith healing features a visual illustration explaining how the point of contact works. At the top of the image sits Roberts himself in front of a large microphone exclaiming, "Rise, the Lord maketh the whole." A bedfast and sickly looking man is located in the bottom corner of the illustration, his feeble hand outstretched and touching the radio, while a gigantic divine hand reaches down from heaven to touch his head and thus communicate "healing virtue." Providing a striking example of the disavowal of the material conduit in the moment of healing cure or efficacious divine communication, the radio loudspeaker, placed prominently in front of the prone patient, voices the ironic words "only believe" (Roberts 1950, 33).

Likewise, a prefiguration or anticipation of the "radio as a point of contact" can be seen in the pictures and descriptions taken from Roberts's massive tent-revival campaigns of the 1940s. Inside what was then the largest tent in the world, sick patients would form a "prayer line" or "healing line" in the front of the sanctuary to be prayed over, one at a time, by Roberts's palpating hand. This massive tent auditorium depended on a large public announcement system to broadcast the voice of the healer throughout the throngs of faithful and expectant audience members. Roberts's praying voice and his right hand of discernment were therefore already mediated by a technological system of voice amplification that was literally inserted between the body of the healer and the patient. The microphone, or technological extension and amplification of the voice, was already mediating the patient-healer complex; Roberts would often hold the microphone in his left hand, its large steel housing held close to his mouth, while the right hand reached out both to "discern" the illness of the patient and to communicate healing virtue. Ironically, the technology of radio broadcasting allowed Roberts to propose a strange mimicking of the healing technique within the amplified space of the revival tent. Roberts asked listeners to put their hands on the apparatus in order to gain access to divine healing power. The materialities of the radio, combined with a need to produce a sensation of "liveness" and immediacy for the distant listening audience (cf. Auslander 1999), initiated a curious reversal or inversion of the tactile healing technique.

In this way, the faithful listeners experienced an artificial or prosthetic embodiment of Roberts's spiritual gift of haptic detection; they literally experienced the tactile sensations of heat and pressure from the vibrating electric diaphragm of the radio loudspeaker. In terms specifically related to the radio apparatus and the challenges of communication at a distance, the point of contact can be seen as a theatrical production of immediacy or "liveness" through a strategic thematization of an unanticipated or unregistered potential of the radio apparatus. Hearing the prayer issuing from the loudspeaker in an experiential condition of "blindness," the listener-participant laid on hands to "fill in" the disembodied and distanced voice. Deploying two sensory modes—the auditory and the haptic—during the performance of healing prayer created a powerful sense of immediacy with the praying voice. More than this, however, the discontinuity or disjuncture between sounds registered by ear and vibrations felt by hand was likely experienced by many tactile listeners as the miraculous healing power of the Holy Ghost.

To experience sound through the hand, as a deaf person palpating the throat of someone speaking in order to "hear," creates a sense of disjuncture between the body's capacity to register and process sound and the sheer materiality of sound experienced through the hand. Thus, this sensation of vibration not only corresponds or co-registers with certain sound-meanings of the radio voice, but the sensitive capacities of the skin are able to register heat, pressure, and vibration that are "unheard" by the ear. Radio tactility, therefore, allows the listener to experience the prayer in a profoundly different sensory mode than is possible in other worship contexts and media environments. Sensations of Holy Ghost power surging through the radio loudspeaker thus reside in this strange space of the experiential gap between the haptic and the audile. This sensation of excess during the practice of radio tactility helps us to understand the healing testimony of Sister Violet and her reliance on tactile and kinesthetic metaphors to describe the miraculous moment when she feels her radio trembling with divine power. At a basic level, Sister Violet's testimony is quite literally a tactile sensation of skein prayer experienced through the hand. Indeed, the tangled excess of noise, percussive pops, and wailing produced through the performance of skein prayer is manually registered through the loudspeaker as a series of warm, trembling vibrations.[3] This particular practice of radio audition seems to emphasize the tactile sensibilities at the expense of aural experience.

In conclusion, historical and ethnographic evidence suggests that radio has had a significant influence on understandings and experiences of prayer, the healing efficacy of tactility, and pious listening practices within the charismatic context. Crucial theurgical techniques within the context of charismatic faith healing, such as the tactile "point of contact," were developed specifically in relation to the radio apparatus and actively incorporated into the worship styles of the Appalachian faithful. Ironically, modes of listening and understandings of faith healing insinuated themselves into the "normal" church context through the mass mediations of the radio apparatus, at least since the early 1930s. Emphasizing the intertwining of charismatic practice and media technologies such as the radio also attests to the thorough modernity of "old-time gospel" and prevents the typical narration of religion in Appalachia as "isolated" or "timeless." Charismatic practices such as skein prayer and radio tactility can be seen as performative negotiations of a specific technologically mediated environment just as much as attempts to influence and instantiate supernatural power. Indeed, I have argued that there are crucial moments within the ritual context when the two seemingly discrete phenomena—the performance of prayer and the technical apparatus—become indistinguishable.

Within the charismatic tradition, the phenomenon of radio tactility points to a "prosthesis of prayer" and an "apparatus of faith" supplementing the spiritualized rhetoric of faith healing. Many of the faithful within the charismatic community and beyond emphasize that prayer is unmediated and free from material conduits, claiming that "there is no distance in prayer." Likewise, on the level of academic analysis, many so-called belief-centered theories of ritual efficacy relegate the force of charismatic healing techniques to internal psychological mechanisms and cognitive processes. In this way, both everyday and scholarly understandings of "faith healing" take for granted the internal, spiritual, and belief-centered characteristics of this curative technique. Yet the prevalence of material "points of contact" such as the radio apparatus suggest otherwise. Perhaps a reconceptualization of the term *faith* in the ubiquitous phrase *faith healing* would be useful.

The exercise of faith—and its visceral, embodied connotations—seems to be activated in material objects and technological apparati exterior to the religious subject. It is as if faith does not reside in the interior structures of cognition and belief but remains hidden within the external object, ready to be "let loose," "unleashed," or "released" through the explosive tactile performance of the "point of contact." Through the machinations of the radio apparatus, for example, the religious subject is able to "reach out and touch faith." Faith therefore seems to make its appearance felt in and through specific processes of objectile and technological mediation.

Yet to conclude by suggesting that faith resides in media radically exterior to the religious subject would be merely to reify what seems to be a peculiar oscillation at work within the term *faith* itself. The precariousness inherent in prayer demands some kind of performance or practice of faith. This performance of faith is not only a spiritual form of volition or belief that would propitiate the precarious contingencies of divine communication. Rather, it is simultaneously a performative revelation and concealment of the material conduits of divine communication. Its power, moreover, depends on a disavowal of the tangible media of prayer in favor of some spiritualized form of belief. The word *faith*, then, encapsulates both the material conduit of prayer and its simultaneous denial. In an ironic self-effacement, the radio loudspeaker voices "only believe" at the very moment when the ailing patient must make tactile contact with the apparatus in order to receive healing power.

Just as haptic and kinesthetic sensations were restored to the necrosed and benumbed finger of Sister Violet through tactile contact with the radio apparatus, the miraculous presence of the Holy Ghost makes its appearance to the particular sensory registers of the religious subject as a specific effect of technological mediation. The apparatus, as a kind of prosthetic sixth sense, attunes the perceptual faculties to specific somatic experiences of the "transcendent." The material and technological prostheses of prayer extend the perceptual capacities of the subject somewhere else, yet this religious experience of *ecstasis* (literally, "talking outside the self") can never be abstracted from the material devotional practices that "stand in" between the everyday and the sacred. The Holy Ghost moves in that ecstatic space between body and apparatus, and thus Sister Violet feels her radio "shakin'" with divine power. To rephrase the ubiquitous passage from the book of Romans (10:17), perhaps it would be more appropriate to conclude that "faith cometh by *touching*."

NOTES

1. I would like to thank Brian Larkin for his insightful commentary and helpful suggestions on an earlier version of this chapter presented at the Scheps Memorial Library in the Columbia University Department of Anthropology.

2. These small independent radio stations are usually owned by members of the local community and operated on a for-profit basis. In addition to the administrative and organizational capacities of the owners of radio station WGTH, they also work in the

studio as DJs throughout the week. Much of the revenue for these stations is generated through advertisements for local businesses.

3. While conducting fieldwork with charismatic listening communities in Appalachia, I had the opportunity several times to participate in radio tactility while listening to live broadcasts in the space of listeners' homes.

REFERENCES

Adorno, Theodor W. 2006. *Current of Music: Elements of a Radio Theory*. Frankfurt am Main: Suhrkamp Verlag.

Arnheim, Rudolf. 1972 [1936]. *Radio: An Art of Sound*. New York: Da Capo.

Auslander, Philip. 1999. *Liveness: Performance in a Mediatized Culture*. London: Routledge.

Baker, Ronald L. 2005. *Miracle Magazine* in the Sixties: Mass Media Narratives of Healings and Blessings. *Journal of American Folklore* 118 (468): 204–218.

Blanton, Ward. 2009. Augustine's Postal Demons: Reflections on a Theologico-Postal History of the West. Paper presented at the European Science Foundation Exploratory Workshop "Technology and Religion: Structural Affinities and Cultural Challenges," Glasgow, October 14–16.

Clements, William. 1974. The Rhetoric of the Radio Ministry. *Journal of American Folklore* 87 (346): 318–327.

Csordas, Thomas. 1994. *The Sacred Self: A Cultural Phenomenology of Charismatic Healing*. Berkeley: University of California Press.

———. 2004. Asymptote of the Ineffable: Embodiment, Alterity, and the Theory of Religion. *Current Anthropology* 45 (2): 163–176.

Dean, Rebecca. 1998. I'll Meet You in the Air: A Cultural Study of Appalachian Pentecostal Radio Preaching. Unpublished manuscript, Department of English, University of Pittsburgh.

de Vries, Hent. 2001. Of Miracles and Special Effects. *International Journal for Philosophy of Religion* 50:41–56.

Dorgan, Howard. 1993. *The Airwaves of Zion: Radio and Religion in Appalachia*. Knoxville: University of Tennessee Press.

Hangen, Tona J. 2002. *Redeeming the Dial: Radio, Religion, and Popular Culture in America*. Chapel Hill: University of North Carolina Press.

Hill, Jonathan. 1978. *The Cat's Whisker: 50 Years of Wireless Design*. London: Universal Books.

Meyer, Birgit, ed. 2009. Introduction: From Imagined Communities to Aesthetic Formations: Religious Mediations, Sensational Forms, and Styles of Binding. In Birgit Meyer, ed., *Aesthetic Formations: Media, Religion, and the Senses*, 1–28. New York: Macmillan.

Muller, F. Max. 1901. *Last Essays by the Right Hon. Professor F. Max Muller*. London: Longmans, Green.

Peters, John D. 1999. *Speaking into the Air: A History of the Idea of Communication*. Chicago: University of Chicago Press.

Roberts, Oral. 1950. *If You Need Healing, Do These Things*. Tulsa, OK: Healing Waters.

Rosenberg, Bruce. 1970. *The Art of the American Folk Preacher*. New York: Oxford University Press.

Schiffer, Michael B. 1991. *The Portable Radio in American Life*. Tucson: University of Arizona Press.

Schivelbusch, Wolfgang. 1977. *The Railway Journey: The Industrialization of Time and Space in the 19th Century*. Berkeley: University of California Press.

Schmidt, Leigh E. 2000. *Hearing Things: Religion, Illusion, and the American Enlightenment*. Cambridge: Harvard University Press.

Sterne, Jonathan. 2003. *The Audible Past: Cultural Origins of Sound Reproduction*. Durham: Duke University Press.

Stewart, Kathleen. 1996. *A Space on the Side of the Road: Cultural Poetics in an "Other" America*. Princeton: Princeton University Press.

Tacchi, Jo. 1998. *Radio Texture: Between Self and Others*. In Daniel Miller, ed., *Material Cultures: Why Some Things Matter*. Chicago: University of Chicago Press.

Titon, Jeff T. 1988. *Powerhouse for God: Speech, Chant, and Song in an Appalachian Baptist Church*. Austin: University of Texas Press.

12

Radio in the (i)Home

Changing Experiences of Domestic Audio Technologies in Britain

JO TACCHI

You make me want to listen to the radio
—Danny, age twenty-eight

Introduction

Recently, I asked a group of four young British people in their mid- to late twenties about their personal perceptions of radio. They each spoke about radio as if its "golden age" had already passed. They reminisced about their parents' listening and associated this with the soundscapes of their child-hoods: "When I was growing up, the radio in the kitchen was always on" (Hannah, age twenty-seven). Teenagers in the late 1990s, these young adults remember listening to the radio as if it were a fixture of that time that is no longer present. In Hannah's words: "I used to listen to Radio 1. . . . I don't any-more. . . . I used to listen to it when I was a teenager. I used to listen like after eleven or after midnight. . . . it was like different people [DJs] each night had a show. I mean, Monday night used to be punk." Rose is a part-time singer. She talks passionately about music but says she rarely listens to the radio anymore. Both Hannah and Rose agree that they will now be found listening to streaming audio, a practice they clearly do not think of as radio. They associate the term *radio* with analogue, real-time radio received through what they consider to be "old-fashioned" radio receivers.

These perceptions point to the ways digital and Internet circuitry has fundamentally transformed radio, while also extending its reach. They talk about podcasts, MP3s, streaming audio, and late-night sounds of comedy and sci-fi listened to through headphones via digital audio channels. The devices they use to listen to audio in their homes range from iPods and other portable MP3 devices to computers with Internet connections and in one case a digital radio receiver. Content listened to via the Internet or digital receiver includes radio programs that are also broadcast to analogue radio receivers, as well as content only received digitally. This is the domestic environment that I refer to as the (*i*)*home*, a digitally enabled private sphere with multiple channels for the reception and circulation of audiovisual media content.

Despite the four young Britons' assertions that radio is no longer relevant, each does still listen to mediated audio, even if it is not what they consider to be radio, and even if it is in different ways from when they were teenagers. One of the four, a young man, talked about how he had recently "been forced" to listen to the radio in his car, since his CD player had broken, and he could not contemplate driving without the accompaniment of music. He had not listened to radio in the car for a very long time, and he talked about the local station he tuned in to as if it was an old friend with whom he had been reunited. He still prefers his "own" music, but he enjoyed the experience of reconnecting, and reknowing that the radio is still there.

Indeed, these young people call attention to the changing definitions of radio itself. If we define radio as the practice of broadcasting or narrowcasting audio content to the public, then much of what these young people listen to qualifies as radio, and some of it still reaches them through radio waves. Yet its users draw a clear distinction between the kinds of mediations associated with digital and Internet audio and those of radio technology. In this chapter, I consider digital and Internet audio to form a part of what I call radio. Across space and time radio has been used differently, demonstrating not only that a global definition of the meanings and uses of radio cannot be assigned but also that evolutions of what I have elsewhere called *radiogenic* technologies should not be dismissed as being different from radio and therefore not a part of the ambit of studies of radio (Tacchi 2000b). It is interesting to note that, in the United Kingdom, radio studies emerged as a strong field of academic study at precisely the time that new digital and networked technologies became widespread (ibid.).

Peter, who is twenty-nine, felt that young people listen less to the radio because they have a lot more choice with the ubiquitous Internet, providing place-based, genre-based, or customized audio on demand. Peter would "never sit in [his] house and listen to the radio." And yet he listens to podcasts and other streaming audio via the Internet—he just does not think of it as radio.

These young people's practices of listening were different in their childhood and teenage years:

> DANNY: I used to tape the radio, on cassette; I've got all the Westwood[1] shows.
> HANNAH: That's a proper teenage thing to do, the latest tunes. You couldn't afford to go and buy the single. You try and cut out the talking by using the record and pause buttons . . . share it with your friends.

And yet similar:

> PETER: Yes, nowadays I listen to streamed shows. And it doesn't matter if you can't listen at a certain time, because you can make MP3 downloads of streamed shows, and I can listen when I want to. People give you links so you know what to listen to.
> DANNY: I suppose podcasts are sort of radio?

In the mid- to late 1990s, precisely the time these young people remember fondly, I conducted an ethnographic study of the role of radio in the home (Tacchi 1998, 2009). The people I talked to then told me similarly nostalgic stories about the "recently passed" golden age of radio and the soundscapes of *their* childhood or teenage lives, ten, twenty, thirty, and forty years before (Tacchi 2003). Some recounted their teenage listening practices which echo Danny's and Hannah's practices of recording music from late-night music-genre radio shows—such as listening to the Top 40 music charts, writing down the artists and songs, to compare notes and talk authoritatively about it the next day on the school playground. For many in the 1990s, just like Hannah, Danny, Peter, and Rose, remembering the radio meant remembering their parents—for example, the comforting memory of a father standing at the kitchen sink shaving every morning to the sound of the radio, always evoked by a certain record heard in 1995 on a local "classic gold" station. One might imagine a future in which Hannah's children will recall with nostalgia their mother listening to BBC Digital Radio 7 late at night to calm her mind and help her sleep, as a defining part of their childhood and a familiar soundscape.

The core data I draw on in this chapter is an ethnographic study of the role of radio in domestic spaces undertaken in the mid- to late 1990s. That study sought to understand something of the *quality* of radio sound. Today this might be referred to as its *affordances*. The idea of affordances is now fairly widespread in studies of new media. With its roots in the phenomenology of Merleau-Ponty and James Gibson, the idea of affordances as the constraining and enabling material possibilities of media seems to have come to new media studies via Donald Norman's *Design of Everyday Things* (2002), first published in 1988. In my earlier work on radio, I explored the inherent qualities of radio sound: Why was it that people often talked about radio as a friend, a companion? What was it that made radio the ideal accompaniment to domestic chores? How did radio work, and in what roles, as an intimate, invisible medium? I used a range of strategies (interviews, participant observation, media-use diaries, sound mapping[2]) to get to know people and find out about their radio-listening habits and associations, as well as their lives and relationships. It was clear from that research that radio was central to domestic soundscapes and the senses of being in the world these engendered. In addition to finding that radio sound has particular characteristics or affordances that make it suitable for the affective management of the everyday, my ethnographic work showed that radio sound was appealing partly because it allowed for moments of "social silence" (Tacchi 1998). More recent interviews suggest that contemporary mediated audio is appealing in much the same ways, which I elaborate in this chapter through exploring concepts of *stillness*. My argument is that while what constitutes the radio has changed, radiolike media and mediated audio continue to permeate domestic spaces and perform a similar role to radio in the mid-1990s, particularly through the affective management of domestic life.

While the technologies of radio transmission have undergone some dramatic changes, and we have largely moved from analogue to digital, the uses and roles of mediated audio in domestic spaces remain strikingly consistent. In this chapter, I explore these underlying similarities. I argue that contemporary mediated audio, including analogue and digital radio, streaming MP3s, and podcasts, continues to display some of the same affordances that radio sound brought to domestic life twenty years ago, even while the social perception of what counts as radio has shifted. On the one hand, I show that it is through the experience of listening that radio and mediated audio becomes meaningful—stressing the importance of context. On the other hand, I suggest that mediated sound has inherent qualities or affordances and historically specific meanings that it brings to those contexts.

In this chapter, to emphasize shifting notions of radio's place in the (i)home, I examine how radio was introduced into British domestic spaces, how the design of early radio as an object and its content intended certain experiences of use, and how radio, as object and content, has always shifted over time, never remaining static for long. There has been a constant shift in the experience of the consumption and use of radio, which accounts for the ways in which it is often nostalgically remembered by generation after generation. I go on to concentrate on one aspect of domestic life—stillness —to highlight both the historical transformation and enduring power of radio as mediated audio in the (i)home. I use the idea of stillness to encompass the practices of *social silence, peace and quiet,* and *tuning out* performed through radio listening in domestic spaces. This is to explore one of the fundamental roles that listening to mediated audio performs in domestic spaces, the maintenance of emotional balance. I begin this chapter by setting out in more detail how we might think about the contrasting pressures of affordances and context.

Contextualized Affordances of Radio

In Gabriella Coleman's (2010) review of ethnographic approaches to digital media, she points to the range of ways in which digital media are shown to matter culturally and yet how they cannot be discussed as a universal experience. Context is important. Digital technologies facilitate and catalyze social reproduction and realizations of self and of culture that are expansive (Coleman, following Miller and Slater 2000). Despite claims about a new, digital, participatory culture (Jenkins 2006), the ethnographic evidence is at best unconvincing that digital media are solely or even primarily responsible for producing "shared subjectivity" or a wholly new sensorium, "still less a life world that might characterize a vast population" (Coleman 2010, 4). On the contrary, while digital media are shown to play an important role in social, linguistic, political, and economic processes, as well as in perceptions and representations of self, the particular details of how they are experienced in the everyday argues against universal and uniform human experience.

The same can be said of analogue media technologies such as the radio, which has performed different roles, in different places, for different people, at different times. Walter Ong has argued that it is "useful to think of cultures in terms of the organization of the sensorium" and that cultural differences can be understood as differences in the sensorium (1991, 28). The sensorium—the operationalization of our "sensory apparatus"—is determined by culture, and at the same time, it makes culture: if one can understand the sensorium, one can understand culture (ibid.). The same might be claimed for media. Just as Coleman's review of digital media tells us how important context is to understanding media, it also demonstrates that there are particular affordances and constraints implicated in these technologies, however heterogeneously in a range of cultural, social, and political contexts the materiality of media is experienced. Sirpa Tenhunen (2008) argues, through close study of mobile use in rural India, that technologies not only amplify ongoing processes of cultural change which we might consider to be a form of local appropriation of technology but also influence social, cultural, and political processes. Media is determined by culture, and at the same time it makes culture.

It is easy to demonstrate that what is understood as radio has varied across time and location and that its affordances and constraints have shifted. If we look at British domestic spaces as our context, across the last ninety or so years, it is possible to observe changes due to emerging technologies, altered domestic spaces, and changing communicative ecologies (Hearn et al. 2009), which in turn are indications of shifting social, economic, and cultural relationships and conditions. The struggle to domesticate technological artifacts, including the wireless in the 1920s, demonstrates this clearly.

Listening to the Past

Radio started as an "unruly guest" inserted into domestic Britain in the early 1920s, transforming into a "good companion" in the following two decades (Moores 1988). The process of integration into the home constituted the family as audience, with reference to historically specific social spaces and divisions of time (ibid., 21). There was no inevitability about the way that radio entered the home. In the beginning, broadcasters thought large crowds at public social gatherings were radio's natural audience. Manufacturers and retailers, however, saw the family unit and the household as their emerging market (ibid., 24).

The affordances of technologies are due in part to their function but also to their design. Artifacts are *designed* to be sold and to make profit. Designs need to appeal to consumer desires (Forty 1986, 7). Adrian Forty looked at the early design of the wireless and argued that design affects how we think. While design historians had, at the time Forty was writing, begun to recognize the need to talk about "social context" or "social background," "the use of 'social context'" was "rarely more than an ornament, allowing the objects themselves still to be regarded as if they had an autonomous existence where all but purely artistic considerations are trivial" (ibid., 8). Forty argued that a history of design must also be a history of societies.

Early radio sets were resistors, wires, and valves, and people spent hours constructing wireless receivers. They had no speakers but single sets of headphones. The main concern was to achieve some sort of reception, however poor. "All you could hear was the sea, you know, like the sound of waves —but oh, there was such a hullabaloo if you could hear one voice, just one voice" (informant account, Moores 1988, 28). It was a technological craze that brought sounds from the outside into the home, but a solitary activity as a (usually) male member of the household listened for hours for the slightest noise, with other members of the household often required to keep quiet: "You couldn't even go and peel potatoes, because he used to say he could hear the sound of droppings in the sink above what was coming through the headphones" (ibid., 30). Although some people devised ways of sharing headphones so that more than one person could listen, in general the early wireless imposed silence on the household.

Forty describes the design of early radio cabinets, which played a key role in making the radio an acceptable and welcome domestic object. It was in the late 1920s that manufacturers started to pay attention to integrating the wireless into the home. Early sets were put away in boxes and sheds when not in use. Manufacturers were interested in designing a wireless that would find a permanent place in the home, and with the increasing availability of mains electricity, they began to design cabinets that would house the apparatus. Speakers were incorporated, and preassembled sets, housed in cabinets, became cheaper and more readily available to more households.

The first cabinets were designed in wood and made to look like any other piece of furniture. The more far-sighted manufacturers soon realized that radios should be distinguishable and began to consider alternatives that "would perhaps fit people's expectations of radio more closely. . . . The problem of the best way of housing wireless sets centred around people's ideas of radio" (Forty 1986, 202). In stark contrast with today, radio was understood as an advance, a product of and for the future. Cabinets began to be designed so that they were immediately recognizable as radio sets. The medium itself was so new that it still posed a threat, and by housing the set in a piece of furniture that was easily integrated into the household furnishings yet modern in design, the "alien and confusing sounds of radio" were given "a place in people's homes" (ibid., 203). In contrast, today, many digital radio receivers are made to look like old-fashioned receivers, reflecting an understanding of the radio receiver as an object of the past.

In the 1930s, one manufacturer began to use the image of technological futurism in its design. Ekco wirelesses in the 1930s used modern plastics such as Bakelite to enhance their futuristic appeal. They used designers of the

Modern Movement rather than cabinetmakers, giving the impression "that the experimental stage was over and it belonged instead to a world that would be made harmonious and comfortable by reliable and smooth-running technology" (Forty 1986, 205). Meanwhile, the broadcast content of radio was able to become integrated into the home because of the wider social situation of the time (Moores 1988).

In the early 1920s, the comfort of the home was to be enhanced by the wireless, with early surveys on the impact of broadcasting in the home pointing to the ways in which it made the home more attractive. There was a move from public to private recreation, encouraged in part by public commentary on the dangers of the working classes hanging around on street corners (Forty 1986, 25). The notion of the home as a place of safety was emphasized in some of the accounts that Moores's respondents gave, for example, the young woman who was not allowed to go to dance halls because of the bad influences she would be subjected to there but was allowed to listen to jazz on the radio at home. For Moores, these accounts "mark a separation of quite distinct public and private domains" (ibid., 26). Radio was introduced into this setting, adding to the recreational activities and helping to constitute a family identity as a discrete and private form. In this way, the use of radio was developing alongside broader movements in society and reflected a changing ideology in which the public was a place of danger and the home a place of safety and comfort.

After the initial craze and novelty which attracted male interest and enthusiasm, women's relation to radio was dramatically transformed with broadcasting discourses constructing "their audience as 'the family,' and addressing the mother as monitor of domestic life" (Forty 1986, 31). The housewife became increasingly important as the broadcaster's way into the daily lives of households. Scheduling was designed to fit in with household chores and activities, with the housewife and mother being seen as broadcasters' target audience. In the early evening, children and working men were seen as the listeners; at mealtimes in the evening and on weekends, it was the family as a whole. In this way, broadcasters established regular listening habits in their audience. "The image of the fireside was common to much broadcasting literature of the time—and the hearth, the radio and the mother between them signified a focus of interior space, family pleasure and domestic life" (ibid., 34). Radio brought into the home a structured time-management schedule based on broadcasters' perceptions of existing structures, and in doing so, it must have itself influenced and helped shape those household activities and their timing.

Radio's Stillness

The idea of stillness emphasizes that radio, as mediated audio, is still meaningful and relevant in everyday lives in Britain, although in different forms from the 1990s and certainly from the 1920s and 1930s. One particular idea I want to focus on is not so much the idea of endurance evoked by radio when we think of it through time but a fully synchronic and diachronic notion of stillness (Bissell and Fuller 2010; Seremetakis 1994) evoked through the practice of listening to radio. My use of the term *stillness* encompasses a few notions, including "social silence" (Tacchi 1998), "peace and quiet" (Gullestad 1992), and "tuning out" (Beer 2007). The idea of stillness as used in this chapter references practices and states of contemplation, halting, reflecting, and stepping back from the fully social flow of life. This can be performed through an endless array of actions and activities and is put forward as an essential component of contemporary life. Here we are concerned with the ways in which radio and other mediated sound is used to achieve stillness and what this means for our understanding of how radio is used and the roles it plays in domestic life.

David Bissell and Gillian Fuller (2010) use the image of a "nail house" in China which defiantly stands alone in the middle of a large cleared building plot in Chongqing to show how the usual semantics of calm and retreat are not the only way to think about stillness. Yang Wu, the owner, stands on the roof demanding to speak with the mayor. It is day seven of this defiant gesture, a tenacious act that represents "an instance of willful unmoving: a stilling that took a stand" (Bissell and Fuller 2010, 2). While the notion of stillness punctuates the flow of everything and is often considered a problem to be dealt with—for example, a problem of missed productivity or of boredom—Bissell and Fuller ask us to consider stillness as polyvalent.

C. Nadia Seremetakis considers stillness in terms of the senses—with the occasional stilling of the senses paying an important personal and social role. In the context of official cultures and memories, she points out that everyday life is conceived of as a "zone of devaluation, forgetfulness, and inattention" (1994, 13). Seremetakis sees it as having been "colonized" and "mythicized" as a "repository of passivity" by political powers and official definitions, precisely because it is in fact the site where "the most elusive depths, obscure corners, transient corridors that evade political grids and controls" are harbored (ibid.). It is within this devalued "zone" that stillness can be generated, as a "resting point," "against the flow of the present" (ibid., 12). Within the mundane, stillness represents contemplation rather than lack of movement:

> I think of the old Greek who halted from his daily activities in the heat of the mid-day to slowly sip his coffee. . . . This was a "resting point," a moment of contemplation, the moment he began to re-taste the day. . . . This was a moment of stillness. . . . Coffee is sintrofiá (friendly companion), as the saying goes. Sintrofiá generates a moment of meta-commentary in which the entire scenography of present and past social landscapes are arrayed before his consciousness: the contemporary political situation, familial events, village circumstances, the weather, crops, international news, all mixed together. (Seremetakis 1994, 13)

We could replace the act of drinking coffee, and coffee itself, with the act of listening to the radio and radio sound. The "friendly companion" is such a common way of describing radio sound and can be used to generate moments of "meta-commentary" in which the past and the present, space and time, are compressed. These moments of stillness are like "tidal pools," where experiential worlds can be "mapped out in miniature" (Seremetakis 1994, 12). Such experiences emphasize the noncontemporaneous aspects of everyday life, drawing on unrecognized and unmarked events and aspects of life, through "interruptive articles, spaces, acts and narratives" (ibid.).

Radio sound can be used to help produce moments of stillness, such as when Trisha (aged thirty-seven in 1995) takes time out to sit down with a cup of coffee and listen to a competition or a favorite radio feature. A shift worker, in some cases she will set her alarm to wake up and listen to a favorite radio feature:

> For instance, the 10 at 10 [feature], which is at the beginning of his show [favorite DJ], . . . this is ten songs with a connecting theme in some way, and Gary Vincent devised a slot in his show whereby we get the opportunity to send in our suggestions. . . . And I really look forward to that everyday. . . . Sometimes I'll set my alarm—shows how silly I am—I'll set my alarm after I've been on nights, for my radio alarm to come on at ten for me to listen to it and lie in bed dozing and listening to it.

Radio and practices of listening can be seen as providing moments of stillness or what I go on to discuss as social silence, peace and quiet, and tuning out (through tuning in). The flow of the day is temporarily halted, sensorily experienced connections are made, and perhaps, feelings of completion achieved. As Bissell and Fuller put is, "*Stillness punctuates the flow of all things*: a queuer in line at the bank; a moment of focus; a passenger in the departure lounge; a suspension before a sneeze; a stability of material forms that assemble; a passport photo" (2010, 3; emphasis in original). According to Seremetakis, such moments "are expressions of non-synchronicity which become material encounters with cultural absence and possibility" (1994, 12), in which the imperceptible may become perceptible in a marked way. In Tricia's life, music radio plays a particular and important role, in a family in which she often feels excluded. Such moments can provide opportunities to create alternative understandings and rationales and can give depth to the experience of everyday life, which is otherwise, and officially, given little attention. Stillness here might be considered as a moment of time out but also as a way of anchoring oneself to something stable, something still, within a web of potential meanings and truths made up of past sensory exchanges and perceptions and object relations.

In this context, "the surround of material culture is neither stable nor fixed, but inherently transitive, demanding connection and completion by the perceiver" (Seremetakis 1994, 7). Soundscapes, including radio sound, if we think of them as part of the material culture of the home and of the sensory landscape, are good for making such connections and completions and for marking out moments of stillness. Radio sound can be seen to make complete, through its connecting power, the domestic, affective environment of the home. Much of its ability to do so is because of its transitory nature and the way in which it is experienced sensorily and affectively. My research participants see radio as a naturalized part of everyday life that needs no explanation or justification. When we think of the many instances of radio sound being used as a background to everyday living, we can see how it can work to make experiential things concrete to some extent—but generally not enough to bring about great self-critical or reflexive attention in a foregrounded way. It may be seen to generate self-reflexivity in a very creative yet highly selective and subtle way, due to the way in which it is experienced—the sensory modality of sound and its flexible character, a pilot to our maneuverings in this web of potential connections and completions.

For Bob (age forty-nine in 1995), radio is a constant companion. He will "turn it on first thing in the morning in the bedroom and listen to it": "If I'm moving around the house, then I've often got both sets on [bedroom and kitchen] quite loud so I can hear it all over the house." For Bob, radio keeps him connected with a world that he wants to know about, and through listening practices, radio helps him to define who he is in such a world. Radio sound anchors Bob through its constant presence when he is at home—so much so that his ex-wife talks about how she used to have to "shut up" when they were still living together, so that he could hear the radio (Tacchi 2000a).

Social Silence, and Peace and Quiet

For many of the people I met in the 1990s, the idea of shutting out the noise (or lack of noise) in their lives through the use of radio sound was important. In many cases, it helped to produce stillness or switching off from anxious thoughts, fears, or repressive responsibilities. In other cases, it helped to provide release from the deafening silence of their lives. When I use the term *social silence*, I am thinking of silence as one end of a scale of sociability. Social silence indicates a lack of social interaction, or stillness from it, but not necessarily a lack of sound. Social silence is a stilling in sociality that allows us to punctuate the flow of all things, as Bissell and Fuller so nicely put it. In some cases, social silence is used to allow for contemplation of sociality. Aspects of life which involve high degrees of sociability—demanding family or work settings—are heard or understood more clearly when reflected on from a situation of nonsociability. It provides the contrast between movement and stillness.

Sound can be used to blast away unwanted thoughts or feelings, so that Sue (age fifty-two in 1995) will sometimes turn the sound up and "blast" the radio in order to clear things: "to clear your mind of what's bothering you and put something else in there. . . . I find it very therapeutic." Radio sound can also be used to compensate for a perceived lack of sociability. Lack of sounds can become a reminder of an undesired social situation to be avoided. Some respondents from the 1990s talked about leaving their radio on, whether or not they were listening actively or even present in the home, and some left it on throughout the night while sleeping. Some people talked about the sound distracting them from their loneliness, which can be thought of as a stilling of a relentless emotional isolation—radio sound as a preventer of social silence.

Deborah, age twenty-seven in 1995, divorced with two young children, used to like it when it was quiet but now actively tries to avoid it: "It is because I'm by myself I know that, whereas before I used to read a lot more, now I watch telly and the radio a lot more because it is company." Having been alone for two years, Deborah now keeps the radio on at night: "It is the silence. That's why I stick the radio on. . . . It is company. The reason I do like talk shows rather than listening to Radio 1 [BBC popular-music radio channel] is that it is someone talking rather than music. That's why I like it when I go up to bed, because I suppose it is a way then of knowing that someone else is around." Radio here is used to cover up unwanted silence, a reminder that there is a world of sociability out there. Deborah also uses radio sound during the day to distract her from her daily tasks and to take her mind off her problems. She chooses music radio in the day, and sometimes when her children are at home, they might all dance and sing along. The sounds she chooses and the ways she uses them help her to get through a difficult time in her life, stilling her loneliness, covering up the social silence.

The idea of radio or mediated sound providing comfort was also talked about in 2009, so that Hannah has a regular listening pattern, emphasizing the comfort provided by her routine: "I listen to digital radio, BBC Radio 7. It is on twenty-four hours. It plays all sorts of shows. I listen to it mostly for comedy and drama, between six p.m. and midnight. It has a crime and thriller hour, lots of classics like the *Goon Show*, lots of stuff made specifically for Radio 7, book adaptations. I listen in the evenings, in bed." It was this description of her listening that prompted Danny to say, "You make me want to listen to the radio."

Marianne Gullestad talks about the rhetorically powerful cultural category of "peace and quiet." These are words often used by ordinary people in Bergen, Norway, to describe interpersonal relationships and to characterize people and actions. In particular, these words are used to "explain, justify, and legitimate withdrawal from social relations" (1992, 140). The notion of peace and quiet is used to "draw boundaries between important cultural domains: around the person, around the home, around the 'immediate family'" (ibid., 145), as well as around the nation itself. Gullestad is not talking about the absence of noise as such but about ideas which are social and cultural and which can be used to describe different qualities in different contexts.

Very much like the notion of stillness discussed earlier, peace and quiet have a dynamic relation to other notions such as life and movement, which are understood in Bergen as positive and controlled, and tension and bother, which are negatively understood states. In Bergen, peace and quite are immaterial and diffuse cultural categories, which are positively value laden and which contribute to structuring thoughts, emotions, and actions (Gullestad 1992, 146). These notions are both void of meaning and saturated with meaning:

> If I start with one category, in this case peace and quiet, I soon come across the other categories: the ideas of independence and of wholeness (helhet) are connected to protection of social boundaries by a reduction of the intensity of social relationships. Social interaction is easily interpreted as a reduction of autonomy and a fragmentation of the self. Therefore it becomes important to cut oneself off from society to get peace and thereby retain in a fundamental sense the control of the self. (Ibid., 158–159)

With regard to media and communication technologies, nowadays we are less likely to think in terms of stillness, social silence, and peace and quiet and more likely to think in terms of connection. Increasingly there is an idea that we are always connected through a series of digital devices. The idea of breaking that connection can be quite powerful.

Tuning Out

The most comprehensive work on practices of the use of mobile audio devices such as the iPod can be found in the work of Michael Bull (2000, 2003, 2007). He considers such devices and their use in public spaces in the city as crucially privatizing. This might be thought of in terms of stillness, as discussed earlier, but Bull's work tends to overemphasize the disconnection. David Beer's (2007) critique of Bull's work and his dissatisfaction with Bull's heavy-handed descriptions of mobile devices being used to screen out the city lead him to propose a subtler "tuning out." To "tune out" means to prioritize the sounds coming through the headphones but to remain cognizant of, and often interrupted by, the complex soundscapes and associated meanings from the urban environment.

Bull describes the use of mobile audio devices for journeys through the city as a way of creating a private, auditory "bubble," signifying the refusal of the "gaze" of others, as a way of managing experience in the public sphere, the creation of an alternative soundworld and urban environment. In Bull's work, engaging with the mobile audio devices is used to create a separate reality, an escape. Rather than a stilling, it suggests an alternative, a rejection, and Bull claims, a substitute for "the subject's sense of the social, community or sense of place" (2003, 363). Bull represents listeners as active in terms of repossessing and occupying time and making it pleasurable through music, in a context that is otherwise mundane and restrictive, where time is taken away from them.

There is a very different interpretation of similar research conversations happening here. In effect, one could understand Bull's position as arguing that privatized soundscapes in public spaces prevent stillness and ensure continued motion and activity despite, and in opposition to, what the urban environment would otherwise prescribe. Beer describes Bull's work as creating an image of a *utopian zone of exclusion formed around the user*" (2007, 857; emphasis in original). Beer prefers the vision of a complex, incomplete, and imperfect process, captured in the term "tuning out." Beer prefers the notion of distraction from the present, rather than Bull's idea that soundscapes are managed to achieve solitude. For Beer, it is about social distance rather than Bull's social withdrawal and soundscape control. While Bull's work suggests that people work to lift themselves out of their immediate environments and escape them, Beer puts forward the notion of tuning out to emphasize the necessary and enduring connections: "This approach towards these technologies is not so much about screening out or controlling, instead to tune out is to prioritize particular aspects of the immediate soundscape (the ones we chose to play back into our ears)" (ibid., 859). Returning to the home as the context for soundscapes that is being considered here, this idea of tuning out, and its implications for maintaining a connection with wider acoustic and social worlds, is important. It can be added to the ways in which we might talk about the polyvalent concept of stillness. It overlaps to an extent with notions of social silence and peace and quiet, and in particular it stresses the importance of the underlying connection in all of this. Unlike in Bull's representations of mobile audio practices, Beer suggests that the "background hum" that is always present in his understanding of tuning out and the understanding on the part of listeners that they will regularly and sometimes abruptly be interrupted by the world outside their "bubble" is important. What is there in the background, the "background hum" in Beer's terminology, is highly significant.

For the respondents whom Bull and Beer talk about in public spaces, that background hum will be opposed to the sounds they play through their audio device. In the homes of many of my respondents, it was radio sound itself that provided this hum. Knowing it is there and is always there is important:

> If I come in from work, I will just switch the radio on automatically, not really listen to it because I've had it on in the car. It would be there in the background, but then I'm busy doing things. It's to do with being on my own here. I'm not always—I mean, there is a lodger here as well, but it's a habit that I've had because I know that my family, my mother and father, did that, and it's kind of a comforting thing; it's always been there, it's always in the background. (Gillian, age thirty-three in 1995)

> I see it as something to relax to, even the debates. I just—it's nice to hear it going on and have a smile, but I wouldn't turn it up loudly. I don't, probably, I don't necessarily wanna hear it, but I just know it's there. (Anne, age thirty-two in 1995)

Gillian and Anne use the radio for relaxation and as a way to take time out but importantly also to stay connected. They might tune out of the world, but they know the world is there—they can hear it in the background hum.

It is important for them to know the world is going on around them and to hear the sounds of that world, but they do not necessarily want to listen to the words, the meanings beyond the meaningfulness of just being there. The way people talk about how they use radio sound can often be understood to describe a certain type of stillness, this time one that allows them simultaneously to keep in touch with life while at the same time to "tune out."

In Conclusion

Mediated audio such as radio has qualities or affordances that make it especially suitable to make connection with, and work in, the affective dimension of everyday life. This, I suggest, is why radio is often characterized as a "friend" and as providing "company." It helps people through their daily lives in a variety of ways. Its capacity to affectively manage the contingencies of the everyday also accounts for its enduring relevance, despite the ways in which it has shifted in how it is received, used, understood, and defined. Mediated sound helps to provide complementary ways of knowing and experiencing—the way it links to the past and the future, to the experienced and imagined outside, and to other worlds. In the webs of memories, connections, sociality, future, fantasy, and feelings that make up our everyday lives and routines, radio and mediated sound, with its particular affordances, is able to work as a pilot or conductor. It can help in a variety of ways to provide stillness for harmonizing the complementary, distinct, different, and conflicting aspects of one's life—a manager of difference. It can be used to create moments of stillness that allow for the important work of reflection, or recognition, of our being in the world.

This chapter has been about the role of radio and mediated sound in the shifting social, technological, and media contexts of British domestic life. History reveals that understandings of radio have been defined by change rather than stability, and it is sensible to think that this pattern will continue ad infinitum. Nevertheless, I argue that contemporary digital sound, received in real time or time delayed through a range of devices not necessarily identified as radio at all, maintains distinctive affordances that also allow us to consider the evolving nature of what we once understood as radio.

NOTES

Thanks to Heather Horst for her suggestion for the title of this work.
1. Tim Westwood, DJ on BBC Radio 1 playing hip hop.
2. Sound mapping involved walking around homes with research participants, drawing

rough sketches of rooms and corridors, and discussing and noting what sounds the participants associated with which spaces.

REFERENCES

Beer, D. 2007. Tune Out: Music, Soundscapes and the Urban Mise-en-Scène. *Information, Communication & Society* 10 (6): 846–866.

Bissell, D., and G. Fuller. 2010. Stillness Unbound. In *Stillness in a Mobile World*, ed. D. Bissell and G. Fuller, 1–17. London: Routledge.

Bull, M. 2000. *Sounding Out the City: Personal Stereos and the Management of Everyday Life.* Oxford, UK: Berg.

———. 2003. Soundscapes of the Car: A Critical Study of Automobile Habitation. In *The Auditory Culture Reader*, ed. M. Bull and L. Back, 357–374. Oxford, UK: Berg.

———. 2007. *Sound Moves: iPod Culture and Urban Experience.* London: Routledge.

Coleman, G. E. 2010. Ethnographic Approaches to Digital Media. *Annual Review of Anthropology* 39:487–505.

Forty, A. 1986. *Objects of Desire: Design and Society since 1750.* London: Thames and Hudson.

Gullestad, M. 1992. *The Art of Social Relations: Essays on Culture, Social Action and Everyday Life in Modern Norway.* Oslo: Scandinavian University Press.

Hearn, G., J. Tacchi, M. Foth, and J. Lennie. 2009. *Action Research and New Media: Concepts, Methods and Cases.* Cresskill, NJ: Hampton.

Jenkins, H. 2006. *Convergence Culture: Where Old and New Media Collide.* New York: NYU Press.

Miller, D., and D. Slater. 2000. *The Internet: An Ethnographic Approach.* Oxford, UK: Berg.

Moores, S. 1988. "The Box on the Dresser": Memories of Early Radio and Everyday Life. *Media, Culture & Society* 10 (1): 23–40.

Norman, D. 2002. *The Design of Everyday Things.* New York: Basic Books.

Ong, W. 1991. The Shifting Sensorium. In *The Varieties of Sensory Experience: A Sourcebook in the Anthropology of the Senses*, ed. D. Howes, 25–30. Toronto: University of Toronto Press.

Seremetakis, C. N. 1994. The Memory of the Senses, Part I: Marks of the Transitory. In *The Senses Still: Perception and Memory as Material Culture in Modernity*, ed. C. N. Seremetakis, 1–18. Chicago: University of Chicago Press.

Tacchi, J. 1998. Radio Texture: Between Self and Others. In *Material Cultures: Why Some Things Matter*, ed. D. Miller, 25–46. Chicago: University of Chicago Press.

———. 2000a. Gender, Fantasy and Radio Consumption: An Ethnographic Case Study. In *Women and Radio: Airing Differences*, ed. C. Mitchell, 152–166. London: Routledge.

———. 2000b. The Need for Radio Theory in the Digital Age. *International Journal of Cultural Studies* 3 (2): 289–298.

———. 2003. Nostalgia and Radio Sound. In *The Auditory Culture Reader*, ed. M. Bull and L. Back. Oxford, UK: Berg.

———. 2009. Radio and Affective Rhythm in the Everyday. *Radio Journal: International Studies in Broadcast and Audio Media* 7 (2): 171–183.

Tenhunen, S. 2008. Mobile Technology in the Village: ICTs, Culture, and Social Logistics in India. *Journal of the Royal Anthropological Institute* (N.S.) 14 (3): 515–534.

13

"A House of Wires upon Wires"

Sensuous and Linguistic Entanglements of Evidence and Epistemologies in the Study of Radio Culture

DEBRA VIDALI-SPITULNIK

When I was a little boy, I listened to programs in my own languages, and in Bemba they used to say *"kuno kuhanda kwashikapepele"* [here at the house of endless activity]. Especially David Yumba. It means "here is a place of many wires." As a kid, I would imagine that you had to crawl under all these wires, and whatever you said there would be picked up. The broadcaster sat there hunched up under the wires and spoke. They also said *"handa ya nsalensale"* [a house of wires upon wires].
—Lawson Chishimba, Zambia National Broadcasting Corporation Radio 4 disc jockey

Competition Quiz No. 3
1. Your wireless set is full of wires. Why, then, do we call it "Wireless"?
2. For what inventions or discoveries were the following men and women famous: (a) Marconi? (b) Priestley? (c) Curie? (d) Whittle? (e) Pasteur? (f) Edison? . . .
—*African Listener* 9 (Northern Rhodesia, September 1952), 16

Media cultures are permeated by the twin discourses of technological mystique and no-nonsense technical manipulation. The idioms of the former: traveling voices and people, activated powers, transformed worlds, enveloped and transported selves. The voice of the latter: push here, move this, connect that, open, close, listen. The juxtaposition in the epigraphs of the personal, lyrical memories of a radio DJ with the dry, colonial voice of authoritative knowledge testing captures this tension between mystery and science, between creative world making and practical technology. It also provides a window into the multidimensional story of radio's meanings in both contemporary Zambia and colonial Zambia (then, Northern Rhodesia). In this chapter, I wish to activate this tension between the voice of imagination and the voice of science and also to activate these metaphors of wires, tangles of wires, and being wireless to open conversations about the nature of evidence and knowledge production in the study of media culture. My questions are just as much about the nature of media anthropology's subject—in this case radio culture—as they are about our work, our writing practices, and our relations to them.

I begin with two sections that explore what it means to document the phenomenology of sound and hearing. In the first, I suggest how researchers might experiment in the documentation of their own media captivations as a way to sharpen their ability to tune in and find language for documenting other people's media captivations. In the second, I argue that the phenomenology of auditory experience, particularly that within radio culture, is entangled with material and ideological meanings and that this necessitates methodologies and research frames that can capture complex nexuses of relations shaping ways-of-hearing, as well as ones that remain modest about their ability to capture subjective realities. Building on these points, the second half of the chapter explores how evidence from language matters for the production of knowledge about sonic cultures. I argue that language can never be taken as a transparent window into subjective experience, thought, or cultural categories. At the same time, I show how different orders of linguistic data—such as nicknames for radio personalities, modes of address, circulating radio phrases, words used by avid radio listeners, and indigenous words for radio—provide important arenas for exploring the complex phenomenology of sonic cultures and ways-of-hearing. All along, the chapter can be read as one that relies on language to argue and to uncover but that remains wary about language's ontological fixity.

Sharpening the Documentation of Media Captivations

Much like the scholars of a different kind of mediation—spirit mediumship —many media anthropologists have been attracted to their subject because of its connections with transformational and imaginative powers. For many of us, there is wonder and aesthetic appreciation much like that suggested by DJ Chishimba's remarks in the epigraph. At the same time, in professional writing, we often downplay these personal attachments, passions, and pleasures. It might be said that we often work as social scientists to balance imagination with fact, to separate juicy from dry, and to allow our research subjects to revel in the former ends of these dyads while downplaying our own emotions and our encounters with mystery.[1]

Several years ago, I accepted an invitation to reflect on my personal attachments with radio and with one Zambian radio broadcaster in particular, within the context of an essay for an edited volume titled *Personal Encounters in Anthropology*. This broadcaster was Lawson Chishimba, quoted in the epigraph. In that essay, I wrote about how "his voice burned a permanent mark on my auditory memory" with its dramatic and unpredictable contours, its hint of mischief, and its unusual blend of sharp and rumbling tonalities (2003, 186). An excerpt:

> His voice had more contours, more ups and downs than those of most Zambians I met. . . . It was a gravely voice, but not deep—more like the voice of a smoker or someone who can't clear his throat. Yet Lawson never sounded congested. It was just as if his voice were flowing over some little pebbles at the back of his throat. And he talked fast, very animated, always making exclamations like "ooh" and "aah." So in the midst of this he would sometimes let out a little bit of a squeak. Kind of like his voice had cracked, like he had strained it across too many fluctuating contours or too much excited delivery. (Ibid., 186)

While my writing centered mainly on Lawson's life—relaying his own love of the magic of broadcasting, ethnographically depicting his work behind the microphone, and narrating a chronology of his career—I also shared how I was a fan of his, how our lives intersected in complex and puzzling ways, and how I grieved over his death in 2000. In the essay, I did not explore the larger epistemological ramifications of my auditory experiences and my search for language to describe both them and Lawson's unique voice qualities. I simply crossed the passion-dispassion divide in a very "normal" genre-sanctioned way: in an essay under the rubric of "personal encounters."

Reflecting now on my attempt to capture auditory recollections and render sounds into language, I am led to larger questions about the production of knowledge in the study of media culture. What might open up for us as scholars, if we were to more directly foreground and interrogate our own relations to the media cultures that we choose to document? What might this open up for an anthropological understanding of media cultures themselves? This entails more than choosing a writing style that is personal or ethnographically reflexive. It is about pushing research toward more phenomenological types of descriptions and discoveries. The magic of being transported by voices and images, the perceived textures of sound, what being riveted feels like—these are difficult to document. They are easily lost in the perfect storm of privacy, the ineffability of experience, delimiting anthropological research frames, and a scarcity of communication resources that can relay and value them.[2] Creating space to explore and express our own magical experiences might sharpen our skills in documenting those of others.

Sharpening the Documentation of Auditory Worlds and Soundscapes

The phenomenology of auditory experience and pleasure (both ethnographic subjects' and researchers') has been treated extensively within the field of ethnomusicology. It also figures prominently within the subfield of the anthropology of the senses. While a growing anthropological literature on radio addresses listener positioning and the affective tenors associated with programs, personalities, and even stations (Fisher 2009; Katriel 2004; Kunreuther 2006), the more experience-near phenomenology of auditory worlds (or ways-of-hearing) is still relatively underdocumented. Paddy Scannell is a useful starting point for thinking about the "complex phenomenological projection[s]" of media (1996, 14), but the challenge remains to explore beyond a text-centered position on media "projection" or beyond an ethnographic/interview-data middle zone that relies mainly on media users' brief comments about their affective attachments.

Here, I propose using Steven Feld's (1996) concept of "acoustemology" (i.e., acoustic epistemology) and Thomas Porcello's (2005) concept of "techoustemology" (i.e., acoustic epistemology as it is interlinked with epistemology about technologies) to move this conversation forward. Both Feld and Porcello argue that forms of knowing about sound are culture and place specific and that the phenomenology of hearing is shaped by culturally specific acoustic epistemologies. Further, for Porcello, technological mediation impacts these acoustic epistemologies. Porcello proposes that it is not possible to disentangle people's knowledge, interpretation, and experiences of technologically produced sound from their knowledge, interpretation, and experiences of the technology that produces it.

Porcello's proposal significantly expands Roger Silverstone's (1994) important concept of media as doubly articulated, that is, simultaneously (1) conveyors of ideological content and (2) material objects with particular cultural meanings. Particularly with regard to the latter type of articulation, the implication of Porcello's approach is that the experience of a medium's materiality on one plane (e.g., as a device with a certain history) affects the experience of the medium's materiality on another plane (e.g., the perception of sound quality). Such entanglements abound for the case of radio. Radio's materiality is multifaceted and complexly overlaid—interpreted in various parts of the world and at different times—as a box that magically speaks, a technology that can be carried, a machine that needs battery or electrical power, a commodity with social status, a commodity within a hierarchy of other electronic commodities, and so on (Crisell 2006; Larkin 2008, 48; Spitulnik 1998–1999, 2002). This materiality crisscrosses the ideological, moral, and affective resonances of radio sounds, voices, personalities, and content, as well as a past-present-future of coexisting voices, sounds, and genres within oral and auditory culture.

One of the earliest theorists to tackle such complexities of radio was film critic Rudolf Arnheim (1936). In his far-reaching book, titled simply *Radio*, Arnheim writes about the dynamic nature of radio broadcasting, with its sounds of different intensities, layers, oscillation from one listening perspective to another, and complex connections to imagination, memory, and thought. Fast-forward five decades plus, and one hears echoes in the field ethnomusicology with Chris Waterman's "densely textured soundscapes" (1990, 214) and Feld's phenomenology of foregrounded and backgrounded relations among sounds which are "multilayered, overlapping, alternating, and interlocking" (1990, 265).

Not only does Arnheim try to explain the "enigma of radiophony" (Cardinal 2007, 23); he captures the mobility of radio sound and its potential for forging connections across public and private spaces. The clever vignette which opens *Radio*'s chapter 11 illustrates these insights:

> While the reader of this book was making himself acquainted with the last pages of the previous chapter, a pleasant baritone voice from the loudspeaker beside him is giving out stock exchange quotations; now there is silence except for the slight noises and cracklings, the reader closes the book and gets ready to go out, and suddenly an entirely different voice from the loudspeaker announces that he will now hear Beethoven's 8th Symphony. The reader puts on his coat and cuts off Beethoven's introductory bars in the middle by a pressure of his finger. But the music persists, though more distant and raucous, drifting up the stair from the hall-porter's room. The reader . . . bangs the front door, but Beethoven follows him down the street, loud and strident from the shoemaker's back room, softly from the second floor of a villa, braying across the market-place from a little café. (1936, 258–259).

While Arnheim moves from this passage to pessimistic mass-culture arguments about the dangers of "all hear[ing] the same thing" (ibid., 259), he nonetheless suggests the complex relationships between the materiality of radio soundscapes and the subjective experience of them in social lives.

As there is no ideal starting point in the documentation of radio sound-scapes and auditory worlds, how does one begin to ethnographically document them and what might be called acoustic practices of "worlding" (cf. Stewart 2007)? One strategy might be to adopt George Marcus's (1995) "follow the X" formula, originally introduced as a framework for research design in multisited research. Marcus proposes that multisited research can be anchored through a selection of one of the following strategies: follow the people, follow the metaphor, follow the thing, follow the plot, follow the life, or follow the conflict. Adapting this to radio, for example, one might "follow the sound," as Arnheim imaginatively does, that is, that persistent broadcast of Beethoven's 8th Symphony. Or one might "follow the person," as Arnheim also does while tracking his own imagined reader. For the case of radio, I would add that an additional strategy is to "follow the machine" (see Spitulnik 2002) or to "follow sounds" in one location. Let me introduce "follow the language" or "follow the labels" as a further permutation of these strategies for object construction and ethnographic entry point. Indeed, if as Feld (1990) argues, a major part of examining the cultural meanings/experiences of sound in a particular place/culture requires investigating the very language and even metalanguage used to describe sound, then language itself can be taken as a powerful entry point and anchor for a wider research agenda into radio cultures. In the remaining half of this chapter, I pursue this strategy on a number of linguistic levels.

Tuning In to Nicknames and Other Linguistic "Captures" of Sound

In colonial Zambia during the 1950s, many radio broadcasters' on-air names were simultaneously about sounds *and* about excitement, fast speed, and constant activity, all features that were strongly tangled up with radio's perceived "modernity" at the time (Spitulnik 1998–1999). These themes resonate with DJ Chishimba's childhood memories in the epigraph, namely, about the broadcasting institution being a place of "endless activity."[3]

In a 1988 interview broadcast on Radio Zambia, former colonial broadcaster Andreya Masiye explained some of these nicknames and their associations: "Kateka was *Mfumfumfu*. In other words: 'Dishing out a lot of information.' Alick Nkhata was known as *Kapandula*: 'One who was very good at analyzing issues.'[4] I was known as *Kabvulumvulu*: 'One who was going around like a whirlwind.' Things like that."[5]

Masiye's name derives directly from the *Kabvulumvulu* (Nyanja language, "Whirlwind") program which he initiated in 1953. In the program, Masiye moved quickly across the country—like a whirlwind—recording ordinary people's opinions about everyday problems and changing social norms. In his onomatopoetic name (eponymous of the program title), one can hear a whirring sound (transliterated as "bvooloo-mvooloo") and envision its busy bearer, both moving fast and traveling remarkable distances. In colonial Zambia, the speaking styles of early broadcasters also became the basis for their popular nicknames, regardless of program titles, as former colonial broadcaster Edward Kateka explains to researcher Graham Mytton in this 1971 interview excerpt:[6]

> GM: *Mfumfumfu*, yes this is what everybody calls you. What is the meaning of this word, *mfumfumfu*?
>
> EK: Well, *mfumfumfu* is a word—"the flow of words without stopping."[7] You see, I used to read the ten pages in five minutes without stopping. You see. This came from the, you know, a four-gallon tin, with only one end open, and you put—you fill it with water, and that sound which it makes—*mfu-mfu-mfu*—which water makes—*mfu-mfu-mfu-mfu*. And well, well, "This person talks like a bucket of water, the flow of that water, as in *mfu-mfu-mfu*."

Emphasizing one syllable at a time (*mfu-mfu-mfu*), Kateka provides a rendering of how "flow" is experienced as both continuous and punctuated. There is a rhythm. A container with a narrow opening has what could be described as punctuated gasps of air along with the sound of pouring liquid. This sound is akin to what is represented in English as *glug-glug-glug*, also an onomatopoetic form that uses syllable reduplication. In the Bemba language (from which *mfumfumfu* derives), the use of onomatopoeia, often conjoined with syllable reduplication, is also present in other words denoting sounds, movements, natural forces, and animal names. This raises questions about the extent to which culturally specific and language-specific habits and patterns of word formation might support such kinds of onomatopoeia when it comes to talk about sound and sound quality. My suggestion is that sonic ways of knowing and being in the world intersect with linguistic habits and grammatical resources. Attending to these intersections potentially generates a whole new arena for understanding radio culture. And the zone of nicknames is just one place where this auditory world opens up.

This material also provides a very brief but vivid snapshot of the enigma of radiophony: Arnheim's fundamental point that radio sound does not have psychological resonance or "meaning" on one plane only. The nicknames and the comments about them highlight the complex *entanglement* of sound, rhythm, speaker's personality, speaker's role, and media content in the experience of radio sound. They also point to the important place of acoustic interconnections and analogies. The phenomenology of radio listening is shaped by experiences with other environmental sounds, natural sounds, whirlwinds, echoing chugs as water is poured out of a container, memories of other voices and attachments to them, and so on.

Such names, labels, and other linguistic practices are revealing of culturally specific meanings and subjective experiences, but they cannot be taken as direct and transparent windows into cultural categories, thought, or experiencing subjectivities (Silverstein 1993). Researchers need to proceed with both caution and creativity, taking linguistic material as clues about acoustemologies and subjective experiences of media, without reifying the linguistic data as evidence of a concrete thing—be it a sound or an experience—that exists outside or prior to language. Such nicknames simply point to a rich relational nexus within what might be called Zambian hearing culture: one that includes natural sounds, one that makes analogies across sound/water/ air flow and movement, and one with a type of acoustemology that includes evaluation of speaker's personality, speaker's role, and content in the experience of sound.

How might a caution around linguistic objectification of sound and sound experiences play out more broadly in the documentation of soundscapes and auditory worlds? Arnheim creates a vivid scene around dynamic textures of sound: "cracklings," "drifting," "braying." But are these the terms—and sound qualities—that matter for the person whom Arnheim follows? If the person and scene were real, would Arnheim's rendition adequately capture what is being experienced? Arriving at more emic terms might require different modalities of research. And perhaps such emic concepts are mainly visible only in pockets, as with highly salient modes of labeling via nicknames, internally within a professional register, or in rich descriptions that a single speaker with particular insight shares with the ethnographer. I leave these as open questions, ones which were not on my radar when I conducted fieldwork in Zambia but ones which I would certainly want to ask about radio culture now.

The larger research agenda that I propose here extends the positions of scholars such as Feld (1996) and Paul Stoller (1997): attending to sensory domains such as sound is not about *adding* a new research topic as much as it is about a potentially radical shift in epistemological frames. For the case of radio culture, this plays out on at least three scales of ethnographic description: the phenomenological, the material, and the sociohistorical. Taking the first, if "one's sonic way of knowing and being in the world" is central to what it means to live as a person (Feld and Brenneis 2004, 462), then this fundamentally informs both radio reception and radio production. Ways of hearing and sounding—and ways of being an acoustically attuned being—may be much more central as organizing and orienting cultural logics than many scholars have yet to give them credit for, even as such techniques of the body are unavoidably central to critical ethnographies of radio (see other contributors in this volume). And it may very well be the case that the familiar Eurocentric and even textcentric frames of talk-based interviewing and collecting self-report about radio worlds, practices, habits, and reactions unduly flattens this phenomenological realm.

The second ethnographic perspective, the material, intersects or is potentially completely enmeshed with the phenomenological realm. So too for the third, the sociohistorical. And the epistemological stakes are parallel. The challenge again is not only to more richly document and explore the meaning of radio or radio programs for a particular people, in a particular place, with more attention to auditory experiences and the meanings of sounds. Nor is it merely about considering how radio, like other public and private sounds, participates in "historically layered relationships in sound" (Feld and Brenneis 2004, 469; also see Kunreuther 2006), although this is crucial. It is about entertaining possibilities for acoustemologies to become manifest in different ways in historical and social formations and experimenting with the language of description in ways that may diverge from familiar Eurocentric and even textcentric frames. It is about simultaneously pushing and reflecting on the limits of commensurability, translation, and inference.

Other Pockets of Insight from the Zone of Language

The zone of language as it relates to the study of media cultures is vast. It is not just about language selection or which language is selected as the preferred variety in a particular medium, be it radio, television, film, novels, or newsprint. It also encompasses rhetorics, the modes of address that are used to construct audiences and publics, and the turns of phrase that are used to hide or elevate interests and ideologies. Attending to language means taking into account the social circulation of media phrases. And finally, it is about our word choices. To illustrate this, we can return to the epigraphs.

The first question in Quiz No. 3, published in the Northern Rhodesian newspaper the *African Listener* (1952), poses a linguistic paradox: "Your wireless set is full of wires. Why, then, do we call it 'Wireless'?" The theme of Quiz No. 3 was "Science," and its author was Mr. R. J. Seal of the Northern Rhodesia African Education Department. The magazine announced that Seal was to judge the answers and that "his decision will be final."[8] A substantial cash prize was promised for the reader who gave the "correct solution" to brain-teaser questions about radio, the causes of measles and malaria, and the famous inventions of Marconi and Pasteur.

Begun in 1952, sixteen years after the introduction of radio into the region, the *African Listener* was a British colonial magazine for the growing radio audience in central and southern Africa. The magazine was full of program schedules, photos of happy listeners, and columns about agriculture and heath care. As part of an ongoing colonial effort in public relations, it invited readers to connect with the project of broadcasting, through friendly, albeit paternalistic, modes of address and numerous competitions based on listeners' participation.

From the perspective of the present, the quiz is a curious artifact representing a Western genre which unites knowledge and pleasure. Truth, expertise, and indoctrination merge with competitive performance, entertainment, and winning money. The quiz, and its embedding in the *African Listener*, is also a microcosm of an entire social field of technologies that worked to shape colonial subjects and establish colonial governmentality. This involved the manufacture of radio consumers and membership in a national collective, as well as the disciplining of regimes of knowledge, such as science and medicine, and, especially, the performance of that knowledge in a competitive format. The two processes converge in the case of the quiz, as an audience-participation genre that relies on previous exposure to science education programs. The modes of address and reference in the first question reveal how this field of relations was mapped out. The radio owner as listener/participant is personalized and directly addressed ("Your wireless"), the first-personal plural and a timeless verb tense are used to establish a broader collectivity and a collective truth ("we call"), and the European male expert ("his decision") is positioned as the arbiter between this "you" and "we."

Much more can be said about this fashioning of early radio and listener participation, particularly as it supported the double-faceted colonial project of "modernizing" Africa and regulating African populations to do productive labor within the imperial economy. But question number one remains unanswered. How ironic that the name of the radio machine was a contradiction of what lay inside. How could wires be inside the wireless? Even early broadcasters, according to DJ Chishimba, talked about the radio station as being *full* of wires. And for enchanted radio listeners such as the young Chishimba, there was probably no other place on earth that was less wireless than the radio workplace.

The answer to the linguistic paradox is that, despite the tangle of wires in the studio and in the radio set, what *was* wireless was the space between these different ends of the communication process. According to the answer from a subsequent issue of the *African Listener,* "The word 'wireless' is used because there is no wire connecting the receiving set to the broadcasting station as is the case in ordinary telegraphy and telephones, where there are wires between the sender and the receiver."[9] There were *no wires* in the space between machines and listeners or in the space between studios and villages. Despite the visible technology of wires, something invisible was happening. This was called wireless.

In addition to the linguistic contradiction (How could something with wires be wireless?), question number one also opens up a broader question about denotation: What does the label "wireless" stand for? Does it denote the radio set itself or something else, like the technology or the transmission? While scholars of radio culture use an updated vocabulary—"wireless" is now "radio"—such questions of denotation continue to trouble talk about radio. And this has implications for both constructing and representing units of analysis. Radio is not necessarily fixed or singular, but the single word *radio* potentially steers thinking this way. Or, perhaps better put, "it" is simultaneously singularly singular, variably singular, and multiplex. *Radio* is the machine, the transmission, the institution, a program, a voice, and/or the sounds.

Language as a Window into Reception History

Experiments in colonial broadcasting in this area date back to the late 1930s, and the first official government broadcasting service for Northern Rhodesia was inaugurated on September 18, 1940.[10] By the time of my field research in the late 1980s, nearly fifty years had passed since radio's introduction. While I attempted to elicit oral histories of people's experiences with early radio, these were difficult to get. Many people could talk about their favorite programs and personalities from the colonial period, but they had dim memories of what their first listening experiences were actually like. Others could not describe their own first encounters with radio but could remember the reactions of others. For example, during a research interview, one woman recalled her grandmother's reaction to radio: "She couldn't believe it. She used to say, 'How could that man be speaking from that box all day without getting tired?'" Significantly, this perception of radio talk as an overflow of speaking resonates strongly with the idea of *mfumfumfu,* "the flow of words without stopping" (the nickname for 1950s broadcaster Edward Kateka), described earlier.

Beyond a report by colonial information officer Harry Franklin (1950) containing excerpts from listeners' letters and the listeners' letters published in the newspaper the *African Listener*, there is little record of how colonial Zambians actually talked about radio and its powers. But traces do remain. According to letter writer Diamon Simukwai, radio is a machine that "speaks" within the domestic space. The speech of this "Wonderful Machine" makes homes "happy," evenings "jolly," and owners such as Joshua Amisi "proud" (ibid., 7–8, 12).[11] These and other early commentators replicated British colonial modes of speaking about radio as a crucial technology for modernizing Africa and Africans, most likely borrowing from the very words of radio broadcasts. For example, in the words of letter writer Henry Kumwenda, radio brings "modern world general knowledge" and is a means for Africans to "wake up" (ibid., 11). By reproducing radio discourse, newly literate and beginning speakers of English such as Kumwenda also helped to canonize a basic set of English-language expressions for talking about both modernity and media technology. In such ways, radio and radio listening provided a crucial enabling technology for modernity's varied forms: as a governmental project, a mode of organizing experience, and a set of wider social discourses.

The language of these early letters, like the language of nicknames, is revealing of acoustemologies and subjective experiences, but it cannot be taken as an unproblematic window into the early reception of radio or colonial consciousness. Rather, it is better understood as pointing toward these ontological realities, ones that may only be approximated. Moreover, the language of the early letters does not stand in isolation but rather needs to be viewed as part of a larger communicative ecology, one with its own conditions of production and circulation and of which we can see a nexus of traces and hints that again inform it only loosely and not deterministically.

Without implying that there is some more pure, or less mediated, way to get at the phenomenology of reception—past or otherwise—I wish to consider what can be illuminated about early reception experiences by looking closely at indigenous Bemba-language words for radio and broadcasting (tables 13.1 and 13.2). A significant majority of early radio listeners in colonial

Table 13.1. Bemba Verbs for Broadcasting

Verb Root	Meaning	Examples
-salanganya	disperse; cause to disperse; distribute; publish; broadcast	*basalanganya ilyashi*, "they broadcast news"
-sabankanya	spread or scatter information; broadcast	*basabankanyapo pamwela*, "they broadcast out on air"

Table 13.2. Bemba Nouns for Radio and Broadcasting

Singular	Plural	Meaning						Class	Class semantics
		radio set	radio broadcasting	radio station	broadcasting station	broadcasting	musical instrument		
waileeshi	*baa-waileeshi*	■	■					1a/2a	human, personal
waileeshi	*ama-waileeshi*	■	■					9a/6	unmarked animacy
leedyo	*baa-leedyo*	■	■	■				1a/2a	human, personal
leedyo	*ama-leedyo*	■	■	■				9a/6	unmarked animacy
cilimba	*baa-cilimba*	■	■					1a/2a	human, personal
ici-limba	*ifi-limba*	■	■				■	7/8	inanimate
umu-labasa	*imi-labasa*				■	■		3/4	agentive, alive

Zambia spoke the Bemba language, which by the 1940s had emerged as the major lingua franca in the Copperbelt and coal-mining towns. Because of its widely recognized political, economic, and social value both for Zambia's migrant labor workforce and for the powerful rural-based Bemba chieftaincy, Bemba was selected as one of the four indigenous languages of colonial Zambia to be used in early radio.

Both verbs in table 13.1 predate the introduction of radio. The first, -*salanganya* (disperse, distribute), is used to describe the distribution of food by a chief among his subjects, the spread of news or gossip across long distances, and electronic broadcasting. The second, -*sabankanya*, describes actions such as the spread of news or rumors, either through face-to-face or electronic communication. The use of these verbs in the new domains of media need not be seen as a case of semantic extension, per se, but rather as a consistent use of primary meanings.

In contrast to the verbs, only one Bemba noun for radio derives from an existing word, namely, the common Bemba word for musical instrument: (*i*)*cilimba*. The other nouns were either borrowed directly from English or newly coined. For example, *waileeshi* (wireless) and *leedyo* (radio) are straightforward cases of loan words assimilated into Bemba from English originals. They illustrate the widespread pattern of word borrowing in which things and the words used to name them are borrowed in tandem.

The origins of *umulabasa*, "broadcasting; broadcasting station," are less certain. The form is built from the root -*labasa* and the singular prefix *umu-*. One plausible origin is that the word was coined after a pronunciation of the radio station's call letters, LBS (Lusaka Broadcasting Station), with *la-ba-sa* being the basis for the root.[12] In this process—similar to the process in which the verb *to xerox* means "to copy"—the proper name for the radio station (LBS) could have become *the* name for broadcasting in general.

The etymological patterns in tables 13.1 and 13.2 illustrate two simultaneous modalities of linguistic innovation. One emphasizes the newness and Europeanness of the radio technology, that is, its unnameability with existing Bemba words and nameability with English ones. The other emphasizes its similarities to what preceded it: musical instruments, spreading out, diffusion, dispersal, and even chiefly redistribution of resources and services.

The realm of grammar is one area that tells still more about word meaning and potential experiential realities. All nouns in table 13.2 are part of the Bemba noun class system, which is a system for grammatically tracking nouns in the language with obligatory agreement markers on adjectives and other parts of speech. Noun class systems are analogous to the gender systems of European languages. Each noun belongs to a noun class and pluralizes according to its noun class pattern. For example, the noun for radio—*ici-limba*—pluralizes as *ifi-limba*. Its noun class membership is indicated by prefixes and the way singular nouns in class 7 always pluralize in class 8. According to standard citation conventions, "class 7/8" is a shorthand for nouns that follow this pluralization pattern. Bantu languages such as Bemba have anywhere between fifteen and approximately twenty-four different noun classes, a dramatic contrast to the much smaller number of noun genders in European languages. Bemba has twenty different noun classes, each characterized by distinct semantic values such as "human," "animate," "inanimate," "long," and "small" (Spitulnik 1987, 1988).

The class memberships of the Bemba nouns for radio technology reveal some intriguing semantic associations. Consider that of *umulabasa/ imilabasa*, "broadcasting," which occur in class 3/4 (*umu-/imi-*). In Bemba, class 3/4 nouns denote phenomena that are agentive, generative, and expansive, such as spiritual beings, natural forces, and other animate entities (Spitulnik 1987, 56–61). Broadcasting is classed alongside *umupashi*, "ancestral spirit"; *umweela*, "air"; *umulopa*, "blood"; *umulumbe*, "story"; *umusowa*, "wailing"; and *umulilo*, "fire." Such groupings suggest a framing of radio as a living, vibrant phenomenon. This resonates with the semantic associations of early listeners' descriptions of radio as an agentive and transformative technology.

A similar perception of broadcasting as agentive and alive is also intimated by the membership of *waileeshi*, *leedyo*, and *cilimba* in a subclass of the human class 1/2, which has the values "human" and "personal" at its semantic core. Class 1a/2a words include most kin terms, most occupational names, and numerous animal names, particularly animals that possess the capacity of speech in folktales. The grammatical grouping of words for radio among the ranks of these nouns suggests that, conceptually, radio was viewed in a similar fashion as humans and other speaking beings.

It should be noted, however, that there is some fluidity to the class statuses of *waileeshi*, *leedyo*, *cilimba*, and their corresponding plurals. The assignments to class 1a/2a are not fixed in stone. The nouns *cilimba/baacilimba* (1a/2a) coexist with the historically prior *icilimba/ifilimba* (7/8), which belong to the generic class of inanimate objects. *Waileeshi* and *leedyo* also occur with the grammatical markings of class 9a/6, which tends to be for nouns denoting inanimate things. In short, the three distinct singular/plural pairs that belong to class 1a/2a, known for its nouns denoting humans and humanlike creatures, all have alternate forms that belong to inanimate or unmarked classes. The dual class memberships thus reflect a tension between radio being perceived as "humanlike" and as "thinglike."

In sum, the linguistic material yields two general insights. First, the new technologies of radio broadcasting were initially intelligible by reference to both indigenous and nonindigenous idioms and practices. They were described through analogies with local practices of information dissemination and music, while entirely new words ("wireless") and discursive practices (reading out radio station call letters) were also assimilated into local languages. The second set of insights is more tentative. The noun class memberships may *suggest* unique interpretations of radio's meanings. However, the data remains inconclusive because with Bantu noun classes, as with the gender systems of European languages, class membership does not transparently indicate semantic value (Spitulnik 1987, 1988). As with the English word *radio*, there is a fluidity of denotation, as well as a polyvocality of connotations that echo through layers of culture and language.

Conclusion

Language, like sound and radio, does not stop in one place. In this chapter, I have attempted to activate conversations about how both language and sound (or, better, ways of languaging and ways of sounding) matter for the study of radio culture. Along one line of thinking, it might be said that looking at language and sonic cultures is just one more arena for research effort to be extended: an option, an add-on, something that gets itemized in an ethnographic division of labor. But in another line of thinking, attending to both language and sound is indispensible for theorizing, methodologically uncovering, and representing radio cultures. This chapter, joining others in this volume, offers a number of suggestions for how such work might be done, what is at stake in it epistemologically, and how it plays out in the investigation of Zambian radio culture. While the twin discourses of technological mystique and no-nonsense technical manipulation typify the poles of mediated experiences, as well as conventional options for investigation and representation, I have suggested here that such poles are better engaged as entanglements with a hermeneutic circle, along with our very language(s) of documentation and evidence.

NOTES

I wish to extend my deepest gratitude to my undergraduate teachers Hubert Dreyfus and Hans Sluga (UC-Berkeley) for bringing me into the work of Heidegger and Wittgenstein, respectively, and to my graduate teachers Michael Silverstein and John Goldsmith (University of Chicago) for their rich training in the complexities of the language-culture interface, issues of evidentiality, and Bantu linguistics. For research support, I am indebted to the Zambia National Broadcasting Corporation, University of Zambia, National Science Foundation, Fulbright-Hays, and Emory University. Special thanks go to Lawson Chishimba, Graham Mytton, volume editors Lucas Bessire and Daniel Fisher, and my father, who first introduced me to the beauty, mystery, and everydayness of sonic cultures.

1. See Van Maanen 1988 on these genre conventions and some well-known exceptions to this personal/scientific dichotomy.
2. Anthropologist Alfred Gell describes his own "methodological deafness" to the rich auditory worlds of Umeda people. Writes Gell, one must approach "the auditory domain, including natural sounds, language and song, as cultural systems in their own right, and not just adjuncts to culture at large, but as foundations, thematic at every level of cultural experience" (1995, 233).
3. It should be noted, however, that Chishimba's childhood dates to the subsequent decade, the 1960s, a period in which colonial rule ended and Zambia gained its independence (1964).
4. Literally, *Kapandula* means "The Analyzer" or "The Splitter" (Bemba language, *-pandula*, "chop, split").
5. Andreya Masiye, speaking in an interview with Maxwell Malawo on Zambia National Broadcasting Corporation, Radio 2, October 1, 1988.
6. Personal audiotape collection of Graham Mytton, London.
7. The onomatopoeic word *mfumfumfu* is used in the Bemba language to describe flowing or gurgling sounds. It does not have a precise literal translation, akin to the one Kateka provides. It is related to the onomatopoeic verb *-fumfumuna* "pour out," "run out."
8. *African Listener* 9 (September 1952), 16.
9. *African Listener* 11 (November 1952), 4.
10. This section is based on Spitulnik 1998–1999; see for more detailed discussion.
11. The word "happy" appears in both the letters of Simukwai and Munthali; the word "jolly" appears in Munthali's letter (Franklin 1950, 8).
12. I thank Michael Mann (London) for this suggestion.

REFERENCES

Arnheim, Rudolf. 1936. *Radio*. London: Faber and Faber.
Cardinal, Serge. 2007. Radiophonic Performance and Abstract Machines: Recasting Arnheim's Art of Sound. *Liminalities: A Journal of Performance Studies* 3 (3): 1–23 (online).
Crisell, Andrew. 2006. *More Than a Music Box: Radio Cultures and Communities in a Multimedia World*. New York: Berghahn.
Feld, Steven. 1990. *Sound and Sentiment: Birds, Weeping, Poetics, and Song in Kalului Expression*. Philadelphia: University of Pennsylvania Press.
———. 1996. Waterfalls of Song: An Acoustemology of Place Resounding in Bosavi, Papua New Guinea. In *Senses of Place*, ed. Steven Feld and Keith Basso, 91–136. Santa Fe, NM: School of American Research.
Feld, Steven, and Donald Brenneis. 2004. Doing Anthropology in Sound. *American Ethnologist* 31 (4): 461–474.
Fisher, Daniel. 2009. Mediating Kinship: Country, Family, and Radio in Northern Australia. *Cultural Anthropology* 24 (2): 280–312.

Franklin, Harry. 1950. *Report on "The Saucepan Special": The Poor Man's Radio for Rural Populations*. Lusaka, Zambia: Government Printer.

Gell, Alfred. 1995. The Language of the Forest: Landscape and Phonological Iconism in Umeda. In *The Anthropology of Landscape: Perspectives on Place and Space*, ed. Eric Hirsch and Michael O'Hanlon, 232–254. Oxford, UK: Clarendon.

Katriel, Tamar. 2004. *Dialogic Moments: From Soul Talks to Talk Radio in Israeli Culture*. Detroit: Wayne State University Press.

Kunreuther, Laura. 2006. Technologies of the Voice: FM Radio, Telephone, and the Nepali Diaspora in Kathmandu. *Cultural Anthropology* 21 (3): 323–353.

Larkin, Brian. 2008. *Signal and Noise: Media, Infrastructure, and Urban Culture in Nigeria*. Durham: Duke University Press.

Marcus, George E. 1995. Ethnography in/of the World System: The Emergence of Multi-sited Ethnography. *Annual Reviews of Anthropology* 24:95–117.

Porcello, Thomas. 2005. Afterword to *Wired for Sound*, ed. Paul D. Greene and Thomas Porcello, 269–279. Middletown, CT: Wesleyan University Press.

Scannell, Paddy. 1996. *Radio, Television, and Modern Life*. New York: Wiley-Blackwell.

Silverstein, Michael. 1993. Of Dynamos and Doorbells: Semiotic Modularity and (Over) determination of Cognitive Representation. *Chicago Linguistic Society* 29 (2): 319–345.

Silverstone, Roger. 1994. *Television and Everyday Life*. London: Routledge.

Spitulnik, Debra. 1987. *Semantic Superstructuring and Infrastructuring: Nominal Class Struggle in ChiBemba*. Studies in African Grammatical Systems, Monograph No. 4. Bloomington: Indiana University Linguistics Club.

———. 1988. Levels of Semantic Structuring in Bantu Noun Classification. In *Current Approaches to African Linguistics*, vol. 5, ed. Paul Newman and Robert D. Botne, 207–220. Dordrecht, Netherlands: Foris.

———. 1998–1999. Mediated Modernities: Encounters with the Electronic in Zambia. *Visual Anthropology Review* 14 (2): 63–84.

———. 2002. Mobile Machines and Fluid Audiences: Rethinking Reception through Zambian Radio Culture. In *Media Worlds: Anthropology on New Terrain*, ed. Faye Ginsburg, Lila Abu-Lughod, and Brian Larkin, 337–354. Berkeley: University of California Press.

———. 2003. Behind the Microphone. In *Personal Encounters in Anthropology: An Introductory Reader*, ed. Linda Walbridge and April Sievert, 185–192. New York: McGraw-Hill.

Stewart, Kathleen. 2007. *Ordinary Affects*. Durham: Duke University Press.

Stoller, Paul. 1997. *Sensuous Scholarship*. Philadelphia: University of Pennsylvania Press.

Van Maanen, John. 1988. *Tales of the Field: On Writing Ethnography*. Chicago: University of Chicago Press.

Waterman, Chris. 1990. *Juju: A Social History and Ethnography of an African Popular Music*. Chicago: University of Chicago Press.

Radio Fields

An Afterword

FAYE GINSBURG

"Truly groundbreaking" is a much overused phrase, but in the case of this volume, I feel confident using it; it is the first to date to bring sustained attention to the innovative work being done on radio as an object of anthropological inquiry. Part of the excitement of this book is its rock-solid connection to the best of current ethnographic theory and method, while also showing the rich contribution that research on radio offers to people in neighboring fields such as media, communications, and sound studies, where scholars are less inclined to work outside their cultural comfort zones than are anthropologists. Despite efforts to think outside the box in these related disciplines, their historical attachments to dominant Western paradigms and practices seem to have grown even stronger with the "digital age"—a term that too often conjures up a view of the whole world as wired—despite the fact that in 2011 70 percent of the world had limited or no access to the Internet.[1] Nonetheless, it is nearly impossible to keep up with the publication of books on one or another aspect of life with so-called new media.

Radio, however, is another matter. Its ubiquity and ease of uptake is well-known.[2] Arguably, it is currently the most widely used media form on earth and certainly one that shaped much of the last century's experience, from Nazi Germany's use of radio as a central propaganda tool in the 1930s (Aylett 2011) to the role of radio in consolidating the affective and political sensibilities of the Civil Rights movement in the United States (Ward 2006), to the current politically polarized "silos" that characterize current talk-radio shows. Knowing that, it is even more remarkable that this book is the first of its kind, given that it is over a century since radio has become a commonplace communications technology and anthropology has become a recognized discipline. Perhaps the neglect of radio in anthropology has been in part because so much of the attention given by the field to media is associated with the visual—film, television, video—too often ignoring the other elements that often constitute those media, such as sound. Meanwhile, the sonic, for many years, has been assigned to ethnomusicology. It is only in the past decade, with the publication of books such as *The Audible Past* (Sterne 2003) and *Aural Cultures* (Drobnick 2004) and a few other works noted in the introduction to this volume that "sound studies" has emerged as an exciting new area of research (Samuels et al. 2010). Indeed, if the 2011 American Anthropological Association meetings were any indicator, the number and quality of panels on this topic suggests that the anthropology of sound is finally coming into its own.[3] Clearly, it is a propitious moment for work on radio to be recognized. As is evident from the chapters in this volume, understanding radio requires attention not only to the sonic—the sound of the human voice, language, music, and even static—but also to the ways that radio is embedded in and sometimes constitutive of "inaudible" social practices such as kinship, religion, technology, personhood, and social movements, to name a few key areas explored in this collection.

In addition to the emergence of work on radio in the present represented by this book, the links between anthropology and radio over the past one hundred years offer a fascinating and underreported story that the introduction provides us, laying out the historical foundations for the work in this volume. Thanks to the editors, Lucas Bessire and Daniel Fisher, as well as the other ten anthropologists whose outstanding work is showcased in this book, the lack of recognition for the significance of radio as an object of ethnographic inquiry and theorization is over.

An Origin Story

I recollect when the idea for this book was first mentioned a number of years ago in a conversation in my office at New York University with Lucas Bessire, when he was just finishing his Ph.D. The possibility of editing a collection of this sort was then a proposal motivated by his dissertation research. Radio had not been part of Lucas's initial plan when he headed out to the Gran Chaco region for extended fieldwork with Ayoreo-speaking people; rather, it was something he encountered while there, the kind of happy inductive accident that so often gives anthropological work its edge. In his case, local two-way radio practice was connecting small groups of Ayoreo speakers across the Bolivian- Paraguayan border not of their making, providing an unexpected and complex form of collective self-production, as Bessire makes clear in his riveting piece in this volume. But it was his concern to make sense of their social practices around radio—and his surprise at how little anthropological literature existed on the topic more generally—that generated that conversation in my office.

As a longstanding radio enthusiast who had encouraged Ph.D. students for years to consider research on radio as a radically understudied yet widespread media form just waiting for ethnographers, I responded to the idea with enormous enthusiasm. I suggested that he partner with Danny Fisher, whose extensive experience studying Aboriginal radio and music in northern Australia, in many ways, made him one of a small group of pioneering scholars (along with some in this volume) carrying out outstanding ethnographic research on this medium, a position which is evident in the sophistication of his piece in this book. Currently teaching in the Department of Anthropology at Macquarie University in Sydney, Australia, Danny is another former NYU Ph.D. student, influenced by his studies with Steve Feld on music and sound. Like Lucas, he had also trained in the Culture and Media Program at NYU,[4] a course of study that provides a broad framework for understanding media ethnographically, theoretically, and with a healthy respect for the insights that practice can offer. Lucas took Danny's email and scribbled down the names of the handful of other anthropologists who had been carrying out research on radio in many different parts of the world, from Europe to the Pacific, to the Arctic, to central Australia. We brainstormed possible book titles, and *Radio Fields* captured the same capacious sensibility of media as a social practice—encompassing the social, the technological, the phenomenological, the material, the transnational—as had the title *Media Worlds* for the book edited by Lila Abu-Lughod, Brian Larkin, and myself in 2002 (Ginsburg, Abu-Lughod, and Larkin 2002).

Like many such talks in which the germ of an idea is planted, it was hard to judge if this one would bear fruit. However, within a month or two, the idea for a book featuring recent ethnographic work on radio started to take shape in earnest as Lucas and Danny went forward with plans for this volume. Together they were able to mobilize a first-rate, wide-ranging group of contributors, from the foundational work of the senior anthropologist Lynn Stephen with indigenous women activists in Oaxaca to the exciting contribution of Andy Blanton, an emerging scholar recently back from his dissertation fieldwork in Appalachia, and of course, everything and everyone in between. As the volume you hold in your hands makes clear, their combined force as editors has been extraordinarily productive, and anthropology—along with media studies—is much enriched by their efforts.

Shaping Radio Fields

Like the contributors in this book, the editors exemplify two key pathways to research on radio among anthropologists: happy accident and strategic choice. As noted earlier, Bessire had never expected to stumble on the surprising and intellectually challenging uptake of two-way radio among Ayoreo speakers in the Gran Chaco region with whom he had been working as an anthropologist and filmmaker. In the case of Fisher, indigenous radio had been at the center of his original and ongoing research with indigenous Australians living in that country's Top End. Despite their different trajectories, both editors carried out the requisite, rewarding, and demanding fieldwork expected of anthropologists, in this case with Indigenous communities in the kind of places that are off the map of most media scholars. Their work renders evident how this kind of anthropological research on media in "out of the way" places—in this case radio—offers a crucial contribution to the "de-Westernizing" as well as decentering of media studies. Indeed, this paradigm-shifting framework characterizes the entire volume and underscores its significance for a greatly enriched understanding of the place of this kind of "small media" in everyday life across the planet, whether among Islamic women radio preachers in Mali or in the experiential sensibilities of radio listening in (i)homes of middle-class multigenerational Britons.

The considerable differences that characterize the radio fields covered in this book make clear the value of this kind of broad perspective that renders this work so lively. The authors collectively offer a wide range of approaches that demonstrate the generativity of the ethnographic approach, from projects based in metropolitan centers, as in Jeffrey Juris's piece on pirate radio in Mexico and Kira Kosnick's work on Radio MultiKulti, to radio in Indigenous communities in Latin America and Australia. At the same time, the editors have structured the volume to demonstrate distinctive overlapping concerns. The grouping of the contributions along five "axes" (a word that draws on the mathematical concept that describes a number of sites that cluster together in a way that resembles an imagined line) underscores this sense of shared orientations. The axes are particularly helpful in calling the reader's attention to some of the key features raised by the study of radio as a social practice and which bear discussion here:

Axis I: The Voice encompasses the actual mediatized voice that is central to radio's form of production, transmission, and interpellation of "listening publics" as well as other collectivities, along with the notion of voice as a trope for ideas of social agency and personhood that are key concepts that shape at least the ideal if not the reality of local radio. This axis includes Laura Kunreuther's piece on the critical role played by FM broadcasting in the 1990s democracy movements in Nepal, calling attention to "voice" as a sign for agency in discussions of ideas of neoliberal citizenship, as well as the inaudible but essential social relations of cultural production, station ownership, and programming. Danny Fisher's chapter based on his work with Indigenous FM radio producers goes to the heart of the matter of "voice consciousness" in his analysis of how voice works simultaneously as an expressive practice and as a location for cultural activism, a project of "Indigenous self-fashioning" which also extends to the appropriation of global musical genres.

Axis II: Radio and Nation draws on the robust notion of "imagined communities" first introduced by Benedict Anderson in 1983 in his foundational study of the role of print media in constituting a sense of national identity beyond face-to-face community. Extending that idea to radio, Bessire and Fisher use this concept to cluster those chapters that demonstrate the different ways in which a sense of a citizenship or at least national belonging is fostered—although not necessarily encompassed—by radio and its capacity to produce not only the infrastructure of mass mediation to people living within the nation but also the sounds, narratives, and sentiments that characterize particular national imaginaries. For example, Danny Kaplan, in this section, focuses on radio engineers and the part that their editorial interventions play in crafting an Israeli national narrative and soundscape, from the mundane "sound" of weather reports to emergency broadcasts, thus playing a crucial though largely unseen role in shaping a sonic sense of Israeli citizenship. In contrast, Dorothea Schulz examines how private FM radio stations in Mali have become the site for Muslim women to take on authority as radio preachers, emphasizing particular attributes of voice that lend them authority in the context of contemporary Islamic moral renewal.

Axis III: Community Radio emphasizes the form most frequently considered to be the site for the formation of a counterpublic/minority sphere in much of the writing on radio by activist scholars in particular. As the editors point out, whether community radio in fact constitutes (or reflects) alternative communities or is built on antihegemonic sentiment—ideological positions strongly attached to the idea of community radio—is an empirical question that is central to the chapters in this section. Such inquiry extends even to the variety of "technological assemblages" that characterize small-scale radio that typically are associated with this form, from low-power radio that targets particular localities to Internet streaming that can bring together constituencies that are geographically dispersed. It is important to recognize that while community radio as such may speak to a particular form of shared identity—that may fall to the left or the right on the political spectrum—people addressed by this form of media may simultaneously hold a range of subject positions. In this section, Lynn Stephen asks why radio became the target for a takeover by Indigenous women in Oaxaca, Mexico, in 2006 during a popular uprising there and shows how that act became a catalyst for expanding the integration of testimonial speech in regional radio as a way of integrating minoritized voices into the political process. Melinda Hinkson covers the history of the Warlpiri Media Association in central Australia from its inception in 1984 to its current status as part of the Pintubi Anmatyerre Warlpiri (PAW) radio network, which operates across eleven communities. She demonstrates how Warlpiri youth, in their on-air dedications, carry out a renewed if transformed expression of Warlpiri cultural imperatives via the novel modes of address offered by radio. Jeff Juris's study of the role of Radio Autónoma, an urban youth pirate radio station in Mexico City advocating "communicational autonomy," explores this case in relation to two distinct models for community radio: AMARC (World Association of Community Radio Broadcasters) is a longstanding group that promotes communication rights, including the legalization of community radio, while the free media movement, including Radio Autónoma, advocates piracy of the airwaves.

Axis IV: Transnational Circuits incorporates chapters that address the capacity of radio technology—and especially but not exclusively airwaves—to cross national borders, creating a mediascape that connects communities separated by geopolitical boundaries but connected by strong ties of language, culture, affect, religion, and kinship. Kira Kosnick, building on her ethnography of Radio MultiKulti, Berlin's public service radio station, shows how radio practices have helped to create new social imaginaries—and expressive modes of cultural citizenship—that render ethnic diversity audible on the airwaves. Lucas Bessire's transnational location is far from the urban multicultural West in his chapter on the solar-powered two-way radio network created by Ayoreo-speaking people of the Bolivian and Paraguayan Gran Chaco. Yet he shows how this technological capacity is deployed as a "transcendent acoustic space" through which Ayoreo alliances are built across the border, via linguistically stylized reports of illness and suffering,

objectifying an Ayoreo sensibility that regards these practices as healing regardless of national context.

Axis V: Language and Perception addresses how radio talk provides a
"sociolinguistic resource" that gives new life to (or stigmatizes) dialects,
new speech genres, and other language practices as they are framed in different political and performative contexts. Andy Blanton's contribution on
Appalachian radio faith healers expands beyond the auditory to the haptic as the faithful receive the healing power of the Holy Ghost through the
act of touching the radio. In a chapter that also concerns radio and affect in
the domestic space most often identified with radio listening in the United
Kingdom, Jo Tacchi analyzes generational change in understandings of the
reception of media in the (i)home (the digitally enabled private sphere).
While young adults associate radio with the past, their use of streamed radio
—while on a different platform than the radio used by their parents—shows
striking continuities with the prior generation in terms of their social practice. Debra Vidali-Spitulnik, in the final chapter, analyzes the "entanglement"
of Bemba language used in radio broadcasting in Zambia as it travels across
a range of social locations in a process that, she argues, has transformed how
modernity is perceived.

As Bessire and Fisher point out in their introduction, the similarities noted
for the chapters arranged along these particular five axes can be redistributed
along other coordinates as well. The social practice of radio raises questions of
affect, kinship, postcolonial politics, religion, gender, social movements, and
infrastructure, to name a few of the topics discussed by the editors in their introduction as areas equally informed by the studies in *Radio Fields*.

Notes from the Field

In closing, I add my own ethnographic notes on the radio fields I inhabit in
New York to see how this media form shapes my own experience and multiple subjectivities. In self-consciously accounting for my encounters with
radio over the past two weeks, I was amazed to find how in so short a time, I
could catalogue a remarkable range of experiences which could easily fit into
as well as extend the analytic frame set out by the editors of this volume.

Radio Field One: In mid-November, I attended an event at the American Mu-
seum of Natural History, an extension of the Margaret Mead Film and Video
Festival held at that institution, that demonstrates how radio is increasingly
linked to actual face-to-face events in places such as Manhattan. Unlike the
radio broadcasts of live performances that characterized an earlier era of

radio (and which still constitute a large portion of radio programming), this event offered the packed audience the opportunity to be part of an immersive "listening party." In this case, we watched the starscape of the planetarium while listening to the most recent episode of a weekly innovative one-hour radio show created by the New York–based group Radio Lab, produced and hosted by Jad Abumrad and Robert Krulwich for National Public Radio. Consistent with theorists working in sound studies, their website explains that "Radiolab believes your ears are a portal to another world."[5] As part of the festival's theme of "Dreams of Outer Space," the show addressed "humanity's paradoxical relationship with space exploration, from wide-eyed romanticism to cynical fear,"[6] including audio interviews with Ann Druyan, widow of Carl Sagan; Brian Greene, host of NOVA's *The Elegant Universe*; and Hayden Planetarium director Neil deGrasse Tyson. Based on some quick ethnographic surveillance of audience members, it appears that the show has developed a cult following that seems to have an epicenter around the Park Slope neighborhood in Brooklyn. Abumrad was on hand to share behind-the-scenes anecdotes about their program and to field questions from the audience, blurring the lines between the sonic storytelling dimensions of radio and live performance.

Radio Field Two: I frequently plug into a sturdy "old-fashioned" Sony Walkman digital radio late at night, distracting myself by listening to the long-standing BBC World Service,[7] which runs from midnight to six a.m. in the United States. In the aural space created by wearing earbuds while lying in bed in a dark room, I am transported to South Sudan as the reporter provides the indexical soundscape as well as analysis of tragic stories of war and displacement, interpellating me (in my pajamas in NYC) as a citizen and subject who could be moved to political action.

Radio Field Three: The next night, my daughter and I watched the movie *Sleepless in Seattle*, a 1993 romantic comedy directed by Nora Ephron, starring Tom Hanks and Meg Ryan, in which the cross-country love affair between the stars is sparked by a radio call-in show.[8] Scenes of Meg Ryan's character, Annie Reed, on the East Coast, weeping in her Baltimore broom closet and later in her car as she listens to Tom Hanks's character, Sam Baldwin, as he describes his loneliness as a widower to the radio "doctor," invoke the indelible historical association between radios, cars, affect, intimacy, and romance in American life.

Radio Field Four: Driving to my father's house for Thanksgiving on Thursday morning, I ended up listening to the weekly morning show *First Voices*

Indigenous Radio on WBAI NY Pacifica Radio, produced by Tiokasin Ghost-horse, a member of the Lakota (Sioux) Nation, a cultural activist, musician, and longtime host of one of the few programs that address the concerns of Native Americans, a cultural world that otherwise is virtually invisible and inaudible to most Americans.[9]

Radio Field Five: As we head north and get out of range of WBAI, my niece, a graduate student in the Interactive Telecommunications Program at NYU, tells me about the class she is taking in which the students are building a micropower radio station for a housing project in NYC so that tenants can easily share information, pointing to the community-building capacities of such low-power technologies that are proliferating in the 21st century.

Radio Field Six: At my father's house, we decide to watch the 2010 movie *The King's Speech*.[10] In that film, the rising role of radio as a key form of political communication in the first half of the 20th century is crucial to the drama. Being able to talk fluidly and frequently via radio in the 1930s is required of any leader. The drama hinges on how King George VI overcame his debilitating speech impediment with the support of an eccentric Australian speech therapist. The film closes with an enactment of his famous radio address that mobilized British citizens on the brink of World War II. The film inspired my father, born in 1919, to reminisce about listening to FDR's evening radio addresses, known as fireside chats, delivered to the American public between 1933 and 1944, as well as his love of Yiddish radio shows that he listened to as a boy in the 1920s with his Russian-immigrant family. While his memories are laden with nostalgia, they also underscore the centrality of radio to political authority and the construction of national subjects as well as collective identity for immigrant/ethnic Americans.

Radio Field Seven: As part of my interest in disability media as an activist parent of a disabled child and as a researcher, I regularly download podcasts of *Disability Beat*, a live weekly public affairs radio program every Wednesday afternoon on WEFT in Champaign, Illinois, a radio station that is out of my range.[11] This week I was able to listen to Leroy Moore and Rob "Da Noize" Temple of Krip Hop Nation discuss their work as part of an international network of musical artists with disabilities. The next day, I brought this podcast into conversation with my students and learned in subsequent dialogue how extensively disability plays a role in many of their lives in ways that are rarely given public expression.

I offer this modest first-person autoethnographic experiment in tracking my radio world over a very short period of time as a final testimony to the value of this volume in revealing radio's remarkable yet underappreciated role in shaping so many aspects of contemporary human experience. We have this book to thank for changing the conversation.

NOTES

1. For statistics on world Internet use, see http://www.internetworldstats.com/stats.htm.
2. In the late 1980s when I was first doing fieldwork on indigenous media making in central Australia, one of the people teaching older Aboriginal women to be DJs for the multilingual radio programs being produced by the Central Australian Aboriginal Media Association (CAAMA) pointed out to me that these women were up and running in their new roles within an hour or two of training, unlike the training required for producing local television.
3. For the full program of the meetings, see http://www.aaanet.org/meetings/2011-AAA -Annual-Meeting.cfm.
4. In 1987, I founded the Certificate Program in Culture and Media at NYU as an interdisciplinary program bringing together graduate students in anthropology and cinema studies. It offers specialized training in the history of cross-cultural representation on film, in ethnographic research on media, and in ethnographic documentary production. See http://anthropology.as.nyu.edu/object/anthro.grad.program .cultmedia.
5. For more information on Radio Lab, see http://www.radiolab.org/about/.
6. For more on this event, see http://www.amnh.org/programs/mead/2011/films/ radiolab.
7. For more on the BBC World Service, see http://www.bbc.co.uk/worldservice/.
8. For more on *Sleepless in Seattle*, see http://www.imdb.com/title/tt0108160/.
9. For more on *First Voices Indigenous Radio*, see http://wbai.org/index. php?option=com_content&task=view&id=394&Itemid=135.
10. For more on this film, see http://www.kingsspeech.com/.
11. For more on *Disability Beat*, see http://www.disabilitybeat.com/.

REFERENCES

Anderson, Benedict. 1983. *Imagined Communities: Reflections on the Origins and Spread of Nationalism*. London: Verso.
Aylett, Glenn. 2011. Hitler's Radio. *Transdiffusion*, November. http://www.transdiffusion.org/ radio/features/hitlers_radio.
Drobnick, Jim, ed. 2004. *Aural Cultures*. Banff Centre, Canada: YYZ Books.
Ginsburg, Faye, Lila Abu-Lughod, Brian Larkin, eds. 2002. *Media Worlds: Anthropology on New Terrain*. Berkeley: University of California Press.
Samuels, David, Louise Meintjes, Ana Maria Ochoa, and Thomas Porcello. 2010. Soundscapes: Toward a Sounded Anthropology. *Annual Review of Anthropology* 39:329–345.

Sterne, Jonathan. 2003. *The Audible Past: Cultural Origins of Sound Production*. Durham: Duke University Press.

Ward, Brian. 2006. *Radio and the Struggle for Civil Rights in the South*. Gainesville: University Press of Florida.

Lucas Bessire is an assistant professor of anthropology at the University of Oklahoma. An award-winning filmmaker and author, he writes widely on indigeneity, biopolitics, and violence in the Gran Chaco region of South America.

Anderson Blanton is a 2011–2012 postdoctoral fellow at the Center for the Study of the American South at the University of North Carolina, Chapel Hill, and the author of the forthcoming book *Until the Stones Cry Out: Materiality, Technology, and Faith in Southern Appalachia*. His research focuses on the interface of religion, tactility, and technology in Appalachia.

Daniel Fisher is a lecturer of anthropology at Macquarie University. He has written broadly on Australian Indigenous media and music production as well as on issues of Indigenous mobility and town camping in Northern Australia. He is completing a monograph on Indigenous Australian media production and public affect and directs Macquarie's ethnographic media program.

Faye Ginsburg is David B. Kriser Professor of Anthropology, director of the Graduate Program in Culture and Media, director of the Center for Media, Culture & History, and codirector of the Center for Religion and Media at New York University. Author and editor of five books, including *Media Worlds: Anthropology on New Terrain*, she has written extensively on indigenous media, documentary film, and gender politics.

Melinda Hinkson is a senior lecturer in anthropology at the Australian National University. She is author of *Aboriginal Sydney: A Guide to Important Places of the Past and Present* (2001) and coeditor (with John Altman) of *Culture Crisis: Anthropology and Politics in Aboriginal Australia* (2010) and *Coercive Reconciliation: Stablise, Normalise, Exit Aboriginal Australia* (2007).

Jeffrey S. Juris is an assistant professor of anthropology at Northeastern University. Author of *Networking Futures: the Movements against Corporate*

Globalization (2008), his research focuses on globalization, social movements, and new digital media, with a geographic focus on Spain and Mexico.

Danny Kaplan is a senior lecturer at Bar Ilan University. The author of *Brothers and Others in Arms: The Making of Love and War in Israeli Combat Units* (2003) and *The Men We Loved: Male Friendship and Nationalism in Israeli Culture* (2006), Kaplan specializes in the anthropology of emotions through the prism of friendship and nationalism.

Kira Kosnick is a professor of sociology in the Faculty of Social Sciences at Goethe-University Frankfurt. Author of *Migrant Media: Turkish Broadcasting and Multicultural Politics in Berlin*, she has written widely on the politics of ethnicity, immigration, and urban space in Europe.

Laura Kunreuther is an associate professor of anthropology at Bard College. Her monograph on public life in Kathmandu after the reestablishment of democracy is forthcoming. Her research interests center on themes of cultural memory, urban public culture, and technology and media.

Dorothea Schulz is a professor of anthropology at the University of Cologne. The author of three books, including *Muslims and New Media in West Africa: Pathways to God*, she has written extensively on Islamic performance and mediation in Mali.

Lynn Stephen is a university distinguished professor of anthropology and ethnic studies at the University of Oregon. The author of four books, including *Transborder Lives: Indigenous Oaxacans in Mexico, California, and Oregon*, she has written extensively on gender inequality, migration, and social movements.

Jo Tacchi is a professor and deputy dean of research and innovation at RMIT University. She has written extensively on radio and on new media technologies and social change.

Debra Vidali-Spitulnik is an associate professor of anthropology at Emory University. Author of numerous essays on radio, she has written extensively on people's relationships with media and language in Zambia.

INDEX

Printed and bound by CPI Group (UK) Ltd, Croydon, CR0 4YY

16/04/2025

14658443-0001